PAMELA COLMAN SMITH
Artist, Feminist, & Mystic

Frontispiece Pamela Colman Smith, from *The Craftsman*, October 1912

PAMELA COLMAN SMITH

Artist, Feminist, & Mystic

ELIZABETH FOLEY O'CONNOR

CLEMSON
UNIVERSITY
PRESS

© 2024 Clemson University
All rights reserved

First Edition, 2021
This paperback edition published 2024

ISBN: 978-1-949979-39-8 (hardback)
ISBN: 978-1-83553-870-8 (paperback)
eISBN: 978-1-949979-40-4 (e-book)

Published by Clemson University Press
in association with Liverpool University Press

Clemson University Press is located in Clemson, SC.
For more information, please visit our website at www.clemson.edu/press.

Library of Congress Cataloging-in-Publication Data

Names: O'Connor, Elizabeth Foley, author.
Title: Pamela Colman Smith : artist, feminist, & mystic / Elizabeth Foley O'Connor.
Description: [Clemson] : Clemson University Press, 2021. | Includes bibliographical references and index. | Summary: "Pamela Colman Smith's illustrations for the Rider Waite tarot deck are known to millions, but her work took her from art galleries to salons with luminaries of the English suffrage movement, the Irish literary revival, and friendships with Ellen Terry, Bram Stoker, and W. B. Yeats among many others"-- Provided by publisher.
Identifiers: LCCN 2021005815 (print) | LCCN 2021005816 (ebook) | ISBN 9781949979398 (hardback) | ISBN 9781949979404 (ebook)
Subjects: LCSH: Smith, Pamela Colman--Criticism and interpretation.
Classification: LCC N6537.S617 O29 2021 (print) | LCC N6537.S617 (ebook) | DDC 709.2--dc23
LC record available at https://lccn.loc.gov/2021005815
LC ebook record available at https://lccn.loc.gov/2021005816

Typeset in Minion Pro by Carnegie Book Production.
Printed and bound by CPI Group (UK) Ltd, Croydon CR0 4YY.

To Michael and Liam O'Connor

Contents

List of Figures   ix

Acknowledgments   xiii

Introduction   1

1   Naming and Identity: Family, Miniature Theater, and Jamaican Residence   21

2   Forging a Path: Critical Reception, Key Influences, and Emergence as an Artist   53

3   Becoming Pixie: Friendship, Synaesthesia, and *The Green Sheaf*   89

4   Art on Her Own Terms: Anansi Stories, the Green Sheaf Press, and "Music Pictures"   127

5   Feminist Symbolic Art: Tarot Designs, Suffrage Posters, and Representations of Women   175

Epilogue   229

Notes   243

Index   295

Figures

Frontispiece Pamela Colman Smith, from *The Craftsman*, October 1912. ii

1.1 Sketch of the procession from *Henry Morgan*, from an October 5, 1896 letter from Pamela Colman Smith to her cousin, Mary "Bobby" Reed. Courtesy of the Pamela Colman Smith Collection, Special Collections Department, Bryn Mawr College Library, box 1, folder 3. 50

2.1 Pamela Colman Smith, illustration for "A School-Girl Song of Spring," *Pratt Institute Monthly* 5, no. 7 (1897), 199. 61

2.2 Pamela Colman Smith, untitled. Private collection. 61

2.3 Sketch of Howard Pyle included in a January 5, 1898 letter from Pamela Colman Smith to her cousin, Mary "Bobby" Reed. Courtesy of the Pamela Colman Smith Collection, Special Collections Department, Bryn Mawr College Library, box 1, folder 11. 64

2.4 Pamela Colman Smith, untitled. Private collection. 76

2.5 Pamela Colman Smith, "A Christmas Carol," included in a portfolio published by R. H. Russell in 1898. Private collection. 77

2.6 Pamela Colman Smith, "The service and the loyalty I owe, in doing it pays itself," *Macbeth*, act 1, scene 4, included in a portfolio published by R. H. Russell in 1898. ART File S528m1 no. 98 (size S). Reproduced by permission of the Folger Shakespeare Library.   79

3.1 Pamela Colman Smith, "Alone," *The Green Sheaf* 4 (April 1903), 9. Reproduced by permission of Stuart R. Kaplan, U.S. Games, Inc.   121

3.2 Pamela Colman Smith, "The Town," *The Green Sheaf* 12 (January 1904), 5. Reproduced by permission of Stuart R. Kaplan, U.S. Games, Inc.   123

4.1 Pamela Colman Smith, "Anansi," from *Annancy Stories* (R. H. Russell, 1899), 3. Reproduced by permission of Stuart R. Kaplan, U.S. Games, Inc.   139

4.2 Cover of Pamela Colman Smith, *Annancy Stories* (R. H. Russell, 1899). Reproduced by permission of Stuart R. Kaplan, U.S. Games, Inc.   141

4.3 Pamela Colman Smith, giant from Seumas MacManus, *In Chimney Corners: Merry Tales of Irish Folklore* (Doubleday, 1899), frontispiece. Reproduced by permission of Stuart R. Kaplan, U.S. Games, Inc.   145

4.4 Pamela Colman Smith, "Five Yam Hill," from *Chim-Chim: Folk Stories from Jamaica* (Green Sheaf Press, 1905), 61. Courtesy of the General Research & Reference Division, Schomberg Center for Research in Black Culture, The New York Public Library, Astor, Lenox and Tilden Foundations.   150

4.5 Pamela Colman Smith, "Annancy and Death," from *Chim-Chim: Folk Stories from Jamaica* (Green Sheaf Press, 1905), 45. Reproduced by permission of Stuart R. Kaplan, U.S. Games, Inc.   164

4.6 Pamela Colman Smith, untitled watercolor of the New York City skyline. Private collection.   168

Figures

5.1	Unsigned, undated sketch of Pamela Colman Smith and A. E. Waite from Colman Smith's visitors' book. Reproduced by permission of Stuart R. Kaplan, U.S. Games, Inc.	192
5.2	Pamela Colman Smith, "Sketch for Glass," 1908. Courtesy Beinecke Rare Book and Manuscript Library, Yale University.	195
5.3	The Sun and Moon cards from the Smith-Waite tarot deck. Reproduced by permission of Stuart R. Kaplan, U.S. Games, Inc.	196
5.4	Pamela Colman Smith, untitled watercolor, 1907. Courtesy Beinecke Rare Book and Manuscript Library, Yale University.	198
5.5	The Tower card from the Smith-Waite tarot deck. Reproduced by permission of Stuart R. Kaplan, U.S. Games, Inc.	201
5.6	Pamela Colman Smith, *Schumann's Noveletten*. Private collection.	203
5.7	Pamela Colman Smith, *Mozart's Sonata in F Major for Violin and Piano, Second Series Duet*, watercolor, 1907. Courtesy Beinecke Rare Book and Manuscript Library, Yale University.	204
5.8	P. S., "What May Happen," cartoon for the Suffrage Atelier. Courtesy of the Women's Library at the London School of Economics.	211
5.9	"The Closed Door," cartoon for the Suffrage Atelier. Courtesy of the Women's Library at the London School of Economics.	212
5.10	"To the Girls' Christmas Tree," cartoon for the Suffrage Atelier. Courtesy of the Museum of London.	213
5.11	"What a Woman may be, and yet not have the Vote," cartoon for the Suffrage Atelier, 1913. Courtesy of the Museum of London.	214
5.12	"Polling Station," cartoon for the Suffrage Atelier, 1913. Courtesy of the Women's Library at the London School of Economics.	215
5.13	Pamela Colman Smith, *The Wave*, watercolor, 1903. Courtesy of the Whitney Museum of American Art.	219

5.14 Pamela Colman Smith, untitled, 1907. Private collection. 220

5.15 Pamela Colman Smith, *Beethoven's Sonata No. 11*, 1907. Courtesy Beinecke Rare Book and Manuscript Library, Yale University. 222

5.16 Pamela Colman Smith, untitled, 1912. Private collection. 223

5.17 Pamela Colman Smith, *Woman in Blue*, 1909. Private collection. 224

5.18 Pamela Colman Smith, untitled, 1906. Private collection. 225

5.19 Pamela Colman Smith, untitled, watercolor, 1911. Private collection. 226

Acknowledgments

I first encountered Pamela Colman Smith, specifically her *Annancy Stories*, in November 2011, days before defending my dissertation on Irish and Caribbean interwar novels of the city. I became fascinated by her personality, achievements, and the multiple struggles that she had to overcome as an early feminist, proto-modernist, and gender-nonconforming person. Over the course of the next nine years, I immersed myself in almost every aspect of this multi-faceted artist and writer's life and work. Attempting to understand her life more closely, I consulted numerous archives, libraries, and databases, and traveled to many places where she lived, including London, Cornwall, and various locations in New York City.

This book would not exist without the assistance of many tireless curators, librarians, and archive assistants at the following institutions who have helped locate resources that have allowed me to piece together a more accurate picture of Colman Smith's life and contributions. They include the Archives of American Art at the Smithsonian Institution, the Archives and Manuscripts department of the British Library, the Pamela Colman Smith Collection at Bryn Mawr College Library, the Brooklyn Historical Society, the Cornwall Record Office, the Rauner Special Collections of Dartmouth College, the Ellen Terry and Edith Craig Database at the University of Essex, the Folger Shakespeare Library, Gillette Castle State Park, the Hathi Trust Digital Library, the Rare Books and Manuscripts divisions of the Huntington Library, the Jesuits in Britain Archive, the Library of Congress Rare Book and

Special Collections, the Women's Library of the London School of Economics, the Museum of London Library, the Manuscripts Department of the National Library of Ireland, the Henry W. and Albert A. Berg Collection of English and American Literature and the Manuscripts and the Archives collections at the New York Public Library, the Bodleian Archives & Manuscripts collections at the University of Oxford, the Philadelphia Museum of Art Archives, the Kislak Center for Special Collections, Rare Books, and Manuscripts at the University of Pennsylvania, the archives at the Roman Catholic Diocese of Plymouth, the Ellen Terry archives and museum at Smallhythe Place, the Schomburg Center for Research in Black Culture, the Special Collections and University Archives at Stony Brook University, the Victoria and Albert Museum Archive, the Museum, Archive, and Library of the Swedenborg Society, and the Beinecke Rare Book and Manuscript Library at Yale University.

My special thanks to Derek and Kimberly Notman for their kindness and graciousness. Most of all, I am indebted to the late Stuart Kaplan for the access he generously provided me to his large private library of Pamela Colman Smith art, books, and memorabilia. Without Stuart's tireless commitment to uncovering once-hidden aspects of Colman Smith's life and work, this volume would not be possible. I am grateful for his help and encouragement as well as for our conversations about Colman Smith and her work.

I am especially grateful to librarians Mary Alice Ball, Jeanne Hamilton, and Cindy Sutton at Washington College's Miller Library, who, over the last seven years, have placed hundreds of interlibrary loan requests on my behalf, remained patient at overdue books, and even helped me locate a volume in the midst of the pandemic. I am also grateful to several friends and acquaintances who took photographs of material for me during their research trips, especially Wayne Chapman, Kate Moncrief, Peter Murray, and Courtney Rydel.

As the research and writing of this volume stretched from the end of my graduate education at Fordham University through my successful completion of the tenure process at Washington College, it has benefitted from the insight and support of a wide range of individuals and institutions. At Fordham I am especially grateful to my dissertation committee: Phil Sicker, Chris GoGwilt, Anne Fernald, and Moshe Gold, who supported this project from its infancy. At Washington College, I am indebted to several Faculty Enhancement Grants, Provost's Travel Grants, and a Junior Leave in the spring semester of 2017 that allowed me the opportunity to travel to archives in England and throughout the U.S. I am also grateful for a supportive English department at Washington College, especially Sean Meehan and Courtney Rydel.

Over the last decade, I have presented material on Colman Smith at numerous conferences. These include the annual meetings of the Modern Language Association (2014), the Modernist Studies Association (2019, 2016, 2015, 2014), the Space Between Society and the Feminist inter/Modernist Association (2018), the Northeast Modern Language Association (2018), the 25th Annual International Conference on Virginia Woolf (2015), and the 2018 Women Writing Decadence: European Perspectives conference at Oxford University. The thoughtful feedback and comments I received contributed immeasurably to this volume. I am especially thankful to the organizers and participants of the inaugural Caribbean Irish Connections conference held in Barbados in 2012, whose extremely positive response to the beginnings of my research into Colman Smith cemented my belief that this was a project worth pursuing. Finally, a word of sincere thanks to Wayne Chapman, Professor Emeritus at Clemson University and former editor of the Clemson University Press, for his unflagging support and encouragement over the last five years.

My research into Colman Smith draws on and continues the important work of recovering her legacy that began in the mid-1970s. I am especially grateful for groundbreaking contributions by Melinda Boyd Parsons and Mary Greer. Mention must also be made of the large group of writers and researchers dedicated to preserving the legacy of Colman Smith and providing adequate recognition for the iconic images she painted for the Smith-Waite deck. These include Dawn Robinson, Ruth Stacey, and Susan Wands.

Like all things in 2020, the global pandemic made finishing this volume more difficult. It was helped immeasurably by the insightful contributions and stalwart support of my writing group partners, Ravenel Richardson and Aimee Armande Wilson. I also thank both the anonymous reviewer for Clemson University Press who offered important suggestions and encouragement near the end of this process, and my editor at Clemson, Alison Mero, who did an excellent job of shepherding this manuscript to completion and getting it ready for press.

While this project at times felt all-encompassing, the support of my family and friends helped sustain me throughout this journey. I thank my parents, Edith and James Foley, for helping to cultivate in me a love of reading, a deep appreciation of museums, libraries, and archives of all sorts, and the courage to persevere even when it seems far easier to give up. I am especially grateful to my father, James Foley, for always being my first, and most patient, editor. I am grateful to my sister, Meredith Foley, for her unfailing support and encouragement and for gamely going along when a trip to Cornwall involved many more visits to graveyards and record offices than traditional tourist destinations. And I commend Oliver for always reminding me that sleep is incredibly necessary and important.

I thank my son, Liam O'Connor, whose growth and development roughly paralleled that of this manuscript. Your imagination, curiosity, and humor constantly remind me what I believe Colman Smith also instinctively knew: that it is important to live each day to the fullest and always be open to the unexpected moments of magic and wonder that surround us. And, most importantly, to my husband, Michael O'Connor, for your unwavering love and support. You have tirelessly listened to my worries and complaints and always know how to cheer me up. Without you, I would not have been able to complete this book.

An early version of material that is covered in Chapter 4 was first published as "Pamela Colman Smith's Performative Primitivism," in *Caribbean Irish Connections: Interdisciplinary Perspectives*, edited by Alison Donnell, Maria McGarrity, and Evelyn O'Callaghan (University Press of the West Indies, 2015). A portion of Chapter 3 was first published as "'We Disgruntled Devils Don't Please Anyone': Pamela Colman Smith, *The Green Sheaf*, and Female Literary Networks," *The South Carolina Review* (Winter 2016). Some of Colman Smith's biographical material was first published in Stuart Kaplan, Mary Greer, Elizabeth Foley O'Connor, and Melinda Boyd Parsons, *Pamela Colman Smith: The Untold Story* (U.S. Games, 2018). Further unauthorized reproduction of all images is prohibited by the rights holders.

Introduction

Today, Pamela Colman Smith is primarily remembered for designing a tarot deck, which has been known for most of the last one hundred and ten years as the Rider-Waite deck. Its name commemorates two men, the mystic A. E. Waite, who is credited with conceiving the deck, and the London publisher, William Rider, rather than the actual designer of the cards. This omission perfectly encapsulates Colman Smith's gendered erasure from the cultural imagination, a type of misogyny that affected many women artists and writers at the turn of the twentieth century. Continuing work done by critics over the last forty years, this literary biography—the first of Colman Smith—sheds new light on the wide range of her contributions beyond the deck, and, in the process, helps reorient the conversation surrounding women's contributions to modernism(s).

Pamela Colman Smith: Feminist, Artist, Mystic contends that Colman Smith was much more than the graphic designer of the storied 1909 tarot deck that served as the model for T. S. Eliot's Madame Sosostris and "her wicked pack of cards" in *The Waste Land*. Active from the mid-1890s through the 1920s, Colman Smith had a burgeoning career as an American artist, writer, folklore performer, editor, publisher, stage designer, and suffrage activist. Her paintings were exhibited in a range of galleries in the U.S. and England, including several major international art exhibitions. She also had the distinction of being the first non-photographic artist (beating out Rodin) to have her work shown at Alfred Stieglitz's 291 gallery in New York. Prolific, Colman Smith illustrated over twenty books and pamphlets, wrote two collections of Afro-Jamaican Anansi folktales, and co-edited *A Broad Sheet* with Jack Yeats from 1902 to 1903. Forging her own path from then on, she created and edited *The Green Sheaf* from 1903 to 1904 by herself, and, after its demise, ran the Green Sheaf Press, which focused particularly on women writers. She was actively involved in the women's suffrage movement, creating multiple posters and postcards, and helping working-class women attend suffrage rallies; in addition, she was arrested for suffrage activities at least once. Colman Smith's letters to friends, patrons, publishers, and gallery owners reveal an irrepressible spirit who was committed to rooting out all types of hypocrisy and prejudice, including classism, sexism, and racism, but who, nonetheless, capitalized on racial stereotypes through her Afro-Jamaican Anansi performances. Taken as a whole, Colman Smith's prodigious body of work is particularly notable for both its hybridity and its ability to take on, and often as quickly cast aside, a range of personas and identities.

Identity and belonging, or the lack thereof, was central to both Colman Smith's work and life as a perceived biracial, gender-nonconforming person. Colman Smith was born in London on February 16, 1878. Her racial identity is uncertain but she was raised as white. However, throughout her life she was consistently viewed as an Other, with contemporaries describing her as Asian, Black, or even an indeterminate "creature." Given her well-documented dark skin, it seems highly likely that Colman Smith was biracial, but I have found no direct evidence to support this through my archival research. In the absence of such confirmation, I concentrate on how her critics and audiences viewed her and how she capitalized on others' perceptions of her as a biracial person through her Afro-Jamaican Anansi performances. Colman Smith also deviated from accepted norms regarding her gender identity and sexuality. She never married nor had children, instead developing close relationships with women. Nicknamed "Pixie" by Ellen Terry, Colman Smith embraced the appellation, constructing a gender-indeterminate persona for herself that persisted into her work.

Although Colman Smith spent her early childhood in England, she resided in Jamaica for a significant part of her childhood and adolescence. She studied at the Pratt Institute in Brooklyn as a teenager before returning to England in the spring of 1900 to make her primary residence. While letters reveal she was close to her parents, especially her father, both parents died before she was twenty-two. Shortly thereafter, Colman Smith wrote to an acquaintance, "I have been on a good many long voyages—twenty-five beginning when I was 3 months old."[1] Her peripatetic childhood exposed her to multiple cultures and laid the groundwork for her eclectic bricolage, contributing to the retreat into imaginative worlds and perpetual quest for belonging that infuses much of her work. For almost twenty years, she frequently traveled between New York and London to pursue exhibitions, publications, and public performances. Eschewing marriage and motherhood, a nontraditional choice at that time, Colman Smith instead surrounded herself with multiple groups of like-minded women artists and writers. However, in 1919 at the age of forty-one she consciously rejected this nomadic, artistic life and permanently settled in Cornwall. Although occasionally at odds with the more conservative locals, Colman Smith continued to pursue her art and forged new communities, establishing a Roman Catholic chapel, Our Lady of the Lizard, in Cornwall. She also settled down with Nora Lake, who became her companion for more than twenty-five years.

Understanding Colman Smith within Feminist Modernism(s)

Despite garnering substantial recognition in the tarot community in recent decades and as a footnote in some studies of occult modernism, Colman Smith's work is largely unknown by both feminist and modernist scholars. However, it is ripe for recovery. Writing in the inaugural issue of *Feminist Modernist Studies*, Jessica Berman stresses the need for transnational feminist recovery projects, as

> [r]econsidering modernism in this way will illuminate the intersecting domains of identity and belonging that motivate and inhabit global modernist work, show the importance of gender as a crucial problematic in the emergence and development of global modernisms, and push us to expand our gendered understanding of modernist literary practices worldwide.[2]

An artist, designer, editor, and writer who was perceived as biracial by contemporaries and deviated from the expected roles of women, Colman Smith personifies the recent widening and broadening of definitions of modernism and the growing focus on intersectionality and the transnational.

Furthermore, re-examining the broad range of her oeuvre in light of her liminality, alienation, and experimentation extends our understanding of the modernist period, especially concerning shifting understandings of race, class, and gender.

Groundbreaking studies by Ann Ardis, Laura Doan, Rita Felski, Jane Garrity, Barbara Green, Sally Ledger, Jane Marcus, Celia Marshik, Sonita Sarker, Bonnie Kime Scott, and Urmila Seshagiri, among many others, have emphasized the important role played by women in the development of modernism. However, in order to more fully map out the complexity, variety, and interpermeability of the full range of modernism(s), we need to appreciate the wide-ranging contributions of women like Colman Smith whose existence has been largely ignored in the narratives of the more famous men and women with whom they collaborated and who often served as mentors and patrons. As Anne Fernald has observed, "It will never be enough to simply note that a writer is neglected. Instead scholars must show how a forgotten or understudied text helps challenge or advance the field."[3] Although Colman Smith has seemingly vanished from our current understanding of modernism, she was far from invisible during the approximately thirty years that she was most active (1896–1927), and her wide-ranging contributions deserve study in their own right. Her early work, especially her magazine *The Green Sheaf*, reflects her unique synthesis of the Arts and Crafts, Art Nouveau, Decadence, and Symbolist movements. Colman Smith's "music pictures," which came to her in synesthetic visions that began on Christmas Day 1900 and that appear to have continued through the 1940s, anticipate elements of both modernism and surrealism. Her Afro-Jamaican Anansi stories are some of the earliest published versions of Caribbean folktales in English and retain much of the Jamaican creole of oral discourse. They are also early examples of the anthropological turn in the early twentieth century that captivated T. S. Eliot, Havelock Ellis, Sigmund Freud, Paul Gauguin, Zora Neale Hurston, D. H. Lawrence, Pablo Picasso, Gertrude Stein, W. B. Yeats, and many others. Colman Smith's cartoons and banners for the British women's suffrage movement, as well as her activism that resulted in at least one arrest and stint in jail, reflect her strong belief that women were equal in every way to men and deserved full citizenship. She was active in the suffrage movement for several years despite being unable to benefit from England's extension of citizenship to propertied women over 30 in 1918 (and all women in 1928), as she retained her American citizenship until her death.[4]

The communities Colman Smith was involved with were far-flung, reflecting both her disparate interests and the changes in her art over her forty-year career. When she was emerging as an artist in the 1890s, her chief influences were Arthur Wesley Dow, her teacher at the Pratt Institute, and Howard Pyle, a prominent American illustrator whose books she loved and with whom she attempted to study, as well as William Morris, Kate Greenaway, Walter Crane, and the British Arts and Crafts movement. During this period, Colman Smith also made important connections with the growing New York City-based community of women artists, including Ida Haskell, Gertrude Käsebier, and Katharine Pyle, who were to remain her friends and collaborators for several years. In 1899 she first met the British actor Ellen Terry, who was to become a long-term friend and benefactor. After leaving the U.S. with Terry in the spring of 1900, Colman Smith toured with the Lyceum Theatre Company, making many drawings of Terry and her partner, Henry Irving, as well as forging a friendship with the company's manager, Bram Stoker. She collaborated on several projects with all of them in the ensuing years and even performed for King Edward VII in 1904.[5]

Colman Smith's web of influence was unusually wide. She contributed in multiple media to disparate networks in London, Dublin, and New York, as well as some brief forays to the Continent.[6] Through Terry, Colman Smith was also introduced to Terry's children, Edith and Gordon Craig, both of whom would become important friends and collaborators. Her interest in Irish myth led her to W. B. Yeats and his family, who in turn introduced her to Lady Augusta Gregory, George Russell (AE), and John Millington Synge, as well as other key members of the Irish Literary Revival, many of whom contributed to her little magazine *The Green Sheaf*. Through her friendship with Yeats, Colman Smith joined his experimental group of Masquers and met Florence Farr. She was initiated in 1901 into the occult group called the Hermetic Order of the Golden Dawn, of which Yeats and Farr were also members. It was through this community, with which she was associated for about a decade, that she met A. E. Waite, her future collaborator on the tarot deck. Colman Smith widely exhibited her "music pictures"—works of art inspired by synesthetic visions she experienced while listening to a range of orchestral music from J. S. Bach to Claude Debussy—in England, Continental Europe, and the United States. This led to three exhibitions at Alfred Stieglitz's experimental 291 gallery in New York between 1907 and 1909, as well as a friendship with Debussy. Colman Smith's long-term friendship with Edy Craig, and Craig's partner, Christopher

St. John, resulted in many collaborations on both stage designs and print projects as well as her entrée into the British women's suffrage movement.

Despite Colman Smith's significant involvement in these important networks, she was continually marginalized and often excluded from these groups by their better-known (often male) leaders. Controversies at times erupted due to her desire to have control over her art and blaze her own path, as these men were often loth to admit a woman as a full collaborator or grant her adequate credit, especially a perceived biracial, gender-nonconforming woman whose class status was often in question. Keeping in mind Colman Smith's acute awareness and at times manipulation of her liminal subject position, I examine her vulnerability but also how she used the bias she encountered as part of her art. Persistently infantilized and exoticized by more established artists and writers, Colman Smith's was unable to fit into pre-existing artistic or social categories. After an initial period of fascination with her creativity and imagination, more established mentors and friends either grew frustrated with her insistence on doing things her own way or became jealous of her creativity. In a continuous feedback loop, this frustration and jealousy then led them to refocus on their inability to clearly place her regarding her gender, race, and class, resulting in her further exoticization and othering, which generally led to the demise of the relationship. While Colman Smith at times attempted to benefit financially from this implicit racism, dressing in Afro-Jamaican peasant garb and telling Anansi stories first at private gatherings and then in public recitals, her embrace of primitivism tended to reduce her to a stereotype and minimize—rather than extend—interest in her art and writing. My intention is neither to excuse nor excoriate Colman Smith but to place her in the context of the stresses associated with the birth of modernism and use her life experiences as a window into the racial, sexual, class, and artistic prejudices of her time. It is my hope that considering the complex interactions surrounding her exoticization will help nuance our understanding of race and gender during the pre-war period.

How Contemporaries Viewed Colman Smith's Racial Origins

Throughout her life, Colman Smith consistently encountered friends, acquaintances, and critics who did not understand her and who had a hard time positioning her within existing gender, class, and racial categories. John Yeats made this assessment in the summer of 1899 after meeting Colman Smith to discuss her proposal to illustrate a collection of Gaelic mythology for children that would be written by his son, W. B. Yeats—a venture that never materialized:

> Pamela Smith and father are the funniest-looking people, the most primitive Americans possible, but I like them much … Her work whether a drawing or the telling of a piece of folklore is very direct and original and therefore sincere – its originality being its naïveté. I should feel safe in getting her to illustrate anything … She looks exactly like a Japanese. Nannie says this Japanese appearance comes from constantly drinking iced water. You at first think her rather elderly, you are surprised to find out that she is very young, quite a girl … I don't think there is anything great or profound in her, or very emotional or practical.[7]

At the time of her visit with Yeats, the "rather elderly" Colman Smith was just 21. John Yeats's comments reflect the conflation of the directness, originality, and sincerity of her art with a perceived naivety, which was to occur repeatedly in discussions of her art. Moreover, his appraisal reflects both his paternalism and his biases against "primitive" Americans, especially those whom he assumed to be a class below him and whose racial origins he had trouble ascertaining.

Similarly, Ellen Terry, the famed Shakespearean actor who was to become a long-time friend and benefactor, termed Colman Smith a "'Japanese toy'" shortly after making her acquaintance.[8] In response to these and other assertions that she had Asian origins, Colman Smith created a sketch of herself in a kimono that was published in *The Critic* magazine in 1900. With characteristic irreverence, she explains in the accompanying article that the Japanese influence on her work is "not so much as people suppose" but the caricature was created "[w]ith a merry recognition of the association."[9] Rather than just let the speculation about her origins pass without public comment, Colman Smith draws attention to it, which reflects her bold personality. She stops short of directly calling out the prejudice but makes clear she finds the whole process highly amusing. While reflecting an awareness of the complexities of race that was more sophisticated than that of many white people at the time, this move also reflects Colman Smith's own privilege, as she had the resources, education, and outlets to confront racism rather than passively accept this dehumanization.

John Yeats's comment also makes clear that Colman Smith's reception was influenced by late nineteenth- and early twentieth-century conceptions of primitivism that, as Elazar Barkan and Ronald Bush have noted, "supplied the necessary 'Other' against whose spectre embattled Victorian society reinforced itself."[10] A product of the ravages of imperialism as it expanded into previously unexplored spaces around the globe, primitivism romanticized indigenous people, using them as a foil to the decadence of Western societies. Influenced by the social thought of Franz Boas, Emile Durkheim, and Max Weber among others, primitivism's effects were wide-ranging. They were apparent in the spoils of conquered empires displayed in European museums as well as the world's fairs and universal expositions that attracted thousands of visitors who gawked at the native peoples confined to zoological replicas of their villages. However, primitivism also centrally influenced a range of early twentieth-century writing from anthropology and evolution to eugenics and sexology. Its impact can also be seen in creative works as disparate as Picasso's *Les Demoiselles d'Avignon* (1907) and Eliot's *The Waste Land* (1922). Colman Smith's long-standing interest in Afro-Jamaican Anansi folktales, which she became aware of during her time in Jamaica, also reflects this increased interest in primitivism.

The day-to-day effects of primitivism on English society, as in much of Europe, were discursive and varied. As Bush explains, there was a "fundamental instability" in the distinctions between civilized and savage.[11] Social critics such as Émile Zola, Scipio Sighele, Gabriel Tarde, and Gustave Le Bon linked the violent potential of modern crowds, which were commonly viewed as consisting primarily of the lower classes, with "the savage barbarism associated with unconscious elements of human nature that had survived evolution."[12] Robert Nye terms this the "modernity" of the savage:

> In the setting of the *fin de siècle*, one can thus understand that the savage energy of crowds might appear in two aspects: as threat and as promise. That was most ancient in crowds, the "residues" they manifested of savage life, was precisely what made them so "modern"—and therefore both a symptom of an effete and decadent civilization and a potential bulwark against it.[13]

The energy and creativity of the crowd—like the "savage" indigenous peoples who were paraded through American and European cities—captivated the imagination of the West, as it represented the spontaneity and creativity that many felt were lacking at the dawn of the twentieth century. However, the violent potential of this difference was always lurking in the shadows.

As Barkan and Bush make clear, "it was but a short step to identifying the savagery of the crowd with the energy of the unconscious, the unconventional, the childlike."[14] I argue that this process mirrors Colman Smith's reception. Contemporaries inability to classify her into clear categories of gender, race, and class helped raise the specter of the primitive Other in many, if not most, of the white Anglo-Americans she encountered. While her difference—often described as her originality, innocence, and childlike naivety—led to her entrance into the diverse groups described above, the members of these groups didn't hesitate to weaponize her difference against her when seeking to delegitimize her for her perceived lack of talent, her rejection of authority, and her deviations from the status quo.

Race was often the primary component of Colman Smith's othering and attendant delegitimization. The clearest written reference to her possible mixed race comes from Alphaeus Cole, who contributed to *The Green Sheaf* and whose book with his wife Margaret, *Saints Among the Animals*, was published by Colman Smith's Green Sheaf Press. He had studied her closely as he painted a portrait of her telling Afro-Jamaican Anansi stories. Cole noted,

> She looked like a Negress. What I think is that she was Jamaican ... a mixture of white and Negress ... She couldn't stay very comfortably in the United States at that time. Negroes were not very welcome ... You know how we treated them ... She went over to England on account of being colored.[15]

Cole, who knew Colman Smith well, is unequivocal on her biracial status and stresses that the widespread racism in the U.S. spurred her to return to England where she had spent the first ten years of her life.

Similarly, the journalist Henry Wood Nevinson called Colman Smith an "exciting little person" and a "native" of Jamaica, noting that he "supposed" she was "touched with negro blood."[16] Nevinson's brief account is, at first glance, complimentary enough—he points out that she could "draw many beautiful and unexpected things"—but he also exoticizes and others her in the process.[17] It is unclear from the passage if Nevinson made his assumption based on the fact that he associated her with Jamaica—she had lived on the island for a better part of a decade—or because "seated on the floor, she would tell unknown negro-folk-tales in a charming negro accent and manner."[18]

Echoing Nevinson's assertions, Earnest Elmo Calkins, who studied with Colman Smith at the Pratt Institute, likened her to "a strange African deity" during her folktale performances.[19] He referenced Nevinson's memoir and stated that while he had "never heard" that Colman Smith was of mixed race, it would "account for her peculiar dramatic power."[20] Calkins was impressed with her performance of her Jamaican folktales but, drawing on the romanticizing discourse of primitivism, assumed that her "peculiar dramatic power" must be a result of race, not skill.

The casualness of these comments makes clear both the ubiquity of contemporaries' speculation about Colman Smith's racial origins and how she often became, consciously or not, associated with the tales she told. Even before Colman Smith became known for her folktale performances, she was described as a Jamaican artist, and the power and originality of her work were attributed to her "exotic" origins rather than her own abilities. This reflects Marianna Torgovnick's observation that the modern West's fascination with the figure of the "primitive" reflects a "transcendental homelessness," an American and Anglo-European anxiety about rapidly changing origins and place in an increasingly alienated and alienating world.[21]

Even friends who reminisced warmly about Colman Smith and her positive contributions either termed her a West Indian or associated her with the Caribbean, which appears to have been coded language to refer to her as biracial. A good example of this comes from Edward A. Carrick, the son of Edward Gordon Craig. Craig was Ellen Terry's son, and Colman Smith contributed illustrations, theater designs, and bookplates to a variety of his projects during the early years of her career. Carrick spent much of his childhood with Terry and his aunt, Edy Craig, who was a close friend and collaborator of Colman Smith. Late in life, Carrick recounted his memories of Colman Smith, whom he called Pixie:

> Here around 1912–1914 Pixie would entertain us and other children– She sat us around her in a circle and, with the aid of little figures that she had made out of wood and paper, she would tell her wonderful stories about a'Nancy [sic]. She generally wound a scarf around her head to add to her West Indian features and the special background to the stories. She was … rather plump and very soft

and lovable—we all adored her ... She taught us [West] Indian songs and games.²²

Like Nevinson and Calkins, Carrick conflates Colman Smith's racial identity with the Anansi stories that she told, but he makes clear that the scarf she wound around her head and the figurines she held augmented her always apparent "West Indian features." However, he does not elaborate on what these might be. Carrick's memories of Colman Smith are far more positive than the other accounts, and it is clear she was a beloved childhood figure even if his assessment does reflect racially charged stereotypes of the Jamaican nurse. In this same vein, George Russell (AE), who contributed to *The Green Sheaf*, referred to Colman Smith as "the little Caribbean Pixie" in a 1902 letter to a friend.²³

Other contemporary accounts passed beyond questioning Colman Smith's racial origins and described her as more animal or even ethereal rather than human. A 1912 *Delineator* profile states that she resembled "a brown squirrel, and a Chinese baby, and a radiant morning..."²⁴ In this bizarre assessment, Colman Smith is stripped of her humanity, infantilized, racialized, and, finally, reduced to an atmospheric phenomenon. The article, like almost all reviews of her work at the time, emphasized how she defied convention and easy categorization. But, unlike most of these accounts, it also stressed how she blazed an important path for female artists: "Before she was twenty, she was an inspiration to American women painters who were working toward something different. Many of our women have since done notable decorative work, but she was the pioneer who gave them courage."²⁵ This assessment highlights that, even when the comments were clearly influenced by racist beliefs about those who did clearly fit into established racial categories, there could still be an appreciation of Colman Smith's important contributions as a feminist artist.

Likewise, Arthur Ransome's generally complimentary description of her in his 1907 *Bohemia in London* also strips Colman Smith of her humanity. He terms her a "strange little creature" and states that, upon welcoming him into her London salon, she described herself as a "goddaughter of a witch and sister to a fairy."²⁶ While it is impossible to know whether Colman Smith actually uttered these words or if they are Ransome's interpretation of what she said, the phrase is fascinating. Emphasizing Colman Smith's Otherness, the description positions her in a liminal space where she appears to have the ability to tap into the unchecked power of the witch and the playfulness of the fairy, but is not restricted to either. Ransome's assessment also reflects the influence of primitivism in his insistence on both romanticizing and othering Colman Smith, reflecting prevalent questions regarding her race, gender, and class.

As the above comments show, Colman Smith was clearly marked as an Other personally and professionally by those she encountered. Her reception and lack of sustained success reflects Sonita Sarker's assertion that "identity illuminates the nature of the position, and position impacts both the practice and the development of that identity."[27] For Colman Smith, her position as a racialized, gendered, and classed Other stymied the development of her professional identity, even, or especially, when she attempted to capitalize on her exoticization through her Afro-Jamaican Anansi performances.

Pixie Identity and Shifting Conceptions of Womanhood

Colman Smith's persona as preserved both in her correspondence and in the recollections of her friends reveals an individual who loved to joke, was quick to laugh, and often poked fun at herself and others. John Masefield's reminiscence of "Blithe Pixie" appears representative.[28] The nickname was bestowed on her by Ellen Terry in December 1899, days after the unexpected death of her father and only months after John Yeats's speculations about her racial origins. The name, as well as the nexus of associations associated with the androgynous fairy, became central to Colman Smith's personal and private life for almost twenty years.

Due to growing interest in both children's literature and folklore, pixies flourished during the Victorian and Edwardian eras. Nora Chesson's 1902 poem "Pixies" synthesizes much of the mythology circulating about the figure, emphasizing their indeterminate nature, mischievousness, freedom, and fearlessness. She writes,

> Have e'er you seen the Pixies, the fold not blest or banned?
> They walk upon the waters; they sail upon the land…
>
> The Pixies know no sorrow, the Pixies feel no fear,
> They take no care for harvest or seedtime of the year;
> Age lays no finger on them, the reaper time goes by
> The Pixies, they who change not, nor grow old or die.[29]

Unaffected by normal human emotions and concerns, pixies exist in a space apart, protected by their magical abilities. As such, it is easy to see why the figure would appeal to Colman Smith. Although "Pixie" calls to mind her puckish sense of humor and willingness to defy social conventions, Colman Smith's creation of an identity through the name shows her response to the racist views on her origins discussed above. If she was not going to fit easily into the established racial categories that structured society at the time, she was going to create a new one for herself. This impetus was similar to, but much longer-lasting than, the motivation for her self-caricature in a Japanese kimono as published in *The Critic* in June 1900. Just as Colman Smith wanted to have the last word on the subject and make clear she was not Asian, her creation of an identity as a racially ambiguous, androgynous Pixie was a way to combat, and even, on her own terms, to profit from, the racism and gender discrimination that she encountered. Rather than struggle to fit into clearly defined categories of race, class, and gender, Colman Smith, as I will discuss throughout this book, decided to jettison those pre-existing classifications and follow her own path.

In almost all expected ways, Colman Smith did not conform to conventional social roles for women but, instead, worked to destabilize and re-envision them. Throughout her life, she eschewed marriage and children in favor of focusing on her creative endeavors. Her closest companions were other women, many, but not all, of whom engaged in various artistic pursuits. Letters reveal that Colman Smith did not conform to expected standards of feminine behavior and deportment. She was outspoken, bold, and did not suffer fools lightly. She positioned herself in opposition to the "feeble females" who "are living well by their inanities!" and stated, consequently, "We disgruntled devils don't please anybody!—"[30] The question remains unanswered whether she was able to please herself.

The last important piece in understanding Colman Smith's identity creation is shifting conceptions of womanhood at the *fin de siècle*, as American and British imperialism rapidly expanded. This is especially important for Colman Smith who was perceived as biracial and did not conform with established views of femininity. Sally Ledger, Jane Garrity, Deborah Cohler, and others have noted that late nineteenth- and early twentieth-century middle- and upper-class British womanhood was defined by and against eugenic motherhood. As Ledger explains, "Feminists were able to exploit the ideological assumptions about women's superior moral strength to enable themselves to take up imperial service in the name of Victorian womanhood. Women's roles as nurturers, child-carers, preservers of purity, could all be put to use as part of the wider imperialist project."[31] Much of this feminist argument was entrenched within imperial discourse, and, as a result, "was preoccupied with race preservation, racial purity, and racial motherhood."[32] This focus on racial preservation and purity increased exponentially in the *fin de siècle* period as the British Empire grew and the domestic birthrate declined. Cohler points out: "The ideological and material production of the British 'race' positioned bourgeois English women as mothers of the nation: maternity rested at the core of ideologies of femininity, and reproduction defined representations of female sexuality. The nation, in other words, constituted gendered ideologies."[33] During the twentieth century, and especially after World War I, modernist women, as Garrity has noted, recapitulated pervasive imperial tropes in "their attempt to re-imagine themselves as full citizens, as legitimate and agency-wielding daughters rather than as subjugated mothers of England."[34] Many of these women identified as lesbian or bisexual. However, at the turn of the twentieth century, many bourgeois women took on well-established masculine tropes in order to more fully assert their female agency and point of view. Before World War I, these masculine strategies were not primarily seen as representative of female homosexuality, which was later to become the standard interpretation.[35] At the turn of the twentieth century, as Cohler notes, "masculine women signified a national or eugenic threat more often than a homosexual symptom."[36]

This book examines how this changing discourse affected "masculine" women like Colman Smith, who came of age in the late 1890s and early 1900s, after the demise of the New Woman but before the sweeping social changes of the interwar period—women who did not bear or raise children and positioned themselves in opposition to heterosexual, bourgeois marriage; women who defiantly exhibited masculine strategies, who wanted to be a part of the public sphere, and who asserted their own agency and identities. This is doubly true for Colman Smith, who, despite living the bulk of her life in England, never became a British citizen, and whose racial origins, as discussed above, were frequently questioned by those she encountered. While letters reveal that Colman Smith often viewed her publications as her children, showing pride as they made their way into the world and protective rage when they were not deemed worthwhile by publishers, the displacement of the maternal instinct onto her art is only half the story. Living through a *fin-de-siècle* period where seemingly unchanging categories and social mores concerning gender, race, and class were increasingly in flux, Colman Smith strove to create a new space for herself that blurred these once-sharp divisions. Her art, which mixed disparate elements with bold use of color, was—like her person—often initially heralded as fresh, original, and exciting. However, this initial enthusiasm was not maintained, often as a result of her refusal (and inability) to conform to still quite clearly demarcated roles for women, even women artists. Women, could, and did, stray from the accepted path, but only up to a point; Colman Smith generally disregarded these conventions entirely and explored uncharted territory.

Unwilling to subordinate herself to the creative vision of others—especially male patrons—Colman Smith strove to retain artistic control over the projects with which she was involved. Continually, however, these attempts proved not to be financially viable, nor did they generate the consistent patronage that funded much of the experimentation of male modernist artists and writers. While the women's suffrage movement provided a glimpse for Colman Smith of what a nurturing, women-centered community could accomplish, the advent of World War I quickly squashed these dreams. After the war, Colman Smith left London—a city that she initially embraced but increasingly associated with frustration and failed expectations—and bought a home on the Lizard at the tip of Cornwall. This remote corner of England likely reminded her of the Jamaica of her childhood and was rich with folklore, much of it centered on pixies, which she loved. Although this move initially provided Colman Smith with the freedom and space to pursue her art on her own terms, increasing poverty, due to changing artistic tastes, and the hostility of her conservative neighbors intruded on her country idyll. Nevertheless, she kept writing, painting, and submitting material throughout the 1930s and early 1940s, though sales were few and far between.

This book illuminates Colman Smith's life and work through five chapters and a biographical epilogue. Chapter 1 explores Colman Smith's origins, arguing that her frequent moves helped create the outsider perspective that was to become a fundamental characteristic of her life and art. Born into an extended New York-based family that included well-known artists, actors, and political figures, Colman Smith spent the first decade of her life primarily in England, which laid the foundation for her decision to return as an adult and settle as an expatriate artist. Her early exposure to Swedenborgianism, a mystical branch of Christianity, helped instill an interest in religious mystery and ritual that continued throughout her life and infused much of her work. After the collapse of her father's mercantile firm, the family moved to Jamaica where she became fascinated with the country, especially its history, folklore, and Obeah spiritual practices. This inspired her to collect Afro-Jamaican Anansi folktales. Her time in Jamaica also provided her with firsthand knowledge of imperialistic primitivism, which fueled both her interest in a wide range of cultures and religious traditions and her, at times, appropriation of Jamaican folktales. This chapter draws heavily upon her letters to her cousin, Mary "Bobby" Reed—a correspondence that began with the pivotal death of Colman Smith's mother in July 1896 and provides a window into both her life in Jamaica and her keen sense of humor. The chapter concludes by arguing that the plays she produced for her miniature theater were important in the development of her feminist voice.

Focused on both Colman Smith's time at the Pratt Institute and her emergence as an artist in 1890s New York, Chapter 2 discusses important influences on her early art and her critical reception. It argues that the two most important influences were Arthur Wesley Dow, her instructor at Pratt, and Howard Pyle, the "Father" of American illustration. The British Arts and Crafts movement was another key influence, especially the work of William Morris, Walter Crane, Kate Greenaway, and Marcus Ward. Furthermore, Colman Smith's life illuminates the ways in which increasing numbers of women navigated a still firmly patriarchal and often misogynistic arts scene. In order to sustain herself, Colman Smith began to surround herself with a network of women artists and writers. At first, this included her cousin "Bobby" Reed, and then expanded to Ida Haskell and Gertrude Käsebier, whom she met at the Pratt Institute. Later she extended this network to include an international network of female friends and acquaintances. These female artistic communities were to provide key support and encouragement to her over the course of her life, especially as she became jaded by the false promises of her male patrons and publishers. The chapter concludes by asserting that we can see the clear feminist focus in her early work through her emphasis on strong female characters, such as her portrayal of Lady Macbeth, as well as her distinctive use of color, movement, shape, and line.

When twenty-two-year-old Colman Smith returned to England in the spring of 1900, she was searching for a new start after the death of her father. Chapter 3 proposes that the embrace of both her new nickname, Pixie, and the friendship of the woman who had bestowed it on her, Ellen Terry, was important to her development of a non-binary gender identity. Colman Smith quickly became enmeshed in the creative worlds of Terry and her children, Edith and Gordon Craig. Indeed, it was while listening to Gordon Craig play Bach that Colman Smith experienced her first musical vision, which led to her most sustained creative output. She also became a long-time friend and collaborator of Edy Craig. During this pivotal period she met W. B. Yeats, was initiated into the Hermetic Order of the Golden Dawn, became a Masquer, and contributed stage designs to several of his productions. This friendship led to other collaborations with his siblings, notably co-editing *A Broad Sheet* with Jack Yeats from 1902 to 1903. Increasingly, Colman Smith realized that she wanted to exert control over her projects and pursue her own artistic vision. To this end, the chapter argues that the thirteen issues of *The Green Sheaf* made important contributions to modernist print culture and show both the influence of and a reaction against W. B. Yeats.

The long-term impact of Afro-Jamaican Anansi stories on Colman Smith's life and work, which has not been previously examined, is the subject of Chapter 4. While there was a growing interest in folktales from both the Caribbean and the American South during this period, her transcriptions of the trickster figure Anansi were set apart by her use of a Jamaican creole, rather than standard English, and her changes to Anansi's temperament and interactions with his animal associates. Looking at Colman Smith's Anansi stories alongside others from the same period, this chapter demonstrates that her novel variations only increased as she matured as a feminist artist and repeatedly returned to these tales both in print and through her Anansi performances. The chapter then considers Colman Smith's "music pictures," which allowed her to experience psychic images that were unleashed through listening to music. Alfred Stieglitz hosted three exhibitions of these paintings at his 291 gallery in New York. Perhaps unsurprisingly, there were many similarities between the reception of her "music pictures" and her Anansi performances. While critics initially praised the imaginative, original, and childlike aspects of Colman Smith's art, they increasingly lamented her supposed technical deficiencies, and lost interest and even mocked them. I argue that this critical reception discloses the connections between racism and misogyny that permeated her critical reception in both the U.S. and Britain.

Chapter 5 demonstrates that throughout the 1910s, Colman Smith's interest in and involvement with the occult revival was an important catalyst for her maturation as a symbolic feminist artist. In November of 1901 she became initiated into the Hermetic Order of the Golden Dawn as the group was beginning to fracture over struggles for control that, at least in part, had their roots in the rapidly changing roles open to women in the early twentieth century. This gendered treatment of women within the occult revival affected Colman Smith in myriad ways, just as the misogynistic atmosphere of the period centrally affected her art and life. While she did not advance beyond the initiatory levels of the Golden Dawn, it was through the group that she met A. E. Waite and designed the images for the storied tarot deck. This chapter asserts that she began working on designs for the deck earlier than previously believed, and that her music paintings of the 1907–08 period share several similarities with her tarot designs, including frequent use of the Rückenfigur technique, depicting figures with their back to the viewer, and tower symbolism. Based on new archival discoveries, this chapter shows that Colman Smith's involvement with the women's suffrage movement, which commenced in earnest in 1909, was an important influence for both her tarot designs and the evolution of her feminist symbolic art. She contributed multiple posters and postcards to the Suffrage Atelier, most of which were unsigned, was jailed at least once for her suffrage activities, and helped working-class women attend suffrage events. The culmination of her myriad interests during this period was the representation of the female figures in her "music pictures," which have not been analyzed as a group. This chapter reveals that moving from women in water, to women in the earth and sky, to, finally, women as trees, Colman Smith created her own symbolic lexicon that allowed her to highlight different aspects of womanhood.

The Epilogue rounds out Colman Smith's life by examining her neglected later years. It examines how her conversion to Roman Catholicism in the summer of 1911 marked a renewed commitment to her feminism and symbolic art, rather than, as has been suggested, a renunciation. The years following her conversion were busy ones. She was an active participant in the women's suffrage movement, had a major solo exhibition at the Berlin Photographic Company in New York, and completed several illustration projects that had a distinct feminist bent. During World War I, Colman Smith was active in a variety of charitable war efforts and participated in a few exhibitions, but interest in her work began to wane. After moving to Cornwall, she was increasingly troubled by financial difficulties. Although there was a resurgence of interest in her work in the mid-1920s, it was short-lived. The constant in her life during this period was Nora Lake, with whom she had a close, intimate relationship, and with whom she lived for at least twenty-five years. After selling her house, Parc Garland, in 1939, she eventually settled in Bude, where she died in 1951.

Pamela Colman Smith: Feminist, Artist, Mystic provides a fuller understanding of the life and work of this important, yet under-appreciated artist and writer, and shows how her contributions revise our understanding of many creative spheres in America and England during the early twentieth century. It focuses primarily on her first forty years, as it was during this period that she made her most important contributions as an artist, writer, folklore performer, editor, publisher, stage designer, and suffrage activist. Colman Smith consistently broke down barriers both small and large, blurring the boundaries between the multiple genres in which she worked. She collaborated with many of the luminaries of the early twentieth century, ranging from Ellen Terry and Bram Stoker to W. B. Yeats, Florence Farr, and A. E. Waite. However, her contemporaries found her racial and gender expression confusing, which led to othering and exoticizing. Although Colman Smith at times attempted to capitalize on this through her performances of Afro-Jamaican Anansi tales, long-term critical and commercial success remained elusive, especially when she stopped following the dictates of the market and pursued art on her own terms through her "music paintings." Her move to Cornwall precipitated the demise of her career, which was compounded by changing artistic tastes after World War I. Nevertheless, Colman Smith continued to create in multiple media through at least the 1940s.

Strikingly, this pattern of female individualism affected countless women artists and writers during the early twentieth century due to the widespread misogyny and racism of the period. Feminist modernist studies has helped re-evaluate the contributions of many of these women artists and writers, so the once-dominant narrative of a few exceptional white men has been transformed into a more nuanced account of the large number of men and women who influenced the multiple networks that compose our understanding of modernism(s). While much important work has been done, the time is right for a more comprehensive appreciation of Colman Smith, a truly dynamic artist and writer. By filling in the contours of her life and career, *Pamela Colman Smith: Feminist, Artist, Mystic* shows that she was much more than a footnote to tarot and modernism. This book returns Colman Smith to her rightful place at the center of multiple transatlantic artist communities, feminist circles, and mystic groups.

CHAPTER ONE

Naming and Identity
Family, Miniature Theater, and Jamaican Residence

On July 25, 1896, an eighteen-year-old Corinne Pamela Mary Colman Smith, who was living at Ambergate in St. Andrew parish, Jamaica, wrote her cousin, Mary Reed, in Brooklyn, New York. The two had attended the Pratt Institute together in Brooklyn and shared interests in theater, art, and literature. Both women were interested in the power and significance of naming, as well as the fluidity of identity that a multiplicity of names can suggest. Each used multiple forms of epistolary address, which demonstrates this preoccupation. Colman Smith addressed her cousin as "Dear Maysie, Bobby, Pickled-mummy and all your other names," a testament to both the deep affection between the two and her love of playful jokes and silly humor.[1] In most of the twenty extant letters that date from July 1896 to December 1900, Colman Smith refers to her cousin as "Bobby,"[2] derived from their shared girlish infatuation with the actor Robert Taber, whom they refer to in their letters as "Bobby," and, even more commonly, "HIM!!!"[3] While Colman Smith's given first name was Corinne, like her mother, she was generally known to her family by her middle name, Pamela, or even Mela; her maternal grandmother was named Pamelia, and Mela was a common family nickname.[4] During the period of Colman Smith's correspondence with her cousin she experimented with a few different names, but she signs the first letter "your Pam—or Ham or Sam."[5] This appellation not only highlights her sense of humor and love of rhyme but also emphasizes fundamental questions about the nature of Colman Smith's identity and her ability to shape

21

and create one for herself, interests that were to prove central to her artistic and personal life, as she moved frequently and took on many personal and professional identities.

Born in London to American parents whose extended New York-based family included well-known artists, actors, and political figures, Colman Smith's adolescent and teenage years were spent primarily in Jamaica. Her time on the island provided her with a transnational perspective and—coupled with significant questions surrounding her racial identity—instilled in her an ethnographic interest in a wide variety of cultures and religious traditions as well as an outsider perspective that was distinctly feminist. As I will detail below, this perspective first emerged from her early forays as an artist and writer during her years in Jamaica, but was pivotal for the rest of her career.

Colman Smith's questioning of her identity and positioning of herself as an outsider was fundamentally shaped by the news she imparted to her cousin in this letter: the death of her mother, Corinne Colman Smith, on July 10, 1896.[6] As she notes in her missive, "I hoped you would write first. I was going to write some time ago. But since the Moon Angel visited here—I have not had time—I have not very much to say."[7] The euphemistic language and short staccato sentences, which do not reflect the typical diction of Colman Smith's normally lengthy and effusive letters, appear to be a way for her to gain psychological distance and protection from the loss she felt at her mother's death. The impact that her mother's death had on her becomes more explicit when taken with the fact that for the next two years she signed all her letters after this one as "Con."[8] By jettisoning her given names and creating a new identity, specifically one that emphasized trickery, play, and the performance of identity, she became a different person who would not have to deal directly with the hurt caused by this loss. Interestingly, after the unexpected death of her father in December 1899, Colman Smith changed names again. This time she did not return to Pamela, her middle name that she consistently used professionally during this period, but adopted the gender-indeterminate appellation Pixie, which had been bestowed on her by a new friend, the Shakespearean actor Ellen Terry.[9] As I will discuss in Chapter 3, pixies are a type of fairy that exist in a parallel world and are able to intrude intermittently on the mundane world of hurt and loss to bring mischief and merriment.[10] This ability to transcend the normal boundaries of space and time was critical to Colman Smith's emerging understanding of herself. Furthermore, the name changes underscore the importance of naming and the fluidity of identity, as well as how deeply affected she was by her parents' deaths.

Swedenborgianism, Howard Pyle, and Processing Death

As a child, Colman Smith's interest in otherworldly happenings and paranormal abilities was fostered through her exposure to Swedenborgianism, which stressed the close connection between the human, angelic, and demonic worlds.[11] Its founder, Emanuel Swedenborg (1688–1772), communicated between these worlds, and many of his followers tried to cultivate this same faculty. According to a 1912 *Craftsman* article, "From childhood she [Colman Smith] has had the gift of the 'second sight.'"[12] Traditionally, people with this type of telepathy can perceive things that are not present to the regular five senses. This ability makes the person privy either to future events or events at distant locations.

Also hinting at her future interests, Colman Smith's halting account to her cousin of her mother's passing reveals her interest in mysticism and alternative views to traditional Christianity. Her euphemistic language in terming her mother's death a "visit from the Moon Angel" is a direct allusion to Howard Pyle's 1895 *The Garden Behind the Moon*.[13] Pyle, a prolific late nineteenth-century writer and illustrator, was best known for his many books on pirates, Robin Hood, and the American Revolution, among other subjects. Most of Pyle's writings can be loosely grouped in the fairy tale and adventure genres and were aimed primarily at children. As I detail in Chapter 2, Pyle's works, and particularly his artistic style, were very influential in Colman Smith's development as both an artist and writer.

Pyle was a follower of Swedenborg. Much more mystical and introspective than most of his other works, *The Garden Behind the Moon* reflects his long-term interest in Swedenborgianism.[14] As Jane Williams-Hogan notes, "The revelation given through Swedenborg was to teach people born at the end of the Christian Church how to see 'through or beyond' the literal understanding of the Bible to the deeper spiritual meaning."[15] Swedenborg wanted the faithful to connect directly with angelic beings through the use of their reason.[16] A defining element in his writings was a belief in a spirit world that directly affected human life, and the possibility of communicating with this world through paranormal means. For Swedenborgians, communicating with this hidden world was not only possible but also key to learning important information that would otherwise be concealed.[17]

It is easy to see why Colman Smith, who even as a teenager was dubious of blind adherence to accepted social mores, was drawn to a religion that promoted close connection to the spirit world, especially after the death of her mother. Swedenborg's teachings are very much in line with Colman Smith's focus on the creative power and potential of the individual. Her exposure to these ideas also likely predisposed her to be more open to non-traditional forms of spirituality, which resulted in her long-term interest in both Afro-Jamaican Obeah and fairies, as well as her decade-long association with the occult group, the Hermetic Order of the Golden Dawn. This mystical background helps explain both her creation of the arresting images for the 1909 Smith-Waite tarot deck, and her otherwise surprising conversion to Roman Catholicism in 1911, a religion she followed until her death forty years later.

The impetus for *The Garden Behind the Moon*—a book of which Pyle wrote that he had "especially strong feelings" and that was a "distinctively Swedenborgian tale"[18]—was the tragic death of his six-year-old son Sellers in 1890, while Pyle was on a research and sketching trip in Jamaica.[19] The text of *The Garden Behind the Moon*, like Swedenborgianism, imagines a very different afterlife than the traditional Christian teaching of a vast gulf between heaven and hell in which the bodily trappings of this world are left behind.[20] In Pyle's work, a beautiful, if aloof, male Moon Angel escorts recently deceased children to the Moon Garden—the book's version of heaven. The Moon Garden closely resembles a well-manicured English country garden and is populated only by children aged three to twelve, who laugh and play, seemingly restored to life. The space, as David, the hero of the tale, attests, is "the best place *out* of the world in which to play."[21] *The Garden Behind the Moon* does contain some familiar fairytale elements: a young boy who overcomes adversity to become a hero, a fantastical villain (in this case a giant Iron Man) who is defeated, magical human and animal guides who help the boy in his quest (notably a winged horse), and a happy ending complete with an advantageous marriage to a princess. Somewhat surprisingly, the book also contains a condemnation of the slave trade and an endorsement of racial equality after death.[22] This sentiment likely resonated with the young Colman Smith, given her perceived biracial status and adolescence spent in the British colony of Jamaica. Although slavery was abolished on the island in 1834, its legacy was still very much apparent in the 1880s and 1890s.

Although Swedenborg's radical views were not accepted in his native country, they were exported to the U.S. almost immediately after that country's founding and gained popularity during the years leading up to and after the Civil War.[23] The roster of U.S. artists and writers influenced by Swedenborgian ideas includes Ralph Waldo Emerson, Henry Thoreau, William Dean Howells, George Inness, Edgar Allan Poe, Harriet Beecher Stowe, and Walt Whitman.[24] Artists and writers outside the U.S. who were influenced by Swedenborg's teachings include William Blake, Henri Balzac, Charles Baudelaire, Fyodor Dostoevsky, Paul Gauguin, August Strindberg, and Jorge Luis Borges.[25] By 1890 the faith claimed 154 American societies and 7,095 adult members, including Colman Smith's parents and her maternal grandparents, who were the primary U.S. publishers of Swedenborg's books in the nineteenth century.[26] As Charles Eldredge has pointed out, the rise in Swedenborgianism after the Civil War was part of a larger American fascination with spiritualism during this period. "While spiritualism as a faith enjoyed fluctuating allegiance by Americans from the mid-century onwards, its greater attention came as a field for scientific investigations."[27] This led to the creation of the U.S. branch of the Society for Psychical Research in 1884, which explored psychic phenomena, telekinesis, spiritualists, and mediums.[28] Furthermore, "[t]he revival of mysticism and the survival of pantheism in late nineteenth-century America paralleled the flourishing of artistic imagination and the birth of Symbolist thought."[29] Although Colman Smith's work from the 1890s and 1900s reflects a range of influences, much of her art and writing from this period shows the influence of this movement.

When Colman Smith's father, Charles Edward Smith, died suddenly in New York on December 1, 1899, Colman Smith returned to the language of Pyle's *The Garden Behind the Moon*. In a letter to her cousin Mary Reed, she notes, "Yes, the Moon Angel has been again—and now they [Colman Smith's parents] are both in the moon house—and can look out of the windows—and we know what they see—Him?"[30] The "Him" appears to refer to the Moon Angel, the god-surrogate in Pyle's story. However, the question mark suggests that Colman Smith at 21 may have had doubts about the afterlife that she did not have at eighteen. A year later, she wrote to Reed on the death of Reed's grandmother, Colman Smith's maternal aunt, whom she called Granny. Colman Smith's difficulty talking about death as well as her reservations about what happens after it are more evident in this letter. She writes, "So the moon angel has visited you this time—& dear Granny has gone—she is happy—& looking out of moon windows with other dear ones of ours—?—we hope." She quickly adds, "I am so sorry—but I can say nothing but I know what it feels like—"[31] After expressing language's inability to adequately convey her emotions, Colman Smith abruptly changes focus to discuss her life in England while on tour with Ellen Terry, Henry Irving, Bram Stoker, and the other members of the Lyceum Theatre Company. Just as in her letter to her cousin following her mother's death, Colman Smith employs similar diversionary tactics, preferring to veer away from an emotionally difficult topic to relate funny stories.

While Colman Smith loved games, laughter, and fairy tales of all sorts, her fondness for Pyle's *The Garden Behind the Moon* had less to do with its joyful, fantastical elements and more with its sympathetic treatment of death and extensive use of both allegory and symbolism. In an October 5, 1896 letter to her cousin Mary Reed, Colman Smith relates the recent visit to her home of a young female friend whom she terms the "rompiest spook I ever saw."[32] The two played games and collaborated on a poem, but Colman Smith expresses surprise at the girl's reaction to Pyle's book:

> I gave her the *Moon Garden* to read and she did not like it at all only as a fairy story!!! Daddy asked her what it meant—and she said nothing—but not to laugh at silly little children[.] I thought she would be the very one to see more—but she does not think of much but her school and romping![33]

The multiple exclamation points, run-on sentences, and heavy underlining in the original emphasize Colman Smith's surprise at the girl's inability, or disinclination, to uncover the deeper meaning of Pyle's text. Her frustration at yet another person failing "to see more," and not just in relation to Pyle's book and Swedenborgianism, would recur at multiple points throughout her life. Moreover, it highlights both Colman Smith's interest in delving deeper into unconventional forms of spirituality and her growing annoyance that many people she encountered did not share this interest and were content to remain on the mundane surface of things.

Origins, Extended Family, and English Childhood

Throughout her life, Colman Smith struggled with those around her who did not understand her and had trouble positioning her within existing gender, class, and racial categories. Published accounts of her art and life also exhibit a tendency to exoticize her background and depict her, and often by extension her art, as simple and naive. A full-page 1904 *Brooklyn Daily Eagle* article is representative:

> There could be no greater contrast to the ordinary dainty young Heights girl, of pretty manners, or normal tendencies, conventional ways and the usual ambitions. Yet were an Iphetonga to be danced to-day, Pamela Coleman [*sic*] Smith, this odd-artist mystic girl, would be trebly qualified for its inmost place.[34]

Here the twenty-six-year-old Colman Smith is described as unusual in both conduct and ambition, as well as mystic, an appellation that was frequently applied to both her and her work. The oddness is seemingly due to her lack of interest in securing a husband and desire to focus instead on an independent life and an artistic career. The unnamed writer could also be insinuating that she might have Native American blood, as "Iphetonga" is both the Native American word for Brooklyn Heights and a reference to the indigenous tribe who inhabited Brooklyn before the arrival of the Europeans.[35] However, "Iphetonga" also alludes to a series of exclusive balls held in Brooklyn Heights in the 1880s and 1890s that were eventually ended due to disagreements over which families had high enough social standing to attend; both Colman Smith's maternal and paternal relatives inhabited the highest echelons of Brooklyn society, which would have guaranteed her an undisputed place at these soirées.[36]

Colman Smith's parents—Charles Edward Smith and Corinne Colman Smith—both came from prominent New York families. Her maternal grandfather, Samuel Colman, was a well-known bookseller, publisher, and etcher, in both Boston and New York City, whose "store in Broadway was a unique depository of pictures, and a favorite resort of artists and *litterateurs*; associated with the Swedenborgians, a sect remarkable for aesthetic proclivities."[37] He is also credited with publishing the first illustrated volume of American verse.[38] His wife, Pamelia Chandler Colman, who published under the name

Mrs. Colman, was a prolific author of children's books, many of them collections of translations of French and German fairy tales or other previously published material, including several William Blake poems that I will discuss in Chapter 5.[39] She collaborated on many of these, notably the long-running series of the Cousin LuLu books, with her eldest daughter, Pamela Atkins Colman (later Howard), who published under the name Miss Colman.[40] In 1846 her *Stories for Corinne: A Book for All Little Girls and Boys* was published by her husband in honor of their daughter, Corinne Chandler Colman, then about 10 years old, who would later become Colman Smith's mother.[41] The eponymous poem that closes the collection reads:

> At hoop and at rope
> She was first of the throng,
> And sweet as the lark
>   Of the woodland her song;
> None who saw the curls fall
> O'er her forehead so fair,
> Could doubt the calm picture
>   Of innocence there.[42]

As was typical of Victorian children's literature, the poem conflates beauty and innocence. In 1856 Mrs. Colman's *Stories for Children: A Book for All Little Girls and Boys* was published by the New York publisher Samuel Raynor; this volume contains almost the exact same content as *Stories for Corinne*, including the closing poem "Corinne."[43] An interesting addition is a frontispiece illustration of a young girl looking jauntily at the reader, captioned "Corinne." In 1856 Corinne Colman would have been a twenty-year-old woman. According to contemporaneous newspaper accounts, Corinne was "very beautiful" and a "great drawing room actress of Brooklyn," whose performances in a private theater hosted by her sister, Pamela Atkins Colman Howard, were acclaimed throughout the borough.[44] It is unknown how Charles and Corinne first became acquainted, but it is fascinating to consider whether they met at one of these private theater performances.

    The best-known of the Colman children was Corinne's older brother, Samuel Colman, who achieved early fame as a landscape artist of the Hudson River School. Some of the most famous members of this school, such as Thomas Cole, George Inness, and Colman himself, were deeply interested in

Swedenborgian mysticism and sought to use their art to express the spiritual reality that lay beyond the surface of nature. Colman first exhibited at the National Academy of Design at the age of eighteen.[45] His long career spanned several styles and periods, and his art took him to France, Spain, Algeria, Mexico, and Japan, where he began to amass his large collection of Chinese and Japanese prints and jades.[46] In the mid-1870s Samuel Colman began etching, and in 1881 ten of his works were included in the *Exhibition of American Etchers* at the Museum of Fine Arts in Boston.[47] Colman was also very interested in interior design, and by 1878 was an associate of Louis Tiffany.[48] The pair decorated many famous homes together in New York and Newport, including the Vanderbilt mansion, and were known for their fusion of exotic influences such as Japanese, Chinese, Moorish, Viking, Celtic, and Byzantine.[49] Although it is unclear how close Colman, who did take long trips to Europe, North Africa, Asia, and the American West, was to his Brooklyn-based relatives, a 1904 *Brooklyn Daily Eagle* article notes that "the chief decoration" of their drawing rooms "comprises a series of paintings of Samuel Coleman [sic] that are highly representative of him."[50] It is likely that Colman Smith saw these paintings during visits to her Brooklyn relatives, if not through direct interaction with her uncle and his work. She also shared an interest in Chinese and Japanese art, and it is possible that this fascination began with the perusal of her uncle's extensive collection. As I discuss in Chapter 2, her appreciation of Japanese art, especially that of the painter and printmaker Hokusai, deepened during her classes with Arthur Wesley Dow at the Pratt Institute and became a key component of her early work.

While Colman Smith's maternal relatives included well-known artists and writers, her paternal family was distinguished by their contributions to government and business. Her father's mother, Lydia Lewis Hooker, was a direct descendant of Thomas Hooker, a Puritan clergyman who established a major colony in Hartford, Connecticut; he was a staunch supporter of uncoupling voting rights from church membership, which was his chief disagreement with the Puritan leadership of the Massachusetts Bay Colony. Colman Smith's paternal grandfather, Cyrus Porter Smith, was an important figure in the development of Brooklyn from a small village in the early nineteenth century to a bustling borough at the time of his death in 1877. He was the fourth appointed mayor of Brooklyn in 1839 and a year later was the first to be popularly elected to that position; he held the office until 1842 and later served as a state senator from New York.[51] A prosperous businessman, Cyrus

Porter Smith helped found the first gas company in Brooklyn, was director of Brooklyn's Union Ferry Company, president of the Brooklyn City Railroad Company, and one of the founding directors of Brooklyn City Hospital.[52] While his older son, Bryan, followed him into business in Brooklyn, his youngest son, Charles Edward, "artist rather than businessman, hardly met with the material success of his brother."[53] Charles, Colman Smith's father, who initially wanted to be an artist and exhibited in Paris as a young man, spent much time in England. Another older brother, Theodore Eanes Smith, known as Teddy, also became a merchant but never married. He remained close to Colman Smith and her father throughout his life, and left her a bequest that spurred her to leave London and purchase a Cornish property, Parc Garland, on the Lizard peninsula in 1919.

The details of Corinne Colman and Charles Smith's courtship are unknown; by December 1870 census records note they are married and living on East 15th Street in Manhattan. Charles is listed as thirty and Corinne thirty-five.[54] However, Charles's baptismal record indicates that he was twenty-four and Corinne, who was very fluid in recording her age, was likely thirty-five or even thirty-six.[55] After their marriage, it appears Corinne made at least two trips to Jamaica by herself; these journeys could indicate that she had family on the island, which would also help explain the family's move to Jamaica in 1889, but the nature and purpose of these trips are unknown.[56] In 1874 Charles joined the New York branch of Cowlishaw, Nicol & Company, manufacturers of silk, worsted, and mixed fabrics. The company's main locations were in London and Manchester, and before Colman Smith's birth in 1878, Charles transferred to the London branch and the family moved to England.[57] While it is possible that the transatlantic move was purely for business reasons, it is also possible, if not likely, that the couple was part of the migration of many artistically inclined Americans to Europe in the 1870s and 1880s, seeking refuge from the Gilded Age.[58] As Charles Eldredge notes, "Armed with imagination, ideal, and soul, reactionaries against the modern condition waged battle internationally with the hegemonic naturalism, empiricism, and rationalism of the late nineteenth century."[59] Although it might seem a stretch to suggest that an employee of a manufacturing firm would oppose materialism, the family, as I discuss below, moved in the highest literary and artistic circles during their time in England. Regardless of their motives, sometime before their daughter's birth on February 16, 1878, Corinne and Charles moved to England, settling just blocks away from Victoria Station in London.[60]

Throughout Colman Smith's life, unsubstantiated rumours swirled around her, alleging that she was adopted, the product of an extramarital affair, or that one of her parents was the product of an interracial extramarital affair.[61] A 1904 *Brooklyn Daily Eagle* article's assessment is typical, and hints at untold secrets when it states that Colman Smith "has always been strange. There is not a page of her life, not an incident, that is not overflowing with romance."[62] The article also mentions that she has "sisters" living in Brooklyn. However, census records show Charles and Corinne had only one child, and there is no indication that either of them married again or had other children.[63] As I detail in the Introduction, there are multiple published and unpublished accounts by people who encountered Colman Smith that state she was of mixed race; however, there was much disagreement over her racial makeup, with some asserting that she was Black or even "West Indian," others claiming she was Asian, and still others that she was an indeterminate "creature."

As a young woman, Colman Smith appears to have internalized the idea that she was different. In a 1902 letter to George Pollexfen, W. B. Yeats's maternal uncle and fellow member of the Hermetic Order of the Golden Dawn, a twenty-four-year-old Colman Smith thanks him for "doing her horoscope" and notes that "I was brought up in a rather unusual way—and there are plenty of people who do not understand me."[64] Responding to a conversation she had with Pollexfen about her parents, she adds that "What you say of my Mother and Father is quite true—I am sure my mother had ideas of her own—and was understood by very few—"[65] Unfortunately, Colman Smith does not elaborate on her own thoughts about her parents or their marriage. Other letters reveal that she was very close with her father, whom she affectionately nicknamed Pig and lived with until his death in December 1899.[66] However, a 1903 article in *The Reader* credits her mother as having the biggest impact on her work, stating that it is "from her mother she derived an intense, individual creative desire, which very early in life began to satisfy itself in a curious sort of drawing."[67]

Another unusual aspect of Colman Smith's childhood was its peripatetic nature. As she noted in a letter to Pollexfen, "I have been [on] a good many long voyages—twenty-five—beginning when I was 3 months old."[68] This would average slightly more than one major trip a year during the twenty-four years prior to her writing this letter, a rather startling number, as the majority of the population at this time did not take any such trips. It is unclear where she went on the infant voyage, although New York to see her Brooklyn relatives is definitely a possibility. We do know that she traveled to Paris in October 1879, presumably with her parents, when she would have been eighteen months old.[69]

Little is known of the family's time in England, but in an October 1896 letter, Colman Smith laments to her cousin, Mary Reed, that it "[s]eems as if all the old friends were going—doesn't it? Sir Frederic Leighton—... William Morris—du Maurier—"[70] Leighton, who died on January 25, 1896, was a noted English painter known for his "classically inspired, realistic nudes."[71] His use of color and frequent depiction of women in profile was an early influence on Colman Smith. William Morris, who died on October 3, 1896, was an English textile designer, poet, novelist, and founder of the British Arts and Crafts movement. His intricate designs of fruit, flowers, and spiraling patterns centrally shaped much of Colman Smith's 1890s art. George du Maurier, who died on October 8, 1896, was a Franco-British *Punch* cartoonist and novelist; Colman Smith read and enjoyed all three of his novels—*Peter Ibbetson* (1891), *Trilby* (1894), and *The Martian* (1897)—exhorting her cousin to read them as well.[72] While it is likely that the Smith family became acquainted with these individuals when they were living in England, the extent of these relationships is unclear.

Colman Smith and her parents lived in Chislehurst, a suburb southeast of London, from 1879 to 1881, and then moved to Didsbury, a suburb of Manchester, where Cowlishaw, Nicol & Company's main plant was located.[73] Due to poor sales resulting from increased American competition, the business was reorganized in May 1887, at which point Charles Smith claimed that he invested £20,510.[74] Court documents record that he earned £1,000 a year and received sixty percent of the firm's profits, significantly more than any of the other partners.[75] Just over a year later, in August 1888, the firm went into receivership, and Smith was named one of the two principal debtors.[76] As the *Manchester Courier and Lancashire General Advertiser* explained, "[t]he immediate cause of the firm's insolvency was the Manchester and Liverpool District Bank refusing to pay any more cheques or meet their acceptances because they were not satisfied with their working of the accounts."[77] In addition, to the heavy losses—approximately £27,000—incurred by the firm, Smith also incurred a personal loss of £667. This debt allegedly accrued because "[h]e lived at the rate of about £2500 a year," which was a rather large sum at the time.[78] Testimony during Smith's bankruptcy trial revealed that he had given preferential treatment to American creditors, most notably his brother

Bryan H. Smith, who had previously been a partner in the firm.[79] Immediately after bankruptcy proceedings were begun against him, Smith sent most of the firm's English inventory to New York in order to prevent seizure of the goods to pay creditors; he also sent all of the family's personal furniture to Boston.[80] Even more tellingly, a telegram sent by Smith to the New York office urged the recipient to "Consult Bryan H. Smith and best legal advice ... Pay no trade creditors ... Keep quiet."[81] The day after these documents were read in court, Charles, Corinne, and Pamela set sail on the *Etruria* from Liverpool bound for New York.[82] While it does not appear that any criminal charges were filed against Charles Smith, it is possible that the bankruptcy proceedings in England motivated him to seek employment in Jamaica, where he would be more geographically remote.

Exposure to the English in Jamaica and Afro-Jamaican Culture

In late 1889 Charles Smith took a job as an auditor with the West India Improvement Company, and the family moved to St. Andrew parish, Jamaica, a suburb northwest of Kingston. It is possible that Colman Smith had relatives on either—or both—her maternal and paternal sides in Jamaica, which could explain the family's move so far away from the cosmopolitan worlds of New York and London that they had previously inhabited. The names Smith and Colman, as well as its frequent variant Coleman, are very common in nineteenth-century Jamaican census records.

Early in 1889 Frederick Wesson began negotiations with the Jamaican government to take over the railway. By late August the West India Improvement Company, led by Wesson, was formed to run the railway system for the government.[83] Charles Smith was hired to be the company's auditor sometime in the late summer or early fall of 1889. Other than them both originally hailing from New York, it is unclear how well Wesson and Smith knew each other; Wesson married Jenny Mills, the widow of Smith's long-time friend Thomas Mills, in 1878, so it is likely that the two were acquainted for some time before the start of their business venture.[84] Wesson may have also been interested in Smith joining the West India Improvement Company because Cyrus Porter Smith, Charles's father, had owned the Brooklyn City Rail Road Company.[85]

Jamaica, which remained a British colony until 1962, had a history of contracting its infrastructure needs to foreign corporations. Two English brothers, William and David Smith, under the auspices of the Jamaica Railway Company, had contracted with the Jamaican government in the 1840s to build a railway line in the country.[86] It does not appear that the brothers were related to Colman Smith or her parents. A fourteen-mile stretch of railroad running from Kingston to Spanish Town was officially opened in November 1845, but Britain's railway boom soon collapsed and plans to extend the railway foundered.[87] The Jamaican government bought the Jamaica Railway Company in 1879 and extended the line to Porus in rural Manchester, as well as north to Ewarton by 1885.[88] However, by the end of the decade the railroad still did not stretch to the end of the island, which led to its transfer back into private hands.[89] By 1894 the West India Improvement Company had laid sixty-six additional miles of track to Montego Bay, and in 1896 a fifty-four-mile extension was completed.[90]

Unlike a governmental body, whose aim is to provide a needed public service, the West Indian Improvement Company had profit as its primary motive, despite its euphemistic name. In order to help finance its operations in Jamaica, the company sold an issue of $1 million of 4 percent bonds that were backed by the Central Trust Company of New York.[91] The majority of the bonds were placed with the English banking firm of Speyer & Co.[92] A second offering was subsequently sold to the Manhattan Trust Company.[93] Litigation records reveal that in October 1896 the West India Improvement Company defaulted on both its contract with the Jamaican government and its other financial obligations. An April 1898 *New York Times* article alleged that the West India Improvement Company had failed to meet its liabilities "owing largely to complications with English capitalists involving jealousies and unfair treatment, and possibly bad management also."[94] The Manhattan Trust Company negotiated with the Jamaican government to transfer the railroad to its control in exchange for the unpaid stock, but this agreement did not last.[95] The Jamaican Legislative Council "strenuously opposed the scheme," and the Imperial Secretary returned the railroad to the control of the government.[96] Subsequently, there were a series of lawsuits between the West India Improvement Company, the Central Trust Company of New York, the Manhattan Trust Company, and the various individuals and corporations that held stock in these companies, which were not resolved until at least 1902. While at least one letter by Charles Smith was entered into testimony as part of the suit, legal records show he did not testify, nor is he named in the statements by Wesson and others who worked with him.[97] Smith died in December 1899 in

New York, but bankruptcy proceedings and litigation continued for several years after his death.[98] It does appear that the return of Colman Smith and her father to New York in March 1897 was precipitated by the West India Improvement Company's default in 1896 and the ensuing legal cases that began the next year.[99]

When Colman Smith and her family arrived in Jamaica in the fall of 1889, they entered a racially stratified and economically depressed colony that was still reeling from the end of slavery fifty years earlier. As Wayne Modest and Tim Barringer note, Queen Victoria's long reign, which is still associated with the zenith of British imperial expansion, "was a period of unresolved transition and crisis" for Jamaica.[100] Although the bulk of the population traced their origin to Africa, a tiny white minority monopolized the wealth and political power.[101] An 1895 *New York Times* report highlighted that out of a population of about 750,000, approximately 15,000 were white, predominantly of English descent.[102] A Black and Brown middle class emerged during the Victorian era, but, as Modest and Barringer explain, the majority "were excluded both by limitations on the voting franchise and by a wider range of informal cultural exclusion, from the political process and from governance of the island …"[103] In addition, approximately 37,000 South Asians, mostly from India, were imported to Jamaica between 1845 and 1921 to work as indentured laborers on the sugar plantations.[104] Colloquially known as "coolies," these workers toiled in harsh conditions and were the focus of much public debate.[105]

Since Jamaica's establishment as a British colony in 1655, the island's economy had depended on imported African slaves who worked the large sugar plantations scattered throughout the island. Although the British slave trade was abolished in 1807, slavery continued until 1834 when it officially ended with a four-year transitional period. With the cessation of slavery, the island's economy faltered.[106] At the same time, the newly emancipated Black residents began a struggle to obtain the same economic, political, and social rights that white residents of the island had always possessed.[107] As Brian Moore and Michele Johnson note, these "diametrically opposed attitudes meant that … 'two Jamaicas' were set on a collision course, for white hegemony could only be maintained by denying black aspirations."[108] This climaxed in the deadly Morant Bay uprising in October 1865 that was brutally suppressed by the colonial government led by Governor Edward John Eyre.[109] What began as a peaceful march by Black protestors led by Peter Bogle to air grievances to the white custos, Baron von Ketelhodt, quickly turned violent when Ketelhodt refused to speak to the group and ordered the militia to open fire.[110] Seven Black people were killed. The protestors retaliated by killing the custos and a few other whites. The riot quickly turned into a massacre as the white settlers killed 450 Blacks and more than 600 men and women were flogged; over 1,000 Afro-Jamaican dwellings were destroyed.[111] As Moore and Johnson point out, "It was a savage retribution by the state, intended to send a clear message to the black population that they should never again attempt any such outbreak of violence."[112] The result was that the Jamaican Assembly, motivated by the fear of future Black uprisings, transferred power to the British Crown and in 1866 a colonial government was appointed. The British Crown was still very much in control of the island when Colman Smith and her parents arrived in 1889, and the environment was often tense with fear of reprisals on both sides.

The Morant Bay uprising marked an economic downturn for the island, which had not eased significantly by the late 1880s. Many former sugar plantations went bankrupt. Some land was sold to Black and Brown Jamaicans under a land-redistribution plan undertaken by the colonial government. A few, predominantly large, British companies consolidated much of this land.[113] As sugar production decreased, the export of fruit, primarily bananas, oranges, coconuts, limes, and pineapples, increased.[114] By the 1890s bananas had replaced sugar as the country's most profitable export.[115] However, the majority of the growing Black and Brown middle class failed to benefit from these profits.

With the advent of the fruit trade came the growth of Jamaica's economic—and burgeoning tourist—relationship with the United States. Although the island is far closer geographically to the U.S. than the U.K., "in 1865, 79 percent of Jamaica's exports went to the United Kingdom, which supplied 61 percent of Jamaica's imports; only 8 percent of Jamaica's exports went to the United States, whence came 26 percent of her imports."[116] After the end of the Civil War, U.S. businesses looked toward Jamaica with renewed focus. An 1895 *New York Times* article speculated as to whether Jamaican oranges—many of which grew freely on government land—could fill the gap in production caused by a Floridian cold snap, and concluded that the island needed more "American money and enterprise and push."[117] This was a not so subtle dig at the perceived lassitude and lack of economic savvy on the part of the Afro-Jamaicans. Many U.S. companies, including the West India

Improvement Company, answered this call.[118] As Mark Nesbitt explains, by 1899 "the United States accounted for 59 percent of Jamaica's exports and 45 percent of her imports."[119] A steamship fleet also brought a growing number of U.S. tourists to the island, and, for expatriates like Colman Smith and her parents, helped facilitate more frequent visits back to the States, a journey that in the 1890s took approximately two weeks.[120]

Even more than twenty years after the 1865 Morant Bay uprising, visitors to Jamaica would have encountered the still widely held view that whites on the island needed to engage in a "civilizing mission" toward Afro-Jamaican residents. According to Moore and Johnson, for missionaries and reformers,

> creole culture, particularly the Afro variant, was characterized by gross immorality, debauchery, superstition, fetish and paganism ... This culture had, therefore, to be eradicated if Jamaica were to become a modern civilized society, and the standard for that would be the incorporation of middle-class Victorian, Christian values and morals which would produce the guiding principles of decency and decorum.[121]

As Elazar Barkan and Ronald Bush have highlighted, the "self-serving function" of this ideology was that "Europeans believed that a natural component of that civilizing was extending European markets to colonized populations."[122] These views, and the economic practices that sustained them, suffused white society in Jamaica at the time, and Colman Smith undoubtedly encountered them.

Although Colman Smith and her parents mingled with the upper echelons of English society in Jamaica, they were not above poking fun at them. In an October 1896 letter to Reed, Colman Smith recounts meeting Henry Blake, the governor of Jamaica, and his wife Edith, who were Anglo-Irish. She tells her cousin that "Daddy calls them Paddy."[123] The use of this derogatory term commonly applied to lower-class Irish Catholics reduced Colman Smith to laughter. The comment also reflects a lifelong distrust of authority and social niceties that she appears to have shared with her father. In the same vein, another letter details her attempts to paint an English girl living on the island. Colman Smith enthuses that "she is very pretty! With big blue eyes and with yellow hair—she plays very well on the piano." However, she quickly tempers this praise by stating that the young girl "is rather stupid [in] other ways!"[124] While she does not elaborate, other comments in her letters to Reed suggest that the young women that Colman Smith met in Jamaica were too focused on decorum and propriety and, as a result, lacked imagination and fun. This view also extended to the majority of the upper- and middle-class young women she met in New York and England.

It is likely that Colman Smith, who was perceived as Asian, Black, or even as an indeterminate Other, would have been targeted, either directly or indirectly, in Jamaica's racially charged environment. A glimpse into this stratified atmosphere can be seen in a January 26, 1897 letter from Colman Smith to Reed in which she discusses a disagreement between herself and Consul Eckford's daughters over dresses she is making for them for an upcoming ball:

> I have been <u>raving</u> mad for the last four days—cause I have been doing the dresses for Polly + Julia Eck—and By Gar! They don't think they are nice enough—! They would not buy any decent stuff! and now they [are] <u>mad</u> cause their things don't look as grand as they think <u>they</u> ought to! Pigs![125]

Colman Smith's rage in the letter—a very rare occurrence in her letters to Reed—is palpable. She does not elaborate on why she was enlisted to design and sew the dresses for the Consul's daughters, if she had done this previously, or if she was given remuneration for the dresses. What is clear is that for reasons not outlined in the letter, and likely due to racial othering, she was not invited to the ball and that she was very annoyed by this oversight. Throughout her life, Colman Smith resisted conservative views associated with the "civilizing mission" mindset of many Anglo-Americans and was generally opposed to hypocrisy and prejudice of all types. She also held a lifelong fascination with Afro-Jamaican culture, especially its folklore and spiritual practices, which undoubtedly began during her residence on the island.

The English "civilizing mission," as well as its economic underpinnings, was on display in the 1891 Jamaica Exhibition. Reminiscent of London's popular nineteenth-century international exhibitions that were grounded in the distinction between the "civilized" and the "savage," the Jamaica Exhibition aimed to increase tourism, bolster agricultural trade, and, as then Governor Henry Blake wrote, "assist the intellectual development of the black population."[126] In the words of *The Jamaica Post*, the exhibition, which was housed at the Kingston Race Course, would "open the eyes" of the island's majority Black population "to the fact of their backward condition."[127] More than 300,000 people visited the Exhibition, and it is likely that Colman Smith and her parents attended.[128]

Despite the fanfare of the 1891 Jamaica Exhibition, the emerging disciplines of anthropology and ethnography largely avoided the colonial Caribbean, which, by the mid-nineteenth century, had been colonized for more than two hundred years. As David Scott has noted, "Neither properly 'primitive' nor 'civilized,' neither 'non-Western' on the conventional criteria nor unambiguously 'Western' (in short, neither fish nor fowl), the Caribbean has never quite fit securely within any anthropological agenda."[129] Quoting Sidney Mintz, a noted Caribbean anthropologist, Scott writes:

> Whereas New Guinea, Africa, Amazonia offered kinship systems, costumes, coiffures, cuisines, languages, beliefs, and customs of dizzying variety and allure, to almost all anthropologists the Caribbean islands and their surrounding shores looked rather too much like a culturally burned-over, second hand, unpristine world. Whether it was kinship or religion or language or anything else, Caribbean people all seemed culturally midway between there and here—everything was alloyed, mixed, ground down, pasted on, the least common denominator.[130]

As a result, the great colonial collections of art and artifacts in both the British Museum and the Victoria and Albert Museum largely neglected the Caribbean in favor of South Asia and Africa.[131]

Colman Smith's previous experience had been limited to England, interspersed with trips to visit New York relatives, and she was fascinated by Jamaica, especially its Afro-Jamaican language, folklore, and cultural traditions. Many of the local customs were suffused with West African traditions. These included Jonkonnu, a performance form "long established under slavery" that interweaves music, dance, and spoken performance.[132] Symbolizing freedom and power, the masquerade, as Nadia Ellis notes, became a "performed rite of freedom" after Emancipation.[133] An Emancipation-era celebration, Bruckins or Bruckins Party, involved procession, music, dance, and re-enactment, at times syncretized with European traditions in subversive ways.[134] Kumina, an African heritage religious culture, was brought to the island by Central African indentured laborers between the 1840s and 1860s. As Dianne M. Stewart explains,

> Kumina rituals encompass a universe of customs pertaining to divination, healing, kindship responsibilities, rites of passage, and so on. Most pivotal for ritual efficacy are the Kumina dances, music, and songs that establish the proper environment for communions with the ancestors, who manifest in the bodies of their descendants during formal ceremonies.[135]

Colman Smith also encountered other Afro-Jamaican religious and spiritual traditions such as Revival, Obeah, and Myal. She would go on to incorporate elements of many of these traditions in her writing and art—especially the close connection with the spirit world—in both overt and covert ways for the rest of her life. However, of all the Afro-Jamaican cultural and religious traditions that Colman Smith encountered during her sojourn in Jamaica, Anansi tales were to become the most central to her oeuvre. In Chapter 4, I will discuss Colman Smith's interest in folklore and the composition of these Anansi tales.

Instead of the standard English Colman Smith would have been familiar with, the majority of the island's residents spoke Jamaican Patois, an English-based creole language intermixed with West African influences. When recording the speech of Afro-Jamaicans in her letters to her cousin, Colman Smith attempts to replicate the creolized language, often with the enhancement of multiple exclamation marks. She peppers her letters to her cousin with examples of the creolized speech of several of the Afro-Jamaican servants who worked on the family's estate, Ambergate, and, as I detail below, she gives this speech to several characters in her miniature theater play, *Henry Morgan*. Although at times Colman Smith employs these voices to inject levity into her writing, there is also an apparent interest in accurately recording their speech at work. This tension between appropriation of and condescension toward "primitive" Afro-Jamaican creolized speech and a genuine ethnographic impulse to preserve and transmit Afro-Jamaican folklore is present both in Colman Smith's two collections of Anansi tales and her folktale performances.

Daily Life in Jamaica

Colman Smith was eleven when she moved to the Caribbean and, as she later recalled, "I lived on & off in Jamaica about seven years."[136] Her education on the island is a matter of conjecture. Although there is no mention of it in any of her surviving letters, Colman Smith could have attended a private school for British expatriates or she might have had a governess. Compared to her early life in England, her educational opportunities would have been severely limited. Periodically she returned to New York, sometimes with her mother, Corinne, and at other times "under the entire charge of a Jamaica negro nurse," when "she made long visits at more than one [Brooklyn] Heights house."[137] It is likely that during these visits she became friendly with her cousin, Mary Reed. It is Colman Smith's letters to Reed, which begin with Corinne Colman's death in July 1896, that provide the clearest picture of her life in Jamaica. The friendship between the cousins was likely cemented during their shared time at the Pratt Institute.

In the 1890s Brooklyn's Pratt Institute served as both a secondary school for students aged twelve and older and as an advanced training program in art and design. Colman Smith first enrolled in October of 1893 when she was fifteen and Jamaica was her primary residence. This is her only documented schooling, but it is likely she attended school in England, since elementary education through age ten was made compulsory beginning in 1880. Early records for Pratt were lost in a fire, and it is unclear how regularly Colman Smith attended, as she frequently returned to Jamaica; I will discuss the artistic impact of her time at Pratt in Chapter 2.

Colman Smith's letters to her cousin are filled with references to Pratt and entreaties to send her love to various friends, teachers, and staff members. She frequently laments that she doesn't have anyone to talk to in Jamaica and implores her cousin to come visit. Overall, her assessment of her island home, which letters reveal she viewed as a temporary stop, is mixed: "Don't know when we will leave this place which is just elegant for some things—air—scenery—rides &c—and piggish for others—no theatres!"[138] However, the overall tone of her letters is upbeat. She frequently expresses sympathy and concern for her cousin's apparent case of the "blues," rather than dwelling on her own unhappiness.[139] To this end, Colman Smith often includes humorous stories, plays, and poems in her letters that she hopes will leave Reed "screaming" with laughter.[140] However, at one point, she expresses incredulity at her cousin's continued unhappiness, especially due to her location: "The idea of being so gruesome when you go to Pratt!" She quickly follows this gentle admonishment with an invitation to join her in Jamaica for the winter, an offer Reed does not seem to have accepted.[141]

Much of Colman Smith's time in Jamaica was spent in pursuits very different from her activities as a Pratt art student, activities that likely contributed to her originality as an artist. As discussed above, she was exposed to Afro-Jamaican culture, which became an important influence for much of her early work, but she also took on duties that the majority of students would not have to, all of which, as letters show, kept her grounded. Before her mother's death, Colman Smith helped nurse her through a prolonged sickness and then kept house for her father. She recounts making breakfast for the household, counting the washing, paying wages to the workers on the estate, and allocating money for groceries. At one point, she laments that "I get terrible mixed up on farthings."[142] However, her life in Jamaica did not consist entirely of domestic duties. She frequently drove around the island in her "little buggy—with her little horse—Grog." As she notes to her cousin, "the only thing that Grog seems afraid of is oxen fastened together and then he stands on his hind legs!"[143] The daughters of the U.S. Consul in Jamaica, Quincy Oliver Eckford, often joined her on these outings.[144] Colman Smith and her father frequently entertained. Among their guests were Sir Henry Blake, the governor of Jamaica from 1889 to 1898, his wife Edith, her elderly parents, and Lord George Fitzgerald, who served as Blake's private secretary.[145] Reflecting an active social life, Colman Smith's letters to her cousin include accounts of polo matches, horseback rides around the island, and overnight visits to other estates.

Letters reveal that Colman Smith read widely, drew, and composed stories, poems, and plays, sometimes with friends, but more often by herself. Her avid reading appears to have been a major feature of her time in Jamaica. In addition to du Maurier's novels, she enjoyed historical fiction, especially works that featured female characters. Favorites included Alexandre Dumas's *The Queen's Necklace* (1849), Rider Haggard's *She* (1887), and Frank R. Stockton's *The Casting Away of Mrs. Lecks and Mrs. Aleshine* (1886), the latter of which she termed "very funny."[146] She was less entranced by Richard Doddridge Blackmore's *Mary Annerley: A Yorkshire Tale* (1880) and reports that after two weeks she is only half way through: "it is very nice—she isn't very—Er—Er—well! Er—she is kind of mamby pamby—! So sweet you know!"¹⁴⁷ A drawing of a very prim, unsmiling woman illustrates what Colman Smith struggles to put into words and reflects her long-term frustration with women, both fictional and flesh and blood, who conform too rigidly to accepted modes of femininity and are less interested in fun and adventure.¹⁴⁸

Colman Smith's art is another frequent subject in her missives to her cousin. She discusses drawings she has undertaken, such as those of Merlin, Vivian, and Guinevere, and asks for new topics.¹⁴⁹ Moreover, her letters are filled with pen-and-ink drawings, and even a few in watercolor, highlighting how she thought visually as well as verbally and often wanted to enhance her words with illustrations. This practice foreshadows the mutually generative relationship between the art and text of her best artistic endeavors. By the end of January 1897 she was participating in a local sketch club.¹⁵⁰ As the fall of 1896 continued, Colman Smith began drawing advertisements for local businesses. She recounts that "Mr. Gardner <u>gave</u> me a whole set of this year's *Academy* pictures for that cricket poster!" and the same letter reproduces parts of a millinery poster she has just completed.¹⁵¹ In early November Colman Smith related that "I finished a poster for Mrs. Vaughn's Restaurant in town of a real nice fat (quite so) girl carrying a bowl of turtle soup with steam arising! ... and in large letters below 'Best Turtle Soup in Town!'"¹⁵² While there is no mention of any payment, the news is accompanied by a large drawing of the soup-carrying young woman.¹⁵³

Miniature Theater Performances and the Emergence of a Feminist Voice

The fusion of images and stories through the performances that Colman Smith put on in her miniature theater were by far the most frequent subject in her letters to her cousin. The plays were written by Colman Smith and took place on a stage that measured approximately eighteen inches square.¹⁵⁴ The toy theater, which even included a trapdoor, was equipped with elaborately painted sets that were moved by means of grooves and strings.¹⁵⁵ An 1899 *Washington Times* article termed it "one of the completest miniature theatres ever seen."¹⁵⁶ Colman Smith manipulated the figures herself, whom she named and often reused in multiple plays. By 1899 she had created more than 300 figures.¹⁵⁷ As Gardner Teall in *Brush & Pencil* explained, "The knights and ladies of the buskin are first drawn on stiff paper and colored, then cut out and made to lead upright lives with a bit of glue and proper manipulation)."[158] Teall adds, "I have never seen a more gorgeous presentation on any stage." Colman Smith created the sets and figures herself, but often had help from her father, servants, and friends who contributed the musical accompaniment and special effects, as well as acting as the plays' narrators.

Miniature theaters first rose to prominence in the Court of Charles II, but they experienced a resurgence in England during the mid-to-late nineteenth century when J. Reddington, a London "bookbinder, tobacconist, and theatrical printer, had set up a miniature stage not three feet wide, yet complete in every detail of mechanical device necessary for a performance."[159] Sara Bernhardt, G. K. Chesterton, Robert Louis Stevenson, Ellen Terry, Sir Henry Irving, and W. B. Yeats all owned miniature theaters.[160] It is unclear when and how Colman Smith obtained her theater and whether it was from Reddington's shop, possibly purchased while she and her family lived in England. The theater could also have been a gift from her cousin, the actor William Gillette, who "employed miniature theatres in the building up of plays for the professional stage."[161] Regardless of its origins, there are many similarities between the description of her miniature theater and Reddington's. The scenery in both "moved easily on grooves," and the actors "glided across the stage on grooves" pulled by strings.[162] In an 1899 article, Albert Bigelow Paine, Colman Smith's friend, detailed that "[r]ecently, however, the strings have been replaced by strips of stiff celluloid which slide easily in the grooves and make it possible for one operator to move the characters of the play in either direction."[163] He also explained that Colman Smith's theater, which was "built of pasteboard and a light wood," had working footlights and incandescent lighting.[164]

During the fall of 1896 and winter of 1897, which Colman Smith spent in Jamaica, she composed and performed several plays for family and friends. These included *The Magic Carbuncle*, which she told Reed that she wrote in one day, and *The Guardsman*.[165] Details of the latter have not been preserved, but after *The Magic Carbuncle* was performed for the first time in November 1896, Colman Smith wrote her cousin that the "people and scenes are ok but the play itself—is—rotten!"[166] She later reworked it and sent the script, figures, and backdrops to her grandmother and cousins in Brooklyn as Christmas presents.[167] Another play, *Herne the Hunter*, depicted the search for a fearsome ghost who inhabited Windsor Forest, and, like others from this period, included several processions of her miniature figures. It is likely these processions were inspired by Colman Smith's exposure to Bruckins, an Afro-Jamaican performance form that centrally figured ritualized processions. Other highlights from the play included a hunting scene, a stone kitchen, Herne's cave, and St. George's chapel in Windsor Castle, where Henry VIII wed Anne Boleyn.[168] Musical accompaniment was a new feature for her theater beginning with this play, and consisted of an accordion, two drums, and a horn.[169] Servants, sometimes aided by Colman Smith herself, would create special effects, such as claps of thunder, the clash of swords, or splashing water.[170] Overall, the performance was a rousing success, with Colman Smith informing her cousin that "we quite galvanized them!"[171]

However, the most popular of Colman Smith's miniature theater plays, and the one that she went on to perform in public for paying audiences, was *Henry Morgan*, which was loosely based on the life of the Welsh privateer.[172] While most famous for his destructive but lucrative raids on the Spanish settlements of Cuba and Panama that have been immortalized in the contemporary imagination through the *Pirates of the Caribbean* movies, Morgan was a celebrity during his lifetime and was knighted for his service to the Crown in 1674.[173] He owned sugar plantations in Jamaica and served as lieutenant governor of the island from 1675 until his death in 1688, including three separate terms as acting governor.[174] By the late nineteenth century he had become one of the most famous figures associated with Jamaica, due in large part to the widespread romanticization of pirates and piracy through works by Howard Pyle, Sir Walter Scott, and Robert Louis Stevenson, among others. Colman Smith drew on this pirate popularity for *Henry Morgan*, and, interestingly, it is the only one of her plays to have a specifically Jamaican subject and setting.

As I will discuss in Chapter 2, Colman Smith read and admired Pyle's work. He published several stories of seventeenth-century pirate activity in both the Atlantic and the Caribbean, beginning with his "Buccaneers and Marooners of the Spanish Main" in 1887, and continuing throughout the 1890s. His "Morgan at Portobello," which appeared in *Harper's New Monthly Magazine* in December 1888, was a likely jumping-off point for Colman Smith's play. Her choice of bold primary colors in the surviving scenes and characters from the play, as well as her later depictions of pirates in "The Green Bed," "The Golden Vanity," *A Broad Sheet*, and *The Green Sheaf*, definitely bear the influence of Pyle's illustrative style. However, as Jill and Robert May note, "Pyle's pirate stories have uncivilized, ruthless villains ... full of bravado but little compassion."[175] In comparison, Colman Smith's Morgan falls in love and turns heroic when the need arises. The reception the play received at an early performance in her Jamaican home appears typical: "At the end ... People were just <u>covered</u> and <u>buried</u> in flowers—and had shouts and applause!"[176] Accounts from public performances in Jamaica, and later in New York, reveal that audiences were captivated by the play's fusion of comedic and melodramatic elements. While the public appetite for pirate lore and Morgan's exploits helped extend the play's acclaim, Colman Smith's skills as a performer, director, and playwright were critical to finding an audience.

Although the text of *Henry Morgan* was never published, it was preserved in a series of letters that Colman Smith sent to her cousin to cheer her up.[177] In some of the letters, she forgets where she had previously left off and makes several changes, highlighting the fluidity and spontaneity that appears to have characterized these performances.[178] In an interesting anachronism, Colman Smith set the play in Port Royal in 1692, four years after Morgan's death and almost twenty years after his knighthood and entry into Jamaican politics. However, 1692 is significant, as on June 7 that year a major earthquake and accompanying tsunami hit Jamaica; Port Royal was destroyed and much of the northern part of the city fell into the sea, including the cemetery in which Morgan was interred. Founded in 1518 by the Spanish, Port Royal was the largest city in the Caribbean during the seventeenth century and served as an epicenter of shipping and commerce as well as piracy. The earthquake lends a dramatic conclusion to Colman Smith's play, and this is likely why she fudged the dates of Morgan's life and governmental service.

Colman Smith's *Henry Morgan* features a swashbuckling hero (Morgan), a beautiful heroine (Julia Bogle—who as I detail below is almost definitely part of Jamaica's Black and Brown middle class), a wealthy, domineering father (Sir William Bogle), pirates, enterprising servants, corrupt police, mistaken identity, and an almost farcical happy ending. The play's dialogue is peppered with Jamaican creole, and Colman Smith's mischievous sense of humor helps bring the characters to life.

Despite the stereotypical nature of much of the plot and characters, there are some unexpected, and occasionally subversive, elements to the play. Jacob

Andrews, a local merchant, agrees to rent a storehouse to Morgan and his fellow pirate Dick Redcastle, who are both on the run from local authorities, to house the spoils from their raids for the high price of "250 doubloons a year in advance!"[179] The trio are celebrating over a bottle of "rare Jamaica" when Martha, Andrews's dark-skinned housekeeper, "rats em all" out to the constables.[180] Morgan escapes but Dick is hauled away to prison. While Martha does what she thinks is right regardless of the potentially negative repercussions from her master, Jane and Benjerman Bingersnoff, Julia Bogle's servants, contemplate ways to dupe their mistress, who has lately fallen in love with Morgan. The pair discover that Morgan has stolen a gray horse from their stables in order to make his escape. Jane's first instinct is to inform her mistress, but Benjermin thinks he could benefit financially by turning him over to the police. Jane disagrees, but only because she thinks it might be more lucrative to work with their mistress. As she notes, "capture a friend of the family! 'A frien of the family!?' Keep your eyes open Benjerman! You could get 800—if you tell her you'll save him!" Benjermin insists, "I am honorable" and that he cannot "be bribed." Unlike Benjermin, Jane's sense of ethics is more malleable, and she insists that such a scheme "Tiwould be better than playing constable!"[181] She then instructs Benjermin "in a stage whisper" to go "[a]fter the gray horse!"[182] Interestingly, Colman Smith's account of *Henry Morgan* does not return to these characters, and they are not mentioned in any of the published accounts.[183]

Julia Bogle is the play's most fully developed, strong, female character, and, unlike Jacob Andrews who is duped by his servants, she is in control of hers, and orders Benjermin and Jane to "cease their wrangling" and follow her commands.[184] Also unlike most women of the day, Julia actively pursues Morgan after she falls in love with him, rather than waiting to be wooed or left behind as Morgan flees from the police. Moreover, she is not troubled either by issues of respectability or by the fact that her father is actively trying to hunt Morgan down in order to turn him over to the police. Julia alone recognizes the disguised Morgan in Spanish Town, and through her ingenuity helps him escape.[185] Interestingly, Julia, whose race is not specified, shares her surname with Paul Bogle, the Black activist who led the peaceful protest that sparked the Morant Bay uprising in 1865, and who would, undoubtedly, have been familiar to Colman Smith's Jamaican audiences. While there is no discussion of the name or its resonances in her letters to her cousin, it seems unlikely that the choice was a mere coincidence;

instead, she likely meant it to signify that her heroine was a member of Jamaica's growing Black and Brown upper middle class. She may have been drawn to the name Bogle for its connotations of strength and leadership, as well as its reputation for defying conventions.

Henry Morgan's only solo scene in the play is his horseback ride to Spanish Town during a thunderstorm. The scene is a darkened wood, and a tree is suddenly illuminated, showing three hanged bodies. Henry exclaims, "Sdeath it looks like a good fellow dancing nothing at all! Surely I know his face!"[186] Colman Smith notes that lightning and "<u>very</u>" loud thunder echo at this point in order to enhance the foreboding mood.[187] When Morgan realizes these bodies are three of his men, he "vows <u>vengeance</u>!", which is accompanied by more thunder, audience applause, and the close.[188] Colman Smith concludes that "[t]his is the most effective scene in the whole play— So they say!"[189] While audiences were likely impressed by the melodramatic pathos of this scene, what is most interesting is that Morgan's success stems far less from his own feats of bravery than from those of the women around him.

As discussed above, Julia Bogle's duplicity is key to Morgan's evasion of the constabulary. However, her accomplice is, arguably, the play's most fascinating character: Morgan's "Aunt Jamima." Her use of Jamaican creole and her name would indicate to contemporary audiences that she was Afro-Jamaican. This is reinforced by the fact that the only other characters in *Henry Morgan* who speak in creole are servants. Interestingly, Colman Smith erases Morgan's Welsh origins and his imperialistic journey to the Caribbean and, instead, provides a back story in which he is the son of an Afro-Jamaican woman— Aunt Jamima's sister Eliza—who ran off to sea as a lad. There is no indication in Colman Smith's letters or in the published accounts of the play that she changed Morgan's race; at one point he is described as red-haired, which was a common attribute of the Welsh Morgan. But it does show that Colman Smith was unperturbed by, and interested in, racial mixing, possibly because of her own biracial heritage. Racial mixing was a very contentious subject in the United States at the *fin de siècle*, and many states had anti-miscegenation laws, which were only struck down in 1967 with the *Loving* v. *Virginia* decision in the U.S. Supreme Court. However, the courtship of a man who appeared white (Morgan) and an upper-class Black woman (Bogle) would be more accepted in late nineteenth-century Jamaica, where there was a growing Black and Brown middle and upper class that had garnered increasing amounts of power and visibility. Once Morgan reveals his identity to his aunt, she is surprised but generally unruffled. She states, "In sooth give Eliza's little boy up to the barbarous constables! <u>Certainly not</u>!" By describing the police as "barbarous," an epithet more commonly applied to pirates, Aunt Jamima comically inverts the expected and displays a canny awareness that appearances and reality do not always align. While she does express some worries that Morgan "may get tired o'keeping still, and smash up all my china and shoot me and kill my cat!", once he informs her that he is planning on renouncing his past life and marrying Julia Bogle, Aunt Jamima's doubts dissipate and she is elated by the impending nuptials.[190]

Near the play's conclusion, Morgan and Julia are in a boat on the Rio Cobre, about to embark on their happy ever after, when they are intercepted by constables who are eager to arrest Henry. However, in a *deus ex machina* moment that rivals both Greek tragedy and the late nineteenth-century sensation novels that Colman Smith read during the period, she writes, "Then earthquake—all known tumble down."[191] In the ensuing melee, Morgan saves Sir Walter Bogle, effectively ending the animosity between them. As Sir Walter states, "Henry, my son, we will call it quits—we will receive you as our son-in-law!" The play concludes with Charles II—magically transported to the Caribbean from beyond the grave—knighting Morgan and naming him captain general and governor of Jamaica.[192] A December 1899 *Puritan* article on Colman Smith's miniature theater recounts a somewhat different staging of *Henry Morgan*, but notes that after Henry's knighting, "over three hundred figures cross the stage, on foot and on horseback, in chariot and in chain, to honor the pirate knight and his bride, the radiant Julia" (Figure 1.1).[193] This lengthy final procession emphasizes how Colman Smith continued to incorporate Afro-Jamaican cultural forms like Bruckins, even after she had left the island.

While Colman Smith performed *Henry Morgan* several times at home during the fall of 1896—often to a wide assortment of guests—the play had its first public performance on December 10, 1896 at the Half Way Tree Infant Kindergarten; Half Way Tree was the capital of St. Andrew parish.[194] More than 200 children and their parents attended, and the performance was accompanied by a guitar, flute, and piccolo that, according to Colman Smith, "make cold shivers run down your back—!"[195] An article in the Kingston *Daily Gleaner* praised her artistic talents and stated, "the beauty and clearness of the performance of the little play called forth unqualified expressions

Figure 1.1 Sketch of the procession from *Henry Morgan*, from an October 5, 1896 letter from Pamela Colman Smith to her cousin, Mary "Bobby" Reed.
Courtesy of the Pamela Colman Smith Collection, Special Collections Department, Bryn Mawr College Library, box 1, folder 3

of appreciation and delight from all present."[196] More than a week after the performance, Colman Smith recounted to her cousin that she was still meeting people who said her play was a "great success."[197]

A year later, Colman Smith performed *Henry Morgan* for her fellow students and teachers as part of a Pratt annual Christmas social. The *Pratt Institute Monthly* notes that the performance netted $95 and terms *Henry Morgan*'s fifteen scenes and thirteen acts "a most original and charming entertainment."[198] The unnamed writer stresses it is difficult to fully express the artistic beauty and effectiveness of the scenes, stating,

> [w]hether one sees the interior of the heroine's chamber, or the blue waters and sunny hillsides of the tropical island, each is a delicately-balanced harmony, constructed on the most refreshingly-original

lines, yet so simply and unerringly true that one feels is a new faculty for seeing life, though it be that of two centuries ago.[199]

As I discuss in Chapter 2, this difficulty of putting into words the full effect of Colman Smith's work and simultaneous focus on the originality and "truth" of her compositions was to become typical of descriptions of her work.

Colman Smith's *Henry Morgan* clearly shows her early interest in both pirates and strong female characters, particularly those who disregard patriarchal authority and social conventions. The play is suffused with humor and attention to language that helps catch the essence of its Jamaican setting. The details of the miniature theater performances included in letters to her cousin make clear that despite her small stage and tiny performers, she envisioned her plays as immersive experiences. This desire to plunge her audiences into settings and traditions they may be completely unfamiliar with, whether Jamaican Bruckins processions, Anansi stories, Irish myths, or English folklore, was an important motivating force behind her *fin-de-siècle* creations.

Although Colman Smith only spent seven years in Jamaica, it was a formative period. Her exposure to Jamaican cultural traditions and modes of expression would repeatedly find expression in her work over the next twenty years, including her 1899 *Annancy Stories*, her 1905 *Chim-Chim: Folk Stories from Jamaica*, and the folktale performances that she gave first at home and then for public groups after her return to England in 1900. She also displayed a persistent interest in seventeenth-century pirates, which she returned to in both *A Broad Sheet* and *The Green Sheaf* as well as in some of her "music pictures." Furthermore, the questions swirling around her racial origins, her peripatetic childhood, and the deaths of both her parents before she was 22 helped form the outsider perspective that was to become a key component of her work, while an early exposure to Swedenborgianism likely predisposed her to be more open to non-traditional forms of spirituality. All these factors helped imbue Colman Smith with an appreciation for the fluidity of identity and the importance of naming that were to prove central to both her construction of a public persona and her critical reception.

CHAPTER TWO

Forging a Path

Critical Reception, Key Influences, and Emergence as an Artist

The mid-to-late 1890s were a pivotal period in Colman Smith's life as both an artist and a writer. She worked tirelessly on a variety of different artistic endeavors, ranging from Christmas cards and lampshades to illustrations and formal paintings. Her interest in English and Irish myth and song emerged as her passion for Jamaican Anansi tales deepened. In December 1897 Colman Smith, who was two months short of her twentieth birthday, had her first joint exhibition at the Macbeth Gallery in New York; she sold four of her watercolors "to connoisseurs who have fine private collections."[1] By the end of the month her Christmas cards, illustrations, and prints were regularly on sale at the gallery. Despite this auspicious beginning, her quest to earn a living from her creative output was often a struggle.

Audiences and critics were initially somewhat receptive but mostly confused as to how to classify Colman Smith's art. The *Brooklyn Daily Eagle* described her work as "pleasures" and stated that her "free and untrammeled style … produces some novel results."[2] A brief notice in the January 1898 *International Studio* identified Colman Smith not as an American artist but as a "designer from Kingston, Jamaica … whose panels in water-colour, half caricatures, half decorations, are extremely interesting even though it is difficult to classify them."[3] The unnamed writer believes Colman Smith's work is less than true art, but what exactly it is—caricature or decoration—appears open to interpretation and debate. And just as her art is marked as difficult to classify, Colman Smith's origins are similarly obscured.[4] While it is possible that the writer was unaware of her American roots, describing her as Jamaican emphasizes her exoticism and reinforces the description of her art as defying categorization. This focus on Colman Smith's originality and the difficulty in classifying her work sets up a critical pattern that was to follow her for the rest of her career. Even James McNeill Whistler reportedly commented, "She can't paint, and she can't draw, but she doesn't have to."[5] This assessment de-emphasizes Colman Smith's technical proficiency, or lack thereof, in favor of her imagination and creativity. It also subtly aligns her with the *fin-de-siécle* Symbolist movement in which artists looked "deeper into the self and to a greater reliance upon individual imagination in lieu of social orientation and an empirical observation."[6] Moreover, Whistler's critical appraisal reflects the highly gendered climate of the *fin-de-siècle* art world, in which male artists like Whistler, Aubrey Beardsley, and Paul Gauguin were largely praised for their innovation and convention-bucking approaches. However, female artists, especially those like Colman Smith who didn't fit into clearly identified racial categories, were critiqued for compositions that did not clearly marry with already-established schools.

Rather than puzzle over her critical reception, Colman Smith's thoughts on her first exhibition were confined to excitement over earning $175 for the sale of a few paintings. As she noted in a letter to her cousin Mary Reed, "Now I can't wait any longer but must tell you about this—*Bill Hart* is sold! for $50. *The Wind* for $25. And *Fruits and Flowers* for $100. Ha Ha! How's that for Christmas Luck?!!!"[7] Colman Smith attributed the sales to "Christmas Luck," rather than talent or hard work, but the rest of the letter makes clear that she was overjoyed at her newfound financial success and the possibility of more sales in other media. Furthermore, this seems to have strengthened her resolve to leave the Pratt Institute in January 1898 without earning a degree and officially commence her artistic career.

Despite this decision, the December 1897 issue of the *Pratt Institute Monthly* was devoted to Colman Smith's work, an honor not bestowed on another student during this period.[8] The issue reproduced three black-and-white images of Colman Smith's compositions that were included in the Macbeth exhibition. A rare photograph of her miniature theater rounded out the spread. In an uncharacteristic display of realism, *The Wind* depicts a Black woman attempting to hang laundry on a very windy day.[9] The setting is likely Jamaica and children play at the edges of the canvas, as a turkey struts across the lawn, the only figure not affected by the gusting wind. This is one of very few Colman Smith images that treat Jamaica—the island where she lived for most of the 1890s—in a more realistic style than her drawings for her Anansi folktale illustrations, which at times verge into Hogarthian caricature. It is also one of very few of her works from any period that could be classified as realist. More evocative of Victorian children's book illustrations, *Our Pets* was created for Arthur Wesley Dow's class at Pratt in the spring of 1897 and features frolicking schoolchildren.[10] The symmetry of the groups of children, many of whom have their backs toward the viewer, shows the influence of Dow's ideas on composition. The movement of the figures, their expressions, and their clothing reflects the work of the Victorian children's book illustrators Walter Crane, Kate Greenaway, and Marcus Ward.[11] As I discuss below, both the flatness and the extreme movement of Colman Smith's figures became a hallmark of her art from the *fin-de-siècle* period.

The cover image for the *Pratt Institute Monthly* article, *Composition— Tropical Fruits*, a slightly retitled *Fruits and Flowers*, depicts a procession of singing, ornately dressed men and women exiting a castle that is reminiscent of the medieval-inspired paintings of the Pre-Raphaelites. The procession, like the ones in *Henry Morgan* and *The Magic Carbuncle*, was likely inspired by the Afro-Jamaican Bruckins masquerades Colman Smith witnessed while living in Jamaica. These processions originated in Emancipation-era celebrations involving music, dance, and re-enactment, at times syncretized with European traditions in subversive ways. As Nadia Ellis explains, Bruckins consisted of "elaborate, formal presentations in which bureaucratic administrations were invented, positions assigned, and speeches given, all in ritualized mimicry of the very forms of colonial power that had long held blacks in slavery and continued to oppress them."[12] Tropical fruits, flowers, brightly colored costumes, songs, and banners were central to the performances, which used mimicry as "a complex co-optation of power."[13] Interestingly, Colman Smith's *Tropical Fruits* is accompanied by a paraphrase of Numbers 13:27, "We came unto the land and this is the fruit thereof," which alludes to the Israelites' long-awaited entry into the Promised Land.[14] The unexpected juxtaposition between the Old Testament verse and the elaborate court procession may also reflect the structural influence of Bruckins. Just like the Bruckins participants, who co-opted the power of the former white slave holders through their mimicry, Colman Smith employs a similar strategy by fusing Victorian fine art and the Bible—both representative of male power and control—with an Afro-Jamaican cultural form that emerged as a response to slavery. This interest in combining disparate times and places, with an eye for rebalancing unequal power relations, would become a hallmark of her art, and, as I detail below, a distinctive characteristic of and vehicle for her feminism.

Prefiguring the important nurturing and supportive roles fellow women artists and writers would have on Colman Smith's career, Ida C. Haskell, the author of the *Pratt Institute Monthly* article and an instructor at the school, complimented both the younger artist's "feeling for color arrangement" and her "comprehension of form in line and design."[15] Her strongest praise was reserved for Colman Smith's "rare gifts" of originality and imagination.[16] Haskell noted, "No doubt she has been influenced and helped by study of the good things in the art world; but she seems to have the power of assimilating these influences and using them as a stimulus in her own growth, not wearing them as a borrowed garment."[17] While not directly quoting Dow, Haskell's assessment brings to mind his assertion that "[a] master in art is always intensely individual, and what he does is an expression of his own peculiar choices."[18] Although Haskell does not specifically name what "good things in the art world" she thinks have influenced Colman Smith, her criticism is astute.

Especially in her art of the 1890s and early 1900s, Colman Smith united disparate artistic approaches—Arts and Crafts, the Pre-Raphaelites, Japonisme, Art Nouveau, and Symbolism—in a unique fusion. Important influences on her early oeuvre included Arthur Wesley Dow (her teacher at Pratt), Howard Pyle (the author and illustrator discussed in Chapter 1), William Morris (who was friendly with Colman Smith's family during their time in England), Marcus Ward (who lived next door to the Colman Smiths when they lived in Chislehurst), Dante Gabriel Rossetti, Walter Crane, and Kate Greenaway.[19] Haskell pointed out that Colman Smith had the "power" to bricolage these eclectic influences together in order to spur her own artistic development, rather than "wear … them like a borrowed garment."[20] As I detail below, this often included critiquing—sometimes overtly, other times through humor, and still others more covertly via mimicry—the power structures and world views that supported and sustained influential male artists.

Moreover, Colman Smith's life illuminates the ways in which increasing numbers of women at the turn of the twentieth century navigated a still firmly patriarchal and often misogynistic arts scene. In order to sustain herself during this early period, Colman Smith began to surround herself with a network of like-minded women artists and writers. At first, this included her cousins Mary Reed and Jessie Wilcox Smith, as well as others like Ida Haskell and Gertrude Käsebier, whom she met at the Pratt Institute. Later she expanded this network to include an international group of female friends and acquaintances. These female artistic communities were to provide key support and encouragement to Colman Smith over the course of her life, especially as she increasingly became jaded by the false promises of her male patrons and publishers. During this early prolific period, we can see a clear feminist focus emerge in her art through her strong female characters, as well as her distinctive use of color, movement, shape, and line.

Influence of Arthur Wesley Dow and Howard Pyle

At the beginning of her emergence as an artist, however, Colman Smith was inspired by two very important American male artists, illustrators, and educators—Howard Pyle and Arthur Wesley Dow. Pyle was a prolific writer and illustrator of children's books and, like Colman Smith and her family, was a follower of Swedenborg. Pyle was a household name by the mid-1890s and, as I will discuss below, taught aspiring artists at what is now Drexel University and later at his own Howard Pyle School of Illustration Art in Wilmington, Delaware. Dow, who was only four years younger than Pyle, was still in the early stages of what was to become an illustrious career. Originally from Ipswich, Massachusetts, he began as an elementary school teacher but spent most of the 1880s studying at the Académie Julian in Paris, which was acclaimed for its avant-garde approach to art and the many famous artists it produced. However, Dow left after he grew dissatisfied with the Parisian art scene.[21] As Nancy E. Green has noted, "Dow gradually assimilated into his work the influences of Japonisme, synthesism, and impressionism. He loathed this last term as he associated it with shoddy workmanship."[22]

After returning to the U.S. in 1889, Dow began to submit designs and illustrations for commercial work, something that would normally have been outside the purview of a fine artist at the time but would serve as a model for Colman Smith's embrace of the opportunities of the mass market. He also began to study Japanese art, especially the *ukiyo-e* ink painting and woodblock printing techniques of Hokusai and Katsushika. This art was not wholly traditionally Japanese in style, but was influenced by the first exposure Japanese artists had to Western art after a long period of enforced isolation. Works like Hokusai's *The Great Wave off Kanagawa* in turn transformed Western artistic sensibilities and helped influence Art Nouveau and Impressionism. Pyle's artistic sensibilities were also shaped by the Japanese conception of art.[23] Writing to his wife, Minnie, he explained, "It is now plain to me that [James McNeill] Whistler and [Joseph] Pennell whom I have admired as great originals are only copying the Japanese. One evening with Hokusai gave me more light on composition and decorative effect than years of studying pictures."[24] In 1893 Dow was named assistant curator of the Japanese collection of the Boston Museum of Fine Arts under Ernest Fenollosa, whose ideas on Japanese spirituality, harmony, and synthesis were to become central to Dow's work.[25]

After giving a well-received public lecture on the importance of integrating Japanese ideas on art into American art education, Dow began teaching at the Pratt Institute in Brooklyn in the fall of 1895. Unlike most art educators of his day, he firmly believed in "the elegance of pure design" that was "based in nature but not a replication of it," and taught his students that paintings should be composed by using color, tone, shape, line, and *notan*—a Japanese word that referred to areas of dark and light.[26] In an age where the aesthetic beauty of art was increasingly valued in and of itself, Dow also stressed utility: "Art is the most useful thing in the world, and the most valued thing."[27] He also contributed articles on art education to the *Pratt Institute Monthly* that became the basis for his popular teaching manual, *Composition*. First published in 1899, *Composition* was used by multiple public school districts, which helped to broadly disseminate Dow's revolutionary views on art education. Dow taught at Pratt until 1903 when he moved uptown to Columbia Teacher's College, where he remained until 1922. It was at Columbia that Dow first taught Georgia O'Keeffe. Almost ten years younger than Colman Smith, O'Keeffe's work and Colman Smith's early artistic creations had important intersections; however, O'Keeffe went on to become the "Mother of American Modernism," while long-term artistic success ultimately eluded Colman Smith.[28] Other prominent artists who studied under Dow and attributed their success to him were Alvin Langdon Colburn, Gertrude Käsebier, Max Weber, and Frank Lloyd Wright.[29] Colburn and Käsebier were to become early friends and collaborators of Colman Smith.

Deeply influenced by William Morris and the Arts and Crafts movement, Dow's central "tenet, like that of his British Arts and Crafts counterparts, was to create objects that were well designed, finely crafted, and beautifully rendered."[30] To this end, he helped expand the art curriculum at Pratt beyond traditional drawing and painting to include pottery, design, photography, and printmaking. In addition, Dow studied early American crafts like basket making, tin work, and embroidery, encouraging his students to explore these media as well. In an age of rapid technological development and industrial growth, Dow was a firm supporter of the handmade object in the ongoing debate regarding whether it or its newer, often cheaper machine-made counterpart, deserved prominence. While mass-produced goods flooded the market during the early twentieth century, Green asserts that Dow's championing of the handmade object as high art "greatly affected the course of modernism in America."[31]

During his eight years at Pratt, Dow instituted changes large and small. These included revolutionizing both the curriculum and its implementation, as well as smaller tweaks, such as having his art students design posters for announcements rather than the more conventional practice of displaying printed notices on bulletin boards.[32] The March 1896 *Pratt Institute Monthly* noted that some of these innovations, such as having students study elementary design principles, initially generated derision among the students. As Jessie Morse noted, "The Girls were at first inclined to laugh at the simplicity of Mr. A. W. Dow's squares and spaces, but already before this writing have found this phase of art a dignified and serious matter."[33] Likely aware of this criticism, Dow explained his system of teaching in a December 1896 *Pratt Institute Monthly* article and stressed that the achievement of aesthetic beauty should be the highest aim of art. Disagreeing with the prevalent view that aspiring artists needed to achieve technical competency before they could express ideas through art, Dow stated, "the effort to express the new idea will show the necessity of being able to draw. Hence good drawing will result naturally from a desire to compose."[34] A year later, Dow expanded upon these ideas, which he now termed the "synthetic method of instruction," and explained that the "most precious attribute of the artist" is the "exercise of the pupil's judgment from the very outset," adding that "the student's personal interpretation or idea of that beauty" is essential.[35] As seen in both Haskell's appraisal of Colman Smith's art and in her letters, Colman Smith had a strong desire to express herself through art, and exhibited seemingly boundless creativity and imagination during the mid-to-late 1890s. While, as I detail below, Dow's views on art had an important influence on Colman Smith's early work, it is likely that his interactions with her during her years at Pratt also helped shape his own developing views on art and the creative process, especially in regards to the judgment and imagination of the artist.

Although Colman Smith's time at Pratt was interrupted by frequent stays in Jamaica, she attended Dow's first composition class in the fall of 1895 in which she earned an A. Through additional classes, she developed her interest in woodcuts and printmaking.[36] This was to become the vehicle for both her little magazine, *The Green Sheaf*, and the Green Sheaf Press.[37] Dow's views on the importance of beautifully designed objects also influenced her creation of lampshade, wallpaper, and textile designs.[38]

At Pratt, Colman Smith was likely first introduced to the concept of synaesthesia, or the merging of senses that are not normally connected, enabling her to apply a name to something she had probably experienced from childhood. This either occurred through Dow's discussions of the ideas of Ernest Fenollosa or, more directly, through Colman Smith's interactions with Fenollosa, or his work, during one of his visits to the Pratt Institute in the 1890s.[39] Fenollosa viewed music as the most important of all the fine arts, as it was, at heart, "pure beauty"; as a result, "space art may be called 'visual music.'"[40] Colman Smith's interest in synaesthesia can most clearly be seen in her attempts to create movement in her compositions. As I will discuss in Chapter 3, her synaesthesia fully took shape in her "music pictures," which began on Christmas Day 1900.[41]

Dow also deepened Colman Smith's knowledge of Japanese *ukiyo-e* prints, with their flat shapes, bright colors, and subjects in action-filled poses. In January 1898 she told her cousin that "we have now a large collection" of Japanese prints.[42] She assimilated these elements into her work from the *fin-de-siècle* period onward.[43] Moreover, Dow's strong support for Colman Smith while she was at the Institute helped forge her reputation as artistically talented, and likely helped her gain the attention of Christopher and William Macbeth, whose gallery hosted her first featured exhibit.

Throughout her three winters at Pratt, Colman Smith's work frequently appeared in the *Pratt Institute Monthly*, an honor not extended to another student during this period.[44] Her first cover was an illustration for a poem, "A School-Girl Song of Spring," in March 1897 (Figure 2.1). The painting depicts a procession of white-clad young girls singing and carrying lilies.[45] The girls, who are identically dressed, walk two-by-two. They are distinguished by their varying heights, walking gaits, and the differences in their skin tones that range from pale porcelain to a medium brown. The smallest

Figure 2.1 Pamela Colman Smith, illustration for "A School-Girl Song of Spring," *Pratt Institute Monthly* 5, no. 7 (1897), 199

girl leads the group on her own. Colman Smith's composition reflects Dow's principle of repetition and belief that beauty consists of "elements of difference harmonized by elements of unity."[46] Colman Smith uses contrasting elements to highlight the individuality of the girls, while providing an overall harmony and unity of movement. The piece is very similar to an untitled painting recently uncovered in a private collection (Figure 2.2). Although in this canvas, the singing girls wear brightly colored dresses and stand next to each other rather than arm-in-arm, the similarities between the two works are striking. Both appear to date from the late 1890s. Moreover, the movement and posture of the girls, most of whom have their mouths open in

Figure 2.2 Pamela Colman Smith, untitled.
Private collection

song, express a very palpable musicality, which would become a hallmark of Colman Smith's art. This also highlights that during this *fin-de-siècle* period, Colman Smith integrated Dow's ideas and techniques into her work alongside her own unique elements.

The poem Colman Smith illustrated, "A School-Girl Song of Spring," which is attributed to the seemingly pseudonymous Betty Botticelli, is rather simplistic in its celebration of the vernal equinox. However, a few lines suggest that Colman Smith herself might have been the author, as well as its illustrator. Early in the first stanza, the girls somewhat surprisingly acknowledge that:

> We do not know exactly why
> Our voices chant this joyful cry;
> We fasten blossoms in our hair,
> Why so, we do not know or care;[47]

This very modern depiction of the girls as automatons who are blindly swept up in a spring celebration is much more typical of the ironic asides found throughout Colman Smith's *Henry Morgan* and her letters to her cousin than in any of the other verse published in the *Pratt Institute Monthly*. The bulletin rarely published students' verse but often reprinted short poems, or parts of poems, by Carlyle, Emerson, and Tennyson, among others. The girls' acknowledgment of their lack of agency is repeated near the end of the poem, but its second and third stanzas are much less transgressive as they focus on hailing "sunshine so sunshiny / rain so moist and wet" as well as "everything" associated with spring. Interestingly, the poem, without Colman Smith's art, was reprinted in the March 18, 1897 edition of the *New York Times* and was again attributed to Botticelli.[48] Whether or not Colman Smith was the author, the illustration's implicit humor and subtle focus on key details that allow the individuality of the girls to stand out against a background of stark similarity reflects Dow's view that "No work has art-value unless it reflects the personality of its author. What everybody can do easily, or by rule, cannot be art."[49]

Colman Smith's interactions with Dow set up a pattern in which she would captivate the interest of an older, more established male artist or writer, and receive instruction, praise, and valuable support as part of a close mentorship that could last anywhere from months to years. Often, as I discuss later in the cases of W. B. Yeats and Alfred Stieglitz, the older male grew impatient with Colman Smith's desire to pursue her own ideas, rather than their recommendations. There is less available evidence regarding Colman Smith's interactions with Dow, and it is unclear why she left Pratt without taking a degree. School officials might have asked her to leave due to her long absences from the school, which included most of the fall of 1897, or she might have felt that after her Macbeth Gallery exhibition she was now ready to become a professional artist. The abrupt nature of her withdrawal, however, suggests that the decision to leave Pratt might have been precipitated by a disagreement with Dow. His only subsequent public comment on Colman Smith's work was a brief mention in a January 1899 *Pratt Institute Monthly* article, in which he stated, "Miss Pamela Colman Smith … has very successfully adapted the language of lines, masses, and color to an imaginative field peculiarly her own."[50] It is unknown if the two communicated after her departure from the school or if Dow used his connections with journal editors or artists to advance her career. A 1902 article in *The Reader* described Colman Smith's reasons for leaving the Institute without a degree in this way: "[a]s no noticeable change showed itself in the character of her work under this tutelage, and as she became more determined to work out her own problems in her own way, she ended her connection with the school."[51] The comment does not specifically mention Dow but, instead, highlights Colman Smith's self-reliance and determination to succeed on her own; it also begins a pattern in which she attempts to shape the narrative of her career and artistic reception.

At the end of the fall 1897 semester, Colman Smith abruptly left Pratt and Dow's educational influence and sought the mentorship of a more established male artist whose support and encouragement—not to mention publishing world connections—would, she hoped, help launch her career. She turned to the author and illustrator Howard Pyle, whom she had admired since childhood. With her father, she traveled in early January 1898 to the Drexel Institute in Philadelphia where Pyle taught, in hopes of joining his class.

As Jill and Robert May note, Pyle is known today as "the father of American illustration." Besides publishing numerous illuminated books and magazine stories of his own, Pyle contributed art to works by Charles Dickens, Nathaniel Hawthorne, William Dean Howells, Thomas Nelson Page, Robert Louis Stevenson, Mark Twain, and Woodrow Wilson, among others.[52] In addition, he trained or influenced many of the central figures of the Golden Age of American magazine illustration such as Maxfield Parrish,

Figure 2.3 Sketch of Howard Pyle included in a January 5, 1898 letter from Pamela Colman Smith to her cousin, Mary "Bobby" Reed. Courtesy of the Pamela Colman Smith Collection, Special Collections Department, Bryn Mawr College Library, box 1, folder 11

Norman Rockwell, and N. C. Wyeth. Among his successful students were "the Red Rose Girls"—Jessie Wilcox Smith, Violet Oakley, and Elizabeth Shippen Green.[53]

Colman Smith was an avid reader of Pyle's work; she owned several of his books and felt that he had not received the acclaim he deserved. As she wrote to her cousin, "Nobody ever appreciates Pyle do they Bobby?" In addition to Pyle's *The Garden Behind the Moon*, which I discussed in Chapter 1, Colman Smith admired his stories and illustrations of pirates, Robin Hood, and King Arthur, especially their ability to captivate her imagination and transport her to distant times and places. Her physical description of Pyle to her cousin captures a larger-than-life quality in both the man and his work. Colman Smith notes that he is a "Great big man—nearer 7 foot than 6—and monstrous broad shouldered—!"[54] She goes on to add that he is clean-shaven, bald, with high cheek bones, a big nose, and both "big round eyes" and "big round glasses."[55] Always one to see through the celebrity of the famous individuals she encountered and grasp the essence of their humanity, she observes that Pyle "just looked as if he wanted to laugh all the time!"[56] The small sketch that she includes in a letter to her cousin highlights these physical characteristics as well as a slight grin and a twinkle in his bespectacled eyes (Figure 2.3).

Pyle had begun teaching at Drexel in the fall of 1894, and Colman Smith's cousin, Jessie Wilcox Smith, attended his first class.[57] Like Dow, Pyle rejected the French-influenced realist school that emphasized precise technical accuracy and asserted that painting should mirror nature. Pyle felt that imitative training was important but not enough, as "it would produce skilled artisans, not creative artists."[58] Instead, he devised a program that prepared students to paint "living pictures," rather than, as he noted, "dead, inert matter in which there is not one single little spark of real life."[59] One of the central principles of this program was the development of what Pyle called the faculty of projection. As Richard Wayne Lykes notes, "Projection was the difference between imitation and creation, between cold and warmth."[60] Elizabeth Shippen Green, who was part of Pyle's first Drexel class, put it this way:

1. To realize as hard as you possibly can the situation that you are about to depict.
2. To realize as hard as you possibly can.
3. To realize![61]

This focus on empathetic connection with subjects and the importance of imagination very closely mirrors Colman Smith's view on art, so it makes sense that she turned to Pyle as her next teacher and mentor. While both Dow and Pyle stressed the importance of the artist's originality and control over a composition, Dow placed much more emphasis on teaching students the importance of color, tone, line, and *notan*. Pyle appears to have privileged artistic imagination over everything else, but, as I detail below, he assumed that his students would already possess a high level of technical proficiency.

Throughout the visit, Colman Smith found Pyle exceeded her expectations. She wrote to her cousin how impressed she was that he talked with her and her father and let them sit in on one of his classes, even though they had apparently traveled to Drexel from New York City without an appointment. This impetuous aspect to her visit seems to indicate that her decision to leave Pratt was forced on her unexpectedly or, at least, was not planned out well in advance. The highlight of the trip was Pyle's perusal of her sketchbook. She notes that he appeared "quite surprised" by her drawings and termed them "very ingenious and interesting."[62] According to Colman Smith, Pyle said he "would be very pleased to have me in the class," but that she would need to submit works for the entrance requirement for the school, which consisted of both a head and a full-length figure in oil.[63] She adds that her father thought that "studying Puritans, Pirates, soldiers, Lords, Ladies, etc." from draped models in costume, as well as the special focus on heads and hands offered by the class, "is just what I need!"[64] However, this dream was not realized. Colman Smith did not attend Pyle's Drexel classes, his Wilmington studio workshops, or the summer classes that he led at Chadds Ford, Pennsylvania. The qualification for admission to Pyle's classes was more extensive than Colman Smith's letter indicates and included three original drawings and three drawings of nude models.[65] Jill and Robert May, Pyle's biographers, explain that his admission criteria "reveals his reluctance to take on beginning students," especially women, who often did not work from nude models.[66] Pyle expected a mastery of basic draftsmanship before a student entered his school. As Colman Smith's letters and published critiques reveal, she struggled with some elements of basic artistic technique, especially in regards to head and hands, which could explain why she never attended Pyle's classes. Whether she failed to submit the paintings or they were deemed to be below the standard required is not known. It is also possible that some other factor, such as her father's ongoing legal troubles stemming from the bankruptcy of the West India Improvement Society, prevented her from attending.

Colman Smith returned to Jamaica with her father by February 1898, but whether that was the reason she did not attend Drexel or a decision after the fact is unknown. What is evident is that while away from the United States, she was still thinking fondly of Pyle. In March 1898 she wrote to her cousin that if she could only get her, Pyle, and a few other friends together, "what a sport we would have!"[67] A few months later, Colman Smith was back in New York, but her tone toward Pyle had altered. In a June 13, 1898 letter to her cousin, Colman Smith notes that, "I might have gone to H-Pyle's summer school—but he said it was full!"[68] She recounts that he had asked to see a manuscript she had recently completed, but that she had refused as it "was already in the hands of a Publisher!", adding "Now won't he be mad! Ha Ha wait till we send him one! [i.e a copy of the published project]"[69] While her playful sense of humor is readily apparent, these lines also hint at lingering resentment over not being able to attend classes with Pyle, and a desire to prove herself as a successful, published artist. Similarly, in a December 13, 1900 letter to Alfred Bigelow Paine, Colman Smith somewhat dismissively references a recent painting by Pyle and alludes to an "article we had the row over."[70]

However, near the end of her life, Colman Smith offered another version of her interactions with Pyle. A handwritten note dating from 1948 on the flyleaf of her copy of the 1898 collection *The Counterpane Fairy* by Katharine Pyle—Howard Pyle's sister—states:

> I met Katharine Pyle about 1899 in N.Y. she is sister of Howard Pyle, an artist. I grew up on <u>his</u> pictures and books. Their grandmother was a Quaker and they lived at Wilmington, Delaware and used to hide the silver at the <u>back</u> of the drawers in the sideboard when they went from home!—H. P. taught at a big art school in Philadelphia. I <u>nearly</u> went there—but he advised my coming to England then with E. T.[71]

The timeline of her interactions with Pyle and his sister in this note differs from what can be pieced together from the three 1898 letters to her cousin. As I note above, Colman Smith expressed a strong desire to attend Pyle's art classes well before the death of her father in December of 1899, and her subsequent decision to leave the U.S. for England in the spring of 1900 with her new friend and benefactor, the actor Ellen Terry. The handwritten note in Katharine Pyle's book, which was adorned with Colman Smith's name, address, and a request to "please return [the book] sometime," could be an attempt to rewrite history and to retroactively make Pyle more supportive of her career. At this point three years before her death Colman Smith was bedridden, and she may well have regretted not being able to study with Pyle and have thought it made an important difference in the ultimate trajectory of her career. It is also possible that her friendship with Katharine Pyle might have reignited Colman Smith's desire to attend Pyle's school, and that she may have been granted admission in early 1900, only to have this plan derailed by her return to England with Terry.

The unexpected note also illuminates a previously unknown friendship between Colman Smith and Katharine Pyle, highlighting the importance of female artistic networks.[72] Colman Smith lived on 18th Street in Manhattan, beginning in the summer of 1898, until her departure for England in May 1900 with Terry, Sir Henry Irving, Bram Stoker, and the other members of the Lyceum Theatre Company. It was likely during this period that she made Katharine's acquaintance, while both were fledgling New York artists. Katharine, who was the youngest of Howard Pyle's three siblings, was a prolific writer and illustrator of works predominantly for children. She lived in Wilmington, Delaware, for most of her life, with the exception of a few years in the late 1890s that she spent in Manhattan, immersing herself in the New York artistic scene of which Colman Smith also was a part. In March 1898 Colman Smith asked her cousin if she had seen Katharine's illustrations for *White Aprons* and *Head of a Hundred*, asking "aren't they scrummy?"[73] This makes clear that Colman Smith admired her work. Katharine, like her brother, was active in the Swedenborgian church that Colman Smith's family were affiliated with, and it is possible that Colman Smith first met her through the church. The two must have been on friendly terms for Colman Smith to have been told stories about Pyle's Quaker grandmother and childhood in Wilmington. Moreover, the fact that Colman Smith remembered them fifty years later highlights her sense of humor, focus on the telling detail, and the importance she placed on her many female friends.

Whatever the exact circumstances surrounding Colman Smith's interactions with Howard Pyle, he was an early, important influence, since he was one of the few illustrators of the time who was also a writer.[74] Like Colman Smith, his first books were not texts that he had created himself but adaptations of earlier stories that were popular in the U.S. and Europe. Pyle also strove to seamlessly integrate his illustrations into the texts in ways that Randolph Caldecott, Walter Crane, and Kate Greenaway—who also influenced Colman Smith—did not.[75] It is clear that Pyle served as an important model not only in Colman Smith's development as an illustrator but also in her desire to create her own words and images, which began shortly after she left Pratt.

Increase in Female Artists and Female Artistic Communities

By 1900 there were approximately 25,000 female artists in the U.S., and women comprised approximately 45 percent of the profession.[76] As Jill and Robert May note, "there were opportunities for women in illustrative art [as opposed to fine art] because a high percentage of the readership of newer illustrated monthlies was female."[77] Pyle's decision, after leaving Drexel following accusations of favoritism, to admit only two women, including his sister, into his Wilmington classes was not unique at the time, but indicates the significant hurdles faced by female artists and illustrators in both publishing and the fine arts well into the twentieth century.[78] Even though there was a growing number of women contributing illustrations to magazines and books, men held the majority of positions as editors, advertisers, and publishers. Despite the many obstacles women artists had to overcome to achieve recognition and financial success, Colman Smith was aware of the growing market for female illustrators and very much wanted to achieve financial and critical success. She experienced this inequity firsthand throughout her career and often railed against the "Pigs! The publishers are all pigs !?!"[79]

To combat this institutionalized sexism, female artists often banded together in communities that helped foster both camaraderie and their art. One of the most famous of these were the previously mentioned trio who were collectively known as the Red Rose Girls—Elizabeth Shippen Green, Violet Oakley, and Jessie Wilcox Smith—who lived together for fourteen years.[80] Even after Shippen Green's marriage in 1911, the three remained close, living within a few blocks of each other for most of their lives.[81] As Charlotte Herzog notes, this "communal living arrangement nurtured a feminist support system that made it possible for them to overcome many of the obstacles faced by their contemporaries. They critiqued each other's projects, promoted each other professionally, and exhibited as a group."[82] Although all three women made a living by their art, Wilcox Smith, who was Colman Smith's cousin on her father's side, was the most successful of the three. Today she is best known for her *Good Housekeeping* illustrations, which monopolized the magazine's covers between 1918 and 1933. Her illustrations were also included in children's books and primarily featured isolated children in natural and domestic settings. As Jill and Robert May note, "in many ways they glorified the clean and tidy middle-class early 20th century white child's life."[83] It is unclear how close Colman Smith was with her cousin—their styles of art were very different, and she never achieved anything near the commercial success Wilcox Smith and her friends enjoyed.[84] However, it is likely that her cousin's artistic successes, as well as her mutually supportive and artistically generative friendship with Shippen Green and Oakley, provided Colman Smith with an important example of successful female artists.

However, the institutionalized sexism these women artists experienced is also evident, even in seemingly positive assessments of their work. In a June 1900 article in *The Critic*, Regina Armstrong discussed what she viewed as the "decorative tendency in pictorial art," focusing on the work of Oakley, Shippen Green, and Wilcox Smith, alongside Colman Smith. Dealing exclusively with women artists, Armstrong explains that "the decorative feeling … is the atmosphere of art, the varying sense of the picturesque, and in its expression reflects mood as well as temperament, so that it may convey the most exquisite delicacy and refinement, or it may be a fantasia of exuberance and exaggeration."[85] Although Armstrong's comments are complimentary, she consistently conflates contemporaneous stereotypes of women as decorative, delicate, exquisite, and refined with their work, and seems to be (silently) comparing them to the unnamed, but readily assumed by readers, alternative of "fine" art, which at the turn of the twentieth century was still seen as a predominantly male realm. Moreover, Armstrong's observations reflect Helen Goodman's assertion in the 1980s that "Then as now, illustration was viewed by many as a stepchild among the arts, several rungs below 'fine art.' Because the work was perceived as practical and commercial, genius was not needed, merely a serviceable talent, training, and on-the-job experience."[86] As a result, artists like Shippen Green, Oakley, and Wilcox Smith flourished because their illustrations more closely reflected commercially established views of art, while others, like Colman Smith, who wanted to transform and transcend traditional modes of representational art, struggled.

Like earlier critiques that had difficulty in pinning down Colman Smith and her work, Armstrong's assessment also seems to be rooted in an inability to classify her as a person. The liberally illustrated *Critic* article includes drawings done by Shippen Green, Oakley, and Wilcox Smith of each other, generally in profile and staring placidly into the distance. In fact, the pieces that represent their illustrative work are very similar to their drawings of each other and—without the captions—it would be quite difficult to differentiate between them. In stark contrast, the article does not reproduce a life-like drawing of Colman Smith, or one of the many photographs of her that were in circulation at the time, but instead presents the caricature, which I discussed in the Introduction, that she drew of herself in a Japanese kimono in response to comments about her possible Asian origins. The example of Colman Smith's illustrative work, an ornate, brightly colored painting of Ellen Terry as Rautendelein in Gerhart Hauptmann's fairy drama *The Sunken Bell*, also emphasizes her difference from the other women artists discussed.

While the bulk of Armstrong's article focuses on the work of Shippen Green, Oakley, and Wilcox Smith, she reserves her strongest praise for Colman Smith:

When one takes up the art of Pamela Colman Smith, so strongly decorative, it is to find that even in consideration with decorative workers, it occupies a distinct, a unique place. No one is doing quite the same kind of work that Miss Smith essays, and it is safe to say that no one could do it in quite her way. She sounds the top note in the gamut of exuberance and exaggeration. But she touches many notes besides,—the humorous, the grotesque, the mystic, the pastoral, and the severe. One who has suffered from her mirthful and clever caricatures will appreciate the latter designation.[87]

Similar to previously discussed critical assessments by Haskell and others, Armstrong, despite her specificity, also emphasizes that Colman Smith's art defies categorization. While convention breaking is generally a positive attribute in a male artist (and was how art was revolutionized at the turn of the twentieth century), in a woman artist, as Colman Smith's life repeatedly illustrates, it proved more challenging. This was especially true for artists whose primary source of income was commercial illustration, which, by definition, needs to fit clear categories and conform to the tastes of a mass public. Interestingly, Armstrong describes Colman Smith's work as both "mystic," a description that was to follow her throughout her career, and the most feminine. Her art is "so strongly decorative" and "sounds the top note in the gamut of exuberance and exaggeration," stereotypical descriptions that would commonly be applied to women and their art during this period. By subtly emphasizing Colman Smith's femininity (and by extension her imagination, exuberance, and inability to conform), Armstrong differentiates her from the other, more sober, more conventional, and more financially successful artists that she discusses.

The differences between Colman Smith and the older and more established Shippen Green, Oakley, and Wilcox Smith are most readily observable in Armstrong's concluding summation: "Miss Oakley with her stable restraint and refined strength may be classed with the warm vigor and dignified handling of Miss Jessie Wilcox Smith, and with the vital and human resources of Miss Green."[88] In comparison, "Miss Colman Smith takes unto herself all the eccentricities of pronounced individuality and shows throughout, an elastic search for the expression of herself and of the wayward fancies and graces that possess her."[89] The older, critically praised, and financially secure women are described as "stable," "dignified," and, "vital"—all traits much more commonly associated with masculinity—while Colman Smith, as discussed above, is a feminized eccentric who is searching for ways to express herself through her art. Thus, even though all the artists Armstrong discusses are women, it is the masculine traits of Shippen Green, Oakley, and Wilcox Smith that are implicitly privileged, even if those traits would not necessarily be valued in a male "fine" artist, who, instead, would be expected to be bold and revolutionary.

While I have not found any detailed references in extant letters about the impact Shippen Green, Oakley, and/or Wilcox Smith had on Colman Smith's art and life, it is likely that the trio served as an important early example of nurturing, female-centered artistic communities. As I discuss in Chapters 3 and 4, these would become more central to Colman Smith once she returned to England in 1900. In addition to her friendship with Katharine Pyle and the influence of Jessie Wilcox Smith, she made important early connections in New York with several other women artists, notably Haskell and Käsebier.

Ida Haskell was born in California in 1861 and trained at the Art Institute of California, the Philadelphia Art Museum, and the Académie Julian in Paris.[90] Known for her landscapes and portraits, she exhibited quite widely in Paris, Philadelphia, and New York City in the 1880s and 1890s.[91] For many years, Haskell taught oil painting and antiques in the Department of Fine Art at Pratt, and Colman Smith likely became acquainted with her while she was a student at the Brooklyn Institute.[92] This acquaintance resulted in a friendship, and the older artist wrote the December 1897 cover story on Colman Smith for the *Pratt Institute Monthly*.[93] Colman Smith reported that Haskell gave her Kenneth Graham's *The Golden Age* that Christmas.[94] In March 1898 Colman Smith named "Miss Haskell" as one of the people whom she missed while in Jamaica, and wished that she would visit her on the island.[95] Three months later she was back in New York City, and reported to her cousin that "Haskie- [her nickname for Haskell] Daddy and I" went to the theater.[96] And in August Colman Smith lamented that "Haskie is out West and I miss her so!"[97] It is unclear how long their friendship lasted, as there are no surviving letters between them, and Colman Smith doesn't mention her again in any of the extant correspondence. However, she did later collaborate with Alice Boughton, Haskell's long-time partner.[98]

Another important artist Colman Smith met during her time at Pratt, who was to become a close friend, was Gertrude Käsebier.[99] An advanced student at the Institute, Käsebier studied under Dow during the 1895–96 period. Her luminous photos of mothers and children are firmly within the pictorialist school and evince the influence of Dow's ideas of light and shadow.[100] In a June 1898 letter to her cousin, Colman Smith notes, "I have a cover for a book of photos by Mrs. Käsebier of Indians."[101] Käsebier's famous photograph of a shadowed Colman Smith, gazing over her shoulder directly into the camera, was first published in *The Critic* in January 1899 as a part of a brief, but very positive, assessment of Colman Smith's early work.[102] It was Käsebier who introduced Colman Smith to Alfred Stieglitz. This acquaintance led to his hosting three important exhibitions of her work at his 291 gallery in New York in the 1907–11 period.

Women, Myth, and Illustrative Power in the Early Works

After Colman Smith and her father returned to Jamaica early in 1898, she embarked on a host of new projects. Rather than returning to more representational works like *The Wind*, she turned toward literature, likely in hopes of advancing her as yet nascent career as an illustrator. Letters reveal that she collaborated on what appears to have been an unfinished play with the headmaster of the Kingston Grammar School, and began work on a Shakespearean Alphabet for children.[103] As Julia Briggs has noted, the "period from 1890 to 1914 was unquestionably the golden age of children's book illustration, when colour printing reached new standards of accuracy."[104] Colman Smith, whom letters reveal was an avid reader of children's literature, repeatedly tried to break into this new, lucrative market during the *fin-de-siécle* period, with only limited success. It is likely that she thought Shakespeare, who was undergoing a resurgence during the late Victorian period, would be an appealing subject for both publishers and consumers, but also provide her with rich material with many strong female characters. By March 1898 she had completed drawings of Banquo from *Macbeth*, Caliban from *The Tempest*, and Hotspur from *Henry IV Part 1*, and had planned illustrations of Katherine from *The Taming of the Shrew*, Viola from *Twelfth Night*, and Mistress Quickly from *Henry IV Parts 1 and 2*, *The Merry Wives of Windsor*, and *Henry V*, among others.[105] Of this grouping, only her painting of Caliban survives; it depicts him in profile as a creature of the sea, replete with scales and barnacles.[106] Like much of her work from this period, the figure displays a lot of movement. Drawing to mind Dow's assertion that "[t]here is a certain beauty in the contrast of large and small. It is the opposite of Monotony," the painting employs an unexpected use of perspective; the seaweed towers over Caliban, and the sand and sea almost morph into each other.[107] Colman Smith was in talks with both R. H. Russell, who published several of her works during this period, and William Heinemann to produce the work.[108] Although the Alphabet was mentioned in both the *Pratt Institute Monthly* and the *Washington Times*, it appears never to have been published.[109]

At some point, the proposed Shakespearean Alphabet project morphed into the 1899 *Shakespeare's Heroines* calendar published by Russell, of which only the cover color lithograph survives.[110] The striking use of red on Portia's cloak, which is picked up in the pattern of the women's clothes, the red of their lips, and the flowers in their hair, emphasizes both the sensuality and the violence that is present in so many of the Bard's plays. The sloping curves of the female figures, all of whom are depicted in profile, are, like many of Colman Smith's women from this period, reminiscent of the work of Edward Burne-Jones and the Pre-Raphaelites. The cover also shows the first published version of Colman Smith's drawing of towers on a mountain; this was to become an important symbol for her, recurring in *The Green Sheaf*, her "music pictures," and her Smith-Waite tarot images. Moreover, both the proposed Shakespearean Alphabet and the *Shakespeare's Heroines* calendar reflect her decision to look to literary sources or her own imagination, rather than nature, for the subjects of her art, a habit that would continue for the rest of her career.

Both Colman Smith's focus on literature as her preferred subject matter and her interest in creating beautiful, deluxe editions that could command higher prices can be seen in the color portfolio that Russell issued of five of her prints for Christmas 1898.[111] The rise of the Arts and Crafts movement created an interest in books as works of art. The *livre d'artiste*, a book containing a collection of an artist's work, became popular in France in the late nineteenth century and served as a vehicle by which early work by Paul Cezanne, Paul Gauguin, Pablo Picasso, and Vincent Van Gogh, among others, circulated.[112] It was likely that Russell, who went on to print several portfolios of Colman Smith's early work, was hoping to capitalize on the middle-class consumer who had some disposable income to buy art gifts during the holiday season.[113] Printed on "Japan paper," hand-colored, and individually retouched, the five color prints included in the portfolio were "Recess," "A Christmas Carol," "The Land of Heart's Desire," "Macbeth," and "Twelfth Night Merry Makers."[114]

Colman Smith's use of color, line, and shading in these Russell portfolios shows Dow's influence, while the focus on story and the movement of the subjects reflects the style of Pyle. Like almost all Colman Smith's work from this period, the figures are outlined with various-sized black lines in a style reminiscent of the flat Japanese *ukiyo-e* prints that Dow felt were important models for his students. As he noted in an 1895 lecture, "the Japanese artist concerns himself chiefly with the flat relations. The Western artist concerns himself … chiefly with round relations," concluding that "It can be shown, logically that the true art lies in the flat relations."[115] However, it is Colman Smith's masterful use of color, which she achieved by mixing colors herself from natural herbs and pigments, that stands out most from this collection and was to become a hallmark of her work from this period. As Dow noted in the December 1896 *Pratt Institute Monthly*, "But color, most of all, gave evidence of living power—it was not nature's accidental colors, nor the impressionist's worsted-like crudities, but the color-mosaic, the harmony resulting from the juxtaposition of spaces varying in hue, in depth of dark, and in quality of tint."[116] This "living power," as created by Colman Smith's innovative use of color, is evident throughout the portfolio.

In "Recess," "A Christmas Carol," and "The Land of Heart's Desire," the power of Colman Smith's use of color takes the form of a liberal use of white contrasted against bright backgrounds in a manner reminiscent of her illustration for "A School-Girl Song of Spring." Many of the children depicted in "Recess" wear white, emphasizing their playfulness and innocence. Their clothes, which call to mind the detailed outfits of Kate Greenaway's children, billow in the wind as they engage in a variety of games in front of a crisply white schoolhouse. Originally exhibited at Pratt as "Our Pets," "Recess" is the only non-illustrative image in the collection.[117] A very similar untitled painting recently discovered in a private collection has almost the same positioning of the frolicking children but different clothes and hair colors (Figure 2.4). The Greenaway influence remains palpable. The biggest difference is that in the upper right there is a young boy with a dunce hat, rather than a girl calling to her friends.

"A Christmas Carol" accompanies the sheet music for Lancashire writer and labor activist Edwin Waugh's adaptation of the sixteenth-century song, "A Long Time Ago in Palestine" (Figure 2.5). Unlike other portrayals of the Holy Family, which focus on Jesus' birth in a Bethlehem manger, Colman Smith's illustration depicts a white-clad Mary and child Jesus set in profile against

Figure 2.4 Pamela Colman Smith, untitled.
Private collection

FORGING A PATH 77

Figure 2.5 Pamela Colman Smith, "A Christmas Carol," included in a portfolio published by R. H. Russell in 1898.
Private collection

vivid bands of blue and green sky.[118] Fluffy clouds double as probable halos and a flock of white doves flutter across the canvas, all emphasizing the purity and holiness of the central figures. Joseph, who is dressed in green and physically distanced from the mother and child, works at his lathe while he gazes lovingly at the pair. The composition also hints at Colman Smith's interpretive abilities as an illustrator, which are also on display in her triptych based on W. B. Yeats's 1894 play *The Land of Heart's Desire*.

In sharp contrast to "Recess" and "A Christmas Carol," in "The Land of Heart's Desire" Colman Smith deviates from the more conventional use of white to emphasize purity and innocence and, instead, employs the color to highlight the ethereality and unconventional nature of both the female sprites and the human woman they seduce.[119] Overall, the piece is notable for the extreme movement of its riotously dancing female fairies, who cavort on the two side panels. In the center image, Shawn Bruin attempts to restrain his wife, Maire, from leaving with the barefoot, red-headed fairy child who leads the dancing, white-gowned sprites. In the background, Shawn's parents, Maurteen and Bridget, physically restrain the priest, Father Hart, from intervening, as even the representative of the Church is powerless in the presence of the fairies, whom the play asserts are the offspring of Satan.[120] The fairy child tempts Maire, telling her that if she stays with her husband, her life will be filled with hard work and frequent childbirth, but in Faery Land all would be different.[121] Colman Smith's excerpts from the play that are included under the triptych emphasize both the freedom and agelessness of the fairies, as well as the lure of Faery Land, a place "Where nobody gets old and crafty and wise, / Where nobody gets old and godly and grave, / Where nobody gets old and bitter of tongue."[122] It sounds like just the type of place Colman Smith herself would enjoy. However, what her triptych, with its focus on the dancing fairies and restrained wife, elides is that once Maire decides to follow the fairy child, she dies. After death Maire transforms into a "little bird with crest of gold!" who then escapes to "a land where even the old are fair, / And even the wise are merry of tongue."[123] This bird, without explanation, is included at the bottom of the triptych.

The Land of Heart's Desire was an important work for Colman Smith. It was likely one of her first introductions to both Yeats's work and Irish myth, as well as the sprites more commonly known as pixies. Colman Smith even performed the role of the fairy child in two London productions in 1904.[124] As I detail in Chapter 3, pixies were to become both an important symbol and identity for her in the early decades of the 1900s. Furthermore, the play marks the first time Yeats drew on Irish folklore as living mythology. As Birgit Bramsbäck notes, "Yeats himself was firmly convinced that folklore in all its manifestations was a living force, a power which should be used to vitalize literature."[125] In Chapter 4, I discuss how this idea of a vibrant, dynamic mythology greatly influenced Colman Smith and resonated with her own growing interest in Afro-Jamaican Anansi tales, as well as pirate lore and the folktales of the Celtic areas of Devon and Cornwall, which she was introduced to during her visit to England in the summer of 1899. The history and lore of very different traditions were extremely important to her, and are often fused in her work from the *fin-de-siècle* period.

FORGING A PATH 79

Figure 2.6 Pamela Colman Smith, "The service and the loyalty I owe, in doing it pays itself," *Macbeth*, act 1, scene 4, included in a portfolio published by R. H. Russell in 1898. ART File S528m1 no. 98 (size S). Reproduced by permission of the Folger Shakespeare Library

Like Colman Smith's triptych for Yeats's *The Land of Heart's Desire*, her illustration for Shakespeare's *Macbeth* reflects Pyle's advice to "realize" imaginatively the fictional world she is creating on paper.[126] Interestingly, both of these images depict female characters who are central to their given works but, especially in the case of Lady Macbeth, not routinely seen as the play's chief focus (Figure 2.6). Colman Smith's illustration portrays Lady Macbeth decorously curtseying to King Duncan. Her elaborate white and pink patterned gown draws the viewer's attention, as does the king's tunic and the texture of the armor of the knights who surround the pair, all of which is reminiscent of both Crane's lavish use of color and Morris's ornate patterns. Lady Macbeth's deferential posture, with her bowed head and closed eyes, is in direct opposition to the lines from Act 1, scene 4 that are printed below: "The service and the loyalty I owe, / In doing it pays itself."[127] In Shakespeare's tragedy, these famous lines are spoken by her husband—Lady Macbeth is not even on stage at the time—and are commonly seen as foreshadowing his murder of the king.[128] This subtle change reflects the importance Colman Smith put on the interpretive abilities of the illustrator as well her lifelong interest in female power and agency, and especially the way in which she felt Lady Macbeth was, in fact, key to understanding the play and the demise of her husband.

Furthermore, this subtle change highlights Colman Smith's interest in refashioning the image of Lady Macbeth. During the nineteenth century she was commonly viewed as a monstrous, murderous woman of "almost peerless malevolence."[129] This mirrors the extent to which Lady Macbeth violated the nineteenth-century ideal of women as nurturing and supportive wives and mothers. This is why Samuel Taylor Coleridge speaks of Lady Macbeth's "superhuman audacity."[130] Early in the nineteenth century, the famed English actor Sara Siddons recounted that when she first learned the part of Lady Macbeth, "a woman in whose bosom the passion of ambition has almost obliterated all the characteristics of human nature," she experienced "a paroxysm of terror."[131] However, as the century progressed, the complexity of women, especially of the fictional variety, slowly became tolerated, if not accepted outright, and there was at least one sympathetic critical study of Lady Macbeth.[132] In 1888 the Lyceum Theatre Company actor Ellen Terry, who was to become a close friend and mentor of Colman Smith, noted that she thought it "strange" that Lady Macbeth should be viewed "as a sort of monster."[133] She went on to assert that "I conceive [her] as a small, slight woman of acute nervous sensibility," who perhaps was "not good, but not much worse than many women you know—me for instance."[134] It is unclear if Colman Smith's illustration of Lady Macbeth was influenced by Terry's interpretation of the character.[135] Her controversial Lady Macbeth was much discussed in the newspapers and magazines of the day, and her performance was immortalized in John Singer Sargent's 1889 painting, which Nina Auerbach has termed the "exaltation of the awesome powers of self-creating womanhood."[136] Colman Smith attended Lyceum Theatre productions in New York during the company's U.S. tours of the 1890s, but did not meet Terry until the fall of 1899. It is fascinating to consider whether their shared interest in Lady Macbeth's complexity and power might have cemented their friendship. Moreover, Colman Smith's

"Macbeth" demonstrates her growing feminist focus and frequent portrayal of women in independent and active roles.

The last print in the collection, "Twelfth Night Merry Makers," depicts riotous dancers at a Christmas party. Like many of Colman Smith's illustrations, most of the people pictured are women. In an early use of the Rückenfigur technique, or the positioning of figures with their backs to the viewer, the woman on the bottom right is facing the dancers, drawing the viewer's eyes toward the partygoers, while her two companions cock their heads at the viewer. Melinda Boyd Parsons has noted that this image's "tilted perspective" displays some of the Japanese influence on Colman Smith's early work.[137]

The Russell portfolio generated Colman Smith's first wholly negative review. The January 1899 edition of the *International Studio* asserted that "[t]he drawing of the designs is animated, but the artist has evidently been influenced by Beardsley, and there is a taint of caricature throughout the compositions."[138] The January 1899 issue of *The Critic* likewise compared her work to Beardsley, but drew a very different conclusion. It stated, "Miss Smith has the cleverness of Aubrey Beardsley without his coarseness. Refinement is the key-note of her work."[139] The fact that both reviewers detected an affinity for Beardsley's drawings in Colman Smith's art is instructive. The two artists share some obvious similarities, and Beardsley's art was an influence on Colman Smith, especially after her return to England in 1900. Like Colman Smith, Beardsley was also strongly influenced by Japanese art and emphasized areas of light and dark. He, too, had a keen sense of humor that is often palpable in his work. However, unlike Colman Smith, the odor of scandal hung over Beardsley. His work was often highly sexually charged, and he was tarred with the same brush as his friend Oscar Wilde after Wilde's 1895 trial for "gross indecency." The fact that Colman Smith's art had a much less pronounced erotic sensibility appears to have been one aspect of *The Critic*'s more positive assessment of her work.

Although Colman Smith's Russell portfolio prints received a mixed reception, they led to a spate of book and illustration projects, many of them focused on folk culture. In 1899 she created *Annancy Stories*, *The Golden Vanity and The Green Bed*, and *Widdicombe Fair* on her own, and illustrated Seumas MacManus's *In Chimney Corners: Merry Tales of Irish Folklore*. She also composed a series of illustrations for Arthur Pinero's 1898 play *Trelawney of the 'Wells'* and a commemorative booklet featuring Sir Henry Irving and

Ellen Terry of the Lyceum Theatre Company.[140] While continuing the innovative use of color and perspective that characterized the Russell portfolio, these works show advances in both technical proficiency and composition, as well as storytelling.

Arguably, the most important work during this prolific year was *Annancy Stories*, which I will discuss in Chapter 4. Excerpts from Colman Smith's *Annancy Stories* were included in the children's pages of both the *New York Herald* and the *Pittsburgh Daily Post*.[141] This marketing reflects Colman Smith's view that the collection's primary audience would be children and that *Annancy Stories* would help launch her on a successful career as a children's writer and illustrator, as it had Joel Chandler Harris with his *Uncle Remus Stories*. Although the sales for *Annancy Stories* were anemic, she did go on to contribute illustrations to the popular children's publication *St. Nicholas Magazine*, whose editor, Alfred Bigelow Paine, was also the children's page editor of the *New York Sunday Herald*. Paine, whom Colman Smith affectionately referred to as "Tutter," became a long-term epistolary confidant. While none of Paine's letters to Colman Smith survive, the comfort and intimacy between the two as displayed in her letters to him is remarkable. At times her inability to sell her work to publishers or magazines led her to humorously negotiate, as she does in an August 1899 letter to Paine: "We are … dead broke so will give St. Nick some old bargains cheap! Ha!"[142] In other letters, she celebrates small victories: "I got $89.80 royalty on Irving Souvenir!! Ha! Much forced!! Perhaps I shall someday get as much as $50.75 out of RHR."[143] RHR refers to Richard H. Russell, representative of the William H. Russell publishing firm that released most of Colman Smith's early work.

However, more than the *Annancy Stories* or any of Colman Smith's other publications up to this point, *In Chimney Corners* had a truly international presence. The collection was widely reviewed in Irish, English, and American newspapers. There were multiple advertisements for it in the *Dublin Daily Mail*, the *Dublin Daily Express*, and the London *Morning Post*. The reviews were, however, mixed. While the *St. Louis Post-Dispatch* noted that "MacManus has caught the elusive spirit of folk lore," and the *Pall Mall Gazette* declared that an "excellent racy teller he makes," the *Brooklyn Life* reviewer stated that the stories "lack imagination" and were "full of repetitions, not only of incident but of phrase, which become wearisome in the reading."[144] The critical responses for Colman Smith's illustrations were even less positive. The *Pall Mall Gazette* stated: "One doubts that the grotesques of Miss Pamela

Colman Smith will add to the book's attractiveness."[145] However, the *Dublin Daily Express* devoted an entire short article to Colman Smith's work, praising her "fantastic imagination" and predicting that her illustrations "will make the book." The unnamed reviewer concluded by suggesting "We hope that some day she will venture into the higher sphere of mythical legend."[146] In fact, as I discuss in Chapter 3, Colman Smith proposed several ideas for works using Yeats's poetry and his retellings of Irish myth, but none of these found their way to print. As I detail in Chapter 4 and 5, she then began to detail her own personal symbology that drew on both Irish mythology and Afro-Jamaican Anansi tales.

Like her *Annancy Stories* and illustrations for *In Chimney Corners*, Colman Smith's twelve full-color illustrations for two Old English ballads, *The Golden Vanity and The Green Bed*, show her growing interest in folktales and folk culture of all sorts.[147] They also echo her growing interest in the interpretive power of the illustrator, one likely honed by her careful study of Pyle's illustrations, as well as Dow's focus on the judgment of the artist. "The Golden Vanity" is a seventeenth-century ballad that details the taking of a famous ship by pirates; the ship is saved by the bravery of a cabin boy who sinks the pirate galley but sacrifices himself in the process. The final verse of the song describes his tragic fate:

> They sewed his body up, all in an old cow's hide,
> And they cast the gallant cabin-boy over the ship's side,
> And they left him without more ado adrifting with the tide,
>   And to sink by the Low-lands low.[148]

While the edition does include an illustration of the boy lying on the deck swathed in burlap-type material, it does not depict his body bobbing on the ocean or sinking to its murky depths. Instead, Colman Smith's final illustration for the song has the boy, seemingly brought back to life, happily swimming with a quartet of mermaids as the ship recedes into the sunset.[149] In this way, using the vocabulary of the folktale, she adds a plausible happy ending to the grim tale.

Like Colman Smith's prints for the Russell portfolio, the illustrations in this collection are notable for their movement, bright colors, and flatness, which is produced by outlining the figures in black. A distinctive feature of Colman Smith's illustrations for *The Golden Vanity and The Green Bed* is a union of foreground and background to create an almost two-dimensional effect due to complicated compositions of swirling lines, variegated color, and areas of pattern and texture. This is most apparent in her depictions of water, which is reminiscent of both Hokusai's *The Great Wave off Kanagawa* and Walter Crane's *The Horses of Neptune*, yet distinctly her own. This is primarily the result of her creative use of color for the sea. She intersperses patches of blue, green, white, and even purple for a unique effect that brings to mind Dow's assessment of Hokusai's use of color: "[his] color is strange and imaginative; sometimes delicate almost to neutrality, sometimes startling and daring."[150] Colman Smith repeatedly returned to depictions of the sea, sometimes adding in mermaids, as she does in her illustrations for "The Golden Vanity," other times depicting women in water, which was to become an important personal symbol.

While "The Golden Vanity" deals with tragedy and self-sacrifice on the high seas, "The Green Bed" depicts both the more raucous aspects of seafaring life and the negative stereotypes surrounding sailors. The ballad tells the story of Dick, a sailor recently in port, who enters a public house wanting to "visit" with the proprietress's daughter and luxuriate in her "best Green Bed." The proprietress immediately inquires as to what gold Dick acquired while at sea. Concerned that she is only interested in his money, he replies that he had "poor luck," which leads her to lie to him:

> My daughter, she's gone out for a walk;
> My beds are all bespoken;
> My larder's bare, like the rum-keg there,
> And my baccy pipes are all broken.[151]

Dick immediately turns to leave the establishment but first pays for his beer, revealing a sizeable pouch of gold. This unexpected development causes the proprietress to change her tune and her daughter to reappear. However, Dick is not swayed and departs, leaving the woman and her daughter in tears. As the *Philadelphia Inquirer*'s "Bookland" column noted, Colman Smith uses the old songs "mainly as a suggestion for studies of the country and sea life in and about early England. In her hands these become more than illustrations; they take rank as remarkably unique and accurate studies of an 'atmosphere' all but lost to the England of to-day."[152] Colman Smith's interest in sailors, nautical themes, and, especially, the color green were to remain important to her and were to feature prominently in her little magazine, *The Green Sheaf*, as well as other works.[153]

Colman Smith's illustrations for both *The Golden Vanity and The Green Bed* and *Widdicombe Fair* display the "spontaneous, intuitive quality" and the "rhythmic syncopation between words and images" that Maurice Sendak traces to Randolph Caldecott as the epitome of children's book illustration.[154] In Colman Smith's work, this synthetic connection between word and image leads to pathos, as in her illustrations for "The Golden Vanity," or humor, as in her drawings for "The Green Bed" and "Widdicombe Fair," all Old English ballads. The wide variety of Colman Smith's subjects is most clearly evident in her *Widdicombe Fair* portfolio, which depicts a diverse group of men and women from all walks of life.[155] Her illustrations show women blushing under the gaze of a nearby male, boldly staring at potential suitors, teasing men as they dance, riotously enjoying themselves, or disdainfully observing the throng. There are several pirates in attendance and at least one dark-skinned performer. Sendak's praise of Walter Crane, whose work he viewed as extremely intricate, can also be applied to Colman Smith in creating pages that "are exquisitely designed with an extraordinary attention to detail."[156] However, unlike Crane, whom Sendak feels does not even attempt to convey character, Colman Smith's illustrations exude personality. This is palpable in all of her folklore projects from the period, but is most evident in *Widdicombe Fair*. In addition to the unnamed man who takes Tom Pearce's old gray mare to Widdicombe Fair where she meets her untimely end, Colman Smith adds a young woman and a burgeoning romance.[157] As the illustrations detail, it is their combined weight that causes the horse to struggle and die. Rather than help the beast or inform her owner, the pair scamper off. The ballad says that Tom "sat down on a stone, and he cried" at the sight of his departed horse.[158] However, Colman Smith adds in small, humorous details that are not in the song, such as the row of mourners, their backs to the viewer, clutching each other in their grief and then visiting the horse's gravestone as the tops of the heads of the man and woman peep mischievously over the cemetery wall. However, her most interesting "projection," to use Pyle's term, into the song is her final depiction of the horse. The ballad informs us that after its death, the beast becomes a ghost that haunts the moors at night with its "rattling bones": "And all the long night be heard skirling and groans, / All along, down along, out along, lee."[159] By contrast, Colman Smith's ghostly horse is sprightly, tossing its head mid-prance as the sun sets in the distance.

Doubleday and McClure issued both *The Golden Vanity and The Green Bed* and *Widdicombe Fair* as limited, hand-colored editions; only 500 numbered copies of each were published in cloth portfolios, often with additional cards and prints.[160] The economics of high-production quality and a limited edition resulted in a relatively high price. Like the Russell portfolio, these ventures appear to have introduced Colman Smith to the value of creating deluxe editions in small runs that would fetch higher prices, something she would explore further in her little magazine *The Green Sheaf*, and her Green Sheaf Press. It was a financial strategy central to William Morris's Kelmscott Press and many other small presses from the *fin de siècle* into the modernist era. However, neither *The Golden Vanity and The Green Bed* nor *Widdicombe Fair* sold their 500 copies, and Colman Smith struggled for years to extract the royalties she felt she was due.

Both *The Golden Vanity and The Green Bed* and *Widdicombe Fair* were part of a *fin-de-siècle* movement of increased interest in traditional West Country English ballads and folklore.[161] Colman Smith loosely based her illustrations on the Rev. Sabine Baring-Gould's transcriptions of songs popular in the West Country English oral tradition.[162] Best known today for writing the hymn "Onward! Christian Soldiers," Baring-Gould published books on Norse mythology, medieval mythology, and werewolves, among many other topics.[163] In fact, his 1865 *Book of Were-Wolves* is believed to have been one of the key sources for Bram Stoker's *Dracula* (1897).[164] Colman Smith and her father had met Baring-Gould at his Devonshire home, Lew Trenchard, during their summer 1899 trip to England and Ireland.[165] Although it was their first time back in Europe since departing from Manchester in 1888 after the bankruptcy of Cowlishaw, Nicol & Company, Colman Smith and her father viewed this trip as primarily a business venture. They met the artist Joseph Pennell, whom Colman Smith described as "rather disgruntled," and who was not favorably inclined to her work, and William Nicholson—half of the Beggarstaff Brothers with James Pryde—who termed the mare from *Widdicombe Fair*, "skippin!"[166] As discussed in the introduction, Colman Smith and her father called on John Yeats—W. B. Yeats's father—with a "scheme" to illustrate a volume of Gaelic mythology, met with Seumas MacManus, the author of *In Chimney Corners*, and visited Baring-Gould, who "liked" her illustrations for *Widdicombe Fair*.[167] However, she had less success with two of his daughters whom she termed "bloomin stupid ... can't see a joke."[168] Despite this encounter, Colman Smith visited Baring-Gould several times and through him met both Henry

Irving, the noted actor and head of the Lyceum Theatre Company, and Bram Stoker, his manager. Irving, Stoker, and especially Ellen Terry were to become an important part of Colman Smith's subsequent personal and artistic life.[169]

Throughout the closing years of the nineteenth century, Colman Smith's career was in the ascendant. Although she cut short her art education at the Pratt Institute under Dow, her skills as an artist and illustrator matured and refined. She fused Dow's ideas of color, movement, shape, and line with Pyle's focus on the imaginative projection of the artist, as well as her appreciation of the Victorian children's illustrators Caldecott, Crane, and Greenaway. Her art was complemented by great narrative achievements and groundbreaking work in Jamaican, Irish, and English folklore. Just as importantly, Colman Smith began creating networks among fellow women artists that would subsequently affect the trajectory of her life and work. Financial success still eluded her, and, most importantly, her beloved father, Charles Edward Smith, who supported and accompanied her emergence as an artist, died unexpectedly in New York at the age of 53 on December 1, 1899.[170] The *Brooklyn Daily Eagle* noted that his passing was a "severe bereavement" for his daughter and that "the companionship between the two was very close and affectionate."[171] Her father's death marked the beginning of Colman Smith's friendship with Ellen Terry, who was to become an important friend, mentor, and surrogate mother. In May 1900 she decided to return with Terry to England, her birthplace, and made that country her primary home for the rest of her life.[172]

CHAPTER THREE

Becoming Pixie

Friendship, Synaesthesia, and *The Green Sheaf*

On Saturday, May 19, 1900, the S.S. *Menominee* set sail from New York harbor bound for England.[1] Pamela Colman Smith, now known as Pixie, along with Sir Henry Irving, Bram Stoker, Ellen Terry, and other members of the Lyceum Theatre Company, was aboard.[2] Her father had died the previous December, and she was still grieving this loss. The appellation "Pixie," which was bestowed on her by Terry, marked the beginning of a close friendship and mentorship between the prominent Lyceum actor, whom Colman Smith termed "a dear," and the fledgling artist and writer.[3] This friendship was a key factor in Colman Smith's decision to return "home" to England after the death of her father.[4] Although Terry was famous for bestowing nicknames on her friends and family, Colman Smith does not elaborate on what motivated the name Pixie. She says only "That's my name ET gave me."[5] However, the moniker became a central part of Colman Smith's identity for at least the next ten years. As I detail below, the Pixie persona played a central role in the creation of a space for herself where she could confront the racism, sexism, and classism she experienced. It also allowed her to both engage more deeply in new facets of her art and take on more leadership roles. In short, the nickname helped Colman Smith tap into the freedom and fearlessness that was pivotal in her becoming an artist, writer, and editor.

During the early years of the twentieth century, Colman Smith became involved with several groups, beliefs, and practices that were to become a key part of her art and life. Her interest in Symbolism and Decadence deepened as she began to experience synesthetic visions while listening to symphonic music. She enmeshed herself in the intertwined worlds of the Lyceum Theatre community, the Irish Literary Revival, and the Hermetic Order of the Golden Dawn. Her performativity also increased as she became a member of W. B. Yeats and Florence Farr's London Masquers. Colman Smith also began giving Afro-Jamaican Anansi performances, first to friends at home, and then, increasingly, in public venues. Importantly, she also took more control over her publication process, co-editing *A Broad Sheet* with Jack Yeats in 1902 and editing her little magazine, *The Green Sheaf*, from 1903 to 1904.

In view of the importance of the Pixie persona for Colman Smith and the key role Terry and her children, Edith and Gordon Craig, played in Colman Smith's life, especially in the years immediately after her return to England, it is worth briefly considering Terry's possible motivations for nicknaming her Pixie. Naming is often a way to assert superiority and impose control over a subordinate's life and work—notable examples are Ezra Pound's christening of Hilda Doolittle as "H.D., Imagiste" and Ford Madox Ford's dubbing Ella Gwendolyn Rees Williams Lenglet as Jean Rhys. This type of subtle gender control, usually involving a man naming a woman, is central to the narrative of modernism.[6] In Terry's naming of Colman Smith, we can see elements of this same type of coercion and control at play, mingled with admiration and support. In a January 15, 1900 letter to her son, Edward Gordon Craig, Terry is impressed by Colman Smith's work ethic, stating that "[s]he is extraordinarily industrious & is ever-lastingly making & selling as fast as she makes."[7] Terry goes on to detail the low prices Colman Smith gets for her lampshades, candleshades, and wooden boxes, concluding that she is "a funny little creature."[8] It is important to keep in mind that Terry was trying to motivate her son, who was perpetually short of funds and repeatedly needed to be bailed out by his mother, to be more industrious. Nevertheless, Terry implicitly views herself and her son as separate from (and superior to) Colman Smith, classifying her as an unidentifiable Other and dismissing her humanity in the process. However, despite the inherent racism and classism buried in Terry's comments, she and her children did much to help Colman Smith assimilate to life in England.

Colman Smith was interested in and aware of the transformative power of naming. There seem to have been multiple reasons behind her adoption of the Pixie nickname bestowed on her by Terry. It obviously already resonated with her and, like Lenglet's embrace of Jean Rhys, Colman Smith imbued the new name with important personal significance. She appears to have been particularly drawn to the sprites' transformative power. By the time Terry gave the nickname in December 1899, pixies had become ubiquitous in popular culture. Colman Smith was acquainted with the lore surrounding Irish fairies, of which pixies were an English variant, through W. B. Yeats's collections of Irish fairy tales, which she had wanted to illustrate for children, and his 1894 play *The Land of Heart's Desire*, which she had illustrated as part of her 1898 Russell portfolio.

Throughout the Victorian and Edwardian periods there was a "veritable explosion" of both interest in the fairy world and reports of alleged sightings at all levels of society. As British anthropologist Paul Manning notes, "the cultural preoccupation with the secret kingdom of the fairies is a hallmark of the era."[9] As belief in conventional religion ebbed during the second half of the nineteenth century, there was a concomitant growth in alternative spiritual belief systems. The fascination with fairyland was an attempt "to reconnect the actual and occult," reflecting the rise in spiritualism and other esoteric interests such as astrology, mesmerism, and the tarot. One element of this renewed interest was the growth of occult groups like the Theosophical Society and the Hermetic Order of the Golden Dawn, besides older organizations like the Freemasons and the Rosicrucians. I will discuss these groups in Chapter 5, along with the role played by Colman Smith in the Golden Dawn after her 1901 initiation.[10]

As Lee O'Brien has noted, "The multifarious Victorian manifestations and appropriations of the fairy world suggest a complex and charged obsession that has an essentially contradictory significance. Fairies are figured as human and not-human, part of social behaviors and rituals, but also entirely 'other.'"[11] This other world, of which pixies were among the most popular denizens, captivated audiences and led to diverse manifestations in art, drama, and literature.[12] Writers from Arthur Conan Doyle to Robert Louis Stevenson and Yeats either included different varieties of elves in their work or publicized their own beliefs.[13] Moreover, fairyland became a space where fantasies regarding gender, race, and class, which otherwise would have been repressed or heavily censored, could take flight. This was especially true for women authors who were interested in discussing same-sex desire.[14]

The rapid rise in all things fairy over the course of the nineteenth century mirrored interest in the emerging fields of anthropology, ethnology, and folklore, as well as the impact of primitivism.[15] Although today these academic studies have little, if anything, in common with interest in fairies, there was then a quasi-scientific interest across disciplines in fairies as possible humanoids, much as we today view the hobbit-like *Homo floresiensis* archeological remains. As Carol Silvers explains, fairies were regarded as a legitimate subject for scientific studies. "By the 1880s such leading folklorists as Sabine Baring-Gould, Andrew Lang, Joseph Jacobs, and Sir John Rhys were examining oral testimony on the nature and the customs of the 'little folk' and the historical and archeological remains left by them."[16] One unexpected outgrowth of this anthropological interest in fairies was the focus on their racial composition. As part of his 1893 "pygmy theory," David MacRitchie "correlated fairy lore with the archeological remains of underground abodes as evidence for the existence of an ancient, dwarflike non-Aryan race in England."[17] Very quickly this interest became centered on the figure of the pixie. As one account detailed, these "little 'stuggy' dark folk" were descended from the Pictish tribes and were "a strange and separate people of the Mongol type."[18] Although it is unclear whether Terry was familiar with the "pygmy theory," the image of pixies as gender- and racially-indeterminate others was prevalent in *fin-de-siècle* popular culture, and this is likely what Terry was drawing on by the nickname.

A friend of Colman Smith, J. M. Barrie, created the most famous example of a pixie, Tinker Bell. This sprite first took flight in Barrie's 1904 play *Peter Pan*, and is today, arguably, the most frequent image conjured up when people hear the word pixie. Tinker Bell is, however, a late and very whimsical sort of pixie. Historically, pixies went back many hundreds of years and were originally relatively obscure sprites who dwelt exclusively in ancient Celtic areas like Cornwall and Devonshire—areas Colman Smith and her father visited during their 1899 trip to England.[19] However, with the rise of the fairy faith over the course of the nineteenth century, pixies garnered their own mythology, with the apex of their popularity occurring during the *fin de siècle*.[20] One of the earliest and fullest descriptions of pixies was recorded by Anna Eliza Bray:

> These tiny elves are said to delight in solitary places, to love pleasant hills and pathless woods; or to disport themselves on the margins of rivers and mountain streams. Of all their amusements, dancing forms their chief delight, and this exercise they are said always to practice, like the Druids of old, in a circle or ring ... These dainty beings, though represented as of exceeding beauty in their higher

or aristocratic order, are nevertheless, in some instances, of strange, uncouth and fantastic figure and visage: though such natural deformity need give them very little uneasiness, since they are traditionally averred to possess the power of assuming various shapes at will; … But whatever changes the outward figures of fairies would undergo, they are, amongst themselves, as consistent in their fashion as a Turk; their dress never varies, it is always green.[21]

Diminutive creatures, pixies were always on the margins. Similarly, Colman Smith, likewise of small stature, was often shunted to the edges of the groups she belonged to due to persistent questions about her race and gender expression. Also like Colman Smith, pixies were known for both their merriment and mischievousness.[22] As I will detail below, green was to become an important color for Colman Smith. She published her little magazine, *The Green Sheaf*, and operated her Green Sheaf Press during this period. For years, her signature, which was almost always written in green ink, was accompanied by a drawing of a small sprite. However, what stands out in Bray's description of pixies—and what likely resonated with Terry—is their otherness. Pixies are "of strange, uncouth and fantastic figure and visage." They are fascinating but, like Colman Smith, otherworldly and inherently uncivilized in comparison to "normal" humans. While Terry and others used the otherness of pixies as a way to categorize Colman Smith as an unclassifiable other, I assert that she embraced the ambiguity and otherness of the pixie nickname, as it allowed her to create her own space, especially in regards to gender, race, and class, outside of pre-existing categories. Moreover, I argue it is the pixie's power to assume different shapes at will that most appealed to Colman Smith and inspired her use of the mischievous sprites in her art and life for more than a decade. She was very interested in transforming both herself and her art in ways that destabilized the stereotypical, and frequently racist, views of those she encountered.

Return to England and Friendship with Terry

Even before Colman Smith first met Ellen Terry in New York during the fall of 1899, she was interested in her career. Colman Smith had seen Terry perform several times in the 1890s and had closely followed her coverage in the press, as well as that of Sir Henry Irving, his son, Henry "Harry" Irving, Jr., and his daughter-in-law, Dorothea "Dolly" Baird. During her time in Jamaica, Colman Smith wrote to her cousin, Mary "Bobby" Reed, while looking at a photograph of Terry in a recent issue of *Academy* magazine:

> Say Ellen as Gwinevere is right in front of me and grins and grins and she <u>must</u> be laughing at Dorothea ... its real <u>fun</u> imagining Henry to make his <u>Pa</u> mad—I wonder what <u>Sir</u> Pa does when he's mad! I guess he goes off and gives it all to <u>Ellen</u> and she feeds him with sweet words and sweet cakes till he comes round! I'm <u>sure</u> you're laughing <u>now</u> ...[23]

Sir Henry Irving was much rumored to disapprove of his oldest son's choice of spouse, and Colman Smith has "real fun" imagining how this act of youthful rebellion played out in private with the aging and notably austere "Sir Pa."[24] Terry, who was romantically linked in the press with Irving, plays the role of ministering angel, assuaging Irving's anger and satiating his appetites until he is restored. However, Colman Smith subtly subverts this traditionally feminine position through her emphasis on Terry's grinning and inference that the expression reveals Terry "<u>must</u> be laughing" at Baird, rather than benignly smiling in support of the young couple. Furthermore, the account highlights both Colman Smith's youthful fascination with actors, who, along with literary figures, made up the celebrity culture of the *fin de siècle*, and her playful imaginativeness. She is interested in the more volatile emotions and details of private life that she implicitly knows were censored from the sanitized images of Terry, Irving, and his family that were presented in the popular press. Her comments also reflect her desire to "see more," whether that was through her interest in Swedenborgianism and the work of Howard Pyle, or her growing interest in synaesthesia, Symbolism, and the occult after her return to England.

Colman Smith was likely first exposed to the New York theater community through her paternal cousin, William Gillette, the noted actor. In January 1900 Colman worked on "two sets of costumes" for Charles Frohman, a well-known New York producer and friend and associate of her cousin.[25] She also contributed to a souvenir theater booklet for Gillette, who achieved prominence in several stage versions of Arthur Conan Doyle's *Sherlock Holmes*.[26] Gillette was the first to portray the fictional detective and endowed him with several attributes that, although absent from the stories, are now commonly associated with him: deerstalker hat, pipe, purple smoking jacket, patterned socks, striped slippers, multiple rings, and a messy Victorian study.[27] The result, as Heather Campbell Coyle notes, is "a rather louche and bohemian Holmes—more Robert Downey Jr. than Basil Rathbone—who is immediately familiar over one-hundred years later."[28] This image of Gillette as Holmes became cemented in the public consciousness through illustrations in *Colliers* and *The Strand*, but Colman Smith's souvenir cover depiction, published in 1901, is believed to have been the first version.[29]

Colman Smith's personal interactions with the principal actors of the Lyceum Theatre appears to have commenced during her 1899 trip to England with her father. In England, Colman Smith met with both Irving and Bram Stoker, the business manager of the Lyceum Theatre, and presented Irving with four large color illustrations and several black-and-white drawings and sketches.[30] These illustrations became part of an eighteen-page souvenir brochure published in November by Doubleday and McClure to coincide with the Lyceum Theatre's American tour.[31] As a syndicated newspaper article relates, Colman Smith was allowed "unusual opportunities to study [Irving's] characters, and those of Miss Terry, from 'behind the scenes.' The result is a collection of drawings altogether remarkable."[32] The text of the souvenir booklet was written by Stoker.

With its heavy outlining in black, movement of the figures, and juxtaposition of areas of vivid color, the Lyceum souvenir booklet is reminiscent of Colman Smith's other work from 1898 and 1899. Although Terry was to become an important friend and mentor, the focus of the portfolio is Irving. His profile graces the cover and he is the subject of three-quarters of the drawings. Stoker's hagiographic text does not mention Terry, who was known during this period as "Our Lady of the Lyceum" and was very popular with fans. Colman Smith's images include Irving in *Robespierre*, Irving and Ellen Terry in *Nance Oldfield*, Terry in *The Amber Heart*, and, the portfolio's final image, both actors in *The Merchant of Venice*.[33] Like the majority of Colman Smith's depictions of Irving, this one emphasizes his ability to transform himself fully into his characters, even to the point of the grotesque. Irving's Shylock glowers in profile, his eyes slightly unfocused. Her use of a distorted perspective depicts him as larger than life but still manages to present Terry's Portia—stately in an all-red ensemble famously made for her by E. W. Godwin—as the center of the piece.[34]

Letters reveal that Terry's son, Edward Gordon Craig, was originally contracted to produce the images for the U.S. souvenir booklet, which might account for her comments about Colman Smith discussed above.[35] On January 16, 1900 Terry wrote to Gordon Craig, "This girl Pamela Smith doesn't get paid nearly as well as you, & <u>she</u> doesn't lose patience—yet the people think a tremendous lot of her over here."[36] Terry also reveals that Colman Smith's payment for the souvenir illustrations was paltry, even in regards to the standards of the day. Although "the souvenirs are selling very well," Colman Smith "just gets 5 cents apiece on each copy sold & no lump sum down."[37] In this way, Terry skillfully assuages her son's annoyance at being passed over for a project when he needed all the income he could procure, while subtly highlighting the significant difference in pay between male and female artists.

As a transgressive woman who had faced significant personal and professional censure for her choices, Terry was no stranger to the unequal treatment of women. She had raised two children as a single parent outside the bonds of marriage and had engaged in five domestic partnerships, actions she committed, according to George Bernard Shaw, "without having the smallest respect for the law."[38] Moreover, as Katharine Cockin has noted,

> Terry claimed the right to roam wherever she pleased—the East End of London or a wood in the countryside—making herself available for new encounters, new experiences. This kind of independence typified the New Woman but Terry had anticipated it by several decades, relishing the novelty of the bicycle and the motor car as well as the toboggan and the hammock.[39]

Undoubtedly, Terry's ability to flout conventions and social mores, yet still gain financial independence and artistic success, provided an important example for Colman Smith. Similarly, the younger woman's burgeoning iconoclasm likely helped forge the bond between the two, which would last for the next twenty years.

While Terry rejected many of the conservative views toward women that typified the Victorian era, she did hold many of the racial and cultural prejudices of her time. The tension between these biases and her appreciation of Colman Smith can be seen in a June 4, 1900 letter to her friend Audrey Campbell:

'The Japanese Toy' is alright, you'll like her—She is clever amusing—such a rum little shute—she has come to settle in England—or Europe rather—& I've asked her to stay with me a long while—she works like mad all the time—her Father—mother both dead—Silly-unclever rich relations—she is glad to get away, after her Father's death, from all of 'em.[40]

As discussed in the Introduction, referring to Colman Smith as a "Japanese Toy," or for that matter an inanimate object, negates her humanity and reduces her to speculation regarding her racial origins. However, the rest of Terry's comments highlight her obvious approval of Colman Smith and appear to urge Campbell to overlook her background and to embrace her as a friend.[41] They also make clear that Colman Smith's New York relatives were not understanding or supportive. Although Terry doesn't elaborate, this was likely due to Colman Smith's desire to pursue a career as an artist and not marry, decisions that at the *fin de siècle* were becoming more common but, especially for upper-class women like Colman Smith's relatives, were not the norm. It's also possible that her "unclever" white relatives, and the upper-class people that they associated with, had racist views regarding mixed-raced individuals, which motivated her to leave the U.S. Also interesting is the detail that Colman Smith's original plan was not necessarily to resettle in England and that Continental Europe—a destination for many American artists and writers during this period who were fleeing the perceived conservatism and parochialism of the United States—was her original aim.[42] While Colman Smith did travel to Bruges in 1902 with Terry, her daughter, Edy Craig, and Craig's partner Christopher St. John (Christabel Marshall), it is unclear if she made any additional trips during this period.[43]

Even before her return to England, Colman Smith was, through her friendship with Terry, predisposed to become friends and collaborators with both Edy and Edward Gordon Craig. This is foreshadowed in Terry's January 15, 1900 letter to her son when she notes: "Everything you do she [Colman Smith] thinks is perfection—& it is 'Teddy' all the time—I have an idea she is writing to you & Edy."[44] Just as she was imagining interactions between Terry, Irving, and his children while she was living in Jamaica, Colman Smith appears to have been practicing a similar type of imaginative projection with Terry's children, specifically Edy, whom she did not meet until she arrived back in England. Colman Smith appears to have spent a significant amount of time with Terry during the fall of 1899 and the winter of 1900, and likely heard many stories about her children, which appear to have captivated her imagination. As a result, two unpublished portfolios she began before leaving the U.S. on the S.S. *Menominee*, and worked on during her transatlantic voyage, include several images of Edy Craig, whom she would befriend shortly after her return to England.[45]

The red portfolio, entitled *Ellen Peg's Book of Merry Joys*, is attributed to "the two little devils Pixie and Puck."[46] However, the role, if any, that Edy Craig, the Puck of the two little devils, had in the creation of the portfolio is unclear. The depictions of Edy appear to be based on Colman Smith's imaginative projections. Most of the portfolio either depicts people Colman Smith met during her interactions with the Lyceum Theatre in the U.S. or the events of the voyage back to England. While it is possible Craig helped Colman Smith with the portfolio after her arrival in England, the entire portfolio is in Colman Smith's distinctive handwriting. Interestingly, the signature for the portfolio's written material—a reversed P and E—differs from Colman Smith's distinctive entwined PCS that she uses as her artistic signature in the portfolio and elsewhere, almost as if she was creating a new, fused persona.

Through Colman Smith's imaginative projection, she depicts Pixie and Puck as children playing pranks. True to the lore surrounding pixies discussed above, which would also extend to Puck, famously immortalized in Shakespeare's *A Midsummer Night's Dream*, the two are depicted as devils rather than angels.[47] However, they are mischievous rather than satanic. Several images show them dressed in black, sneaking about or engaging in stage magic, often with goofy grins on their faces. In others, they are sprawled on the ground, their limbs entwined, watching Terry or other members of the Lyceum Theatre perform. It is important to keep in mind that although both portfolios present Colman Smith and Craig as children, they were adults. Colman Smith was 22 in the spring of 1900 and Craig was 30. The change in age is important, as it more closely links them to their "mother" Terry who, at 53, was still youthful. It also helps position the portfolios as potential children's books, which, as I discuss below, was a market Colman Smith was still hoping to break into.

Consisting of thirty-seven loose sheets, the red portfolio is primarily a collection of portraits and is an introduction to the story told in the green portfolio. Many of the portraits have a distortion of perspective, specifically enlarged heads and truncated bodies, which are reminiscent of Frederick

Watty's *Cartoon Portraits and Biographical Sketches of Men of the Day* (1873). The red portfolio portraits include "The Pixie," Colman Smith wearing a kimono, which I discuss in the Introduction, and which was likely motivated by speculation about her supposed Asian ancestry; "The Puck," Edy Craig writing with a quill pen and looking very much like a young Ellen Terry; "The Brodribb," Sir Henry Irving, who was born John Henry Brodribb, wearing a voluminous black cloak emblazoned with many of his Lyceum costumes; "The Brammy Joker," Bram Stoker costumed as a bat—complete with hooks for arms—in reference to his popular 1899 novel, *Dracula*; "The Ted Pecker," a red-cheeked Edward Gordon Craig wearing a blue cobbler's apron and engraving wooden blocks; and "The Irving Irvingovitch," Laurence Irving, Henry's son, who was interested in the work of Russian novelists, painting dreams. Colman Smith's paintings include key items that help convey an important dimension of the subject's personality.

Providing important insight into the dating of the red portfolio, at least two of the portraits were almost definitely completed before Colman Smith left New York, as the subjects did not sail on S.S. *Menominee* back to England. "The Gillie" depicts William Gillette, Colman Smith's cousin, wearing a purple dressing gown and carrying a gun, like his dramatic alter ego Sherlock Holmes. Gillette was in New York, as his *Sherlock Holmes* made its Broadway debut at the Garrick Theater on November 6, 1899 and ran until June 16, 1900. Similarly, "The Goodhap" shows Norman Hapgood, a dramatic critic for the New York City *Commercial Advertiser* and *The Bookman*. A similar portrait of Hapgood by Colman Smith, also with an enlarged head but only showing his upper body, appeared in the June 1900 issue of *The Critic*.[48] Although not as clearly in the distinctive "portrait" style of the red portfolio, another image, dated May 13, 1900, presents Colman Smith and Craig, replete with paints and a pin cushion, joined by a young boy carrying a very large box identified as containing Terry's hats. Interestingly, the portfolio also contains an image dated May 13, 1916, 5 p.m.—long after the rest of the portfolio was completed and ostensibly given to Terry—of Colman Smith and Craig visibly sweating from the rays of an oversized sun. In this image, they are depicted normally—gone are the extended limbs and black clothes of the rest of the portfolio—wearing the garb of conventional early twentieth-century women. The addition of this late image raises the question of whether Colman Smith continued to edit, add to, or even subtract from the portfolio, or if the image was added afterwards by Terry or Craig.

By far the most frequent subject in the red portfolio is Terry, the Ellen Peg of its title. In one image, she is depicted with brightly colored clothespins—the pegs in the portfolio's title—in her hair and as her feet.[49] She wears a bright floral coat and blue and white striped dress that was part of her costume for *Nance Oldfield*, and she has a plate of clams and a barrel marked cocaine at her side. In another drawing, Terry smokes a cigarette in bed—still a taboo activity for a woman in 1900—with her green bag next to her and a pile of letters sliding off her lap onto the floor. A third presents her as Nance Young-Meadow, a nod to her starring turn in *Nance Oldfield*, and poised to slide down a bannister. The final image reprises Terry as Portia from *The Merchant of Venice*, one of the images that Colman Smith included in the Lyceum souvenir program, but with a slightly enlarged head that is closer to the style of the other portrait subjects.

The portraits are interspersed with a humorous narrative that appears to be a parody of a nature guide. For example, "The Ellen Peg" description explains, "She is a tall fair animal—its apt to take long journeys—it plays and plays and often likes to play that it isn't Peggy at all."[50] We also learn that "The Peg is seldom seen without two little Devils nearby—they are not always there, but they would like to be."[51] Thus, the narrative alludes to the fact that Craig remained in England and was not actually with Terry when Colman Smith created the portfolio. Regardless of their geographical proximity, it is only Pixie and Peg who know "all about the habits of this animal … and they never tell."[52] These secrets include, as Colman Smith's drawing highlights, clams, a noted aphrodisiac, and cocaine, which was seen as a popular medicinal support and, until 1904, was even included in the original recipe for Coca Cola.[53] Mixed with alcohol, it was known as Vin Mariani, a tonic popular with Victorians from Jules Verne and Queen Victoria to Ulysses S. Grant and Pope Leo XIII. Sir Henry Irving even endorsed the drink in an 1894 advertisement in *Harper's Weekly*, as did actors Sandra Bernhardt and Eleonora Duse, who were both friends of Terry.[54]

The red and green portfolios were designed as complements to each other. The red portfolio is an introduction to the characters who take part in the events described in the green portfolio. The bulk of the green portfolio is a parodic reworking of "The Golden Vanity," a West Country folk song collected by Sabine Baring-Gould that Colman Smith illustrated in 1899. Substituting humor for the melodrama in the original, this version tells the story of "how High Lord Admiral Sir Henry Irving KCB and his goody Company set sail from the Lowlands low to the Highlands high by way of the Atmosphere and setting forth what befell them and their renowned vessel on their voyage."[55] Various members of the Lyceum Company speculate whether the boat can hold the contents of Terry's voluminous green bag, when "Up spake two Little Devils who were clinging on behind."[56] They volunteer to "speak to Stoker Brammy Joker down below," but not before partaking in "a nice hot cup [of] tea" with Terry. Below deck, Pixie and Puck discover stowaways but quickly come up with a plan to remove them from the ship:

> ... out they put their horns and they opened all the ports,
> And the atmosphere came pouring in by buckets full and quarts
> And it floated out the stowaways in spite of their efforts
> And they sunk into the water down below.[57]

The rest of the company bands together and bails out the ship, with the portholes closed just in time to stop the devils from being swept overboard. The whole group celebrates with a grand concert and recitation.

In addition to the four-page illustrated version of "The Golden Vanity," the green portfolio includes seven additional illustrations of various scenes mentioned in the song. Unlike the images in the red portfolio, which are primarily portraits, these include experiments with perspective, such as a boat floating on top of a globe that turns into a newspaper, and liberal use of gold leaf. The largest piece in the portfolio is a three-page spread dedicated to the celebratory performance the Lyceum Theatre Company puts on after the stowaways are removed and the boat is saved from flooding. It includes Bram Stoker singing, Ellen Terry reciting, and Sir Henry Irving playing the piano, while Lawrence Irving strums his lute and Pixie and Puck watch from the corner.[58] A poster version of this scene was included in the Industrial and Fine Art Exhibition held at Grantham, England in 1902.[59]

Upon Colman Smith's arrival in England, she quickly turned the imaginings she created in her red and green portfolios into reality and became close friends and collaborators with both Edy Craig—the Puck of the portfolios—and her partner Christopher St. John.[60] She also befriended Terry's son Edward Gordon Craig—the Ted Pecker of the red portfolio—and contributed to several of his publications. However, she remained close to Terry.[61] In the fall of 1900 Colman Smith embarked on a tour of England with Terry and the Lyceum Theatre Company, for which she played in crowd scenes.[62]

During the nine-week tour, she visited Brighton, Edinburgh, Glasgow, Manchester, and Liverpool, "a very American place—and of course I didn't like it."[63] This time on the stage undoubtedly helped Colman Smith to hone her performative streak, which was first sparked during her miniature theater performances.

"Music Pictures," Synaesthesia, and the Influence of Gordon Craig

After Colman Smith's return to England, she spent a lot of time with Terry, her two children, and their respective partners. While listening to Gordon Craig play Bach on Christmas Day 1900 at Terry's house, Colman Smith had her first vision to music that she then used to produce art. These visions were to catapult her, albeit briefly, to avant-garde artistic prominence, and recurred, after a two-year hiatus, for the remainder of her life. She described the experience in a 1927 *Illustrated London News* article:

> ... a shutter clicked back and left a hole in the air about an inch square, and through it I saw a bank and broken ground, the smooth trunks of trees with dark leaves; across from left to right came dancing and frolicking little elfin people with the wind blowing through their hair and billowing their dresses. The picture was very vivid and clear, and of beautiful colour, with bluish mist behind the tree trunks. I drew an outline in pencil of what I saw on the edge of a newspaper, and as I finished—in perhaps a minute—the shutter clicked back again.[64]

Although couched in the modern language of photography, Colman Smith's first musical vision gave her a brief window into fairyland. Her memory of this fleeting experience is closely entwined with her interest in pixies— "the frolicking little elfin people with the wind blowing through their hair and billowing their dresses"—which was so central to her creation of a new identity for herself after her return to England. Her brief description calls to mind her depiction of the female sprites who carry Maire away in her triptych for Yeats's *The Land of Heart's Desire*, as well as Yeats's own discussions of "trooping fairies."[65] In this way, Colman Smith links these musical visions with the world of fairies that she also explored through her Pixie persona. This is reflected in magazine interviews given during the most prolific period of her "music pictures," where Colman Smith reported that "from childhood she has had the gift of the 'second sight'" and that after her first visit to Ireland in the summer of 1899, "the power of her early childhood returned to her."[66] However, what this power exactly entailed, and the difference between it and what she termed her "music pictures," is unclear, and the press coverage leaves the reader with the distinct impression that all of these mystical experiences are connected.

After her first musical vision, Colman Smith "apparently did no more drawings to music for about two years."[67] She reported that the images returned when she attended a series of concerts by the musician and conductor Arnold Dolmetsch. However, what the *Illustrated London News* account omits is the important personal and professional growth that occurred during the ensuing two years. She became friends and collaborators with W. B. Yeats, whose work she had long admired from afar. Dolmetsch, like Colman Smith and Florence Farr, was associated with the London Masquers, a group who chanted Yeats's poetry. Colman Smith's involvement with the theater deepened as she also made costumes and stage designs for multiple productions, including several at the Abbey Theatre. Her friendship with Yeats led to her induction in November 1901 into the Hermetic Order of the Golden Dawn, the occult group she was to be associated with for at least the next nine years. In addition, through Yeats, the other members of the Irish Literary Revival, and Gordon Craig, Colman Smith became better acquainted with the Symbolist and Decadent movements and began incorporating elements of these into her work, especially once her musical visions resumed.

While Colman Smith describes her visions in mystical terms—a window suddenly opening into another world due to the impact of the music she listened to—her descriptions of her visions reflect synaesthesia. As Donielle Johnson, Carrie Allison, and Simon Baron-Cohen outline, "Traditionally, the term synaesthesia describes a condition in which the stimulation of one sensory modality automatically evokes a perception in an unstimulated modality."[68] People with synaesthesia most commonly perceive letters or numbers as colors, but synaesthetic associations can occur with any number of crossed senses of cognitive pathways.[69] The first variant of music-color synaesthesia was recognized in 1812.[70] Generally, this type of synaesthesia relates color to the timbre of music or associates a color with a musical note.[71] However, Colman Smith appears to have experienced an atypical form of synaesthesia where music evokes a complex visual image.

Press coverage, such as that discussed above, emphasized Colman Smith's mysticism due to her musical visions and interest in fairyland, but her synaesthesia was not an isolated, unique occurrence. During the late nineteenth century, a diverse group of artists, writers, and scientists became interested in the connections between music and painting. An outgrowth of Romantic and Symbolist aesthetics, the interest was predominantly focused on the possibility of a "correspondence of the senses," whether "it was possible that in the act of perception there could be a merging of these equivalent senses a literal syn- (or pan-) aesthesia."[72] Charles Baudelaire describes this synthetic ideal in his 1857 poem "Correspondences": "Like long echoes that mingle in the distance / In a profound tenebrous unity, / Vast as the night and vast as light, / Perfumes, sounds, and colors respond to one another."[73] Baudelaire highlights the interconnections between smell, sound, and sight to create a unified experience. In Colman Smith's case, the sense of sound stimulated by orchestral music resulted in a mental image that she quickly transferred onto paper. As I will discuss in Chapter 5, the Symbolist interest in synaesthesia greatly influenced many late nineteenth- and early twentieth-century occult groups.

Colman Smith was first exposed to synaesthesia through the work of Ernest Fenollosa, the mentor of Arthur Wesley Dow, her teacher at the Pratt Institute in Brooklyn. Dow explains Fenollosa's theories in his work *Composition*:

> He [Fenollosa] vigorously advocated a radically different idea, based as in music, upon synthetic principles. He believed music to be, in a sense, the key to the other fine arts, since its essence is pure beauty; that space art may be called "visual music," and may be studied and criticized from this point of view.[74]

Dow incorporated these ideas into many of the exercises he gave his students, and Colman Smith likely encountered it during her time at Pratt.[75] Although there is no record of Fenollosa teaching at Pratt, he did give several invited talks, and in a brief biography Colman Smith wrote in the 1930s, she states that she studied under both Fenollosa and Dow.[76]

While Fenollosa and Dow referred to the phenomenon as "visual music," others termed it "musical painting" or even "color music."[77] Regardless of the name, some artists used this manifestation of synaesthesia as a way to distinguish between "high" art and the growing rise of its more commercial cousin.

In 1878 James Whistler, the American expatriate artist and friend of Dow, proclaimed in a letter to the London *World*:

> As music is the poetry of sound, so is painting the poetry of sight, and subject-matter has nothing to do with harmony of sound or of colour. The great musicians knew this. Beethoven and the rest wrote music – simply music: symphony in this, concerto or sonata in that ... Art should be independent of all clap-trap – should stand alone, and appeal to the artistic sense of eye or ear, without confounding this with emotions entirely foreign to it, as devotion, pity, love, patriotism, and the like. All these have no kind of concern with it, and that is why I insist on calling my works "arrangements" and "harmonies."[78]

Whistler takes as a given the interchangeability of music, poetry, and painting, seeing them as different manifestations of the same impulse to create beauty. He differentiates between "Art," which should "appeal to the artistic sense of eye or ear," and "clap-trap," which exemplifies popular "airs," like "Yankee Doodle," that are focused on emotions.[79] He views his art as separate from this, hence the musical titles of some of his most famous works, such as *Symphony in White, No. 1* and *Nocturne: Blue and Gold*. Judith Zilczer points out that "Whistler adopted musical titles for his paintings as a declaration of creative freedom."[80]

Unlike Whistler, most of those interested in the connections between music and painting were not overly focused on the fusion as a way to demarcate high art from mass culture. According to Zilczer, there were two primary views of synaesthesia-influenced musical painting at the *fin de siècle*: quasi-mystical and pseudo-scientific. "According to the more romantically inclined artists and writers, the interchangeability of the senses was evidence of mystical correspondence to a higher reality."[81] Members of this mystical group included Alfred Stieglitz, who would host three exhibitions of Colman Smith's work between 1907 and 1911, and Stieglitz's associates, the photographer Edward Steichen and the artist Francis Picabia.[82] Almost as if he was elaborating on the work of Fenollosa and Dow, Picabia asserted that "We understand without any difficulty the meaning and logic of a piece of music because this work is based on laws of harmony and composition..."[83] This music analogy inspired Wassily Kandinsky and Grantisek Kupka, among others.[84] As I detail in Chapter 4, Colman Smith's view of the power of music was also mystical, but the narrative around her musical compositions emphasized her innocence, naivety, and otherness rather than her artistry.

Several of Dow's later students, such as Georgia O'Keeffe and Max Weber, also subscribed to the quasi-mystical view and linked its start to their studies under Dow, where they were required to paint to music in class. Through this experience, O'Keeffe explained that she acquired "the idea that music could be translated into something for the eye."[85] However, none of these artists reported "musical visions" of quite the same type as Colman Smith. Artists such as John Covert, Arthur Dove, and Charles Sheeler experimented with different technical ways to translate music onto canvas, while still others, like Morgan Russell and Stanton Macdonald-Wright, joined forces with scientific researchers to study synaesthesia as a phenomenon of human perception.[86] Furthermore, one major difference between Colman Smith's musical visions and the artists just discussed is that these later compositions look markedly different; in comparison to Colman Smith's more ethereal and Symbolist-inspired canvases, they were almost all bold and abstract. As I will discuss below, although Colman Smith's work never fully ventured into abstraction, there are several discernible stages within her musical visions. Moreover, the later artists were seen as embodying different facets of a new, revolutionary trend in art, while Colman Smith's musical visions, which were initially heralded as harbingers of the artistic future, were ultimately dismissed as backward-looking outliers.

In contemplating the roots of Colman Smith's "music pictures," it is important not to overlook the person playing Bach when she experienced her first, Edward Gordon Craig.[87] The younger of Terry's two children, he spent his childhood and teenage years "surrounded by the colorful Pre-Raphaelite-like stage sets" of the Lyceum Theatre. As Melinda Boyd Parsons notes, "This stimulating, multi-sensory environment undoubtedly planted the seeds of a synaesthetic awareness in young Craig's mind…"[88] He was interested in Whistler's theories of musicality, as well as the work of the "eccentric painter and stage designer" Sir Herbert von Herkomer, visiting his experimental theater outside of London and attending his lectures.[89] In the 1890s Gordon Craig became friends with the musician Martin Fallis Shaw, who introduced him to the work of Bach but also the idea that music could have mood.[90] In the 1900–01 period, the pair collaborated on several productions of *Dido and Aeneas* and *The Mask of Love*, presented by the Purcell Operatic Society that they co-founded.[91] Gordon Craig created backdrops illuminated by projections of colored lights for theses productions. W. B. Yeats was "transfixed" by this, noting in a letter that "It was like watching people wavering on the edge of infinity, somewhere at the Worlds End."[92] Gordon Craig's stage effects for this production resulted in a friendship and some collaboration with Yeats.[93] As I detail below, this connection helped forge the collaborations and friendships between Edy Craig, Colman Smith, and Yeats. Furthermore, the joint productions of *Dido and Aeneas* and *The Mask of Love* were likely among the many artistic ventures Colman Smith was exposed to during this period, which, ultimately, helped spark her own experimentation with plumbing the border between the world of reality and the world of dreams through her "music pictures."

While the extent of Colman Smith's friendship with Gordon Craig is not as fully documented as her friendship with Edy Craig or Terry, she did spend time with him between her return to England in the spring of 1900 and his move to Germany in the summer of 1904.[94] This friendship helped further expose Colman Smith to both Symbolism and the synthetic application of sound, mood, and color that was to prove central to her musical visions. However, this was a gradual process that developed over several years. We do know that Colman Smith contributed three items to the last issue of Gordon Craig's little magazine, *The Page*, in 1901. These included a new Jamaican folktale transcription, "Turkle and Pigeon," which would become part of her 1905 *Chim-Chim* collection, as well as an illustration entitled "The Wind" that accompanied Anna Laetitia Barbauld's poem of the same name.[95]

Moreover, *The Page* was a key influence in Colman Smith's decision to edit her own publications and, eventually, start her own press. Since it was his own magazine, Gordon Craig had creative freedom in what to publish and created most of the content himself. This provided an important model of an individual who, when faced with a publishing environment that did not reflect his own artistic tastes, decided to circumvent the establishment. By the early 1900s Colman Smith had also grown frustrated with exploitative publishers and an industry whose realist tastes, increasingly, did not match her interests. At Pratt, she had focused on book illustration, and the work of Howard Pyle was an important influence. However, many of the illustrative projects Colman Smith created in the 1890s—*Annancy Stories*, *The Golden Vanity and The Green Bed*, and *Widdicombe Fair*—did not sell well and she received very little profit. Elkin Matthews published *The Golden Vanity and The Green Bed* in England in 1903, also to lackluster sales.⁹⁶ Whether the poor sales were due to a lack of promotion or exploitative payment agreements, the adult, often tongue-in-cheek, humor of these works, or—specifically with *Annancy Stories*—the use of dialect and focus on Jamaican folktales, is unclear.

After Colman Smith's return to England, she conceived of several book-length projects, including an illustrated collection of sixty fairy poems tentatively titled *Pixie's Poetry Book*, and at least two different editions of Anna Laetitia Barbauld's writings for children—an untitled edition of her 1778 *Lessons for Children* and a mini-book entitled *The Basket Maker and Other Tales*. A six-page version of the latter was test printed, which included "The Wind" poem and illustration, previously published in *The Page*, in addition to two other illustrations and short tales.⁹⁷ Barbauld, a transgressive and iconoclastic woman of letters, was both "revered and reviled by her contemporaries."⁹⁸ William Blake admired her poetry, especially her *Hymns in Prose for Children*, which inspired his *Songs of Innocence and of Experience*, but by the 1890s her work, which had helped to revolutionize children's literature a century earlier, had fallen out of favor and was out of print, a fate that would continue for most of the twentieth century.⁹⁹ Unsurprisingly, none of Colman Smith's book-length Barbauld projects ever found a publisher. However, as I discuss below, several of the illustrations were published in *A Broad Sheet* and *The Green Sheaf*.¹⁰⁰ Less is known about *Pixie's Poetry Book*, as no draft copies have survived.

Barbauld dedicated her most famous children's books to her son, Charles, and a Little Charles is featured in *Lessons for Children* and other works. Colman Smith habitually referred to her edition of Barbauld's *Lessons for Children* as Little Charles. Her frustrations over her difficulty in placing the manuscript with a publisher is indicative of her view of the industry during this period. As she wrote to Alfred Bigelow Paine in May 1901,

> That bloomin pig! [Grant] Richards! Kept Little Charles 6 weeks and then returned him! Then sent him to Heinemann and Lane and Duckworth in turn. And he came back from each! An older and a wiser Charles! But still he is in a neat little red portfolio and no publisher is likely to take him! Dam!!!!!!!!!!!!¹⁰¹

Later that summer she expressed her exhaustion over the whole process, especially her distance from many of the New York publishers: "Has RR [Russell] been over here [England] this year? Or Doubleday? I can't find out anything! Dam publishers any way!—I am tired of 'em."[102] Thus, it is not difficult to see why Colman Smith would be interested in gaining more control over the publication process, as she did through editing *A Broad Sheet* and *The Green Sheaf*. While this new control moved her seemingly beyond the dictates of the publishing world, it also shifted her further away from the cultural mainstream.

W. B. Yeats, Involvement in the Masquers, and Afro-Jamaican Anansi Performances

By the winter of 1901 Colman Smith had settled at 14 Milbourne Grove, The Boltons, in South Kensington. After a short time, she rented the flat next door for her studio. These rooms soon became the site of a weekly gathering of artists, writers, actors, and other Chelsea bohemians. According to Arthur Ransome's *Bohemia in London* (1907), Colman Smith and her guests drank opal hush and recited poems as part of her involvement with the London Masquers. She also began reciting Anansi stories at these gatherings, which helped set the stage for her public Anansi folktale performances.

Another key development of this period was her growing interest in convention-breaking women, likely sparked by her friendship with Terry and Edy Craig. Colman Smith and Craig collaborated on costume and stage designs for several productions. These included *The Sacrament of Judas* and *Nicandra* in the spring of 1901.[103] The latter play, whose central character is a monstrous snake woman, was to prove a recurring subject for Colman Smith that culminated in her 1911 illustrations for Bram Stoker's *The Lair of the White Worm*.[104] She also contributed a series of costume designs for Terry's ill-fated 1903 production of Ibsen's *The Vikings at Helgeland*, in which Terry played "the fierce warrior wife" Hiordis, who "denounces her weak son as a bastard, murders her husband, and drowns herself."[105] While fans rejected Terry in a "wicked woman part," Colman Smith did multiple sketches and paintings of her in this powerful role.[106]

One of Colman Smith's first published projects after her return to England was a series of five prints for *Kensington Magazine*, several of which take women as their subject matter.[107] Craig, Christopher St. John, and W. B. Yeats all contributed to the short-lived publication edited by Beatrice Erskine and R. J. Richardson.[108] At a March 1901 studio tea given by Erskine Colman

Smith finally met Yeats. She described her first encounter with the eminent poet and dramatist thus:

> W. B. Y. was there and he is a rummy critter! Seemed most stupid and had on a tea party air and posed about and looked bored— And when all the ladies with ermine collars had gone, who all told him how very much they liked his bloomin poetry, which probably they had never read or heard of … then WB began to talk! Folklore—songs, plays, Irish, language, and lots more—reciting a sort of folksong which was splendid.[109]

Colman Smith's powers of perception and her quickness to see through the artifice of the social niceties on display during the tea are immediately apparent in her humorous account. There is a marked difference in how Yeats acted in front of the upper-class "ladies with ermine collars," who well might become potential patrons, as opposed to the more unvarnished self that emerged once they left. It is no surprise that Colman Smith greatly preferred the latter. Her palpable interest in Yeats's discourse on everything from Irish folklore and his plays to the study of the Irish language is clear. Moreover, this tea was likely her first exposure to Yeats's chanting, which she tentatively categorizes as "reciting a sort of folksong," but does not hesitate to call "splendid." Through her friendship with Yeats, she was to become directly involved in these recitations.

As Ronald Schuchard details in *The Last Minstrels: Yeats and the Revival of the Bardic Arts*, Yeats held a deep interest in reviving the lost bardic arts of chanting and musical speech throughout his life.[110] During the *fin-de-siècle* period, he was helped in this quest by Florence Farr, an actor and fellow adept of the Hermetic Order of the Golden Dawn, and Arnold Dolmetsch, a musician and "consummate crafter of old English instruments."[111] In the summer of 1901 Dolmetsch created a prototype of a twelve-string psaltery, and taught Farr how to regulate her voice so it would best resonate with the instrument.[112] Yeats described the unique capabilities of this type of musical speech in his essay, "Speaking to the Psaltery," first published in 1902:

> A friend [Farr], who was here a few minutes ago, has sat with a beautiful stringed instrument upon her knee, her fingers passing over the strings, and has spoken to me some verses … Wherever the rhythm

was most delicate, wherever the emotion was most ecstatic, her art was the most beautiful, and yet, although she sometimes spoke to a little tune, it was never singing, as we sing to-day, never anything but speech. A singing note, a word chanted as they chant in churches, would have spoiled everything; nor was it reciting, for she spoke to a notation as definite as that of song, using the instrument, which murmured sweetly and faintly, under the spoken sounds, to give her the changing notes.[113]

While Yeats extols the beauty, delicacy, and emotionality of this form, critics, collaborators, and even family were less supportive, as many believed the chanting detracted from his dramas.[114] However, Colman Smith was one of the first outside of Farr to embrace Yeats's musical speech. She was likely drawn to the form due to the Jamaican Anansi performances that she had recently started giving, which contemporaries reported as having a riveting, musical quality.

Shortly after their initial meeting at the studio tea at the mews, Yeats saw Colman Smith's stage designs for the *Countess Cathleen* and watched parts of a performance of the play in her miniature theater, and was "much pleased."[115] In November 1901 Colman Smith joined the Isis-Urania Temple of the Hermetic Order of the Golden Dawn, of which both Yeats and Farr were members. While Colman Smith did not become an adept like Yeats or Farr, and, in fact, never advanced beyond the first level, the group undoubtedly helped deepen her interests in ritual, mystery, and the spiritual world.

Colman Smith and Yeats's shared interest in musical speech resulted in her joining first the Irish Literary Society and then the London Masquers.[116] She was in attendance at Yeats's famous June 1902 London lecture on the psaltery and wrote to Lady Augusta Gregory that it "was a great success; people packed like herrings in a box!"[117] She traveled to Dublin in October of that year for the Samhain Festival in the Antient Concert Rooms and, along with Lady Gregory, Douglas Hyde, and probably James Joyce, watched Farr chant to the psaltery.[118] The next night Colman Smith did the stage makeup for a performance of Yeats's *Cathleen ni Houlihan*. It was so effective that three years later her way of blackening the face of Cathleen—originally played by Maud Gonne—had become "a holy tradition."[119] During the winter of 1903 Colman Smith's involvement with Yeats and his growing group of chanters deepened, and in March 1903 he appointed her librarian of "a new sort of Stage Society," whose members included Edy Craig, Walter Crane, Sturge Moore, and Arthur Symons.[120] Yeats explained that the new group would "have little dealing with the problem plays & shall try to bring back beauty and beautiful speech—."[121] By May 1903 Colman Smith had begun chanting in public, joining Farr on stage to illustrate examples as part of Yeats's lectures on "Heroic and Folk Literature."[122] A *Christian Commonwealth* article described her as a "quaint little lady, rich in Indian jewels and girlish shyness," while a *Speaker* account praised her "charming lilting" of Yeats's "The Song of Wandering Aengus."[123]

After the Masquers disbanded in November 1903 due to Yeats's extended trip to the U.S. and Farr's creation of the short-lived Dancers, Colman Smith pronounced that "The Masquers is dead—at least for the present—" and expressed her lack of interest in joining the new group.[124] However, her interest in musical speech as an art form did not abate. In December 1903 she consciously linked her chanting with her telling of Jamaican Anansi tales, and wrote to Yeats that "I am lilting and storytelling at a great rate!" She alludes to an "amusing argument" she had with the artist John Singer Sargent, regarding their differing interpretations of the little red fox in Yeats's "The Happy Townland."[125] Although Colman Smith does not elaborate on their conflicting views, she concludes that "I think the sale of your books should go up!" due to "the number of people who have asked where the Red Fox comes from."[126] This reflects both her long-term interest in sales—for both herself and her friends—and her growing realization that speculation and controversy can increase sales of both books and tickets. As I will discuss in Chapter 4, Colman Smith began to incorporate the lilting of Yeats's poems into her Anansi storytelling performances and her art exhibitions, with controversial results.

During this period, a close mentorship developed between Colman Smith and Yeats, and she consulted him on all of her major editorial endeavors. She discussed plans for a projected illustrated edition of Blake's *Songs of Innocence and Experience*—they both admired Blake—and suggested that she design a book of Gaelic mythology for children—with text written by Yeats and Lady Gregory—but nothing came of either plan.[127] Colman Smith collaborated on stage designs and costumes with her close friend Edy Craig for Yeats's *Where There is Nothing* in a production that premiered at the Royal Court Theatre in London in November 1904, which Yeats termed "impressive."[128] He also gave her the task of stage designs for J. M. Synge's *The Well of the Saints*, which were originally promised to his brother Jack, as "Pixie Smith ... alone seems to understand what I want."[129] However, this appears to have been one of the last collaborations between the two. One possible reason for the break was the split in the Golden Dawn that occurred that year, with Colman Smith remaining with Waite in the Isis-Urania chapter and Yeats leaving to form the *Stella Matutina* group.[130] Another possibility is an item in *The Lamp* that outed him as the physical model of George Moore's *Evelyn Innes*, which included Yeats's assertion that "A man's morals are from God, but his opinions he is personally responsible for ... it's not always pleasant to have my portrait saying things I never even thought of."[131] This was accompanied by Colman Smith's somewhat unflattering 1901 drawing of Yeats, that closely matched the novel's description, and a 1904 photograph by Alice Boughton.[132]

Editing *A Broad Sheet* and *The Green Sheaf*

Even before she began lilting Yeats's poems in public, Colman Smith quickly became part of the constellation of artists, writers, and musicians associated with Yeats and his family. She contributed Christmas cards, lace, wallpaper, and other designs to the Dun Emer Press, run by Elizabeth and Susan "Lily" Yeats and Evelyn Gleeson, and contributed banner designs for Loughrea Cathedral in Galway, worked by Lily and her assistants.[133] One of the first of these collaborative friendships was with Jack Yeats and his wife, "Cottie," which was likely sparked by their shared love of miniature theater. In June 1901 Colman Smith visited the couple at their Devonshire cottage, watched Jack's performance of his miniature circus, and regaled them with performances of Jamaican folktales, replete with handmade cardboard cutouts of the key characters, such as the ones that she used at her weekly gatherings.[134] This visit led to her co-editing *A Broad Sheet* with Jack for twelve monthly issues from January to December 1902.

A Broad Sheet, as its name implies, was a one-page publication that was published and sold by Elkin Mathews.[135] A subscription was twelve shillings a year and three dollars in the U.S. Originally a format for public notices, the large single sheet was favored in the seventeenth and eighteenth centuries by balladeers, poets, and political activists. The little magazine primarily featured large, hand-colored drawings by Jack Yeats and Colman Smith, accompanied by poetry and prose from many prominent figures of the Irish Literary Revival such as Lady Augusta Gregory, George Moore, George Russell (AE), and W. B. Yeats.

114   PAMELA COLMAN SMITH

Overall, Colman Smith's contributions to *A Broad Sheet* reflect her varied interests; excerpts from Barbauld's *Poems for Children* mingle with illustrations and stories of pirates and the sea, a preoccupation since her time in Jamaica in the 1890s. Highlights from Colman Smith's tenure at *A Broad Sheet* include her self-portrait, "The Recitation," which depicts "Pamela Prettijohn on her birthday declaiming, 'The Brigand's Bride' for Grandmamma and Grandpapa Prettijohn and the assembled family."[136] The illustration is marked by both its undifferentiated background—a unique departure for Colman Smith during this period—and the wide hoop skirts of the ladies in attendance that harken back to an earlier era. Her illustration for AE's "The Gates of Dreamland" features a clutch of floating female sprites waiting to take the male speaker away to "the Land of Youth."[137] According to Schuchard, the poem was one of the first that Yeats had Farr arrange for the psaltery.[138] Two excerpts from Barbauld's poems are accompanied by illustrations of little children that are likely taken from her unpublished "Little Charles" portfolio discussed above.[139] Seven Colman Smith illustrations of various poems and songs connected to pirates and the sea are scattered throughout the run of *A Broad Sheet*, making it the little magazine's most common topic.[140] One of the most striking depicts a woman, her back to the viewer, staring wistfully at a series of ships as they sail into the distance. She is framed by a thick border of spider webs in which a mask-like human face is hidden. The illustration is accompanied by a short, untitled poem by Colman Smith: "The cobweb cloak of Time has dropped between the world and me, / The Rainbow ships of memory have drifted out to sea."[141] The picture and caption suggest the ability of a clairvoyant to see events unfolding in the past as if they were happening today. Both the poem and illustration are more dreamy and introspective than much of Colman Smith's other art for *A Broad Sheet* and, with her illustration for AE's play *Deirdre* in the penultimate issue, foreshadow the much more symbolic turn in her art that is evident in *The Green Sheaf*.[142]

However, the collaboration between Yeats and Colman Smith did not persist beyond 1902. Of the twelve issues on which Colman Smith served as co-editor for *A Broad Sheet*, seven feature large drawings by her at the top of the page, which, along with more positive assessments of her in the press, may have contributed to the end of her involvement with the publication.[143] A brief mention of the publication in the November 29, 1902 edition of *The Sphere* proclaims that Colman Smith is "a true artist, with a great literary gift," while Jack Yeats's "art is of what I call the 'poster' variety; that is to say, it lends itself most effectively to use in posters ... while less satisfactory in books."[144] A few days later, Jack Yeats wrote to John Quinn stressing that "Pamela Smith did *not* start the Broad Sheet. I did." He went on to elaborate that she didn't do her share of the work:

> Between you and me and the wall, as they say, Miss Pamela Smith (though I think her a fine illustrator with a fine eye for colour and just the artist for illuminating verse) is a little bit lazy, and she being a woman I can't take a very high hand with things, so there is often a lot of fuss about the numbers, and I don't like to be responsible for anything that I have not got absolute control of.[145]

His sister Lily later recounted going to Colman Smith's studio once a month to hand-color issues of *A Broad Sheet* for her brother, and recounts that Colman Smith "often lay on the sofa and cried because, she said, I was bullying her and making her work when she did not feel like work."[146] However, Lily's account completely overlooks how many, if any, issues Jack Yeats had colored, as well as Colman Smith's other projects, which undoubtedly contributed to her fatigue.[147] There were likely also personality clashes that led to Colman Smith's decision to leave *A Broad Sheet* and launch her own little magazine, which she would have sole control over.[148] It is unclear how the end to their collaboration affected their friendship, but Yeats did contribute a drawing to the tenth edition of *The Green Sheaf*, and she did contribute drawings to *Broadsides*, which he produced for his sisters' Dun Emer Press.[149]

In January 1903 Colman Smith launched her little magazine after lengthy discussions with W. B. Yeats during the planning stages; ultimately, in a move that is reflective of her growing feminism and independence, she did not incorporate many of his suggestions. She replaced his choice of *The Hour-Glass* for the title with *The Green Sheaf*.[150] Moreover, she did not dedicate the little magazine to "the Art of Happy Desire," as Yeats suggested, but more simply to "pleasure."[151] Where Yeats wanted the subject matter to be confined to dreams of an ideal state, "beautiful or charming or in some other way desirable," Colman Smith chose to have her magazine contain "pictures, verses, ballads, of love and war; tales of pirates and the sea ... ballads of the old world."[152] Similar to *A Broad Sheet*, *The Green Sheaf* was printed on thick, handmade paper.[153] The magazine had a run of thirteen issues, an annual subscription of thirteen shillings, and a single issue price of 13 pence, all likely due to the importance of the number thirteen to the Hermetic Order of the Golden Dawn, of which Colman Smith was a member. In a 1902 letter to George Pollexfen, W. B. Yeats's uncle and a fellow member of the Golden Dawn, Colman Smith noted that thirteen was her "lucky number."[154] Regardless of the motivation, the pricing "ranked [it] among the most expensive publications of the kind in the world, a distinction which it shares with *A Broad Sheet*."[155]

An enigmatic title, *The Green Sheaf* and its accompanying image of a sheaf of green pages tied with a red ribbon brings to mind U.S. currency, of which Colman Smith often lamented her shortage, but also the green sheaves of grain that in the Bible the Israelites offer to God in order that he might bless the spring harvest.[156] While grain is the most commonly discussed meaning, a sheaf, as the *Oxford English Dictionary* notes, can also refer to "a cluster or bundle of things tied up together."[157] In this respect the title is apt, as the magazine contained a range of art, poetry, fiction, translations, and nonfiction prose.

There are many potential reasons why Colman Smith might have decided to pick green as the title for her magazine, and the choice was likely multivalent. As George Schoolfield has noted, by the early 1890s "[g]reen had already become the color of decadence—not the green of blooming nature but the green of decay."[158] This was mirrored in the color of the Decadents' favorite drink, absinthe. In his 1889 essay "The Boom in Yellow," Richard Le Gallienne explained that "Green must always have a large following among artists and art lovers; for, as has been pointed out, an appreciation of it is a sure sign of a subtle artistic temperament," quickly adding that "[t]there is something not quite good, something almost sinister, about it."[159] The same year Oscar Wilde discussed the color in his essay on the writer and poisoner Thomas Wainwright: "He had the curious love of green, which in individuals is always the sign of a subtle artistic temperament, and in nations is said to denote a laxity if not a decadence of morals."[160] This hints at the color's long association with homosexuality. In Latin, the adjective *galbinatus* meant both a shade of green and effeminate.[161] The color, and especially the "unnatural" green carnation that was created with arsenic, began to be specifically associated with homosexuality in London after Wilde reportedly asked male friends to wear the flower for the 1892 premiere of *Lady Windermere's Fan*, a practice he continued through his 1895 trial for gross indecency.[162] It is unclear if Colman Smith was familiar with Wilde's practice and its covert meaning—she may well have been, because her friend, the London actor W. Graham Robertson, was one of the main propagators of the story—or if she just associated the color with artists and Decadence more broadly.[163] As discussed above, green was also associated with pixies, which had been Colman Smith's nickname since December 1899, and was an important component of her independent, gender-nonconforming identity. It was also the color of Ireland, popularized as part of the Irish Literary Revival, many of whose members were friends and contributors to *The Green Sheaf*. Furthermore, Colman Smith liked the color and wrote almost all her business and personal correspondence in green ink from 1900 to at least 1907.

While not as well-known as *The Yellow Book* or *The Savoy*—whose editor Arthur Symons was a friend and fellow Masquer—*The Green Sheaf* was influenced by these Decadent publications. It was sold by Elkin Mathews, one of the two publishers of *The Yellow Book*, in London and in Brentano's bookstore in New York. The influence of the art of Aubrey Beardsley is also a palpable link. As noted in Chapter 2, several critics emphasized the affinities between Colman Smith and Beardsley. Both were influenced by Art Nouveau and Japanese art, and both employed an emphasis of light and dark areas, which accounts for at least some of the similarities between their work. While the influence of Beardsley can be seen in a range of Colman Smith's work from the *fin-de-siècle* period, including her cover illustrations for the *Celtic Christmas* magazine and several drawings included in *The Green Sheaf*, her art is marked by a vibrant use of color, more diversity in the size and shape of the figures, and, after the resumption of her "music pictures," a sharp decrease in the ornate patterns of her early work.

Furthermore, *The Green Sheaf*'s pages have a focus on sensations, exoticism, and alternate forms of spirituality, all undergirded with a feminist insistence on female agency that had decided Decadent reverberations. Numbers were dedicated to topics ranging from dreams to pirates to death. Moreover, the little magazine was notable for bringing together artists and writers from disparate groups such as the Irish Literary Revival and the London stage, as well as for the inclusion of a whole host of otherwise unknown women artists and writers.

As Liz Constable, Dennis Denisoff, and Matthew Potolsky have noted, Decadence, and its closely connected foremother Symbolism, is much more than its well-known themes, tropes, and characters: "decadent textual strategies interfere with the boundaries and borders (national, sexual, definitional, historical, to name but a few) that criticism normally relies upon to make its judgements, producing what we call a 'perennial decay' of those boundaries and borders."[164] In *The Green Sheaf* this took the form of Laurence Irving's narrative of Prince Siddhartha's transformation into the Buddha sharing the same issue with an excerpt from Barbauld's *Lessons for Children*, accompanied by a Colman Smith illustration, and a lithograph of W. B. Yeats's painting "The Lake at Coole."[165] Short stories, lavish full-color artwork, and poems intermingled with sheet music, reproductions of masques, and dream fragments. More traditionally Decadent laments on death and the superficiality of women are juxtaposed with fairy tales emphasizing the power and agency of women. In this way, *The Green Sheaf* reflects Sally Ledger's claim that "there was a discursive and aesthetic resonance between aestheticism, Decadence, and the New Woman" as "the cultural movement that embraced aestheticism and Decadence was broader and more eclectic than is sometimes allowed."[166] Like *The Yellow Book* before it, *The Green Sheaf*'s "conflicting cultural trends" reflect the clash between old and new that plays out in its pages.[167]

In the early decades of the twentieth century, "periodicals were becoming complex visual texts, changing the reading experience in hard-to-fathom ways even as the rise of a modern advertising industry contributed to the transformation of older business models in publishing."[168] *The Green Sheaf*, which has not been discussed in relation to this wider movement, definitely reflects the trends of "the rapidly changing 'Atlantic Scene'" of English-language publishing at the turn of the twentieth century that Ann Ardis and Patrick Collier discuss. Like *The Yellow Book* and *The Savoy*, *The Green Sheaf* appeared in a large format, on handmade paper, and was hand-colored. As Carolyn Burdett has noted of *The Yellow Book*, "the volumes drew attention to their appeal as objects."[169] Like *A Broad Sheet*, *The Green Sheaf* was hand-colored, relatively expensive, and produced in limited numbers. Its target audience was the middle- to upper-class reader who was interested in and knowledgeable about the avant-garde.

Although some issues of *The Green Sheaf* have a unifying theme, such as the second, which focuses on dreams and the supernatural, most numbers were more loosely conceived. Early issues saw poetry, fiction, and drama by many of those who graced the pages of *A Broad Sheet*, such as W. B. Yeats, AE, Lady Gregory, and F. York Powell. It also continued and extended the earlier journal's practice of publishing work by deceased artists and writers. To that end, *The Green Sheaf* printed several works by Blake, short stories by Barbauld, and poems by John Keats, as well as a short translation by Friedrich Nietzsche and a painting by Dante Gabriel Rossetti. Like the earlier publication, each issue featured multiple drawings and poems by Colman Smith. Names more commonly associated with the theater such as Gordon Craig, Laurence Irving, Martin Shaw, Mary Brown, and E. Harcourt Williams also graced its pages. Other contributors included Victor Bridges, Lady Alix Egerton, Cecil French, W. T. Horton, John Masefield, Yone Noguchi, Ernest Radford, Reginald Rigby, John Millington Synge, and John Todhunter.

The Green Sheaf also published the work of a host of seemingly unknown women writers, as well as anonymous contributions, which increased as the numbers progressed. Some of these female names appear to be pseudonyms, possibly even for Colman Smith herself. However, no formal records from the operation of the magazine remain. As Ardis notes, "the phenomenon of anonymous, pseudonymous, and semi-pseudonymous publication is far more common in the early twentieth century than scholarship in modernist studies trains us to expect."[170] Many if not most turn-of-the-twentieth-century writers multiplied their authorial identities in ways that "defy a Foucauldian conceptualization of the author function or a modernist notion of an authorial imprimatur."[171] As Leonard Koos attests, this use of pseudonyms was also popular among French Decadent writers, particularly women, in the 1880s and 1890s.[172] As no business records of *The Green Sheaf* appear to have been saved, it appears unlikely we will ever know the full extent of the magazine's use of pseudonyms. Christopher St. John, a noted campaigner for women's suffrage, a playwright, and novelist, contributed a range of fiction and translations in almost every issue under their birth name of Christabel Marshall. Leslie Moore, the pen name of the South African novelist and memoirist Ida Constance Baker, who is best known for her long-term relationship with Katherine Mansfield, contributed the short story "Will o' the Wisp" to the fifth issue.[173]

Notably, *The Green Sheaf* did not include any of Colman Smith's retellings of Jamaican folktales, although beginning with the sixth issue the magazine did contain advertisements for readers to hire "Gelukiezanger"—Colman Smith's name for herself, which I discuss in Chapter 4, for these performances—to tell these stories at parties.[174] One possible explanation for this omission is that Colman Smith felt strongly that her retellings of Anansi stories needed to be written in a language that reflected Jamaican creole. While this is now standard practice, it was not the case when Colman Smith first began publishing her versions of these tales in the mid-1890s. *The Green Sheaf*, as its editorial statement affirms, was very catholic in its content and printed a wide variety of fairy and folktales from several different countries. However, all its content was written in standard English, and it might have been the fear of losing subscribers that caused Colman Smith to refrain from publishing any of her retellings in the pages of her magazine. Despite having persistent problems with money throughout her adult life, her letters reveal that she was attuned to financial concerns.

The first issue of *The Green Sheaf* commenced with a full-page illustration by E. Monsell entitled "The Book-worm."[175] It features a portly gentleman, dressed in a light green waistcoat and breeches, peering through spectacles at a large pile of finely bound books at his feet. Before him is a blue globe that is almost completely blank; there is only a pink corner of what appears to be Europe that remains visible. By choosing this image as the first in the inaugural issue of her little magazine, Colman Smith pokes fun at old men, and patriarchal culture more broadly, who insist on looking for answers to the problems of the day by peering into old books rather than direct action; this applies to both the blank spaces on the map and those excluded from the discussion: women, the working class, colonial subjects, and immigrants.

Colman Smith's editorial direction seems to have been to present the widest range of content possible. For example, the third issue begins with "The Harvest Home Masque" by Gordon Craig and Martin Shaw, which is part an explanation of this dramatic representation of the peasant celebration of the end of the harvest and part advertisement for a modern version the authors could present in a home or theater setting; it is accompanied by an unattributed full-page illustration.[176] This is followed by Alix Egerton's poem "The Lament of the Dead Knight," which explores the supernatural love between the dead speaker and his bereaved lady love; a Cecil French drawing of grieving lovers separated by coils of snaky brambles can be found at the bottom of the page.[177] Ernest Radford's poem "Eventide" follows and is accompanied by one of Colman Smith's more mystical illustrations—an androgynous figure wrapped in a shawl who is being pulled along by cavorting red-headed pixies while pairs of lovers embrace on clouds scattered throughout the darkening sky.[178] This image, along with her illustration of her dream vision, which depicts a group of floating spirits carrying "a red heart from which dropped a pearl—hung by a golden chain," gestures toward her more mystical musical visions, which she was experiencing regularly during this period.[179]

Figure 3.1 Pamela Colman Smith, "Alone,"
The Green Sheaf 4 (April 1903), 9.
Reproduced by permission of Stuart R. Kaplan, U.S. Games, Inc.

However, a few issues of the magazine contain poetry and drawings that deal with contemporary life and, notably, they were created by Colman Smith herself. For example, the fourth issue contains her stark illustration of a woman walking by herself in a field that is barren, except for two leafless trees standing watch (Figure 3.1). The woman is depicted in profile, with bent head, wearing a brown dress, cloak, and bonnet that matches the desolate trees. Even taking into consideration the fashion styles of the nineteenth century, which the illustration appears to harken back to, the woman appears distinctly pregnant. While her marital status is not clear from the image, the poem that accompanies the image, "Alone," clearly implies that she is unmarried and has experienced social and psychological isolation as a result. The poem concludes with the speaker lamenting that she feels alienated regardless of the setting:

> In cities large—in country lane,
> Around the world—tis all the same;
> Across the sea from shore to shore,
> Alone—alone, for evermore.[180]

While the position of women was rapidly changing in the early twentieth century and would continue to do so in unprecedented ways, pregnancy outside of marriage was still very much a taboo subject in 1903, which is likely why the poem does not explicitly name the woman's condition. At the time, unwed pregnancy often led to isolation from family, friends, and society, and when it was depicted at all in nineteenth-century literature, it resulted in either death or a life of sex work, which often culminated in disease and death. It is the only work in the thirteen numbers of *The Green Sheaf* to deal with pregnancy outside the bounds of marriage. Moreover, "Alone" foreshadows the bleaker, more introspective, turn in poetry of the modernist period.

Colman Smith returned to realism—a very rare occurrence in *The Green Sheaf*—in the penultimate issue, number 12, through the large illustration and accompanying poem, "The Town" (Figure 3.2). Featuring an early example of her use of the Rückenfigur technique, a woman is in profile, caught in a rare moment of repose while she contemplates the talking men and dancing lovers who surround her. The illustration is set at twilight and a vivid blue hue, accented by red and yellow, envelops the scene. The drawing conveys the

The Green Sheaf

THE TOWN.

O DEARY me how idle is
This great and weary town.
For people talk and never do
As they go up and down.

P. C. S.

5

Figure 3.2 Pamela Colman Smith, "The Town,"
The Green Sheaf 12 (January 1904), 5.
Reproduced by permission of Stuart R. Kaplan, U.S. Games, Inc.

glamor and bustle of city life, as well as the dissatisfaction many of its inhabitants likely experienced. Rather than convey the romantic assignations taking place or even the peacefulness of the evening, the speaker expresses the ennui that was to typify the modernist experience:

> O DEARY me how idle is
> This great and weary town.
> For people talk and never do
> As they go up and down.[181]

In this short stanza, even "the great" town is "weary." Interestingly, this lassitude is not due to the hustle and bustle of the thousands of people who flood its streets every day, but the emptiness of their talk and their failure to follow through their pronouncements.

Reception and Demise of *The Green Sheaf*

Contemporaneous reviews of *The Green Sheaf* were infrequent. A brief mention of the magazine did appear in the February 6, 1904 issue of *The Academy & Literature*. The unnamed writer noted that "The Green Sheaf is a refreshing publication, as its name implies … the literary contents are quaint and sometimes beautiful, but the chiefest charm lies in the hand-coloured prints, which are highly-decorative, simple in treatment and of a pleasant old-world flavour."[182] A month later in the same publication another unnamed writer (or possibly the same person who has undergone a change in view) struck a different tone: "I have been flipping through the dandified leaves of the ninth number of that strange little periodical 'The Green Sheaf' published and edited and sold by the strange personality whom we call Pamela Colman Smith."[183] The author goes on to state that "some of the designs, by far the best, are from her own whimsical hands," but it is impossible to ignore the repeated use of "strange" to describe both Colman Smith and her publication. This bemusement, which often manifests in condescension and infantilization, is in keeping with other Anglo-American views of Colman Smith and her work. While the first account stressed the beauty and "old world charm" of *The Green Sheaf*'s contents, the second terms it "dandified," emphasizing its links to Decadence and Aestheticism, and stresses that even the best drawings are merely "whimsical."

Colman Smith's own view of the magazine also changed dramatically over the course of its life. In April 1903 she wrote to gallery owner William Macbeth, thanking him for subscribing to *The Green Sheaf* and agreeing that "it <u>does</u> look well!", and adding that "It is exciting getting it out every month—planning it all out…"[184] She also points out that she has recently opened a school for hand coloring, a venture that "I have had in mind for long."[185] The school is frequently advertised in the back pages of *The Green Sheaf* and seems to have been one of several money-making ventures that Colman Smith conceived of during this period. It is also possible—though it is not addressed in this letter nor any others that I have found—that pupils of the school may have helped her color *The Green Sheaf* illustrations as part of their training, thus lightening the burden of having to color each copy by hand and providing valuable experience. However, it is unclear how many students, if any, signed up for this school.

By February 1904 Colman Smith's initial optimism and excitement regarding *The Green Sheaf* had cooled considerably. As she wrote to Paine,

> The Green Sheaf will probably go on semi annually because there are many other things to do more important … I am telling Annancy stories very often now and hope in time to make some money by it—Green Sheaf does not pay yet—It is most discouraging to go on working at it.[186]

Discouraged and frustrated by *The Green Sheaf*'s inability to live up to her economic dreams and, undoubtedly, by the amount of work it took to single-handedly edit, publish, and sell even a small-circulation literary magazine, Colman Smith wrote W. B. Yeats in February of 1904 with a new plan. She wanted his advice on a scheme to set up a small press with her close friend, Mrs. Fortescue: "We want very much to set up a hand press to print small editions of books (by subscription) hand-coloured."[187] She raised two potential projects—Blake's *Songs of Innocence and Songs of Experience* and a book devoted to the work of the Victorian painter, printmaker, and engraver Edward Calvert, whose work was heavily influenced by Blake. Colman Smith did her homework and knew that other publishing companies were working on editions of each; Methuen on an edition of Blake using a three-color printing process and with an introduction by Laurence Binyon, and a long-announced edition of the Calvert by the Unicorn Press.[188] Colman Smith requested Yeats's help, in the form of an introduction for the Blake and "what text there is" for the Calvert, and the prestige—and accompanying sales—his name would bring to either project. She knows that secrecy is important and implores Yeats to "<u>Please</u> keep this to <u>yourself</u>."[189] Neither of these projects came to fruition. However, as I will discuss in Chapter 4, Colman Smith did operate a Green Sheaf shop in Knightsbridge that sold hand-colored prints, drawings, cards, and programs as well as a range of books that she published through her Green Sheaf Press.[190]

The period after Colman Smith's return to England in May 1901 was an extremely prolific one that was to have long-lasting personal and artistic ramifications. She cemented her long-term collaborative friendships with Ellen Terry and her children, Edy and Gordon Craig, and initiated new ones with W. B. Yeats and his brother Jack. Her network included many of the figures of the Irish Literary Revival and the Hermetic Order of the Golden Dawn, which she was inducted into in November 1901. Her performativity increased as she worked as an extra in Lyceum Theatre productions and contributed stage and costume designs. She became a member of Yeats's Masquers and chanted his poems in public, while at the same time she began giving public performances of her Jamaican Anansi tales. Taking control over her publication process, she co-edited *A Broad Sheet* with Jack Yeats in 1902 and edited *The Green Sheaf* by herself in 1903–04. These experiences helped her to become Pixie—a gender- and racially-indeterminate sprite—and begin the next stage of her career: her "music pictures" and the operation of her Green Sheaf Press.

CHAPTER FOUR

Art on Her Own Terms
Anansi Stories, the Green Sheaf Press, and "Music Pictures"

Colman Smith's growing confidence in both herself and her artistic vision is evident in a short manifesto she wrote in March 1907 for *The Craftsman* magazine, a publication dedicated to the Arts and Crafts movement. Entitled "A Protest Against Fear," the statement directly appeals to young American artists:

> It seems to me that fear has got hold of all this land. Each one has a great fear of himself, a fear to believe, to think, to do, to be, to act.
>
> Who dares to do anything without fear of what some other will think or say? How can a country have a living, growing art when it is so bound down by fear, the most dreadful of all evils?[1]

Colman Smith's impassioned defense of artistic freedom calls to mind William Blake—a key influence during this period—and prefigures the Futurist, Imagist, and other artistic manifestos that proliferated before World War I.[2] Moreover, the statement's rhythm, repetition, and use of rhetorical questions reflect her rhetorical skill honed through her Jamaican Anansi performances. Addressing artists whose creativity is stymied by doubts over the direction and shape of their art, she calls on them to break down barriers imposed by fear; these constraints can be externally placed by teachers, publishers, or critics, internally imposed, or, more commonly, a combination thereof. Certainly,

Colman Smith had to contend with both external and internal detractors as she embarked on her artistic career. However, flush from the success of her January 1907 exhibit at Alfred Stieglitz's 291 gallery in New York City, which prominently displayed seventy-two of her drawings, many of them her "music pictures," she exhorts her fellow artists to be bold, stressing that fear, and by extension convention, is "the most dreadful of all evils."

Having lived in London since the spring of 1900, Colman Smith viewed the U.S., the country of which she remained a citizen until her death, from the remove of an expatriate. Through this perspective, she implicitly positions the U.S. as more conservative and artistically limited than Europe, which, she notes, has resulted in her home country "producing almost no freedom of thought or work."[3] However, cognizant of the narrative of westward expansion that was so central to the emergence of an American identity in the early twentieth century, Colman Smith praises "[t]his marvelous, great country, big in all its feeling and full of energy," subtly linking the freedom of movement and the promise of the American Dream with the need for artistic freedom. She concludes by urging students to look within:

> You, younger students, who are entering this garden of toil, where flowers are grown by love and patience, why do you not try to be true to your better selves, why do you not try to see the finer, bigger things that are all about you, and to kill in your garden those mawkish weeds of sugar-sweet sentimentality and shallow feeling. Try to feel truly one thought, one scene, and make others feel it as keenly as you do—thus is art born.[4]

Drawing on the long-standing trope of likening the production of art to the cultivation of a garden, Colman Smith acknowledges the love, care, and hard work that art demands. She then asserts that artists are betraying themselves— and killing their carefully tended gardens—by catering to the mercurial, if at times financially remunerative, whims of the marketplace with its "mawkish weeds of sugar-sweet sentimentality and shallow feeling." Instead, she alludes to the ideas of both Arthur Wesley Dow and Howard Pyle, encouraging artists to feel deep emotions and depict them empathetically through their work. Only in this way, Colman Smith asserts, can there be an inclusive, expansive, and truly American art. She was to return to, and expand on, these ideas the following year in "Should the Art Student Think?"

An expatriate artist who spent most of her life outside of the United States, Colman Smith's work does not generally engage with "traditional" American themes such as colonial revolutionary history, westward expansion, or the immigrant experience. However, all her creative work from this period reflects her catholicity of interests, especially her growing commitment to recasting and reshaping material from various traditions into a unique fusion. This bold determination to blaze a new path is at the heart of Colman Smith's "A Protest Against Fear" and is distinctly American. It reflects her developing interest in freedom, individuality, and personal transformation that, I argue, crystalized after her return to the U.S.

This chapter investigates the central importance of myth and mysticism to all facets of Colman Smith's creative life. I argue that the resumption of her musical visions, which returned in the winter of 1903 after a two-year hiatus, proved pivotal in the maturation of her art.[5] Colman Smith's musical visions provided her with the means to create a personal mythology that allowed her to take disparate elements and reshape them, increasingly emphasizing the importance of female agency. This embrace of her independence and individuality, which at heart is very American, empowered Colman Smith to confront the artistic, social, and financial conditions that had been holding her back. She began making bold creative decisions that helped turn her attention toward creating art for art's sake. As a result, her fine art career, arguably, reached its apex. Colman Smith also expanded her public Anansi performances, which allowed her to confront racist speculation about her origins as well as take on many of the characteristics of the trickster figure. As a result, she experienced renewed confidence and passion for her art during this creatively fertile decade.

Colman Smith's interest in myth and mysticism began early and took various forms. In childhood she was introduced to a range of American and European fairy tales through the numerous collections published by her maternal grandmother and aunt. Her exposure to Swedenborgianism also helped cement her interest in the spirit world and the direct connection between earthly existence and the hereafter, which was to become a persistent interest as she matured. During her time in Jamaica, she became familiar with the rich Afro-Caribbean cultural legacy of the island, especially Revival, Obeah, and Myal, which featured interactions with the spirit world. Her stay on the island also introduced her to Afro-Jamaican Anansi folktales and pirate lore. Colman Smith soon began writing and performing her versions of pirate tales for her miniature theater, an important precursor to her public Anansi performances. She began traveling around the island collecting versions of Afro-Jamaican folktales. Colman Smith published her first transcription of an Anansi tale in 1896 and followed this up with a full-length collection, *Annancy Stories*, in 1899.[6] Her exploration of Anansi tales quickly sparked interest in folklore from other places, including Devon, which served as the subject of some of her early work, and, most importantly, Irish myth, which she became acquainted with primarily through the poetry, plays, and folktales of W. B. Yeats. Her fascination with Irish myths, particularly those connected with women and sprites, crystalized in her creation of her Pixie persona—one that emphasized her mischievousness and sense of fun as well as allowing her to reject constricting ideas of heterosexual femininity and embrace androgyny.

After her return to England in the spring of 1900, Colman Smith began to unite some of these varied approaches to myth and mysticism by becoming associated with both the Hermetic Order of the Golden Dawn and the Irish Literary Revival. These endeavors helped lay the foundation for two of her most important creative projects of this period: her performances of Jamaican folktales and her magazine, *The Green Sheaf*. Telling Anansi tales in public allowed Colman Smith to bring to life the stories and characters that most intrigued her, making important changes that reflected her new, increasingly feminist, perspective. This is best embodied by her 1905 publication of *Chim-Chim: Folk Stories from Jamaica*, which draws upon Anansi tales, many of which she had been performing in public for years, to emphasize gender fluidity and female empowerment.[7] Similarly, *The Green Sheaf*, which ran for thirteen issues from 1903 to 1904, was a unique fusion of Colman Smith's interests in the occult revival, the theater, pirates, romanticism, and Irish myth, among other things.

While *The Green Sheaf* marked the first—and only—time Colman Smith brought together so many of her disparate interests in one publication, it was also time-consuming to produce. Every issue was hand-colored, and the publication met with a mixed critical response. Ultimately, she decided to end the little magazine in order to devote more time to both her growing fine art career, which had taken off since the resumption of her musical visions, and her public performances of Anansi folktales in both England and the U.S. To supplement this income, she created the Green Sheaf store and press in Knightsbridge, almost directly across the street from Harrods, which by the early twentieth century was a bustling department store. She had grown progressively frustrated with a publishing industry whose tastes did not reflect her own, and which she felt was much more focused on its own profits than on adequately compensating its authors. By taking control of the publication process, Colman Smith could pursue the types of art she was most interested in. Although the Green Sheaf Press survived longer than the eponymous store, both outlets provided her with greater freedom to disseminate her work and that of like-minded friends, free from the dictates of the publishing world. Moreover, this prefigures the activities of Virginia and Leonard Woolf's Hogarth Press and Sylvia Beach's Shakespeare & Company, among many others.

Arguably it was through her musical visions that Colman Smith was best able to combine her growing interest in mythology, feminism, and the occult. As I will discuss in Chapter 5, there are many interconnections between these paintings and the images she created for the 1909 Smith-Waite tarot deck. Initially, the art world embraced her musical visions, and Alfred Stieglitz exhibited her art three times between 1907 and 1909 at his 291 gallery. Her work was favorably compared to Blake's, and Colman Smith was hailed as a mystical visionary. However, these accolades were relatively short-lived and, increasingly, turned to mockery as she did not neatly fit into received categories. This was especially true when she attempted to combine her fine art exhibitions with her Afro-Jamaican Anansi performances. However, this response only served to cement her feminism and motivated both her work for the women's suffrage movement and the creation of her symbolic lexicon with her "music pictures."

Exposure to Anansi Tales and Folktale Collections

The vibrant, dynamic folk culture Colman Smith encountered when she moved to Jamaica as an impressionable eleven-year-old greatly influenced her view of the spiritual world as a palpable reality. It also gave her a better understanding of myth and folklore as living and ever-changing windows into the unseen world of the subconscious. Rather than viewing Anansi folktales, Irish myths, and European fairy tales as discrete entities, she was interested in their underlying common elements. When the teenaged Colman Smith began collecting and writing down her own tales of Anansi, whom she calls Annancy using a common variant of the time, she drew on many different cultural elements. This type of borrowing and recombination was to become a hallmark of not only Colman Smith's two Anansi collections and folktale performances but also most of her creative output from the early twentieth century. This strategy anticipates Jung's concept of the archetype or the belief that fairy tales and myths contain repeating motifs that transcend a particular time or culture.[8]

Anansi himself is an almost perfect example of what Jung was later to describe as the trickster archetype. The trickster is one of Jung's central archetypes, and he emphasizes that the "phantom of the trickster haunts the mythology of all ages."[9] However, Colman Smith was obviously not drawing upon Jung—his work on archetypes was first published in 1919—but rather homes in on a conception she independently arrived at through her interest in and co-option of trickster figures such as the Cornish pixie, the Afro-Jamaican Anansi, and the Irish giant, among others. Colman Smith's own hybridity—she appeared to be of mixed race—set her apart and seemingly shaped her attraction to these outsider figures.

Traced back to the Akan people of Ghana in West Africa, the stories of Anansi and his friends were transported to the Caribbean by African slaves who were forced to work on the plantations. Operating in a middle space, Anansi is neither a god nor a human but can assume the form of both a man and a spider. As Emily Zobel Marshall notes, Anansi, and his U.S. counterpart Brer Rabbit, "can shape-shift, transcend gender boundaries and remove their body parts, and above all, they are the breakers of taboos and socials norms."[10] Due to this deliberate refusal to follow established rules, Anansi, as Cynthia James points out, is "a paradigm for the West Indian ethos of survival" and "has become a synecdoche for Caribbean ingenuity, endurance, and commitment to self-preservation."[11] A creature of contradictions, Anansi is, ultimately, an "unfathomable, ambiguous character that with roguish delight evades every attempt at describing him."[12] Thus it is not hard to see why the iconoclastic Colman Smith would be drawn to this gender-indeterminate, protean figure, who consistently, and often against great odds, flouts established social mores, nor why Anansi was an important model for her convention breaking in both her personal and artistic life. Moreover, it is fitting that Colman Smith's first professional forays as a writer, which came only months after the July 1896 death of her mother, were Anansi tales, as this marked an important new phase of her life and appears to have signaled an important maturation for the 18-year-old. This section will discuss some important differences between Colman Smith's *Annancy Stories* and contemporaneous volumes, highlight her contributions as the first known illustrator of these tales, and explore her representation of the Afro-Jamaican practice of Obeah.

Colman Smith published her first two transcriptions of the exploits of the humanoid spider—"Annancy and the Yam Hills" and "De Story of de Man and Six Poached Eggs"—in the October–December 1896 issue of *Journal of American Folklore*.[13] Like the majority of the Jamaican Anansi tales published in the late nineteenth century,[14] Colman Smith's versions employ creole dialect throughout, a practice she adhered to in her two book-length collections.

Colman Smith does not attempt to situate the narrative for the reader. This decision to present her transcriptions without comment is in stark contrast to Ada Wilson Trowbridge's "Negro Customs and Folk-Stories of Jamaica," which directly follows Colman Smith's tales in this issue of the *Journal of American Folklore*. Trowbridge, who was living in Illinois at the time of publication but had spent time in Jamaica as a child, prefigures her four transcriptions of Anansi tales with a lengthy, quasi-ethnographic essay that draws on common primitivist stereotypes of Afro-Jamaicans to highlight their perceived lack of intelligence, naivety, and immorality, as well as their close association with the supernatural.[15] This is most clearly evident in her description of an Afro-Jamaican "sit up" in which the family and friends of a dying individual help them pass their final hours with music, stories, and songs:

> Each person present takes some part in the singing,—apparently selecting the time and tune as his spirit moves him, without regard for the laws of harmony,—chanting to vociferous accompaniment of groans and wails of lamentation. A more grim or grotesque spectacle cannot be imagined or music more discordant and weird.
>
> Give the imagination full play, and the dusky faces contorted by simulated grief, the minor discords and monotony of the chanting, the moans from the dying soul, the wails from the mourners,—all this carried on through the long, dark hours of the night, under the fitful firelight, will conjure up more grim fancies than even the strongest mind could deem agreeable.[16]

Trowbridge is clearly writing for a white audience, whom she believes will share her racist beliefs about Afro-Jamaicans. While she is highlighting what she believes to be the otherworldly quality of the event and its participants, she also points out, seemingly needlessly, the inability of the Afro-Jamaicans to keep tune, their lack of harmony, and that their grief is "simulated" rather than genuine. As I will discuss more fully below, contemporaneous accounts of Colman Smith's Anansi performances similarly highlighted the primitive aspects of these stories, often expressing similar racist views and/or underscoring their otherworldly qualities. However, just as frequently reviewers emphasized the truth and sincerity of her performances, with many accounts taking as a given that she was Afro-Jamaican.

According to Marshall, the primary collectors of Jamaican Anansi stories in the late nineteenth and early twentieth centuries were white middle-class women, like Trowbridge, whose "Euro-Christian values ... unavoidably influenced the content of the collections they chose to assemble."[17] The first book-length collection, *Mama's Black Nurse Stories*, was written by Pamela Milne-Home, an English woman from a military family whose father was stationed in Jamaica, and published in 1890. Milne-Home's collection contains a lengthy introductory essay that also reflects a distinctly white Euro-Christian bias. However, she takes pains to connect Anansi and the other characters in the stories she collects with more familiar elements in Irish, German, Indian, Japanese, Russian, and Scandinavian folklore, as well as highlighting the stories' West African roots. Although not as blatantly as Trowbridge, Milne-Home also emphasizes the racial divides in Jamaica. She stresses "the difficulty ... these days of obtaining any information on this subject from a West India negro," speculating that this reticence to discuss Anansi could be due to "the great spread of education [that] causes them to fear ridicule on the part of white questioners, or that the systematic discouragement of the clergy of all sects is beginning to take effect at last."[18] Milne-Home does not suggest the likely truth: that this hesitancy was due to a desire to preserve an important element of Afro-Jamaican culture and protect it from censure.

In direct contrast to both Milne-Home and Trowbridge, Colman Smith's first book-length collection of twenty-two of these tales, *Annancy Stories*, published in 1899, does not include any introductory material by the author. Rather than attempting to situate and "explain" Anansi tales to white audiences, a move that emphasizes both racial difference and the spectacle of the tales, Colman Smith offers them without comment, letting readers make their own inferences and connections. However, the volume does include a short prefatory note by Thomas Nelson Page, one of the founders of the literary plantation tradition in the U.S., which focuses on romanticized views of plantation life. Page praises the collection as "perhaps the most original contribution to negro folk-lore literature since the day when 'Uncle Remus' gave us his imperishable record of 'Brer Rabbit.'"[19] He takes as a given that Colman Smith was inspired to collect the tales after reading Joel Chandler Harris's stories, which are steeped in the white plantation fantasy where, as Zobel Marshall notes, "slaves were happy being slaves and they understood their place in the world—they were fiercely loyal and pleased to serve their benevolent, chivalrous, morally upstanding masters."[20] It is not known if Colman Smith sought out Page's preface or if it was an insertion made by the publisher, R. H. Russell, in order to increase the cachet of the book. It is also not known if she read any of Chandler Harris's Brer Rabbit stories before writing *Annancy Stories*; the only copies of these tales in her library date from 1906.[21] Colman Smith does not mention Page or Harris in her extensive correspondence with her cousin during this period, nor do their names pop up in any of the later extant letters. Unlike Harris's popular Brer Rabbit tales, Colman Smith does not include a frame narration in standard English in which Uncle Remus, a kindly ex-slave, tells the tales to white children. The only gesture to this tradition in *Annancy Stories* is a frontispiece in which Mother Calbee, an Afro-Jamaican Obeah figure, tells a story to a group of enraptured white girls and animals.[22] However, Colman Smith then presents readers with unfiltered access to the tales, encouraging them to enjoy them on their own terms. Reflecting her decision to fully immerse her readers in the world of Anansi and his friends without attempting to explain the cultural significance of the tales, Colman Smith wrote them in a distinctive creole, without any narration in standard English. While she does gloss a few words that could not be readily understood, the choice to use only creole plunges readers more fully into another cultural and imaginative landscape.

Other contemporaneous collections of Anansi tales, such as *A Selection of Anancy Stories* (1899) by Wona (a pseudonym for Una Jeffrey-Smith) and *Jamaican Song and Stories* (1907) by the Englishman Walter Jekyll, employed the opposite tactic by writing a narrative in standard English that was interspersed with creole dialogue. Jekyll's version was very popular and was republished multiple times over the course of the twentieth century.[23] Jeffrey-Smith's preface to her volume, which, like *Annancy Stories*, was published in 1899, emphasizes the shame that she assumes Afro-Jamaicans feel when asked by whites to relate Anansi tales.

> Now-a-days, the nurse is scarcely to be met with who, when asked to tell an Anancy story, will not promptly answer that she 'don't know none'; for the average Negro woman, like the average woman

everywhere, dreads being laughed at. She knows that her dialect is not a beautiful one, and that 'Missus' won't like to hear it from the lips of her darlings; so even if she does know one, she remains discreetly silent.[24]

Reminiscent of Trowbridge's and Milne-Home's comments, Jeffrey-Smith's racist views of Afro-Jamaicans are clearly evident, as is a complete inability, or unwillingness, to understand the nurse's perspective, despite trying to convince her white audience that she fully understands her feelings. A Kingston *Daily Gleaner* review of Jeffrey-Smith's collection, which also deals extensively with Colman Smith's *Annancy Stories*, points out that the two volumes "each chose a different plan" in regards to dialect and that "of the two we very much prefer Wona's."[25] The supposition that Afro-Jamaican creole was too difficult and disorienting for white readers undergirds Jeffrey-Smith's collection, as well as Milne-Home's and Trowbridge's essays. However, this view is completely absent from Colman Smith's collection, which revels in the distinctive elements of creole speech. The tales are ostensibly told by Afro-Jamaican narrators, and all the humans and animals, including the white characters, speak in creole.

Colman Smith's embrace of creole speech likely contributed to *Annancy Stories*' poor sales. Martha Warren Beckwith's scholarly 1924 edition, *Anansi: Jamaican Stories of the Spider God*, which is today viewed as the standard Anansi text due to its extensive comparative indices, employed the same narrative and linguistic strategies as Colman Smith and initially met with the same lackluster response.[26] Similarly, Zora Neale Hurston received intense criticism for her decision to use black vernacular for both her 1935 folktale collection *Of Mules and Men* and, especially, her 1937 novel, *Their Eyes Were Watching God*.[27] Although Colman Smith was frustrated by the tepid critical and popular response in America and England to *Annancy Stories*—the collection was reissued by Grant Allen in England in 1903—she was inspired by her chanting work for W. B. Yeats to try another way of disseminating the stories. She began telling Anansi tales in person to paying audiences, something she had been doing for years for friends informally, and was proven correct in her assumption that white audiences would respond more positively to spoken than to written creole.

After performing Anansi tales in public for several years, Colman Smith published her second collection, *Chim-Chim: Folk Stories from Jamaica*, in

1905 through her Green Sheaf Press. In it she employs the same narrative and linguistic strategies that she utilized in *Annancy Stories*. However, there is no comparable frontispiece of an Afro-Jamaican character telling stories to white children, likely because by this point Colman Smith had been in this position hundreds of times herself, as she frequently performed at children's parties and bazaars.[28] The volume does contain a brief prefatory note in which she states:

> These are Stories told in Jamaica by the people among themselves, or by the old nurses to their charges.
>
> I have tried to write them down exactly as I heard them from many different people and in different parts of the island, where they vary more or less. In the hills, in the North-West, they are chiefly about birds; in other parts, about fish and rabbits, as well as the spiders Annancy and Tiger, and other animals.[29]

Unlike Milne-Home's and Trowbridge's prefaces, Colman Smith's introductory material does not display a noticeable Euro-Christian bias. She refers to Afro-Jamaicans simply as "the people." Gesturing toward the stratified nature of late nineteenth-century Jamaica, she explains that Anansi tales are generally told "among themselves" or to white children, who, presumably, would be more easily entertained and less judgmental than their parents. However, unlike Milne-Home and Jeffrey-Smith, Colman Smith does not elaborate as to why this might be the case. She also points out geographical variants in the tales, something missing from the other contemporaneous collections.[30] Her focus on transcription is important, as it gives credence to her use of Jamaican creole, especially as her using creole was criticized as being difficult for white audiences.[31] The more scholarly tone of Colman Smith's note is reflected by a brief endorsement she includes from Fredrick York Powell, a past president of the English Folklore Society. Colman Smith had attended a meeting of the group in June 1904 and recited several of her Anansi stories and participated in an ensuing discussion.[32]

Innovations in *Annancy Stories*

In both of Colman Smith's Anansi collections, her transcriptions highlight Anansi's wily tricks, pronounced sense of humor, and deliberate refusal to follow established rules. Her Anansi is not as aggressive as other contemporaneous accounts and is often bested by other animals. While the stories do contain murder and other forms of cruelty, Colman Smith emphasizes the playfulness and mischievousness of Anansi and his animal compatriots. This is reflected in her copious drawings. In contrast to Milne-Home's Anansi, who is described as "a hairy old man with long nails, very ugly," Colman Smith's is much younger, without long nails and with only a few wisps of facial hair (Figure 4.1).[33] More spider than human, he, like almost all the animals in the collection, is gender-indeterminate, with a large, rounded lower half that is reminiscent of a spider's abdomen. He walks upright and only has two arms and legs, unlike contemporary illustrations that often give him spider-like appendages. The most salient feature of Colman Smith's Anansi, which appears to be one of her distinctive additions, is a pair of large, protuberant ears that highlight his ability to listen carefully and, thus, trick his animal associates. This Anansi does not wear clothes but has black-and-white patterned skin reminiscent of a spider's markings. However, other characters wear clothing. For instance, the bird, Chim-Chim, at one point puts on a "long-tail-blue coat" to go to Anansi's sham funeral, and Toad struts on two legs in a frock coat, floral-patterned vest, and the plumed hat of an eighteenth-century white Jamaican planter.[34]

Printed in black and white, *Annancy Stories* contains multiple full-page illustrations as well as other smaller drawings that are scattered throughout the text. Like Colman Smith's other works from the *fin-de-siècle* period, the illustrations reflect the influence of Arthur Wesley Dow, her teacher at the Pratt Institute, with their varying areas of light and dark, shading, and outlining. Many of the clothes of both the European and Jamaican characters are ornately patterned—showing the influence of both Walter Crane and William Morris as well as the design exercises that Dow put all his students through.

One of the key differences between *Annancy Stories* and Colman Smith's other work is her depiction of dark- and light-complexioned characters. The dark-skinned characters have strikingly different facial features, with wider faces, broader noses, and thicker lips that call to mind both Hogarthian caricature and racist stereotypes of the type popularized in the U.S. by the plantation literary tradition and the rise of minstrelsy. In comparison, the light-skinned characters have traditional European features and generally wear ornately patterned clothes. Throughout the collection, Colman Smith makes copious use of shading, and this is most apparent in the Afro-Jamaican

Figure 4.1 Pamela Colman Smith, "Anansi," from *Annancy Stories* (R. H. Russell, 1899), 3. Reproduced by permission of Stuart R. Kaplan, U.S. Games, Inc.

characters' faces. This stylistic choice appears to have been one of the ways she chose to emphasize racial difference in the absence of color. The cover, the only image that is reproduced in color, shows how, if given the opportunity, she would have complemented the shaded black areas with a cocoa color for the skin tones of the Afro-Jamaicans, which does much to soften the stark black/white contrast throughout the book. Interestingly, when Colman Smith returned to Jamaican folktales for her 1905 *Chim-Chim* collection, her full-color illustrations depict almost exclusively humanoid and animal characters.[35] Throughout the rest of her career, Colman Smith did not employ this type of caricature when drawing dark-skinned people, including representations of herself. She likely made this decision in order to disassociate her Anansi tales from the pejorative stereotypes surrounding Black individuals, especially as the popularity of the Black minstrel figure increased in the early twentieth century. The exception to this is her illustration for Oolanga, an African servant obsessed with death and torture and quite clearly meant as a caricature of the minstrelsy tradition, in Bram Stoker's *Lair of the White Worm* (1911).[36]

Despite including images of Afro-Jamaicans that draw on stereotypical facial features, *Annancy Stories* breaks from convention and is more nuanced in its depictions of Obeah. As I have previously mentioned, this term refers to a series of popular magical and spiritual practices, which were brought to the Caribbean by slaves transported from West Africa. The slaves believed that Obeah's spells and supernatural powers provided them with their strongest means of resisting the power of the white ruling class. The British colonial authorities in Jamaica likewise regarded Obeah as a serious threat to their control of the island. Obeah was connected to both the 1823 Boxing Day conspiracy and the 1865 Morant Bay uprising. Despite repeated British efforts to suppress Obeah, these practices were still widespread in the late nineteenth century when Colman Smith lived on the island.[37] As Faith Smith has pointed out, throughout the 1890s "the Jamaican reading public was treated to police logs and court cases covered by the newspapers, and sensational pamphlets purporting to contain the true confessions of alleged practitioners and the lurid acts perpetrated on their victims."[38] In 1898, during Colman Smith's last year in Jamaica, a new Obeah Law (No. 5) banned the publication and dissemination of these sensational tracts and tightened the punishments for Obeah-related crimes.[39]

While several famous literary depictions of Obeah focus on the evils of Obeah men, practitioners, in reality, were both men and women.[40] One of Jamaica's national heroines is an Obeah woman called Nanny of the Maroons, whose face appears on the island's $500 banknote. She led a group of runaway slaves who conducted guerrilla warfare against the British in the early eighteenth century, and it was claimed that she used her magical powers to catch bullets with her buttocks.[41] *Annancy Stories* prominently features several examples of an Obeah woman, at times identified as Mother Calbee, but no Obeah men.[42] An important boundary-crossing figure in the collection, the Obeah woman appears both in stories that centrally focus on Anansi and his animal friends, as well as in others that draw on European fairy tales and primarily feature white characters. Therefore it is not surprising, especially

Figure 4.2 Cover of Pamela Colman Smith, *Annancy Stories* (R. H. Russell, 1899).
Reproduced by permission of Stuart R. Kaplan, U.S. Games, Inc.

when taken with Colman Smith's long-term interest in strong female characters, that she decided to put Mother Calbee on the cover of her first book, rather than the eponymous humanoid spider Anansi.

One major stylistic innovation in *Annancy Stories* is the distortion of perspective. Colman Smith often zooms in on a few key characters, making their heads and upper torsos much larger than normal, similar to a close-up with a still camera. This is most evident in the cover image of the "Obeah woman," Mother Calbee, who is depicted as larger than life (Figure 4.2).[43] This technique is reminiscent of Dow's instructions to his students to "shap[e] the view" of their compositions "by framing and cropping the object so that the space moved up or across the surface in an interesting way to harmonize with the movement of the form."[44] Rather than uncomplicated harmony, Colman Smith's method forces the viewer to confront Mother Calbee's unabashed gaze. This boldness is in clear contrast to the white characters of both genders who are either depicted in profile or else stare mistily off into the distance.

Transcultural Myth Making: Jamaican Anansi and the Irish Giant

One of the distinctive elements of Colman Smith's *Annancy Stories* is that it includes elements from Grimm and Hans Christian Anderson fairy tales, as well as Aesop's fables. This reflects her deep interest in connecting and recombining folk and fairy tales from different cultures to create something new. A *Brooklyn Life* reviewer noted that Colman Smith's illustrations "arrest the attention immediately," but quickly adds, "If by some blunder of the binder they had been included in a copy of the 'Arabian Nights,' they would have seemed more appropriate than they do here."[45] However, the large number of illustrations focused on Anansi and his animal friends, the numerous Afro-Jamaican characters depicted, and the distinctive Jamaican setting make this comment highly improbable. Colman Smith did blend European fairy tales with Anansi stories, such as "Mr. Titman," her version of Rumpelstiltskin. However, her incorporation of European elements could be subversive, such as in her final illustration for "Annancy An' Tiger Ridin' Horse." In this, a small, non-threatening, gender-indeterminate Tiger is rebuffed by a tall, haughty white woman, dressed in a flowing dress and flowered crown, whose affections he had been pursuing.[46] By depicting Tiger, usually seen as the fierce king of the jungle, as so fully bested by the towering white woman, Colman Smith emphasized the racial power imbalance that pervaded Jamaica in the late nineteenth century and, at the same time, upended the traditional gender balance. In other contemporaneous versions of the story, the young woman is decidedly ancillary or, in the case of Milne-Home's version, nonexistent, the focus being the rivalry between Anansi and Tiger that culminates in Anansi riding Tiger like a horse. In these versions, the emphasis is on the wily Anansi triumphing over the strong but dim-witted Tiger. Ultimately, Colman Smith's changes to the more familiar Anansi stories reflect what Cynthia James has described as the spirit of "the indigenous Creole-Caribbean storytelling tradition, these trickster tales are almost inseparable from creation myths, animal tales, imaginative lies, outrageous fabrications, and stories of forest and supernatural happenings."[47] Colman Smith drew on tales she learned from Afro-Jamaicans, some of which incorporate elements of European fairy tales, and then emphasized elements, such as imbalances in racial and gender power, that were important to her. When she returned to these Anansi tales in her 1905 *Chim-Chim* collection, she did not include any stories that contain elements of European fairy tales, likely a result of her years telling Anansi stories in public.

Colman Smith's 1899 *Annancy Stories* reflected her interest in cross-cultural representation between Afro-Jamaican Anansi stories and European myths, especially those from Ireland. Her illustrations for *Annancy Stories* bear several similarities to both the female dancing figures in her triptych of Yeats's *The Land of Heart's Desire* and her drawings for Seumas MacManus's *In Chimney Corners: Merry Tales of Irish Folklore*, which were all published within a year of each other.[48] This suggests that Colman Smith was beginning to create a transcultural representational code. For example, her final illustration of three sisters seemingly bewitched by Anansi's fiddling in "How Annancy Win De Five Doubloon" is similar to the riotous dancers in her illustration for Yeats's play; both groups of figures are consumed by the otherworldly magic of music.[49] In Yeats's play, the sprites seduce the young woman into going with them to fairyland, leading to her death, but this decision is presented as part of her avoidance of responsibility as a wife and mother. In Colman Smith's story, the wily Anansi gains access to a previously off-limits house—and the mistress's three white daughters—through his fiddling outside their door. Entranced by the music, the girls beg their mother to allow him inside, which she begrudgingly does: "An' den he come in, an' play, an play, an' dance, an' dance, an' had a bery nice time. An' den dey had a gran' supper, an' dey dance all night till before day."[50] The riotous merriment sparked by

Anansi's magical music allows him to transgress racial divisions and results in him earning the five doubloons of the story's title from his friends, who had bet him that he would never gain entrance. Colman Smith's moral, "Dis story show dat dere is notting dat a man can't do if he try!", emphasizes that persistence does pay off.[51]

Throughout *Annancy Stories* and *In Chimney Corners* there are some marked similarities, but also key differences, in Colman Smith's depiction of white characters, especially women. In both collections the influence of the Pre-Raphaelites is evident. Colman Smith's women tend to be tall, often as tall or taller than their male counterparts, and wear long, flowing dresses, often ornately patterned, with flowers in their hair. However, in *Annancy Stories*, Colman Smith's white women are very static and are generally depicted in profile as they stare mistily into the distance.[52] This is in direct contrast to the active poses and animated expressions of both the animals and the Afro-Jamaicans of both sexes that pepper the text, and likely reflects racial and gender stereotypes surrounding the deportment of women in the *fin de siècle*. While the white women in *In Chimney Corners* often wear similar clothes to their *Annancy Stories* counterparts, their stances are much more active and their facial features more animated, making them much more similar to the female dancing figure in "How Annancy Win De Five Doubloon" and the triptych for Yeats's *The Land of Heart's Desire*.[53] One interesting exception is Colman Smith's depiction of the hen-wife in "Billy Beg and the Bull" in *In Chimney Corners*.[54] Shown sitting on a bench surrounded by her fowl, the hen-wife is hunched over, with much darker skin than the other women.[55] Her red-rimmed eyes are closed, and she is dressed in black to highlight her otherness in comparison to the King's brightly clothed daughter, who seeks her help. Like the Obeah women and other magical figures found in *Annancy Stories*, the hen-wife is a figure of magic and mystery, and, as such, her depiction is much closer to those figures than Colman Smith's portrayal of other white women in either text.[56]

The clearest example of Colman Smith's transcultural representation code can be found in her drawings of Anansi and of the Irish giant that features on the cover and frontispiece of *In Chimney Corners*. Interestingly, the giant only appears as a central character in the final story of the collection, "The Giant of the Band Beggar's Hall," and is not physically described other than the repeated refrain that he is "the greatest giant over all of them" (Figure 4.3).[57] In fact, the giant shown calling a flock of birds in

Figure 4.3 Pamela Colman Smith, giant from Seumas MacManus, *In Chimney Corners: Merry Tales of Irish Folklore* (Doubleday, 1899), frontispiece.
Reproduced by permission of Stuart R. Kaplan, U.S. Games, Inc.

the volume's frontispiece is actually the brother of the titular giant. Colman Smith's drawings of both Anansi and the giant include large ears, upturned eyes, sloping brows, and flyaway hair to indicate that, despite their culturally specific differences, she saw both of these characters as trickster figures.[58] Although his physical strength far surpasses that of the diminutive Anansi, the giant loves to engage in trickery and is only narrowly bested by Jack, the king of Ireland's son. Jack, the story's main protagonist, embodies a twenty-first-century definition of toxic masculinity. Spoiled and petulant, he kicks a harmless cat and terrifies his mother, the queen, in his anger. He only meets the giant and is tricked into his quest after becoming enraged that a bridge he commanded his father to build, because the trout in the stream are "wagging their tails" at him, has been repeatedly destroyed.[59] It is not clear whether the decision to put the giant on the cover and frontispiece of the collection, rather than the more obvious Jack, who is the protagonist of several of the tales and the closest to a unifying figure, was made by Colman Smith, the author Seumas MacManus, the publisher, or some combination thereof. A much smaller male figure, probably Jack, appears in the center bottom of the frontispiece, but rather than aggressively confronting the giant, as Jack does in the story, he stares at him with amazed, upturned eyes.[60] While Jack could be showing his appreciation toward the giant for the gifts he receives after locating his secret castle, it is equally plausible that Colman Smith is subtly mocking Jack and trying to reorient the collection away from him and toward the giant, whom she views as a more interesting trickster figure.

Unfortunately, no known correspondence between Colman Smith and MacManus exists that could shed light on these illustrative choices, or even how Colman Smith became acquainted with MacManus and obtained the job. In the late 1890s MacManus, who was married to the Irish Literary Revival poet Ethna Carbery, was at the beginning of his literary career. However, he would quickly gain a wide following in the U.S. for his retellings of Irish folklore. Although he had lived in New York in the 1890s, where he published his first two collections and possibly met Colman Smith, MacManus returned to his native Ireland in the spring of 1899 and resumed work as a schoolteacher as he prepared *In Chimney Corners* for publication. Colman Smith notes in an August 1899 letter to Alfred Bigelow Paine that she and her father had traveled to Mountcharles, a village in Donegal, to see MacManus and were not impressed: "he is a bloomin school master and

<u>awful</u> stupid."⁶¹ Colman Smith does not elaborate on what provoked this evaluation, but it is fascinating to speculate that some of her negative opinion might have been due to disagreements over their varying approaches to the folklore collection, especially the decision to place the giant on the cover and the frontispiece.

Even more importantly, it was during this first visit to Ireland in the summer of 1899 "that the power to see clearly the invisible realm," which Colman Smith claimed to have possessed in early childhood, returned to her.⁶² Through these visions and by reading a wide variety of Irish myths and legends, Colman Smith became well-versed in Irish mythology, learning to distinguish between "the gnomes, goblins, wraiths, leprechauns, pixies, salamanders, and people of the sea."⁶³ These visions helped her develop both her Pixie persona and her close friendship with W. B. Yeats, which resulted in her quickly becoming a member of his Masquers. This involvement seems to have been a direct catalyst in Colman Smith's decision to start giving public performances of the Anansi tales that she had been delivering at home to friends and acquaintances for several years.

Roots of Gelukiezanger and Gender Fluidity in the *Chim-Chim* Collection

During the spring of 1903 Colman Smith began advertising her performances of Afro-Jamaican Anansi stories in the back pages of her *Green Sheaf*, under the name of Gelukiezanger.⁶⁴ The word appears to derive from the Dutch *geluk* meaning happy and *zanger* meaning singer. However, it is unclear if the word was brought to Jamaica by Dutch settlers and was in local usage on the island in the 1890s, or if it is something that Colman Smith created.

The only print usage of Gelukiezanger appears in the story "Paarat, Tiger An' Annancy," which is included in *Annancy Stories*. In structure, Colman Smith's story is quite similar to both Martha Warren Beckwith's Jamaican "New Names" and Elsie Clew Parson's Bahamian variant that includes Monkey and Elephant with Anansi.⁶⁵ Colman Smith's tale begins with a famished Parrot, Tiger, and Anansi agreeing to play a game. They travel to each of their mothers, asking if they know their child's new name, and, if not, they eat the unsuspecting women. In typical fashion, Anansi cheats and secretly informs his mother that his name is now Checherebanja.⁶⁶ She survives, while the other two mothers fall victim to the game and are consumed.[67] The story highlights how extreme violence, which in Colman Smith's collections is either undercut by humor or otherwise de-emphasized, is present in most, if not all, Anansi tales. However, what is most surprising about this short tale is the new name Colman Smith bestows on Tiger: Gelukiezanger.[68] None of the other known variants use this name for Tiger, and as it is the name that Colman Smith chose to advertise her Anansi storytelling performances, it implies a link between Tiger and herself.

Tiger, as the king of the jungle, is depicted in most Anansi tales as fierce and warlike; he is one of the chief rivals of Anansi, who is regarded as the weakest, but also the cleverest, of all the animals.[69] However, in Colman Smith's two collections, she makes substantial changes to this common characterization in order to render Tiger both more likeable and more clearly linked with Colman Smith herself. Her Tiger is almost identical in size and shape to Anansi, differing only in the fact that his body is covered in stripes. Like Colman Smith's Anansi, her Tiger is similarly gender-indeterminate, and Tiger's hair is much longer and more freely flowing; at times he even wears a head wrap similar to those worn by clearly female characters, such as Anansi's mother, despite the fact that he is referred to as male.[70] Although the similarities between the two characters are not explicitly discussed in *Annancy Stories*, Colman Smith touches on the issue in *Chim-Chim: Folk Stories from Jamaica*, which she published in 1905 through her Green Sheaf Press. "Chim-Chim," the first story in the collection, notes that Tiger "is anoder Spider."[71] This is reinforced in Colman Smith's introduction to the volume where she terms both Anansi and Tiger "spiders."[72] She does not clarify or extend the discussion in other stories, but the two references reflect the relationship between the two, as presented in both collections, as a friendly rivalry rather than a deadly vendetta.

Reflecting Colman Smith's inclusion of the key detail regarding Tiger's true form, *Chim-Chim* revisits much of the same material that was first collected in *Annancy Stories* but refines it. Although Colman Smith continues to tell her tales exclusively in creole, the grammar and sentence structure is regularized, and the extensive use of dialogue, which typified the first collection, is streamlined for increased readability. She also includes telling, often humorous details, such as in "Chim-Chim" where, before Tiger's funeral, Chim-Chim dons his "second-best-two-tailed-blue-coat (fe' him best coat is too good fe' Tiger)."[73] The collection is substantially smaller, but in full-color, and only includes stories that feature Anansi and his animal friends. Of the eight stories in the collection, six are slightly expanded versions of tales from *Annancy Stories*. "Kissander" is an expansion of "Dog An' De Duckanoo," with a cat, Colman Smith's favorite animal, in the place of man's best friend.[74] The only substantially new story in the collection, "Turkle and Pigeon," is closely related to other known versions.[75] However, in Colman Smith's retelling, Turkle tricks her captors on her own and not through advice given by Anansi. Similarly, after Turkle escapes from the devil's cook, the woman tricks the devil and his friends by feeding them goat instead of their expected meal of turtle, which causes them to "dance till they fall down dead."[76]

Colman Smith's consistent emphasis on female agency in her retelling of Anansi tales is most evident in the evolution of her three different versions of "Annancy and the Yam Hills." The first version, which was not illustrated, was published, along with "De Story of de Man and Six Poached Eggs," in *Journal of American Folklore* in 1896.[77] Although this was an American publication, the journal frequently published folk stories from around the globe. Colman Smith's first version is quite short; however, it does include a key difference from other known variants: the animal that tricks Anansi into saying "Five," the Obeah Queen's name, and, thus, falling down dead, is a female guinea fowl rather than the male monkey that is Anansi's traditional adversary.[78] In some variants, Anansi emerges unscathed after tricking a variety of animals into saying "Five,"[79] but in Colman Smith's "Annancy an' de Nyam Hills," which first appears in *Annancy Stories*, Guinea Fowl eats Anansi after he dies.[80] The tale concludes with the moral, "Dis story show dat 'greedy choke puppy'!"[81] Interestingly, Colman Smith's title illustration depicts six Afro-Jamaican women yelling and shaking their fists at a shrugging Anansi, even though Afro-Jamaican characters do not appear in the story.[82] It is as if Anansi's tricks raise so much ire from Afro-Jamaican women that they have to express their displeasure, even if they aren't specifically mentioned. In *Chim-Chim*, the story is retitled "Five Yam Hill," but it closely follows the text in *Annancy Stories* with the exception of the closing motto: "Dis show how man stupid!"[83] Guinea Fowl is also far more overtly feminine. Here she is called Mrs. Guinea Fowl—in the previous versions the honorific is lacking—and she wears a bonnet and frilly shawl, while Anansi crouches in the corner and wears a long-sleeved, high-necked black dress in order to emphasize his emasculation (Figure 4.4).[84] Colman Smith began to play with representations of gender in

Figure 4.4 Pamela Colman Smith, "Five Yam Hill,"
from *Chim-Chim: Folk Stories from Jamaica* (Green Sheaf Press, 1905), 61.
Courtesy of the General Research & Reference Division, Schomberg
Center for Research in Black Culture, The New York Public Library, Astor,
Lenox and Tilden Foundations

Annancy Stories and then, as she grew in confidence and had greater control over the publication process, she experimented more fully with gender fluidity in her *Chim-Chim* collection.

Importance of the Green Sheaf Press

Colman Smith used her own Green Sheaf Press to publish *Chim-Chim*, one of the most experimental of her writing projects. Sidestepping her increasingly fraught experiences with publishers, the Press allowed her to publish what she chose without opposition—or, at least, what she could afford to print. Although no records of the Green Sheaf Press exist, it published at least ten volumes in two years. It is fascinating to consider what Colman Smith could have achieved if she had had the economic resources to continue the Press, which appears to have stopped operation in 1906; as I detail below, it was during the latter part of this decade that her feminist sensibility began to really develop. Undoubtedly, the Press had an important effect on the rest of Colman Smith's artistic career and gave her confidence to take risks with less clearly financially viable art, such as her "music pictures," which she began widely exhibiting after the Press ceased operations. Little is known about the Green Sheaf store in Knightsbridge, which sold Colman Smith's designs as well as sculpture by other women artists. It was in operation until at least December 1905.[85]

The wide-ranging authors Colman Smith published through the Green Sheaf Press reflect the same eclecticism that characterized *The Green Sheaf*, her little magazine. Although her planned editions of William Blake and Edward Calvert never materialized, the Green Sheaf Press produced a variety of short stories, fairy tales, poems, and plays, many by women writers.[86] Colman Smith's friend Christopher St. John, who was the long-time partner of Edy Craig, wrote *Henry Irving*, a biography of the Lyceum Theatre owner, which was published by the Press a few months after Irving's October 1905 death. In this "elegiac monograph," St. John "objected to inaccurate and hackneyed obituaries, to criticism of Irving's diction, his conventional approach to Shakespeare, [and] the dominance of his personality in every role."[87] Colman Smith contributed the cover image of a still-smoking lantern that had just been snuffed out.[88]

Other authors published by the Green Sheaf Press included Dollie Radford, the wife of Ernest Radford, an organizer of the Arts and Crafts movement and member of the Rhymers Club. A poet in her own right, Dollie, along with Gertrude M. Bradley, wrote the children's book *Shadow Rabbit: A Story of Adventure*, which was published by the Press in 1906. A book of fairy stories, *Tales for Philip and Paul*, by the Lyceum actor E. Harcourt Williams, was published in July 1905. Later that summer Colman Smith published *A Sheaf of Song* by Alfred C. Calmour. A dramatist who is best known for *The Amber Heart*, Calmour dedicated his verses, which primarily focus on thwarted love, to Ellen Terry, who regularly starred in *The Amber Heart* as part of her Lyceum Theatre repertoire. The Green Sheaf Press published another, more mystical work in 1906, *In the Valley of Stars There Is a Tower of Silence: A Persian Tragedy.* Written by Smara Khamara, a pseudonym for F. Hadland Davis, a writer best known for his later volumes of Japanese myths and legends, the work was the result of a "period of interest in Egyptology and Sufi thought."[89]

The wide and disparate transatlantic networks to which Colman Smith was connected in the early twentieth century are also reflected in the volumes published by the Green Sheaf Press, many of which were the works of friends who had also contributed to *The Green Sheaf*. These included *Saints Among the Animals* (1906), with text by Margaret Ward Cole and illustrations by her husband, and *Green Sheaf* contributor, Alpheus Philemon Cole.[90] The book, seemingly directed at children, tells short stories of medieval saints' interactions with a wide variety of animals. The Coles, who like Colman Smith were American, were frequent guests at her weekly "at home" evenings, and Alpheus painted a portrait of Colman Smith during this period.[91] Children's book author and *Green Sheaf* illustrator Reginald Rigby contributed *The Book of Good Advice* (1906). The Press also published *The Book of the Hours* (1905) by Lady Alix Egerton, which was extensively illustrated by Colman Smith. Egerton contributed several medieval-influenced poems and stories to *The Green Sheaf* and was a close friend of Colman Smith's during this period. She is best known for her introductions to the Ellesmere manuscript of Chaucer's *Canterbury Tales* and the Bridgewater manuscript of John Milton's *Comus*, both of which had been in her family since the seventeenth century.[92]

Another long-time friend and *Green Sheaf* contributor, Laurence Alma-Tadema, had two works published by Colman Smith's Press: *Four Plays* (1905) and *Tales from My Garden* (1906). The first volume includes a full-color frontispiece while the second contains multiple illustrations by Colman Smith. Her final illustration for *Tales from My Garden* depicts two women locked in a passionate embrace. Although the two are ostensibly sisters who have been long separated, their kiss is anything but sisterly. As Alma-Tadema's narrator notes, "looking down from the tower's height, hand in hand, at both their worlds—the wide and the narrow—there in the dawn they kissed, seeming to touch on wings still mortal, the confines of eternity."[93] They board a waiting boat to sail into the future, "hand in hand" and "inseparable." Colman Smith's illustration emphasizes the women's passion; they bend into each other as they clutch shoulders, the folds of their flowing gowns melting together. This depiction is in marked contrast to her relatively rare portrayals of heterosexual couples, which are generally noteworthy for their stiffness and lack of movement. Alma-Tadema, the eldest daughter of the noted Victorian painter Sir Lawrence Alma-Tadema, did not disguise her lesbian orientation and was well connected in literary circles. In July 1907 she introduced Colman Smith to Frances Hodgson Burnett. Burnett achieved lasting fame with her classic children's novels *Little Lord Fauntleroy* (1886) and *The Secret Garden* (1911). She talked to her son Vivian Burnett, who was editor of the *Children's Magazine*, about publishing Colman Smith's Anansi stories. The stories appear never to have been published, but Burnett wrote to Alma-Tadema that Vivian, who was based in New York, "jumped" at Colman Smith's name and recounted that "she is a personage here among those who know things."[94] Vivian's comment reflects the impact that both Colman Smith's Anansi storytelling and her art were making among New York's literary elite.

Return to the United States, Anansi Performances, and Primitivism

In the spring of 1906 Colman Smith returned to the U.S. after an absence of almost six years. As she wrote to her friend Albert Bigelow Paine, one of the reasons she kept away was the negative impression that she had received of Americans abroad: "What people from America I've seen- seem to be very much stick in the mud, hampered, weighted down, dull- narrow without feeling sort of people! And those that have feeling are so dull! So empty!"[95] The first half of the trip was a prolonged vacation in which she reconnected with family and friends.[96] This enjoyable visit appears to have led Colman Smith to reassess her view of Americans. According to a *Craftsman* article, within three months in New York she had "filled a dozen note books with sketches for paintings all born of the appeal made to her imagination by the tremendously significant conditions which she has felt all about her."[97] She traveled back to England briefly in the summer to give several Anansi performances, but returned to New York in early fall.[98] The second half of Colman Smith's 1906 trip was primarily business. The Green Sheaf Press had not garnered the sales or the critical notice she had hoped,[99] and she wanted to break into the lucrative American market. Using the networks of her well-known New York-based family, as well as friends in the publishing industry that she had made when living in the city in the late 1890s, Colman Smith quickly began telling Anansi stories, reconnecting with American publishers, and meeting with gallery owners.[100] This culminated in her first exhibition at Alfred Stieglitz's 291 gallery in January 1907.[101]

Colman Smith began regaling audiences in Brooklyn, Manhattan, and Boston with her Afro-Jamaican Anansi performances in the winter of 1907.[102] By this time she had been telling the tales for audiences in England for several years and had perfected her performance. Instead of the more traditional "In a long before time," with which she begins the majority of her tales in *Annancy Stories*, Colman Smith commenced her performances of these tales with "In a long-before time—before Queen Victoria came to reign over we."[103] This phrasing, which she uses extensively in her *Chim-Chim* collection, transports listeners back to a seemingly simpler time when Great Britain was uncontested as the world's greatest imperial power, and highlights Jamaica's colonial status, thus emphasizing the "otherness" of these deceptively simple Anansi stories. It also makes clear that Colman Smith wanted to point out, if only subtly, the unequal power dynamic between her predominantly white audiences and the Afro-Jamaicans whose Anansi stories she was telling.

Colman Smith's careful curation of these performances in respect to set, props, and costuming undoubtedly played into her audience's stereotypically primitivist views of Afro-Jamaicans.[104] Eschewing scenery, she "sat upon a low platform with her feet tucked under her" surrounded by "a half-dozen big fat candles before her to serve as footlights."[105] Contemporary accounts reveal that she wore several costumes for her performances, such as a long green or blue hooded cloak for her chanting of W. B. Yeats's poems and a gray and white or green and white striped gown for her recitation of Old English ballads. However, for her telling of Anansi stories, Colman Smith always wore the same costume, which drew on primitivist ideas of Afro-Jamaicans: "a loose robe of flame colored silk with an arrangement of tulle and beads bound about her head like a kerchief."[106] Contemporary reviewers repeatedly pointed out Colman Smith's racial otherness, highlighting her "astonishing arrangement of head gear," her "capital West Indian dialect," and that she did not just act out the stories but fully "portrays" them.[107] Other accounts noted the inclusion of a stuffed alligator from Jamaica that was endowed "with a singularly congenial expression of countenance."[108] These U.S. accounts echo a 1904 *London Mail* article that states, "the scene is curiously barbaric as the storyteller bends over the primitive stage."[109] All of these reports emphasize the spectacle of these performances, which seems to have been as much, if not more, of a draw for audiences as the Anansi stories themselves.[110]

Colman Smith captivated a range of audiences, from respectable Packer Collegiate women alumnae and bohemian Pratt Institute Art Club members to well-heeled guests at a benefit for the Italian Ambassador at the Waldorf Astoria.[111] The response to these performances was so uniformly positive that it led a *Brooklyn Life* writer to assert:

> Even with the prestige of English approval, Miss Smith's instant success here is a bit unusual. I think it is largely due to her absence of all pose; queer, unexpected, absolutely original as Miss Smith is, one realizes her quite unmistakable genuineness as well as appreciates her talents. She is a gentlewoman, presenting an odd type of thoroughly unconventional femininity—therein lies her greatest charm.[112]

While Colman Smith was clearly appropriating Afro-Jamaican Anansi stories for her own professional gain, the confusion that she, granddaughter of two very powerful, politically connected white Brooklyn families, generated as the seemingly authentic teller of these tales is palpable. The reviewer runs through a number of descriptors ranging from queer to gentlewoman, with the latter quietly alluding to Colman Smith's well-known family. Although the writer is unable to articulate what exactly has contributed to Colman Smith's "instant success," he finally settles on the idea that her "greatest charm" lies in her "unconventional femininity." The type of unconventionality is not discussed, but the subtle sexualization of Colman Smith, like so many descriptions of her and her Anansi performances, reflects the racist, sexualized view of the Afro-Jamaican woman who were seen as the traditional tellers of these tales, as well as the trouble reviewers had in reconciling Colman Smith with those stereotypes.

A similar response can be seen in coverage of Colman Smith's New Year's Eve performance for Mark Twain. As the *New York World* noted, "an exotic young woman with melting dark eyes and a sweet, crooning voice made the veteran humorist laugh like a child, and all his distinguished company of guests forgot time, space and the everyday world of commonplace reality."[113] Colman Smith's power to transport her audience is evident; like the *Brooklyn Life* account, the *New York World* critic emphasizes both her exoticism and her sexuality. A later review makes her primitivist appeal even more apparent. The article states that Colman Smith delivered these

> fairy folk-tales ... in the weird dialect of the Jamaican negroes—a sort of cockney English with Spanish colouring, a rhythmic rising inflection at the end of each sentence, and barbaric words and idioms sprinkled through it that must have come directly from the voodoo worshippers of the African jungle.[114]

Neither writer notes exactly what reduced Twain to laughter, but both emphasize the power of Colman Smith's performance, which, according to the critic from *The Nelson Mail*, derived from Obeah. And, as powerful Obeah women are scattered throughout Colman Smith's Anansi stories, it is possible that the writer was so swept away by her performance that he conflated Colman Smith with the characters in her stories.

This writer also homes in on the racist stereotypes that some audience members evidently found amusing, and highlights at least some in attendance who apparently interpreted Colman Smith as enacting a type of blackface minstrelsy that was popular during the early twentieth century. None of the numerous accounts of her performances mention her darkening her face or changing her appearance, other than through costume. However, Colman Smith, as Wendy Martin notes of Josephine Baker's French music hall performances, took "advantage of the situation by deliberately manipulating the conventions of primitivism to gain a considerable measure of control over her audience."[115] Although Colman Smith did not employ grass skirts, bananas, or nudity to appeal to her audiences' primitivist interests, she did use lighting, costume, and Afro-Jamaican creole speech.

In one of the relatively rare interviews that Colman Smith gave about her Anansi performances, she emphasizes both the importance of the oral transmission of the tales and their universality. She explains that while Anansi stories can be painted, sung, or written, the spoken word surpasses the other media.

> All stories can be told, and told so that every human being can understand them. When I tell the Jamaica stories to very young children, I illustrate them with dolls, which I make myself—saw them out of wood with a fret-saw, then paint them and stick on feathers

and beads, Jamaica mammy style. These are to the little kiddies what book illustrations are to grown-ups. But the real, universal world-old way is to tell the stories orally, and put the illustrations in as you go along, by sign language, facial expression, intonation, gesture, and all that sort of thing.[116]

Colman Smith's focus on the similarities between different modes of artistic output is key here, as it highlights that she viewed these very different modes of expression as part of the same continuum. The accouterments—whether dolls, images, animals, or words—only serve to enhance the experience. It's the human element of the oral performance that she views as most important in order to connect with audiences and transmit ideas and emotions. Moreover, her comments suggest that she was well aware of both the importance of oral tradition and the dramatic power she could wield over her audiences. However, the casual racism in her reference to the traditional Afro-Jamaican women tellers of these tales shows that, regardless of how she was viewed by critics, she viewed herself as separate from these tellers and was appropriating the material for her own benefit.

Nature, Content, and Reception of the Music Visions

Just as Colman Smith exerted power over her audiences through her Anansi performances, her musical visions also provided her with an opportunity to create new worlds for her viewers. However, her musical visions differed from the oral performances in that they also had power over her. Although Colman Smith said she was endowed with the gift of second sight since childhood, published accounts note that her first musical vision occurred on Christmas Day 1900 while Gordon Craig, Ellen Terry's son, was playing Bach.[117] The visions then stopped for two years and began again at the end of 1902 when she attended a series of concerts by friend and fellow Masquer Arnold Dolmetsch. Shortly thereafter, Colman Smith began making larger drawings at Queen's Hall concerts in London, producing as many as twenty to thirty drawings in one sitting.[118] During a prolific week in February 1908, she noted that she had done ninety-four drawings, "almost all of them useable ones."[119] The visions would appear to her in color, but in order to get them down quickly, Colman Smith would sketch in pencil. However, after "some people in the audience objected to the scratching of her pencil," she took to using a brush with ink in sepia, blue, or black.[120] If a sketch appealed to her, she would then return to it, enlarging and finishing it as well as adding color.[121] It is unclear what this process entailed and whether she added elements, although it is definitely possible.

As discussed in Chapter 3, the ability to translate music into pictures is a rare variant of synaesthesia. People who experience synaesthesia are usually born with it or develop it early in childhood. Colman Smith was twenty-two when she said she experienced her first musical vision. However, she had reportedly experienced second sight from childhood and these visions can be seen as part of a larger constellation of extrasensory gifts. It is also possible that she had previously experienced some sort of combination of sound-induced fusion of colors and/or images, but that these new visions were heightened and, as such, seemed unique to her. What is important to keep in mind is that these musical visions reappeared at a very important time in Colman Smith's life, a period when her study of myth, mysticism, and her Anansi performances had all reached a critical mass.

Colman Smith's musical visions took several forms. While the most common was the "living and moving picture," which immediately materialized upon hearing a musical piece, at other times the picture emerged and grew in color and form upon the page as she drew.[122] Speed was of the utmost importance for this "lightning artist," as the images would disappear as soon as the last notes of the music faded. According to an *Illustrated London News* feature, the action of drawing these images was entirely subconscious, and "if [Colman Smith] ever alters her drawing in the least detail from what she sees, the picture instantly breaks up and disappears."[123]

Press accounts of Colman Smith's musical visions are not entirely consistent. *The Craftsman* noted that if the music did not appeal to her, she either drew nothing at all or left only a half-finished sketch, thus highlighting that she had at least some role in this process.[124] In a 1909 *Boston Sunday Post* article, Colman Smith attempted to connect her visions with the scientific writings of William James, noting that "Professor James says that there is a border of the mind where all sound becomes visible, and my work proves that this is so."[125] This is a fairly accurate description of James's views on the workings of the brain. He famously proposed that if the eyes were forced to connect to the auditory centers of the brain, and the ears with the visual centers, we would "hear the lightning and see the thunder, see the symphony and hear the conductor's movements."[126] This explained for Colman Smith exactly what was happening in her brain when she experienced her musical visions.

Colman Smith elaborated most fully on her musical visions in a draft manuscript, part of which was included in a 1908 *Strand Magazine* article:

> They are not pictures of the music theme—pictures of the flying notes—not conscious illustrations of the name given to a piece of music, but just what I see when I hear music—thoughts loosened and set free by the spell of sound. I put them down with haste, sometimes they are so strange they almost shock me as they come. Subconscious energy lives in them all. (Sand makes patterns by vibrations on a drum). When I take a brush in hand and the music begins, it is like looking into a beautiful country. There stretched far away are plains and mountains and the billowy sea.[127]

Colman Smith emphasizes that what she sees is not an illustration of either the notes or the name of a given piece of music, but "thoughts loosened and set free by the spell of sound." Significantly, she understands that these visions are mediated by her subconscious. In a section that was not included in the *Strand* article, she goes on to highlight the energy created through these experiences, the unconscious material they drew on, and that the process was a shock to her nervous system. Closely echoing the language she used in a 1927 *Illustrated London News* article, Colman Smith concludes that what occurs in her mind is like a window "into a beautiful country," and the landscapes that she sees through this process—plains with distant mountains and rolling seas—recur over and over again in her musical visions. Interestingly, the *Strand* changed Colman Smith's original language of "looking into a beautiful country" to "unlocking the door into," which emphasizes the mystical nature of these visions.[128] Similarly, the parts of the manuscript that the *Strand* omitted highlight Colman Smith's agency in this process and how it makes her feel. This language undercuts the otherworldly theme of this article as well as that of almost all the other press coverage on Colman Smith, whether devoted to her musical visions, her Anansi tales, or another facet of her career.

Over the course of her twenty-five years of exhibiting and discussing these musical visions with the press—although the visions appear to have continued into at least the 1940s—Colman Smith created paintings from a wide range of orchestral music, including Bach, Beethoven, Brahms, Chopin, Debussy, Franck, Greig, Mozart, Ravel, Schumann, and Tchaikovsky among others. Only the music of Wagner consistently failed to elicit any consistent images, but instead sparked anger: "my scalp tingles and my hair pricks; I feel so full of rage that I want to crack the heads of people together like nuts. When it is played in a room, thick curtains of brown spiders' webs appear; sticky and evil smelling."[129] She does not elaborate as to why, but an article by M. Irwin MacDonald states that the German composer's "colossal images of gods and heroes, and the profoundly sensuous appeal of his stupendous orchestration, brings ... a passionate revolt from all that the music means." While MacDonald clearly preferred Wagner's music to the "formless musical fancies of Debussy" that inspired many of Colman Smith's "music pictures" from 1908 onward, it is clear that Colman Smith was responding instinctually to the patriarchal, often pompous characters that Wagner's music brings to life.

A few of Colman Smith's early musical visions portray relatively prosaic, even heartwarming surroundings in bright watercolor, such as the 1905 *Catch Me* based on Schumann's Fantasy Pieces, op. 10, no. 4, which depicts a mother and child in a playful half embrace on a windy day.[130] This reflects the large number of children, occasionally accompanied by maternal figures, in Colman Smith's early art. However, as her musical visions progressed, she moved almost entirely away from children toward canvases that depicted adults and, increasingly, women or androgynous figures. Interestingly, when Colman Smith returned to Schumann's Fantasy Pieces, op. 10, no. 4, in 1915, the playfulness remained, but the tenor and composition of the painting have changed completely, as she has discarded the watercolors in favor of dark figures in outline against a barren landscape.[131] Playing more clearly with perspective, Colman Smith replaces the mother and child with a dancing man, who appears to be running away from a central woman, while a third figure cavorts away in the other direction.

As Colman Smith began to associate different composers with specific images, her music visions became more personally symbolic. Bach's Chromatic Fantasy was linked with brown-clad maidens ringing bells, while Chopin's Ballade No. 1 in G minor, op. 23 called to mind gardens at night "where mystery and dread lurk under every bush, but joy and passion throb within the air, and the cold moon bewitches all the scene."[132] The catalog to Colman Smith's 1907 exhibition at Stieglitz's 291 gallery lists this painting as *The Fugitive*, which encapsulates the music's visual connotations for her.[133] However, the retitling also reflects the tension in her early musical visions between the desire only to associate the paintings with the music that inspired them, allowing viewers to come to their own conclusions, and the push by gallery owners and critics to have more evocative titles that unpacked the paintings for viewers.

As noted, reviewers emphasized the mystical, visionary aspects of Colman Smith's paintings. Like the reception of her Anansi performances and her early illustrative work, critics stressed her sincerity, naivety, and truthfulness. Reflecting this trend, MacDonald's complimentary assessment from 1912 emphasizes that her work contains both "the open mind and vivid perception of the child" and "the coordination and control of both conscious and subconscious faculties."[134] However, in an unexpected move that must have been inspired by her "otherness," he asserts that Colman Smith's art is "simply another application of the powers held in the old time by the master weavers of Kashmir." He goes on to detail the story of an English traveler who marveled that the singing workers could produce such a "brilliant, intricate web ... without a chart or pattern of any kind." Questioning the master weaver on how this was possible, the English man received the answer: "Sahib, we see the colors and patterns as we sign and so we weave the shawl." The English traveler cannot move beyond his primitivist views and finds it impossible that the dark-skinned Kashmiris could possibly create such beautiful designs on their own. MacDonald applies this anecdote to his topic, stating that "Pamela Colman Smith sees the thronging images as she listens, and so she makes her pictures."[135] Like the English traveler, MacDonald is amazed that the skill and intricacy of Colman Smith's musical visions were produced by an artist, not to mention a woman, who possessed "the open mind and vivid perception of the child." While MacDonald does not mention her racial origins, her time spent in Jamaica, or her Anansi performances, the only photograph of Colman Smith in the article is the now famous one of her in costume for her folktale performances, included as the frontispiece for this book. Described in the caption only as "a recent photograph," it depicts her in her peasant-style dress, with a turban on her head, multiple strands of beads around her neck, and a mischievous glint in her eye as, with crossed arms, she boldly stares into the camera. As discussed above, Colman Smith's costume, and the Anansi performances themselves, catered to the primitivist views of her audiences. Even though MacDonald does not address her Anansi performances explicitly, the captivating image, which exudes both feminist power and "otherness," clearly influenced his decision to liken her to Kashmiri weavers and, undoubtedly, influenced her reception by readers.

Three Stieglitz Exhibitions and Advice for Art Students

Arguably the most important exhibitions in Colman Smith's career, and the ones that helped shape both her critical and popular reception, were the three shows held at Alfred Stieglitz's 291 gallery, which was originally known as the Little Galleries of the Photo-Secession. Well-known for his championing of pictorialist photography in his 5th Avenue gallery, Stieglitz was beginning to pack up his space for good after repeated clashes with others in the movement when, in the fall of 1906, Colman Smith unexpectedly walked in with her portfolio of paintings.[136] He was "so impressed that he decided then and there to give her an exhibit."[137] In January 1907 seventy-two of Colman Smith's watercolors went on display in Stieglitz's attic gallery, becoming the gallery's first solo exhibition of non-photographic art.[138] Stieglitz's close friend and associate Edward Steichen was outraged when he heard this news, as he was facilitating a planned exhibition of August Rodin's drawings that was to have been the gallery's first foray into non-photographic art.[139] Writing in *Camera Work*, Stieglitz defended his decision as not a departure from the ideas of the Photo-Secession, but as their manifestation:

> The Secession Idea is neither the servant nor the product of a medium ... it is the Spirit of the Lamp ... The Photo-Secession is not the keeper of this Lamp, but lights it when it may; and when these pictures of Miss Smith's, conceived in this spirit and no other, came to us, although they came unheralded and unexpectant, we but tended the Lamp in tendering them hospitality.[140]

Drawing on Ruskin's *Seven Lamps of Architecture*, Stieglitz presents the exhibition of Colman Smith's work as fated, almost as something out of his control, that as a humble promoter of the ideals of the spirit of the Photo-Secession—a group that was in the process of fracturing—he felt duty-bound to promote.

Initially, Colman Smith's show drew more journalists than art patrons. However, this changed when, ten days into the exhibition, art critic James Huneker visited the gallery and praised her work in the *New York Sun*.[141] Favorably comparing her art to that of well-known European artists such Aubrey Beardsley, Blake, Edvard Munch, and Odilon Redon, he stated that her paintings "reveal the workings of a strangely organized imagination.

Poetic in the accepted sense it is, and something more, something more unearthly."[142] He particularly highlighted an affinity with Blake. As Dennis Denisoff has pointed out, Huneker "appears to have recognized [that] Dow's and Pater's idealisation of music becomes, in Smith's formulation, two types of synaesthesia: first, the painterly reproduction of the music she hears and, second, her experience in this reality of the beauty of the otherworldly soul."[143] However, Huneker did not name these connections explicitly and, like the majority of Colman Smith's critics, focused most of his assessment on the mystical aspects of her work.

Huneker singled out *Death in the House* as "absolutely nerve shuddering," explaining that the painting was not typically gruesome but, like the work of Munch, subtly conveyed a sense of horror through suggestion. However, he completely overlooks the humor in the image, which first appeared as an illustration for her short story "Annancy and Death" in her *Chim-Chim* collection (Figure 4.5).[144] Like the close variant "How Annancy Fooled Death" that was included in *Annancy Stories*, the story details how the trickster spider, while clinging to the rafters of his home, convinces Death to move a flour barrel under him. Anansi safely drops into the barrel, flour flies up into Death's eyes, and Anansi absconds.[145] Taken out of context, the dark painting of a small, frail-looking Anansi peeking down at a cadaverous Death, whose bulging bag holds the rest of Anansi's family, is unsettling. Although Colman Smith's illustrations often highlight the lighter, more humorous side of the Anansi stories, the painting makes clear the thin line between death and life that Anansi straddles. The decision to remove any reference to Anansi from the title of the painting also brings into focus the potential of Colman Smith's images to transport viewers into different times and places, even when there is confusion surrounding the details.

Despite the overall positive tenor of his review, Huneker, like many of her critics, finds fault with Colman Smith's technique. "Her mastery of her material leaves much to be desired. She is naively crude; she often stumbles; she is too hallucinatory"; but he concludes "Yet she has fantasy, and fantasy covers a wilderness of technical shortcomings."[146] Huneker's favorable comparisons to famous male artists generated popular interest and resulted in the extension of the exhibition for an additional ten days.[147] As Stieglitz remembered, "[t]he exhibition created a sensation ... [bringing] the Whitneys and Havemeyers, Vanderbilts and all classes of people into these tiny rooms of ours. The place was literally mobbed."[148] Many of the paintings

Figure 4.5 Pamela Colman Smith, "Annancy and Death," from *Chim-Chim: Folk Stories from Jamaica* (Green Sheaf Press, 1905), 45. Reproduced by permission of Stuart R. Kaplan, U.S. Games, Inc.

from the exhibition sold and "nearly all of the most significant magazines" published Colman Smith's work.[149]

The 291 show was quickly followed by inclusion in a prestigious national exhibit at the Pennsylvania Academy in Philadelphia in April.[150] Colman Smith did not attend, as she returned to England at the end of March. Curious about her reception, she wrote Stieglitz, asking, "Did people shout with glee? Or were they just scornful?"[151] Stieglitz's response is unrecorded. Colman Smith's paintings received only brief mentions at best in coverage of this large exhibition.[152] At the end of 1907 she was still concerned with negative views of her work. As she was preparing for a group show at the Baillie Gallery in London and a joint exhibition in Edinburgh, she wrote Stieglitz that British art patrons would likely react to her musical paintings with "wild rage."[153] Although this feared violence does not appear to have materialized, Colman Smith reported only a few sales from either show.[154]

Always attempting to widen her appeal and her profits, Colman Smith united her Anansi performances with an exhibition of her musical visions—facets of her professional life that she had previously kept separate—at the Baillie Gallery in February 1908. Terming the event "a charmingly unconventional little entertainment," *The Times* noted that Colman Smith delivered the tales with "delightful gusto and spirit," but, likely relating to her use of dialect, explained that they were told in a "curiously homely fashion."[155] While this first, seemingly unplanned recitation was, as the reviewer points out, delivered "on the spot," Colman Smith sporadically continued to combine her telling of Anansi stories with her art exhibitions. Throughout 1908 she performed Anansi stories at a range of venues, including benefits and Christmas concerts.[156]

American audiences continued to be more receptive to Colman Smith's art than their British contemporaries, but the financial and critical success of her 1907 return was not soon matched. Four of her drawings were included as part of the National Art Club's January 1908 Special Exhibition of Contemporary Art, but they received little attention among the larger canvases by Mary Cassatt, Childe Hassam, and John Sloan, and photography by Käsebier, Stieglitz, and Steichen.[157] In March 1908 Colman Smith's work appeared in a second exhibition at Stieglitz's 291 gallery, this time as part of a group show with Will Geiger and D. S. McLaughlin.[158] For financial reasons, Colman Smith did not return to New York for the show but eagerly wrote Stieglitz for both news on sales from the exhibition and whether he believed her work had "improved."[159] Although more publications reviewed this show as compared to her solo exhibition, the response was more mixed, with some critics confused by the increased number of paintings that were identified only by the musical composition that had inspired them. Huneker, writing in the *New York Sun*, was far less effusive than the previous year. While still favorably comparing Colman Smith's work to Blake, he "sadly ... confess[ed] to missing the significance of the titles. The cold truth is that music can't be successfully transposed thus."[160] Huneker went on to question why certain images were linked with specific pieces of music, such as "a man with a bird on his wrist" titled "Bach's Brandenburg Concerto No. 2."[161] The *New York Tribune*'s critic voiced a similar complaint, noting that "[t]he compositions suggest fancy rather than imagination, and they waken no memories of the music associated with them in the catalogue."[162] Stieglitz appears also to have raised the issue of the musical composition titles not substantially illuminating the subjects of her canvases. However, as Colman Smith defiantly wrote, apparently in answer to such a query, "If you want other titles than music ones, you must make em up!"[163] Catalogs for both the 1907 and 1908 exhibitions at 291 show that in 1907 the majority of the paintings had non-musical titles, although a few indicated which musical work had inspired them, while the majority in 1908 were identified solely by musical composition.[164] However, in the second show there were a number of more conventionally titled pieces intermingled with the musical ones, indicating that Stieglitz likely followed Colman Smith's advice. This type of criticism reflects the tension between Colman Smith's repeated assertion that she was just recording the visions revealed to her through sound, and art critics and patrons who were habituated to look for "meaning" in art and wanted illustrative titles to guide them through this process.

Despite the criticism levied at Colman Smith as part of the second 291 show, New York press reports show that she was making a significant impact in artistic and literary circles. *The Craftsman* singled her out as one of very few American artists who were providing "a different, new, intelligent understanding point of view toward our country as it exists."[165] The *New York Sun* favorably compared Colman Smith's work when reviewing Dutch symbolist Jan Toorop's visionary paintings.[166] Similarly, *The Craftsman*, reviewing an Arthur B. Davies exhibit, favorably compared her paintings to Davies's work: "I do not always understand exactly what Miss Pamela Colman Smith has dreamed of in some of her strange fantastic drawings, but almost invariably

I catch a glimpse of another land and find my imagination stirred and feel an extra heart beat."[167] Furthermore, reflecting how well known she had become, her friend the photographer Alice Boughton included a portrait of Colman Smith, alongside those of literary celebrities such as Henry James, William James, and Yeats, in her July exhibition at the Pratt Institute.[168]

Colman Smith's attitude toward the country of her citizenship also improved and she filled multiple notebooks with sketches. At least a few of these found their way into a series of "Impressions of New York" that were included in the 1907 exhibition at the 291 gallery. A *Brooklyn Life* reviewer noted that "the huge skyscrapers, the smoky atmosphere, the crowded streets, and the night effects—are the more remarkable."[169] One of the paintings depicts the New York skyline at night framed by the East River and the Brooklyn Bridge (Figure 4.6). A man stands in profile on the Brooklyn Heights shore, where many of Colman Smith's relatives lived. Large puffs of smoke swirl around the skyline, most emanating from two ferry boats chugging back to Brooklyn from Manhattan, likely harkening back to the fleet of ferry boats that her grandfather, Cyrus Smith, controlled as director of Brooklyn's Union Ferry Company. Reflecting the positive impression that the U.S. had made on her, Colman Smith told *The Craftsman* in March 1907 that "there has never been a time or nation fuller of meaning to the thinking artist than America is to-day."[170] However, she also became increasingly critical that the art industry wasn't reflecting this depth and diversity. That same month, and in the same magazine, Colman Smith published the short manifesto "A Protest Against Fear," which I discussed above, in which she expressed outrage at the hesitancy that she saw in American art students to embrace the wide and varied material their country provided.

Colman Smith returned to the same subject in a July 1908 *Craftsman* essay, "Should the Art Student Think?" She expanded on many of the ideas in the first, short essay, urging students to think more fully about the ends they wanted to achieve as working artists during their training. If important planning was left to the uncertain future, students could leave art school as "crippled tool[s]," who have no clear direction and, as a result, must blindly follow the whims of the market. Exhorting students to observe and listen to the world around them, Colman Smith wrote, "Learn from everything, see everything, and above all *feel* everything! And make other people when they look at your drawing feel it too!"[171] She then explicitly connected this advice with the varied American cultural landscape, telling students to drink in the

Figure 4.6 Pamela Colman Smith, untitled watercolor of the New York City skyline. Private collection

world around them. In this way, she was propounding the view that American artists were not creating works that adequately reflected the power of their country. She states:

> Lift up your ideals, you weaklings, and force a way out of that thunderous clamor of the steam press, the hurrying herd of blind humanity, noise, dust, strife, seething toil—there is power! The imprisoned Titans underneath the soil, grinding, writhing—take your strength from them, throw aside your petty drawing room point of view.[172]

The appeal to the senses is palpable in her critique of emerging artists. She stresses the need for power and strength in weeding out the entrenched, less radical views of both society and the publishing industry that, in her experience, primarily catered to conventional, middle-class tastes. Urging students to take their cue from "the imprisoned Titans underneath the soil," she exhorts students to pick new, more vibrant subjects for their compositions.

The impassioned, even accusatory tone of Colman Smith's essay contrasts strongly with the critical reception of her paintings as dreamy and mystical windows into other worlds. However, the voice of "Should the Art Student Think?" reflects her letters, where she often rails about a publishing industry and art world that she felt was stacked against her. In order to combat this injustice, she constantly tried to find different outlets and sympathetic collaborators and patrons for her creative endeavors, whether editing avant-garde little magazines, chanting Yeats's poetry, joining an occult group, operating her own press and store, or, as I will detail in Chapter 5, becoming active in the British women's suffrage movement. In this first half of her career, Colman Smith constantly found new ways to assert her own power through art in order to combat what she terms "the hard crust of convention," and, in this essay, she imparted that hard-won knowledge to a new generation of art students.[173] However, her attempts to apply this advice to her own life and work yielded mixed results at best.

Colman Smith's last show at the 291 gallery took place in March 1909 and received far less media attention than her first two exhibitions. A brief mention in the *New York Times* noted that "Miss Smith's style has always a touch of the bizarre united to elements of greater dignity."[174] Writing in the July 1909 issue of *Camera Work*, Benjamin De Casseres praised Colman

Smith's one-woman show, stating "[n]o more curious and fascinating exhibition has ever been held in New York." He continued:

> She is a blender of visions, a mystic, a symbolist, one who transfigures the world she lives in by the overwhelming simplicity of her imagination. To me, these wonderful little drawings are not merely art; they are poems, ideas, life-values and cosmic values that have long gestated within the subconscious world of their creator—a wizard's world of intoxicating evocations—here and now accouched on their vibrating, colored beds, to mystify and awe the mind of some few beholders; to project their souls from off this little Springboard of Time into the stupendous unbegotten thing we name the Infinite.[175]

Like the earlier assessments of Huneker and others, De Casseres stresses that Colman Smith's art is suffused with both mysticism and symbolism that taps into the subconscious. However, while praising the visionary aspects of her paintings and terming her "the evocatrice of wonder," De Casseres also discusses the "'overwhelming simplicity' of her work" that borders on "lunacy."[176] Even when it was being praised, critics consistently emphasized what they saw as the childlike qualities of her art, which, undoubtedly, reflected their primitivist perception of both her and her work. This was heightened during this last Stieglitz exhibition when she appeared at the opening reception dressed in her West Indian costume and gave an unexpected performance of Anansi stories and Yeats's poems, a practice she had begun in England the previous year.[177] Reflecting the consistently racist reception that Colman Smith received, her performance was caricatured by Marius de Zayas, a close friend of Stieglitz during this period. In a drawing that was first published in *The Critic*, de Zayas contorts Colman Smith's features and depicts her as an otherworldly apparition.[178]

Although Stieglitz's championing of Colman Smith abruptly ended after this third show, the support he provided during the years she exhibited at the 291 gallery was significant for both the maturation of her art and Stieglitz's own embrace of modern art. As we have seen, he accorded Colman Smith the honor of his first non-photographic solo show. In January 1908 Stieglitz hosted the first U.S. exhibition of Rodin's sculpture and drawings.[179] He then went on to exhibit work by Henri Matisse, Paul Cezanne, Pablo Picasso, and Francis Picabia, which introduced New York audiences—and

America more broadly—to the work of these important modernist artists, cementing Stieglitz's reputation as an important early proponent of this groundbreaking art.[180] Colman Smith was one of only six women Stieglitz featured in exhibitions from 1905 to 1917. Her friends, the photographers Gertrude Käsebier (1906) and Alice Boughton (1907), each had a solo show, and Georgia O'Keeffe was exhibited twice (1915, 1917). However, Colman Smith was the only woman included in three shows.[181] As Melinda Boyd Parsons points out, "This indicates Stieglitz's on-going interest in her art, as does his creation of a limited-edition portfolio of platinum prints of her visionary paintings (one of which he kept until his death)."[182] While Stieglitz publicly disavowed Colman Smith and her work shortly after her last exhibition at the 291 gallery, her "proto-modernism played a catalytic role in the development of theories of art at 291."[183] When he first saw Colman Smith's work, it appeared as "modern" to an art world struggling to cast off the strictures of nineteenth-century Impressionism and still unaware of the coming abstract phase.

It is possible that after exhibitions highlighting the work of Rodin, Matisse, and Picasso, Stieglitz's opinion of Colman Smith's more mystical and symbolist paintings changed. Her decision to include an Anansi performance as part of the 1909 exhibition's opening night reception might also have negatively influenced his perception of her and her work. In Colman Smith's last two letters to Stieglitz, she repeatedly inquires about money she thought was due to her. On November 19, 1909 she wrote, "I wonder where you are !!—I want some money for Christmas—!" She then goes on to inquire about payments owed and offers to send several new works for him to sell.[184] At one point she interjects that "I hope you are doing well—& the Little Galleries are still there!"[185] Stieglitz's response to this letter, if there was one, is not recorded, and it is likely that he, like Yeats and several other of Colman Smith's male mentors, grew tired of her requests for money and support and broke off contact.

Colman Smith's 1909 New York visit was not nearly as filled with public appearances and press coverage as her 1907 sojourn, during which her Anansi performances caused "such a furore."[186] However, she returned to the Pratt Art Club to deliver a lecture on the importance of imagination in art. Entitled "Magic Spectacles," her talk was accompanied by a stereopticon or magic lantern presentation of French, Italian, Chinese, and Japanese art that she felt was dominated by imagination.[187] Although the press coverage barely mentioned it, Colman Smith combined her discussion of art with Anansi performances.

In addition to her show at the 291 gallery and lecture at Pratt, Colman Smith also traveled to Boston, where twenty of her pictures were on exhibit at the Twentieth Century Club. She also gave a "Magic Spectacles" talk on the opening evening.[188] This event produced a lavishly illustrated article in the *Boston Sunday Post*, the text of which was predominantly drawn from the same draft manuscript that Colman Smith had given to Stieglitz at the end of 1907 and that had been part-published in *The Strand Magazine* in 1908. The review's chief addition was to frame Colman Smith and her musical visions as the "newest psychological pastime," stating that many celebrities and socialites now dabbled with this "infectious" pursuit.[189] While she generally favored publicity of any kind, especially the kind that positively promoted her and her art, it is hard to fathom why Colman Smith would have supported framing what she described as a mystical window "into a beautiful country" as a new fad.

Nevertheless, by 1909 this type of response, which misinterpreted, misconstrued, and even outright rejected Colman Smith and her art, had become the norm for both her popular and critical reception. The prevailing primitivist, and often racist, views of the Anglo-American public she encountered reinforced the impression of hostility. However, by the end of the year, she seems to have been far less personally affected by this response than she had been earlier. While no doubt time and familiarity with this type of reception had inured her to it, she was now also heavily invested in new projects, specifically her tarot images. This project both developed and extended recurrent symbolism and techniques in her "music pictures" from 1906 onward. This period was also marked by increased political engagement. She became active in the Suffrage Atelier and, more broadly, the British women's suffrage movement, which gained momentum in the pre-World War I period.

Although she remained an American citizen, Colman Smith turned away from the U.S., which she had visited for extended periods between 1906 and 1909, and embraced English life and, most importantly, the crusade for women's rights. This political engagement, in turn, had an effect on her art. Colman Smith appears to have concluded that the fear she noted in her March 1907 *Craftsman* essay as infecting her country of origin was, despite hopes to the contrary, beyond repair. The critical and popular reception of both her Anansi performances and the exhibitions of her "music pictures," which were marked by primitivist, often racist, assumptions and feminized stereotypes, likely cemented this decision. This chapter has highlighted how Colman Smith's interest in transcultural myth, which began through her editions and performances of Afro-Jamaican Anansi stories, fused with the resumption of her musical visions to produce a period of extreme productivity, Chapter 5 will explore how her increased involvement in mystical traditions and suffrage activities heightened her growing feminism and enriched her art.

CHAPTER FIVE

Feminist Symbolic Art
Tarot Designs, Suffrage Posters, and Representations of Women

On November 19, 1909, Pamela Colman Smith was excited about a new project. She wrote to Alfred Stieglitz, "I've just finished a big job for very little cash! A set of designs for a pack of Tarot cards—80 designs."[1] Colman Smith goes on to detail that the cards would be "printed in color by lithography—probably very badly!" and would be ready by December 1. She promises to send him a pack, as well as some of the original designs, to be sold in his gallery, as "some people may like them!"[2] This is the last extant letter between Colman Smith and Stieglitz, the friend and patron who had hosted three exhibitions of her work at his 291 gallery in Manhattan, and it is tantalizing to contemplate whether she ever did forward any of the original tarot card designs, which have not been located. This brief exchange, at the end of a letter primarily concerned with Stieglitz's silence in response to other letters, is Colman Smith's only known comment on her best-known work. The monetary nature of these remarks could give the impression that the tarot project was not important to her and that the cards had very little personal significance. However, like most things in Colman Smith's life and legacy, this is far from the whole story.

By comparison with Colman Smith's short discussion, Arthur Edward Waite, the man who commissioned the tarot deck, wrote extensively on both the deck and Colman Smith's involvement with the project. It was under his name, along with that of the publisher Rider & Sons, that the deck first achieved acclaim. Colman Smith first met Waite when she was initiated into the Hermetic Order of the Golden Dawn in November 1901 and followed him to his Independent and Rectified Order after the group's split in 1903. In a pattern that was repeated in almost all of Colman Smith's interactions with famous men, Waite's remarks, which are dismissive of her contribution, have dominated the received narrative. As he noted in his autobiography, *Shadows of Life and Thought*:

> Now, in those days there was a most imaginative and abnormally psychic artist, named Pamela Colman Smith, who had drifted into the Golden Dawn and loved its Ceremonies—as transformed by myself—without pretending or indeed attempting to understand their sub-surface consequence. It seemed to some of us in the circle that there was a draughtswoman among us who, under proper guidance, could produce a Tarot with an appeal in the world of art and a suggestion of significance behind the Symbols which would put on them another construction than had ever been dreamed by those who, through many generations, had produced and used them for mere divinatory purposes. My province was to see that the designs—especially those of the important Trumps Major—kept that in the hiddenness which belonged to certain Greater Mysteries, in the Paths of which I was travelling. I am not of course intimating that the Golden Dawn had at that time any deep understanding by inheritance of Tarot Cards; but, if I may so say, it was getting to know under my auspices that their Symbols—or some at least among them—were gates which opened on realms of vision beyond occult dreams. I saw to it therefore that Pamela Colman Smith should not be picking up casually any floating images from my own or another mind. She had to be spoon-fed carefully over the Priestess Card, over that which is called the Fool and over the Hanged Man.[3]

In a condescending tone that calls to mind comments by male critics on her musical visions, her Afro-Jamaican Anansi performances, and her illustrative work, Waite diminishes Colman Smith's creative, mystic, and intellectual contributions to the tarot deck, essentially writing her out of a process that she was integral to and taking undue credit himself. While Waite's initial description of Colman Smith as "most imaginative" is positive and seems apt, he quickly adds that she is "abnormally psychic." As previously discussed, Colman Smith claimed that she had had second sight since childhood, which reportedly returned when she first visited Ireland in 1899. By the winter of 1903 she had begun regularly experiencing her musical visions. A 1907 *Occult Review* article details an extended vision she and her friend, Lady Alix Egerton, experienced at Peacock's Well in Ireland.[4] All of these extrasensory events would classify her as "abnormally psychic" in a positive sense. However, when taken in context with Waite's diction in the rest of the passage—he notes that she "drifted" into the group without consciously choosing membership for herself, did not attempt to understand the deeper meaning of the cards, and terms her a "draughtswoman" rather than an accomplished fine artist and illustrator—"abnormally psychic" takes on a decidedly negative tone.

It is true that when Colman Smith began work on the cards, she had only advanced to the Zelator, or second level, of the Golden Dawn and, as such, would likely only have seen two Golden Dawn tarot cards, as the full meaning behind the cards was only revealed at the sixth initiation. It is possible that Colman Smith's friends, Florence Farr and W. B. Yeats, who, like Waite, were advanced students of the Golden Dawn, could have been "the other mind" that Waite is concerned could have contaminated Colman Smith's ideas for the cards with "floating images." Waite took the vows of secrecy around the Golden Dawn initiation rites seriously. He recalls having to "spoon feed" Colman Smith symbols he had acquired through his own extensive esoteric research into the Priestess card, the Fool, the Hanged Man, and the nineteen other cards of the Major Arcana, just as if she were an artistically inclined baby.

Furthermore, Waite's comments hinge on his belief that he alone could interpret the cards, as "their Symbols—or some at least among them—were gates which opened on realms of vision beyond occult dreams." Waite's blindness to Colman Smith's own ability to construct symbolic gates that could open portals into visionary dreams led him to leave her relatively alone with the fifty-six cards of the Minor Arcana. The result is that the deck she created was the first, since the Sola Busca deck in the fifteenth century, to include a Minor Arcana with pictorial scenes illustrating the cards' meanings.

I argue that she began work on the deck much earlier than previously thought, likely in 1908, and incorporated important elements and symbolism from her "music pictures" from the 1907–08 period. There are many examples of this, but the two I focus on are her extensive use of the Rückenfigur technique, or a central figure positioned with their back to the viewer, through which she conveys a range of emotions from joy to contemplation to pain, and the symbolism of the white tower. Drawing on the nexus of meanings associated with the Tower card, she associates the building with systems of oppression that need to be destroyed.

Like the vast majority of the male Anglo-Americans Colman Smith encountered during her life, Waite completely underestimated her ability to interpret, create, and synthesize meaning. To some extent, this was a natural outgrowth of the gendered climate of the early twentieth century. Although the occult revival was more forward-thinking and egalitarian than the norm, with many individuals supporting women's suffrage, the same gender prejudices were prevalent. Women members of the occult revival were seen as passively mystical while men were viewed as actively searching out hidden truths. This reflects Waite's retrospective assessment of Colman Smith. However, despite his later statements, Colman Smith, working with Waite, created a tarot deck with both nuance and playfulness, which has allowed generations of tarot readers to discover individual symbolism and meaning.

This chapter argues that Colman Smith's creative role in the 1909 tarot deck was a catalytic moment in her artistic and spiritual life that both tapped into and helped fuel her growing feminism. It is significant that as Colman Smith was creating the tarot designs, she was also becoming more active in the women's suffrage movement. During the 1909–13 period, she contributed multiple posters and cartoons to the Suffrage Atelier, was jailed at least once for her suffrage activities, and helped working-class suburban women in getting financial assistance to attend a London rally. Colman Smith's work on the tarot deck helped her to imbue her suffrage posters with symbolism. This culminated in the development of a symbolic lexicon for the depiction of women in her "musical vision" paintings. Drawing on years of mythological study, including, but not limited to, Afro-Jamaican Anansi tales, Cornish pixie tales, and Irish folklore, Colman Smith created a complex symbolic system involving women as waves, mountains, vegetation, clouds, and, increasingly, trees. In doing this, however, she drew on subtle overtones of meaning to create her own distinct symbols rather than rely on traditional mythological scenes like many of her male contemporaries. In this way, she closely resembled William Blake, an artist she admired, and an important influence on Britain's occult revival.

Blake's Mysticism and Influence on Colman Smith

Blake, the well-known painter and poet, is today one of the towering figures in British mysticism. A radical in both religion and politics, he regarded the French Revolution highly and sought similar changes in religious thought.[5] Blake followed a unique type of radical Gnostic Christianity that led him to become interested in communing with spirits. In the 1780s he discovered the writings of Emanuel Swedenborg, a philosopher, scientist, and mystic, and was drawn to both Swedenborg's teachings on angels and his description of the spirit world. Blake praised Swedenborg on several occasions and was a founding member of the London New Church, which was made up of Swedenborg's followers. The influence of Swedenborg's teachings is found throughout Blake's poetry, prose, and visual art.[6] Although Blake took issue with a number of Swedenborg's teachings and stopped attending services, the Swedenborgians were key champions of his work after his death.[7] Blake was also fascinated by the occult. He regularly attended séances, frequently entered trances to converse with spirits, and several of his poems are infused with Hermetic and Kabbalistic ideas.[8] So familiar was Blake with esoteric tradition that Yeats thought that he had "received initiation into an order of Christian Kabbalists, then established in London and known as 'The Hermetic Students of the G[olden] D[awn].'"[9]

Colman Smith was likely first exposed to Blake by her maternal grandparents. Samuel and Pamelia Colman were Swedenborgians, who had joined the Boston Society of the New Jerusalem on April 7, 1833. Colman Smith likely attended Swedenborgian services with her parents in Manchester and while visiting her maternal relatives in Brooklyn.[10] In 1841 Samuel Colman's printing firm published Swedenborg's *Writings*, as well as excerpts from his *Apocalypse Examined*.[11] Colman's New York store also sold many editions of Swedenborg's works along with the *New Jerusalem Magazine*.[12] As late as 1850 Pamelia Colman, who published under the name Mrs. Samuel Colman, wrote *The Innocence of Childhood*, which contained "fairly direct references to Swedenborg's teachings," and was advertised and reviewed in several Swedenborgian periodicals.[13]

Pamelia Colman also published nine different poems from Blake's *Songs of Innocence* in four separate publications, several of which included illustrations based on Blake's drawings in his illuminated originals.[14] As Raymond Deck explains, "Taken together, these printings constitute a remarkable 'edition' of

Blake's poems, both for their text and for their accompanying illustrations."[15] A Christmas gift book that Pamelia Colman edited, *The Little Keepsake for 1844*, which was jointly published by Samuel Colman and T. H. Carter, included Blake's "A Dream" and "A Cradle Song," while the July 1844 edition of the *Boys' and Girls' Library* contained "The Lamb," and a small Christmas gift book, *The Child's Gem for 1845*, featured "Little Boy Found."[16] Her reproductions of Blake's work contain relatively minor changes in capitalization, punctuation, and word choice but they are unmistakably his poems.[17]

Although the extent of Colman Smith's childhood exposure to Blake is unclear, it is likely that she perused some of her grandmother's books and periodicals on her visits to her Brooklyn relatives and had, at least, a passing acquaintance with his work. This increased once she returned to England in the spring of 1900 and met Yeats, who had recently finished a three-volume work on Blake with former fellow Theosophist Edwin Ellis.[18] As discussed in Chapter 3, Colman Smith consulted with Yeats about the possibility of publishing an illustrated edition of Blake's work through her Green Sheaf Press, but it never materialized.[19] A few months later, she wrote to her friend Alfred Bigelow Paine that she had recently visited an exhibition of Blake's art in London and was entranced: "I never knew his colour was so rich!"[20] She goes on to state that she hoped to obtain permission to reproduce a few paintings through her Green Sheaf Press, referencing a possible introduction by Oxford professor Frederick York Powell. However, Powell died shortly after and the edition never materialized.[21]

Gender Disparities within the Occult Revival

By the end of the nineteenth century, occultism in Britain had permeated into many facets of personal and public life to an extent only previously seen in the sixteenth century.[22] As Christine Ferguson notes, "This revival was characterized by a flourishing of popular interest, if not necessarily widespread belief, in forms of knowledge considered to lie beyond the fold of scientific rationalism or contemporary Judeo-Christian orthodoxy, including magic, mesmerism, spirit communication, alchemy, astrology, ancient or non-Western religions, palmistry and reincarnation, to name just a few" of the movement's varied influences.[23] Varied in practice and eclectic in doctrine, the occult revival was non-hierarchal and diffuse.[24]

The origins of this movement can be traced to the receding tide of popular religion in England and western Europe that began around 1750 and accelerated steadily as the forces of secularism gained ground. Concurrently, mesmerism, astrology, and spiritualism experienced a steady increase. The rise of spiritualism was especially pronounced in mid-nineteenth-century England and advanced with the founding of the theosophy movement. Helena Petrovna Blavatsky (known as Madame Blavatsky), a Russian émigré, originally founded the Theosophical Society in the United States in 1875, but the movement soon spread to India and then to England in 1887.[25] Blavatsky herself relocated to England in 1887 and was the source of a great deal of the public's growing occult interest.

An important element in the occult revival's domination of the cultural imagination during the *fin de siècle* was the rapid emergence of occult topics into public discourse. In contrast to the clandestine diffusion of occultism during the Middle Ages, it was now a very open affair, occurring in the realm of public deliberation and popular culture and becoming widely disseminated through the periodical press and the publishing industry.[26] And women, especially unmarried women like Colman Smith, who were pursuing professional careers, entered the public sphere in record numbers in the late nineteenth and early twentieth centuries.

Women had always been disproportionately associated with the spread of occult practices, going back at least to the early modern period.[27] Large numbers of women participated in esoteric organizations in the early twentieth century, at least in part because these groups were more receptive to the women's suffrage movement and unorthodox ways of thinking more broadly.[28] In *The Divine Feminine: Theosophy and Feminism in England*, Joy Dixon explains that "Esoteric religion—what we might now call alternative or New Age spirituality—provided a crucial space for the articulation of this unorthodox vision."[29] Despite this close interrelationship, most accounts focus on either the suffrage movement or the occult revival, rather than their intersection.[30] As a result, the contributions of individuals like Colman Smith, who were involved in both, have been minimized as they have been viewed as separate entities.[31]

While the links between women's involvement in esoteric religion and feminist politics are clear, it is important to keep in mind that even the occult revival was subject to gender-related tensions. As Dixon points out,

> The spiritual was itself a site of struggle; feminist versions of theosophy or esotericism existed in tension with other, often explicitly antifeminist interpretations of the esoteric tradition. Women's spirituality emerged from these struggles as a precarious, contradictory, and unstable formation; its mobilization within feminist political culture was also inflected by these struggles.[32]

This was doubly true for a woman like Colman Smith, who was consistently raced as an indeterminate other. Moreover, the contested environment Dixon describes reflects Colman Smith's involvement in the Hermetic Order of the Golden Dawn, especially her relationships with Yeats and Waite, and is one of the chief reasons why the tarot deck she created was not associated with her name until relatively recently. Yeats's close mentorship of Colman Smith appears to have cooled in the year after the break in the Hermetic Order of the Golden Dawn, and her decision to follow Waite to his Independent and Rectified Order rather than join Yeats in the *Stella Matutina*.

The Hermetic Order of the Golden Dawn

The fraught and quickly changing relationships between the sexes in the late nineteenth century also affected the Hermetic Order of the Golden Dawn, one of the most important groups of the occult revival, and the first to allow men and women to perform rituals together. The group was founded in October 1887 by three leading British occultists: Samuel Liddell "McGregor" Mathers, William Wynn Westcott, and William Robert Woodman, who were all Freemasons and members of the esoteric Christian group Societas Rosicruciana in Anglia (S.R.I.A.).[33] Westcott, who was also a member of the Theosophical Society and the deputy coroner of London, began the group after allegedly receiving an ancient manuscript written in cipher that detailed quasi-masonic rituals that became the basis for the group's co-ed magical rituals.[34] The Golden Dawn differed from other Hermetic organizations, such as the Rosicrucians and Freemasons, in allowing women as well as men to join on an equal basis.[35] Chic and Sandra Tabatha Cicero contend that Westcott invented both the cipher manuscripts and Anna Sprengel, a German woman who allegedly chartered the Isis Urania Temple of the Golden Dawn, in order to provide both ancient magical and feminine support for involving women.[36] As Ferguson has noted, "[w]omen certainly had access to forms of spiritual authority and power within the revival that they could not otherwise attain, but frequently, if not always, this accreditation was staked on their association with male proxies or senior adepts."[37] These unequal gender dynamics were especially true for a "self-consciously elitist" group like the Hermetic Order of the Golden Dawn, which was grappling with "changing notions of class and race."[38] Women were involved in all levels of the Golden Dawn, but in the early twentieth century the group fractured due to power conflicts and scandals that often broke down along gender lines.

In addition to the principles of occult science, Golden Dawn practitioners learned the magic of Hermes, sometimes known as Trismegistus, Thoth, and Mercurius. As Mary Greer notes, "The students' goal was to unite the Will with the highest Self,"[39] where "Will" was the intention of an individual's "highest, divine, or God-like Self" that was free of selfishness and achieved through an imaginative use of the senses.[40] Influences on the group were diverse and included ancient Egyptian religion, Christianity, Freemasonry, the Kabbalah, paganism, and theurgy.[41] Membership was divided into three orders and ten grades. The first or Outer Order consisted of four grades where initiates studied spiritual philosophy.[42] Initially, this was the extent of the Golden Dawn's levels. However, after Woodman's death in 1891, Westcott abruptly stopped receiving letters from Sprengel, disassociating himself from the management of the Temple. Mathers then began the second or Inner Order, in which members learned practical magic such as divining and scrying.[43] Mathers subsequently told select members of the Inner Order that he had been contacted by a group of Secret Chiefs who had shared information on alchemy and sexual magic. While several women including Moina Mathers (née Bergson), Florence Farr, Maud Gonne, and Annie Horniman were initiated into the Secret Chiefs, the majority of the members of the Golden Dawn, especially those in the second and third Orders, were male.[44] After Westcott officially severed ties with the group in 1896, Mathers was left in complete control, but operated the group remotely from Paris. Farr was named the Chief Adept in Anglia and soon began to question Mathers's authority, and especially why only he was allowed to correspond with the Secret Chiefs.[45] The group began to fracture in the early years of the twentieth century, first over the initiation of the notorious Aleister Crowley, and then over a very public scandal. An American con artist couple deceived Mathers into believing that the woman was the incarnation of Anna Sprengel and stole secret Golden Dawn papers; after a notorious trial in England, they were convicted of multiple crimes.[46]

Colman Smith's initiation occurred in the midst of this turmoil. She likely joined the group because she was friends with several members, including Yeats, Farr, and W. T. Horton. She was inducted with Ethel Fryer-Fortescue, who was a relative of Ellen Terry.[47] Census records from 1901 reveal that Colman Smith was living with the Davis family at 14 Milborne Grove, The Boltons, in South Kensington.[48] Fryer-Fortescue, whose maiden name was Davis, was also residing in this house.[49] The friendship between the two continued for several years, and in 1904 they began the Green Sheaf Press and Green Sheaf store together.[50] Colman Smith took as her magical motto in the Golden Dawn *Quod tibi id alium*, "what is to others, is to you."[51] This saying, a version of the biblical Golden Rule, is fitting, as she was always quick to drop pretense and formality, focusing instead on fairness in all things. Although the reasons why Colman Smith decided to join the Golden Dawn are unknown, she had been interested in spiritualism and alternative forms of religion since her childhood exposure to Swedenborgianism and Obeah. As a young artist, Colman Smith began signing her work PCS, with the letters intertwined on a caduceus. She began this practice in 1898, and she continued to do so for the rest of her life. The impetus for this distinctive signature is not known, but it is likely she knew of its link to Hermes—the winged messenger of the gods who carried a serpent-entwined staff—and might have become interested in the Golden Dawn, at least in part, because it was devoted to the study of his magic. Similarly, the group's focus on the imaginative use of the will might also have appealed to her.

During her time in South Kensington, Colman Smith's rooms—she also rented a room in the adjoining house for her studio—became the site of a weekly gathering of artists, writers, actors, and other Chelsea bohemians. According to Arthur Ransome's *Bohemia in London* (1907), Colman Smith and her guests drank opal hush, claret mixed with lemonade "so that a beautiful amethystine foam rose shimmering to the brim."[52] James Joyce lampooned this drink, which is believed to have been created by Yeats, in *Ulysses*. In the "Lestrygonians" episode, Leopold Bloom thinks, "What do you think really of that hermetic crowd, the opal hush poets: A. E. the master-mystic? That Blavatsky woman started it."[53] In this brief aside, Bloom conflates Madame Helena Blavatsky, who founded the Theosophical Society in 1875, with the Hermetic Order of the Golden Dawn. George Russell (AE) was a follower of theosophy and a contributor to *The Green Sheaf*, while Yeats and Colman Smith were members of the Golden Dawn, which is likely how she became acquainted with the drink. Her visitors' book reveals that many members of the Golden Dawn, including Farr, Fortescue, Horton, and Yeats, attended these weekly gatherings during which Colman Smith recited her Afro-Jamaican Anansi stories and poems by Yeats.[54] This also demonstrates the interconnectedness between Colman Smith's various pursuits, and how many of Yeats's Masquers, such as Colman Smith, Farr, and Horton, were also members of the Golden Dawn.

Colman Smith does not discuss her involvement in the Golden Dawn in any extant letters; as a result, her views on the group and why she did not advance beyond the Zelator grade are unknown. As discussed above, Waite later characterized her decision to remain at an introductory level as lack of interest or even an inability to grasp the depth and complexity of mystical thought. I think it is far more probable that Colman Smith did not advance because she was pursuing other interests—editing little magazines, operating the Green Sheaf Press, painting musical visions, designing theater costumes and sets, and performing Afro-Jamaican Anansi stories—and rejected the male atmosphere that characterized the Golden Dawn. Maybe most importantly, she accepted Waite's invitation to design the tarot deck because it gave her another opportunity to showcase her work.

By 1903 the Isis-Urania Temple of the Hermetic Order of the Golden Dawn had broken up into feuding factions, which resulted in a split into three separate and independent groups. Waite characterized the group during this period as "the pseudo-occult."[55] Those who remained loyal to Mathers formed the Order of the Alpha et Omega Temple, while Waite eventually took over as head of the original Isis-Urania Temple. Yeats, R. W. Felkin, and other London members created a new *Stella Matutina* or Morning Star order that emphasized magical rituals. Many of the original Golden Dawn members, including Colman Smith, stayed with Waite's group, which he renamed the Independent and Rectified Rite of the Golden Dawn, which placed its focus on mysticism over magic.

During the approximately three years of Colman Smith's close friendship and mentorship with Yeats, both within and beyond the Golden Dawn, one of the key interests they shared was a deep love and appreciation for the work of Blake. The occult revival was inspired by the work of Paracelsus, Swedenborg, Plato, Plotinus, Dante, Blake, Shelley, and Balzac, with Swedenborg and Blake being two of the most important influences.[56] Colman Smith was first introduced to both of these figures during childhood. After her return to England in 1900 and subsequent friendship with Yeats, the work of the latter was to become especially important in her artistic and spiritual life.

For Yeats, Swedenborg was the prototype for spiritual revelations and the model for Blake, who, as Leon Surette notes, "was the most important recipient of astral communications in English literary history prior to Yeats."[57] Surette goes on to assert that while Swedenborg was content to restrict his spiritual communications to angels, Blake, Swedenborg's "disciple and antagonist," was not.[58] According to Yeats, this desire to associate with the full range of spirits consumed Blake: "he carried it to a passion and made it the foundation of his thought."[59] This is also, Yeats argues, why Blake, in his rejection of authority and valuation of "the antiquities of all peoples," was far more of a visionary then Swedenborg.[60] Yeats yokes this desire to connect with the full spectrum of the spirit world both to the increased interest in séances, which Yeats himself frequently participated in during the *fin-de-siécle* period, and the idea of fairyland in Irish mythology. "It is the other world of the early races, of those whose dead are in the rath or faery hill, of all who see no place of reward and punishment but a continuance of the life of cattle, sheep, markets and war."[61] In this way, Yeats emphasizes that the links between the past and present, the living and the spirit realm, are most visible to "the folk," or the common people.[62]

Although Yeats first published his essay on Swedenborg, Blake, and the spirit world in 1914, he became interested in the connections between them during the period when he was in close communication with Colman Smith.[63] It is likely that Yeats saw links between Blake, Colman Smith, and himself in their shared "imaginative energy" and rejection of authority.[64] As discussed in Chapter 3, Yeats viewed Colman Smith, because of her lack of education, her gender, and ambiguities regarding her race, as much closer to the "common people"—and by extension the spirit world—than a "scholar" like himself.

As we have seen, Colman Smith possessed what Yeats called the "power of vision," despite the fact it went largely unrecognized and misunderstood during her lifetime, not least because many at the time felt that those qualities could not reside in a young woman of ambiguous race. An exception to this was *New York Sun* art critic James Huneker. He readily admitted Colman Smith to "the favored choir" of William Blake and his mystics in his review of her first exhibition at Stieglitz's 291 gallery.[65] The connections between Colman Smith and Blake are remarkable. Like Blake, Colman Smith rejected the status quo and attempted to capture realms beyond the physical through her "music pictures." Blake often painted from mental images, if not actual visions. As he wrote to a friend on August 23, 1799, "This world is a world of imagination and vision. I see everything I paint in this world, but everybody does not see alike."[66] Both viewed the world as imbued with imagination. This mindset fundamentally inspired all Colman Smith's art. The dearth of people who shared her perspective negatively impacted her critical and commercial success during her lifetime.

Colman Smith began the second number of *The Green Sheaf* with an excerpt from Blake that emphasizes their shared interests:

> The world of imagination is the world of eternity. It is the divine bosom into which we shall go after the death of the vegetated body.
> The world of imagination is infinite and eternal, whereas the world of generation or vegetation is finite and temporal.
> There exist in that eternal world the eternal realities of everything which we see reflected in this vegetable glass of nature.[67]

The passage, which first appeared in Blake's 1809 Descriptive Catalogue that accompanied his now lost painting, *A Vision of the Last Judgement*, was included in the second volume of Yeats and Ellis's treatise on Blake.[68] Very Swedenborgian in spirit, it makes explicit the connections between the spirit world and the imagination, which Yeats highlights in his essay, as well as providing an interesting lens through which to view Colman Smith's "music pictures": they provide windows into an eternal, infinite world of imagination.

The Tarot, Arthur Edward Waite, and the 1909 Smith-Waite Deck

The search for connections between the eternal world and Blake's "vegetable glass of nature" is also at root the crux of the tarot deck. As Waite noted, "the Tarot is a research in symbolism; its study is a mystic experiment; and though it has been, is and will be used for divination, it belongs to another realm and began therein."[69] It makes sense that Colman Smith, who from 1907 onward was firmly invested in her "music pictures," would be interested in connections between the spiritual and physical worlds. Tarot decks were originally used as playing cards and later for fortune telling. The cups correspond to the hearts, the wands to the diamonds, the swords to the spades, and the pentacles to the clubs in the better-known suits of playing cards.[70] The earliest known tarot decks are the Boiardo Viti and the Sola Busca decks from northern Italy in the late fifteenth century.[71] The Sola Busca deck is the only known example of a deck with a fully illustrated Major and Minor Arcana before the Smith-Waite deck.[72] Commissioned by a wealthy Milanese family, the Sola Busca deck "is characterized by a great precision of outline; it is neatly cut with regular parallels and cross-hatching."[73] The British Museum had maintained photographic copies of the deck since 1907 and engravings since 1845, and Colman Smith consulted them while formulating her designs.[74] The influence appears most strongly in regards to the fifty-six cards that comprise the Minor Arcana, and like the Sola Busca deck, the Smith-Waite deck includes detailed outlines throughout.[75] However, as discussed in Chapter 2, outlining in black was a feature of Colman Smith's work from the 1890s onward, especially in illustrative projects.

Before discussing the Smith-Waite deck in more detail, I will briefly trace the history of the tarot that influenced its publication. The occult history of the tarot dates to the late eighteenth century and the publication of Antoine Court de Gébelin's *The Primitive World*, which traces the tarot cards to Egyptian priests and the ancient *Book of Thoth* or the *Book of Thrice Great Hermes*. This esoteric learning was then brought to ancient Rome, and, after the fall of Rome, the popes allegedly preserved this knowledge in secret and brought it to Avignon with them in the Middle Ages. De Gébelin was also responsible for the mystical connection of the tarot's twenty-one trumps and the Fool with the twenty-two letters of the Hebrew alphabet.[76] In the late eighteenth century, Jean-Baptiste Alliette, known as Etteilla, expounded the importance of the occult and explained the first use the tarot deck in a specifically divinatory context, as well as writing about the interrelationship between the tarot, astrology, and the four classical elements and humors.[77] Many of Etteilla's divinatory meanings were used by Mathers for the Golden Dawn tarot and by Waite for the 1909 deck.[78] However, in an essay advertising his new deck, Waite disparaged Etteilla, stating that the earlier deck's "symbolism has been confused" by Etellia's "reveries," as his zeal surpassed both his discretion and his occult knowledge.[79] Waite attempted to distance himself, and the Smith-Waite deck, from the Ettellia deck, which was widely available in France, asserting both his own superior mystical learning and discretion. When coupled with his assessment of Colman Smith, Waite's comments suggest that he had a pattern of dismissing the contributions of others that were important to his creative process.

The last major influence on the Smith-Waite deck was Éliphas Lévi, an ordained Roman Catholic deacon and radical socialist in nineteenth-century France, who was the first to amalgamate tarot, astrology, and the Catholic tradition.[80] Despite the long-term hostility between Roman Catholicism and tarot—and the occult more broadly—in the nineteenth century there emerged a mystical Catholic tradition that overlapped with at least some of the interests of the occult revival, including members of the Golden Dawn. This mystical interconnection between the Roman Catholic tradition and the occult fascinated Waite. His mother had converted to Roman Catholicism after the death of her husband, and raised her children in the faith. Although Waite did not practice as an adult, he became increasingly fascinated by what he termed the "Secret Tradition" of Western Christian mysticism of which tarot was a part.[81] In the introduction to *The Pictorial Key to the Tarot* (1911), Waite outlines his understanding of the importance of the cards:

> The Tarot embodies symbolical presentations of universal ideas, behind which lie all the implicits of the human mind, and it is in this sense that they contain secret doctrine … this doctrine has always existed—that is to say, has been excogitated in the consciousness of an elect minority; that it has been perpetuated in secrecy from one to another and has been recorded in secret literatures, like those of Alchemy and Kabalism; that it is contained also in those Instituted Mysteries of which Rosicrucianism offers an example near to our hand in the past, and Craft Masonry a living summary, or general memorial, for those who can interpret its real meaning.[82]

As Melinda Boyd Parsons has noted, this interest in a secret tradition was a result of Waite's fascination with the Grail Legend, which was the subject of his *The Hidden Church of the Holy Grail*, which was published while he was working with Colman Smith.[83] However, this interest in a secret order began much earlier and reflects Waite's belief that there was a hidden form of Christianity, beyond what was conveyed through the Bible or taught by the Church, which had been transferred verbally from generation to generation and had become scattered in various secret societies and hermetic texts. This led him to join the Hermetic Order of the Golden Dawn in 1891. He subsequently joined multiple different groups, including the Freemasons, Societas Rociscruciana in Anglia, the Knights Templar, the Knights of Malta, the Red Cross of Constantine, and the Swedenborgian Rite, among many others.[84] His quest to uncover the secret tradition also led him to the work of the eighteenth-century French Catholic mystic Louis Claude de Saint-Martin, the subject of Waite's 1901 biography, whose thought was centrally influenced by Emanuel Swedenborg.[85]

A shared interest in Roman Catholicism was one of several connections between Colman Smith and Waite. Colman Smith converted to Roman Catholicism in July 1911, approximately eighteen months after finishing the Smith-Waite deck. Conversion is a lengthy process, and she likely began it either while she was drafting the designs or right after their completion. I contend that her Roman Catholicism was more a continuation of the mystical and occult interests that she held from childhood than a renunciation of them. While Colman Smith likely had many influences in choosing to become a Roman Catholic, including Edy Craig's partner Christopher St. John, who also converted during this period, Waite may have been an influence in exposing her to Catholic mysticism. Even after he stopped actively practicing the Catholic faith and moved into Freemasonry, Waite continued to have a strong attraction to the liturgy and mysticism of the Church and thought Christian mysticism was a path into the same veiled world as the tarot. He speculated in *The Pictorial Key to the Tarot* that its rich symbolism might have originated "as a secret symbolical language of the Albigensian [Gnostic Christian] sects."[86] Waite also placed the tarot in a wider matrix that included the Holy Grail legends and the Arthurian romances. Colman Smith remained a devout Roman Catholic for the rest of her life but, as I will discuss in the Epilogue, her faith was encompassing. At her death, her Bible was found to contain drawings of both tarot symbols and religious iconography.

Another key link between Colman Smith and Waite was their shared outsider status. Both were American by birth but spent most of their lives in England. Waite was born in Brooklyn on October 2, 1857, but after the death of his father at sea, his mother returned with her small children to her native England, where Waite spent the rest of his life. R. A. Gilbert, Waite's biographer, asserts that Waite's parents were unmarried and that his mother, Emma Lovell, faced disapproval from her family after her return home.[87] It

Feminist Symbolic Art 191

is fascinating to consider whether Colman Smith and Waite ever discussed these questions about their parentage or shared outsider status.

What exactly spurred Waite and Colman Smith to collaborate on the iconic tarot deck is unknown, but it resulted in a "marriage" of their unique skill sets. As Gertrude Moakley, an early investigator of the collaboration, has noted, neither appeared to realize the deck's lasting impact:

> How often this happens! The little thing which is just "tossed off" turns out to be the epitome of all its author stood for, still alive and fresh when all of his work has begun to smell of dried lavender. And when a brilliant man and woman like Waite and Pamela Smith work together, his masculinity and her femininity are sometimes flint and steel to produce new brilliance.[88]

While Waite emphasized the importance of his occult scholarship in the tarot project, it is obvious that it was also the product of Colman Smith's psychic abilities and artistic skill. An unsigned drawing from her visitors' book depicts Colman Smith, wearing a pointed hat bedecked with the moon and stars, and Waite bending over an image on her desk, presumably designs for the tarot images. An angry demon faces them in mid-air, possibly the original inhabitant of the skull that is on the desk, as a bat flutters off to the side (Figure 5.1).[89] In a December 1909 *Occult Review* essay advertising the deck's publication, Waite explained that as "the Tarot … is in the air," he "embraced an opportunity which has been somewhat of the unexpected kind and have interested a very skillful and original artist in the proposal to design a set."[90] Much more positive in his assessment of Colman Smith than in his later account, Waite points out that "in addition to her obvious gifts, [she] has some knowledge of Tarot values; [and] has lent a sympathetic ear to my proposal to rectify the symbolism by reference to channels of knowledge which are not in the open day."[91] This resulted "in a marriage of art and symbolism for the production of a true Tarot under one of its aspects."[92] However, like most marriages, the individual contributions of both parties became blurred. Colman Smith contributed more than just the art; she imbued the deck, especially the Minor Arcana, with her own intuitive gifts and symbolism.

The timeframe for the completion of the tarot project is unclear, but it has generally been viewed as quite abbreviated. Each of the seventy-eight

Figure 5.1 Unsigned, undated sketch of Pamela Colman Smith and A. E. Waite from Colman Smith's visitors' book.
Reproduced by permission of Stuart R. Kaplan, U.S. Games, Inc.

cards in the deck, plus two additional decorative cards, had to be designed by hand. As discussed in Chapter 4, Colman Smith spent the spring of 1909 in the U.S. for her last show at Stieglitz's 291 gallery. She returned to London at the end of May and is believed to have then begun work on the designs in earnest.[93] Since she had to complete the project by late October or very early November for the lithographers, Sprague & Company, to do their work, Colman Smith only had about five months to do her research, consult with Waite, and complete eighty designs.[94] Her November 19, 1909 letter to Stieglitz discussed above confirms the end of this timeline.[95] The December 1909 *Occult Review* issue that announced the deck included black-and-white versions of several of the cards. Ralph Shirley, the journal's editor who was also the director of William Rider & Sons, the publisher of the deck, announced that the tarot would go on sale that month.[96] However, there is no reference in any extant document from Colman Smith or Waite as to when she began to design the cards, and it is highly likely she began to design them before her 1908 trip to New York.

My exploration of the connections between Colman Smith's musical visions and tarot iconography extends work by several critics into how she drew on people and places that she knew when creating designs for the deck. Boyd Parsons has written most extensively on this, pointing out Colman Smith's use of androgynous figures on several of the cards, her insertion of portraits of some of her friends into the deck—notably Ellen Terry and Edy Craig—and her development of Catholic symbolism within the cards.[97] The latter is best seen on the X of Swords, where the figure appears to be impaled on ten swords, but a close examination reveals that their right hand is making the symbol of Christ Pantocrator, the risen Christ almighty.[98] Marcus Katz and Tali Goodwin have noted connections between the landscape depicted in the deck and specific locations in the south of England, especially the area surrounding Terry's Smallhythe House and nearby Tower Cottage in Winchelsea, where Colman Smith stayed during the summer and fall of 1909 when she was completing the project.[99] Katharine Cockin has also noted that Colman Smith's depiction of the Devil's wings—"the anatomically correct depiction of the bat's thumb, the hook-like structure half-way along the wing"—closely resembles her caricature of Bram Stoker, or as she termed him Brammy Joker, in formal evening dress and a bat-like cloak.[100]

Connections Between the "Music Paintings" and the Tarot Deck

A close examination of Colman Smith's musical visions from the 1907–08 period reveals several key links with the Smith-Wait tarot deck. I contend that Colman Smith likely had conversations with Waite about the deck as early as 1908, if not before, and incorporated tarot iconography into her paintings during this period, as well as including important symbols and techniques from these paintings into the tarot deck. An untitled "Sketch for Glass," which is dated to 1908 and held in the Alfred Stieglitz/Georgia O'Keeffe Archive at Yale University, shows that Colman Smith created at least one full-color painting that centrally includes tarot symbolism much earlier than previously thought.[101] The image may have been used as part of an advertising display for either Colman Smith's 1908 or 1909 shows at Stieglitz's 291 gallery (Figure 5.2). The sketch depicts an androgynous person clothed in flowing patchwork gray and brown, standing with outstretched arms with their back to the viewer. The rays of a glowing yellow sun—reminiscent of both the Sun and the Moon cards—are visible in the upper quarter of the painting (Figure 5.3). Numerous orbs of glowing light, which call to mind both the drops of light on the Moon card and those that surround the 1907 sketch of Maud Adams as Peter Pan, extend down toward a ground littered with three skulls and numerous stars.[102] The stars are smaller but similar to the ones that adorn the Star card. In the "Sketch for Glass," the figure's outstretched arms appear to embrace the balls of light, like the dog and wolf with upstretched noses on the Moon card, rather than in "Peter Pan," where the figure seems oblivious to their presence. In *The Pictorial Key to the Tarot*, Waite states that the Sun "appears to shed its influence on earth not only by light and heat—like the moon—but by drops of dew. Court de Gebélin termed these tears of gold and pearl."[103] Waite elaborates that the orbs of light on the Moon card are "intellectual light, which is a reflection and beyond it is the unknown mystery."[104] The Sun card does not include these drops of dew, just the rays emanating from the sun, which disappear into a patch of cheerful sunflowers. The earlier "Sketch for Glass" more readily conveys the sun's influence on humans, with the orbs, which here resemble tongues of fire, radiating from the sun and seemingly transmitting both influence and knowledge to the person with outstretched arms. Kathleen Pyne sees the individual as analogous to Colman Smith as "she

FEMINIST SYMBOLIC ART 195

Figure 5.2 Pamela Colman Smith, "Sketch for Glass," 1908.
Courtesy Beinecke Rare Book and Manuscript Library, Yale University

Figure 5.3 The Sun and Moon cards from the Smith-Waite tarot deck. Reproduced by permission of Stuart R. Kaplan, U.S. Games, Inc.

triumphantly faces the sun ... Turning her back on the past, which is figured as a death, the seeker is reborn into a state of spiritual enlightenment."[105] Furthermore, the lavender background of the "Sketch for Glass" calls to mind the pastel backgrounds of the 1909 tarot deck, which are predominantly yellow, blue, and dove gray.

Androgynous figures clothed in flowing garments with their backs to the viewer occur several times in Colman Smith's "music pictures" from the 1907–08 period, suggesting that she was fascinated by individuals turning inward and away from the public, whether in release, introspection, or pain. The technique, known as Rückenfigur or "figure from the back" in German, was popularized by the German Romanticist Caspar David Friedrich in the early nineteenth century, but dates as far back as Giotto in the fourteenth century, and was occasionally utilized by Raphael and Vermeer among others. The positioning creates tension as it both attracts viewers into a location and emphasizes the barrier between them and the scene.[106] As Elizabeth Prettejohn has pointed out, "The Rückenfigur is unlike any previous figure in the one crucial respect: he (or she…) is not just a represented object in a picture, but also the embodied subject of the aesthetic experience of the picture—we look *with*, rather than merely *at*, the Rückenfigur."[107] This focus on looking with the figure is key to both Colman Smith's "music pictures" and the tarot designs. She didn't want viewers to merely gaze at her art but to participate in it and to find a new perspective, often into an imaginative or symbolic world, through the process.

Through her "music pictures," Colman Smith worked out the connections between ideas and images and—consciously or not—developed a symbolic language. As I discuss below, this symbol system is, when taken as a whole, primarily focused on the depiction of female figures. However, during this extremely fertile 1907–09 period, Colman Smith extensively experimented with androgynous figures, including those in the designs for the Smith-Waite deck. In a "Sketch for Glass," the figure appears exultant, wanting to embrace the light streaming from the sun, even if this impulsiveness yields the same outcome—death—that met the skulls scattered around their feet. A 1907 watercolor drawn to an untitled Robert Schumann piece depicts an androgynous figure in similar flowing, dark, ragged robes, also utilizing the Rückenfigur positioning (Figure 5.4).[108] In this piece, the figure is smaller and stands on a low hill overlooking a pale blue sea and a light brown sky. A silvery moon, whose nose and mouth are visible and which is reminiscent of the moon in George Méliès' 1902 silent film *A Trip to the Moon*, looms in the right corner. Similarly, Colman Smith's musical vision inspired by Beethoven's Piano Sonata Pathétique, and created in 1907, prominently features the Rückenfigur technique.[109] A tall figure in a long, dark robe stands with their back to the viewer, gazing down at a mountain and sea dotted with small islands. However, this figure is much more introspective than either of the others, and, in keeping with many of the figures in the musical visions from this period, is depicted in a pose reminiscent of Rodin's *The Thinker*.[110] Another untitled platinotype from the 1907 Stieglitz exhibition shows a similar androgynous individual with raised arms, clothed in a ragged, flowing gown, who is flanked by an androgynous robed and hooded figure holding a sword in the air, and a woman in a long, white flowing gown.[111] The image exudes foreboding,

Figure 5.4 Pamela Colman Smith, untitled watercolor, 1907.
Courtesy Beinecke Rare Book and Manuscript Library, Yale University

even imminent death, as the central figure is poised on a precipice with their hands raised and only partially visible over their shoulders, evoking fear and surrender, rather than the embrace of death in "Sketch for Glass."

Colman Smith's development of a private symbol system carried over into her designs for the tarot deck, especially the cards associated with the Minor Arcana. Waite, in his collaboration with Colman Smith, was primarily focused on the Major Arcana. As he pointed out, "The meanings attributed to the Trumps Major, or Greater Arcana, when taken, as they usually are, apart from the ordinary numbered and court cards, depend upon the worlds or spheres of consciousness to which particular interpretations have referred them."[112] As he posited in the *Occult Review*:

> The question remains whether there is an integral connection between the Greater and Lesser Arcana and in this case how to establish their respective offices in higher Tarot symbolism. If, however, their connection is arbitrary, a separation should be effected, the Lesser Arcana being allocated to their proper place in cartomancy and the Trumps Major to their own, which is to seership of another order.[113]

While Colman Smith and Waite likely discussed the images for the Minor Arcana, it appears she had much more freedom with these cards. This can be seen in the many ways she employs the Rückenfigur technique. Just as with her "music pictures," this positioning can take on several meanings depending on the movement of the figures and the other elements in the design. For example, its use on the X of Cups expresses joy. The card depicts a man and woman standing together with outstretched hands raised to greet a rainbow on which the cups are displayed. The couple's children dance with clasped hands nearby and a red-roofed farm is nestled in leafy trees, flanked by a small stream. The scene calls to mind the woman and child in "The Wind," an illustration from 1901, which was part of a planned but never realized book highlighting the work of Anna Laetitia Barbauld. The image is one of Colman Smith's first uses of the Rückenfigur technique to highlight the mother and son's joy at the billowing clouds.[114] Both of these drawings correspond with Waite's meaning for the X of Cups, which he says represents, "Contentment, repose of the entire heart, [and] the perfection of that state."[115] Another example where Colman Smith's use of Rückenfigur positioning closely correlates with Waite's interpretation is the X of Wands, which depicts a man bent over carrying heavy staves, his body emanating pain and exhaustion. This directly links with the card's chief meaning of oppression.[116]

For many of the Minor Arcana, Colman Smith's design choices increase the multiplicity of meanings in the cards. The figures on the VIII of Cups and the II and III of Wands, which all utilize the Rückenfigur positioning, are introspective, reminiscent of her painting for Beethoven's Sonata Pathétique. Unlike the earlier figures, whose hands are at their sides as they pensively gaze into the distance, all of these figures have one arm out in support, leaning either on one of the wands or on a hiking staff on the VIII of Cups, in order to gain strength for the future.[117] Colman Smith's images roughly correspond with Waite's brief discussion of the divinatory meanings of these cards, but often increase their nexus of meanings. This is especially true of the II of Wands, where Colman Smith's design choices can help shed light on what Waite says can be the dual, conflicting meaning of the card, which can symbolize both a lord overlooking his dominion, and malady and mortification.[118] The globe he holds in his right hand, coupled with the staff he grasps with his left, emphasizes the figure's worry and concern as he contemplates both physical and mental journeys. In this same vein, Colman Smith's use of small, telling details helps imbue the cards with added meanings. Waite asserts that the III of Wands symbolizes trade, commerce, and established strength, stating that the richly dressed figure is male and is surveying his ships, which are visible in the right corner, as they sail off for ports unknown.[119] One of the deck's many examples of androgyny, the figure on the III of Wands could as easily be male as female. They could be gazing at distant ships or staring at a lone figure (a lost love?) in the left-hand corner of the card. The individual's right hand appears to be wearing armor, which could signify conquest or war, either in support of trade or another aim, such as love, hate, or power.

However, it is the Tower card that provides the best example of how Colman Smith fuses tarot iconography with important symbols from her "music pictures" to create a series of references across several cards that she continued to utilize in her paintings well after the completion of the deck. The Tower card features a tall white tower—its crown-like dome already jettisoned—struck by lightning and surrounded by tongues of fire on a dark background (Figure 5.5). It symbolizes impending destructive change, perhaps leading to liberation from former constraints, which, among other

Figure 5.5 The Tower card from the Smith-Waite tarot deck. Reproduced by permission of Stuart R. Kaplan, U.S. Games, Inc.

possibilities, could be the destruction of papal Rome, the Castle of Plutus, God's House, or the Tower of Babel.[120] It can also signify misery, distress, and adversity.[121] However, as Waite noted, the Tower "is assuredly a card of confusion," and "[i]t is idle to indicate that it depicts ruin in all of its aspects."[122] He elaborates: "it is the ruin of the House of Life when evil has prevailed therein, and above all it is the rending of the House of Doctrine. I understand, however, that the reference is to a House of Falsehood."[123] Colman Smith, who hated artifice and deceit of all types, would likely have been interested in this card, especially during this period when she was becoming active in the suffrage movement and wanted to upend the patriarchal system of oppression toward women and create a new, more equal and transparent society based on truth and justice for all.

A very similar white tower on a hill appears in several of Colman Smith's musically inspired paintings from the 1907 period, such as *Castle of Pain*, inspired by Robert Schumann's Piano Concerto in A Minor.[124] Goodwin and

Katz have pointed out that the Tower card in the Smith-Waite deck is close to the Golden Dawn tarot's design for the card.[125] Using the Rückenfigur technique, the canvas focuses on a female figure slumped on the rocks, gazing up at a lone white tower separated from her by a body of water.[126] Male heads and that of a horned figure reminiscent of a bull adorn the rocks behind her. These symbols of patriarchy surround the woman, even in her escape beyond the bonds of society to the natural world, which Colman Smith generally depicts as feminine. The positioning of her body suggests pain and sadness at the obstacles that confront her, even in a beautiful natural landscape. A recently discovered painting, which was inspired by Robert Schumann's *Noveletten*, depicts seemingly the same woman, this time positioned more upright and in less obvious distress, gazing at an identical, but much closer white tower (Figure 5.6). Female faces that are deep in thought peer down at her from the large tree to her right, possibly signifying the ways women working together can surmount injustice. A very similar use of a looming white tower, this time with a mountain in the distance and a woman in deep repose in the foreground, can be seen in Colman Smith's watercolor to Mozart's Sonata in F Major for Violin and Piano, also from 1907 (Figure 5.7).[127] Unlike the others, this painting includes a close-up of her face, showing her closed eyes as she turns away from the tower to face the viewer.[128]

In the Smith-Waite tarot deck, towers appear on several cards, including the background of the V of Cups and the Ace of Wands.[129] Both the Moon and Death cards include two white towers. On the Moon card, two towers flank the conjoined sun and moon as a dog and wolf turn their heads upwards to reach the falling drops of dew. As Waite notes,

> The card represents life of the imagination apart from life of the spirit. The path between the towers is the issue into the unknown. The dog and wolf are the fears of the natural mind in the presence of that place of exit, when there is only reflected light to guide it.[130]

The two towers again appear in the right margin of the Death card, this time on either side of the rising sun, which symbolizes immortality.[131] The dark knight, with his banner of a mystic rose that signifies life, dominates the card.[132] However, like the Tower card, the Death card's meaning is not as ruinous as it first appears and, like the collapse of the tower, old ideas, doctrines, and orders need to die before new ones can emerge.[133]

Figure 5.6 Pamela Colman Smith, *Schumann's Noveletten*.
Private collection

Figure 5.7 Pamela Colman Smith, *Mozart's Sonata in F Major for Violin and Piano, Second Series Duet*, watercolor, 1907.
Courtesy Beinecke Rare Book and Manuscript Library, Yale University

Even well after the completion of the tarot deck in December 1909, white towers appear to have continued to capture Colman Smith's symbolic imagination. Her musical vision inspired by Beethoven's Symphony No. 5 in C minor was displayed at her 1912 exhibition at the Berlin Photographic Company in New York.[134] The painting depicts three women in long flowing robes with hands raised, seemingly in protest, against a shore littered with white towers, symbolizing the pervasive and diffuse influence of the patriarchy. The three central women are standing on and emerging out of the water, and two others are bent double as they return to it, all emphasizing women's close connection with nature. As I will discuss below, women emerging from and disappearing into water are recurring features in many of Colman Smith's "music pictures" from this period. At the right of the canvas, a woman carrying two children, one of the relatively rare examples of maternity in her paintings, gazes at the protesting women over her shoulder. In the foreground, another woman, this one with outstretched arms, invites the viewer into this grouping of female solidarity and dissent.

Involvement in the Suffrage Movement and Poster Designs for the Suffrage Atelier

Taken as a whole, the Smith-Waite tarot deck reflects Colman Smith's involvement in the suffrage movement in 1909. The cards' bright colors evoke the elaborate costumes of the suffrage processionals that she witnessed and possibly took part in.[135] The relatively flat figures outlined in black that adorn the tarot deck also bear similarities to poster designs that Colman Smith produced as part of her work for the Suffrage Atelier. While her contributions to Laurence Housman's 1911 *Anti-Suffrage Alphabet*[136] and membership in Edith Craig's Pioneer Players theater society are relatively well known, the extent of Colman Smith's connection with the suffrage movement has long been unclear. This is primarily because most of her work for the Suffrage Atelier was unsigned, as was the group's practice. My analysis of the organization's posters and cartoons demonstrates that many of the posters show the hallmarks of Colman Smith's style, and that her political involvement in the movement was much more extensive than originally believed. In addition, I have found archival material in the Women's Library at the London School of Economics showing that Colman Smith actively helped working-class women to attend suffrage meetings, contacted suffrage leaders for help on their behalf, and was imprisoned in Royal Holloway for her suffrage activities. I contend that Colman Smith's involvement in the suffrage movement was essential to the development of her feminist consciousness and the evolution of her symbolic depiction of women.

Letters from the 1890s through the 1910s show that Colman Smith was fiercely independent, hated injustice and hypocrisy in all its forms, and believed that women were just as capable and creative as men. These inclinations were likely strengthened through her friendships and artistic partnerships with many like-minded individuals. The most important of Colman Smith's friendships during the early twentieth century were with Ellen Terry, her daughter Edith Craig, and Craig's long-time partner Christopher St. John. As Cockin has noted, "Terry had become an icon as the archetypal 'free woman'" who inspired many to agitate for increased rights.[137] Craig and St. John were actively involved in the British women's suffrage movement. As early as July 1906 St. John's suffrage-related play, *The Decision: A Dramatic Incident*, was performed at Stafford House in the West End.[138] Although the extent of Colman Smith's involvement with the production is unclear, an advertisement for her "afternoon of folklore" with Marion Gordon Kerby did appear in the program.[139] St. John then went on to co-write with Cicely Hamilton at least two suffrage plays during the 1908–09 period: *How the Vote Was Won* and *The Pot and the Kettle*. St. John continued to actively participate in the movement, serving as a committee member for the Catholic Women's Suffrage Society and the Women Writers' Suffrage League, and she was arrested in 1909 for setting fire to a mailbox.[140]

However, it was Craig who "became a highly valued figure in the women's suffrage movement—as a director, performer, leader—and she lent her skills and time to numerous activities and organizations."[141] These included organizing street processions, attending political meetings, selling suffrage newspapers on the street, promoting the publication and performance of women's suffrage plays, and, most importantly, directing several of these plays herself.[142] One of the most important of these was Cicely Hamilton's *A Pageant of Great Women*, which was inspired by a tableau of famous historic women that Craig first put on for the Women's Freedom League.[143] From 1909 to 1911 *A Pageant of Great Women* was performed at least fifteen times throughout England, often as part of large pro-suffrage rallies.[144] In addition to directing, Craig often took the role of nineteenth-century French artist Rosa Bonheur; St. John was often Hannah Snell, an eighteenth-century British woman who dressed as a man and became a soldier.[145] At *A Pageant of Great Women*'s first performance in 1909 at London's Scala Theatre, Terry played eighteenth-century actor Nance Oldfield, the only speaking role among the "great women" and a figure she had often portrayed for the Lyceum Theatre.[146] The cast for the *Pageant* ranged between fifty-three and ninety women, the majority of whom were amateurs, and it is likely that Colman Smith participated at some point, but if so, this is undocumented.[147]

Building on the success of *A Pageant of Great Women*, Craig and St. John formed the Pioneer Players in 1911.[148] With Ellen Terry as its president, the group became London's alternative to the Stage Society, and was committed to producing "the play of ideas."[149] Although the extent of Colman Smith's participation is unclear, she designed the organization's logo and from 1915 to 1918 was on its executive council.[150] She also created cover illustrations for several play programs, designed costumes for a 1918 performance of *An Early English Nativity Play*, assisted in a 1919 staging of Herman Heijerman's *The Rising Sun*, and served as a judge at the Mi-Carême costume ball in 1913 and 1914.[151]

While she was likely introduced to the women's suffrage movement through the work of Craig and St. John, Colman Smith's largest and most substantial contributions were made through the Suffrage Atelier. Formed in the spring of 1909 by Laurence and Clemence Housman—siblings of the poet A. E. Housman—along with Agnes Hope Joseph and Ethel Willis to prepare for the upcoming Women's Social and Political Union (W.S.P.U.) demonstration, the Suffrage Atelier was part of the more militant side of the suffrage movement.[152] By 1910 the group had about one hundred members whose aim, as *Votes for Women* noted, was to create "effective picture propaganda for the suffrage."[153] The group became a major political entity and encouraged professional and non-professional artists to submit work, paying them a small percentage of the profits.[154] This was highly unusual for suffrage organizations which generally relied on voluntary contributions from members.[155] One reason for this was that the group included members from the working classes, as well as the middle and upper classes.[156] The Atelier produced plays in addition to artwork. Craig was a key link in bringing the Suffrage Atelier, and the closely aligned Artist Suffrage League, together with the Actresses' Franchise League.[157]

From its official home in Kensington—a shed at the end of the Housman siblings' garden—the Suffrage Atelier offered a range of activities that focused both on developing women's artistic skills and shaping their suffrage identities.[158] References in *Votes for Women* make clear that this included educational and creative classes, but a significant part of the Atelier's time was devoted to making textile banners for suffrage rallies and processions. Laurence Housman designed many of them while his sister, Clemence, led the teams of workers who embroidered them.[159] As Tara Morton has noted, "Working cooperatively on banners meant that new relationships could be forged between women based upon a commonality of interests in craft and the suffrage, rather than on normative family relations."[160] While it is unclear to what extent, if any, Colman Smith participated in the Atelier's banner-making projects—she did have some experience making banners with Yeats's sisters—we do know that she contributed many posters and cartoons to the printmaking wing of the organization. In addition to selling these print materials, the Suffrage Atelier taught women how to design and print them using traditional materials. As Lisa Tickner has detailed, unlike the Artists' Suffrage League, which relied primarily on commercial lithographs, the Suffrage Atelier used much older engraving processes and, from at least 1910, the group owned its own printing press.[161] It is fascinating to speculate whether Colman Smith, who had owned a press at least during the 1904–06 period when she operated her Green Sheaf Press, was involved in the training of these women and the printing of the materials.

Colman Smith did contribute at least two identifiable postcards, which are signed with her initials rather than the distinctive caduceus that adorns her other work.[162] The most famous is entitled "A Bird in the Hand is Worth Two Mocking-Birds in the Bush." It depicts a woman in profile firmly holding a bird while two sneering birds with human faces—the Liberal Prime Minister Herbert Henry Asquith and the Chancellor of the Exchequer David Lloyd George (identified by helpful tags around their necks)—perch in an ivy tree.[163] Text on the bottom that is attributed to "A. and L.G." states, "If you drop the Conciliation Bill we may do something for you in the dim and speculative future." The historical events that inspired this cartoon appear to have been two comments by the politicians in 1908. On May 27, Asquith, who a week earlier had promised a women's suffrage amendment before the end of the parliamentary session if a Conciliation Bill was dropped, was asked by an anti-suffragist when such an amendment would occur and answered: "My honourable friend has asked me a contingent question with regard to a remote and speculative future."[164] Six months later, on December 5, Asquith addressed members of the W.S.P.U. in the Albert Hall, many of whom had grown frustrated by the delays in his promises and heckled him loudly, leading to forcible ejections.[165] He then repeated his "old worn-out promise" to introduce a Reform Bill and not to oppose a women's suffrage amendment.[166] As Sylvia Pankhurst recalled in *The Suffragette*:

> The women reminded the Chancellor that the Prime Minister had relegated the introduction of the Reform Bill to "the dim and speculative future," but he protested that it would be introduced before the

Parliament came to an end. He was asked how women were to prove the "demand" for their enfranchisement which was one of the conditions of the promise and his reply was, "as the men showed their desire," but the women answered:—"Men burnt down buildings, they shed blood," and, "the Government has ignored our demonstrations." He was questioned as to the second condition that the Votes for Women amendment must be drafted on "democratic lines," but though asked again and again "What is democratic?" he vouchsafed no reply and at last the cry, "Where is the message?" broke out once more and a great white banner, with the inscription, "Be honest," was hung out from one of the boxes.[167]

Pankhurst's recollection of the Albert Hall event emphasizes the growing frustration of the women with a prime minister and chancellor who paid lip service to the importance of women's suffrage but were unwilling to commit fully.

Like the women who draped the banner emblazoned with "Be honest" over the railings, Colman Smith's postcard cuts to the chase. Long-term frustration over male publishers and mentors who had made repeated promises but had not followed through had made her circumspect and weary of the empty assurances of men. Drawing on the adage "a bird in the hand is worth two in the bush," the cartoon urges women not to give in to the angry squawking of the political "birds" who mock the woman with their false promises but, instead, push forward with the Conciliation Bill. The woman's erect posture is noticeable as she firmly holds onto her bird—this one with a Conciliation Bill tag— and keeps it safely away from the Asquith and Lloyd George birds that rest on an incongruous ivy tree, likely chosen because the plant's malignant berries symbolized the politicians' destructive promises. The cartoon enacts the artist Louisa Jopling Rowe's statement that the value of pictorial art in political propaganda is "to hold up to ridicule the Members of Parliament who think that women, having no sense of humour, cannot register votes."[168] In her suffrage cartoons, Colman Smith clearly demonstrates her often biting humor, and, as Marian Sawyer notes of the Suffrage Atelier as a whole, she engaged in "what feminist cartoonists have done ever since—wresting control so that the butt of the joke is no longer the woman, but rather the self-interested arguments used to keep women in their place."[169] For a variety of reasons, the women's suffrage movement did not follow the cartoon's advice, and between 1910 and 1912 three Conciliation Bills, which would have extended the right to vote to more than a million property-owning women in Great Britain, were promised but eventually dropped. Colman Smith's cartoon showcases the clean, unornamented style that was to become the hallmark of her suffrage posters and, as I discuss below, more broadly heralds a shift in her illustrative style. It is also a reflection of her tarot designs, as that project likewise required her to convey messages symbolically in a compressed amount of space.

Another signed postcard also explicitly deals with political wrangling between women's suffrage supporters and Asquith and Lloyd George.[170] Entitled "What May Happen," it depicts a woman in profile turning away a boy who is presenting her with a pie emblazoned "Servants Tax" and a basket labelled L-George and Co. The caption reads, "Take it away, my boy! I've not been consulted in the making of this pie & as it's a present I must pay for, I won't accept it!" (Figure 5.8). The postcard refers to Lloyd George's controversial 1909 budget, which proposed a 20 percent tax on the wealthy but also imposed levies on servants' licenses and dogs. With its similar typeface, copious use of white space, and black shading in the left corner for emphasis, it closely resembles Colman Smith's "A Bird in the Hand" postcard.[171]

Colman Smith's suffrage posters and postcards fall into three main categories: those that support women's suffrage broadly, often with a political bent; those focused on the negative economic impact the inability to vote had on women; and those that detail gender disparities between women and men. Although not explicitly referencing women's suffrage, "The Closed Door," an undated, anonymous Suffrage Atelier postcard that I believe is Colman Smith's work, responded to the proposed 1911 National Insurance Act that based health insurance for all on contributions from employers (Figure 5.9). It depicts female servants being turned away from a hospital by a male doctor because they are not sick enough to be admitted, and by a woman employer because she cannot afford to pay the new tax. A male figure with a Robin Hood style hat and outfit, but wearing bat wings and brandishing an upturned sword, bars their way. The male figure's idiosyncratic wings closely resemble Colman Smith's wings for both the Devil tarot card and her caricature of Bram Stoker, "Brammy Joker."

The injustice of gender disparities is the last major category of Colman Smith's suffrage postcards. "To the Girls' Christmas Tree," which is reminiscent of the style of "A Bird in the Hand," focuses on how gender disparities

Figure 5.8 P. S., "What May Happen," cartoon for the Suffrage Atelier. Courtesy of the Women's Library at the London School of Economics

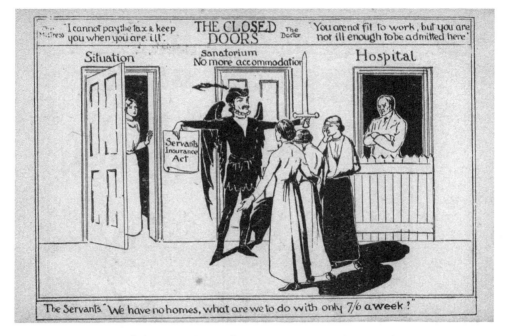

Figure 5.9 "The Closed Door," cartoon for the Suffrage Atelier.
Courtesy of the Women's Library at the London School of Economics

begin in childhood, creating a culture of second-class citizens (Figure 5.10). It depicts older, wealthy men blocking young girls from enjoying a beautifully bedecked Christmas tree. The text at the bottom admonishes the girls—several of whom are visibly wiping away tears—that "We have let you see this nice tree, so go home quietly the boys may want all the presents but perhaps there may be something left for you." The long string of unpunctuated text, which appears to be in the same typeface as "A Bird in the Hand," emphasizes that the girls need to behave and, if they are lucky, they might be rewarded with some of the boys' presents; the boys, the cartoon sardonically implies, will get them whether or not their actions merit rewards.

The last two suffrage cartoons I will discuss are probably the most familiar, even if they are not generally associated with Colman Smith. Created in 1913, they are both anonymously credited to the Suffrage Atelier and highlight the vast gulf between the men who were allowed to vote and the high-achieving, dedicated women who were not. Unlike most of Colman Smith's extant

FEMINIST SYMBOLIC ART 213

Figure 5.10 "To the Girls' Christmas Tree," cartoon for the Suffrage Atelier. Courtesy of the Museum of London

Figure 5.11 "What a Woman may be, and yet not have the Vote," cartoon for the Suffrage Atelier, 1913.
Courtesy of the Museum of London

suffrage postcards, these experimented with spot color. The first, "What a Woman may be, and yet not have the Vote," consists of a relatively simple ten-panel design (Figure 5.11).[172] The top five panels illustrate various professions held by women, including mayor, nurse, mother, doctor or teacher, and factory worker. These are contrasted with the bottom five panels that display "What a Man may have been & yet not lose the Vote." These include a convict, a lunatic, a proprietor of white slaves, a man unfit for service, and a drunkard. Similar to her other postcards from 1913, this does not rely heavily on text, like 'A Bird in the Hand" or "The Girls' Christmas Tree," to convey its meaning, but instead works through the sharp, if humorous, juxtaposition of the accomplished women and the broken or exploitative men. The second color cartoon, "Polling Station," elaborates on the previous work (Figure 5.12).[173] Dispensing with the traditional cartoon panels, this postcard depicts a line of men from all walks of life entering a polling station to cast

FEMINIST SYMBOLIC ART   215

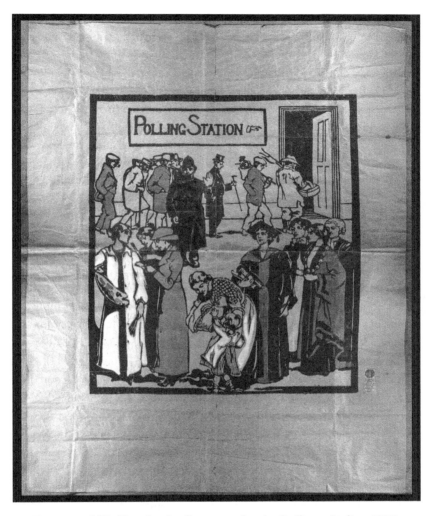

Figure 5.12 "Polling Station," cartoon for the Suffrage Atelier, 1913.
Courtesy of the Women's Library at the London School of Economics

their ballots, while a procession of accomplished women that includes artists, writers, and college professors are prevented from doing the same by a beadle with an upraised palm. Interestingly, the women appear to ignore him. This work features even less text than "What a Woman may be," but still effectively transmits its message that women are intelligent, competent, and, most importantly, deserving of the vote.

In addition to creating these cartoons and posters, Colman Smith was also involved in other suffrage activities. Her name was included on a published Roll of Honor of women arrested for participating in suffrage protests and embroidered on a sash with other women who had spent at least one night in Royal Holloway prison.[174] However, there is no other documentation about this arrest, nor any record of whether Colman Smith was arrested more than once. In addition, a series of 1911 letters between Colman Smith and Philippa Strachey, the secretary of the National Union of Women's Suffrage Societies, demonstrates her commitment to helping working-class women participate in suffrage activities.[175] Colman Smith, who was the secretary of the Plumstead branch of the Women's Co-operative Guild, was attempting to get travel expenses for twelve working-class women who attended a June 2, 1911 Queen's Hall suffrage meeting.[176] She writes that initially a local suffrage leader had assured them that their bus and train fares would be covered; however, at the door of the meeting they were informed that their travel expenses would not be reimbursed, and they would have to appeal to Strachey in writing. When no response was received to Colman Smith's first two letters (only the second of which has been preserved), a "very indignant" Mrs. Kidd, one of the women who had attended the meeting and on whose behalf Colman Smith had written, followed up on July 8. Kidd writes, "Am I to understand that the ladies I came in contact with on that night were all humbugs and would ... by any back door to get out of paying their debts?" She concludes that "if there is no reply to this letter by Thursday," she will contact the newspapers.[177] Interestingly, despite Mrs. Kidd's name and signature, the handwriting is very obviously Colman Smith's, just in a somewhat larger and sloppier variant than her first letter. It is impossible to know whether the real Mrs. Kidd, who was listed as one of the attendees Colman Smith brought with her to the Queen's Hall meeting, dictated the letter or if it was a combined effort. However, its outrage tinged with humor mirrors other letters by Colman Smith. According to carbon copies of internal correspondence included in the file, the women did eventually receive their travel expenses.[178]

While the record of Colman Smith's involvement with the suffrage movement remains incomplete, it provides valuable insight into cross-class cooperation between women both within and beyond the Suffrage Atelier. Moreover, it highlights Colman Smith's commitment to helping working-class women and to combatting injustice, even if it came from within a suffrage organization.

Symbolic Representations of Women in the "Music Pictures"

Increasingly during this period, Colman Smith's "music pictures" feature women and transport viewers into a variety of imaginative, often ethereal and sometimes dystopian landscapes. Because she discussed these paintings as almost out-of-body experiences that occurred when she listened to orchestral music, critics have rarely focused on patterns of representation in them.[179] This is due in part to Colman Smith's assertion that her "music pictures" were "thoughts loosened and set free by the spell of sound."[180] However, whether her musical visions were the manifestation of her conscious or unconscious mind, or some combination thereof, they do contain their own symbolic lexicon. As I discussed in relation to connections with the Smith-Waite tarot deck, this lexicon includes her adoption of the Rückenfigur positioning and extensive use of the tower image. What can be difficult about Colman Smith's symbology is that it is not static but shifts over time. There are always exceptions, but distinctive patterns do arise. The most important of these evolving symbols is Colman Smith's representation of women in the natural world. She reimagined mythological figures like the mermaid, the sidhe, and the dryad to create her own symbolic system. This progresses from women as part of the sea, emphasizing both rebirth and the ever-changing flux of life, to women superimposed on the earth and sky, highlighting both their connection to the natural world and elemental power, to women as trees, showcasing their stability and interconnectedness.

Representations of women in water, specifically as mermaids, first appear in Colman Smith's illustrative work of the 1890s. For example, at the end of "The Golden Vanity," which I discussed in Chapter 2, five mermaids with green skin and seaweed-encrusted hair—a few embellished with a fish or sea star—greet the drowned cabin boy after he plunges into the ocean to save the ship.[181] Mermaids were a ubiquitous presence in art and literature in the late nineteenth century and early twentieth century.[182] Most of the popular representations of these women, such as Howard Pyle's "The Mermaid" (1910), fuse a woman's face and voluptuous upper torso with a scaly, fish-tailed lower half, a representation that is still present in today's mermaid resurgence. In comparison, Colman Smith's mermaids look much more like fish, and their green skin is very close to her coloration of the sea that is their home.[183]

Colman Smith's depiction of women as water in her "music pictures" is very different. They do not resemble representations, humorous or sexualized, of mermaids. Nor do these paintings clearly align with any of the many portrayals of women in water in late nineteenth- and early twentieth-century art that drew on mythological or classical subjects to show women as naiads, nymphs, or enchantresses, such as John William Waterhouse's *A Naiad* (1893) or his *Hylas and the Nymphs* (1896), and Sir Lawrence Alma-Tadema's *A Favourite Custom* (1909). These paintings, and others like them, feature nude women and generally closely adhere to a specific source text that they visually represent. Moreover, the women are highly sexualized and are presented as objects for the male gaze.

In contrast, Colman Smith, through the very nature of her "music pictures," discouraged any direct mythological sources. However, her water women paintings evoke several different types of female water spirit, and she looks beyond the Greek and Roman myths of her male contemporaries. She appears to draw on undines, elemental beings associated with water and first discussed by Paracelsus; the Germanic nixies, or water spirits; the Irish selkie; and from Norse mythology, the nine daughters of Ægir and Rán who personify waves. Colman Smith read widely in mythology and it is possible that her musical visions drew on and synthesized these various water sprites, possibly even subconsciously, into a nexus of overlapping possible meanings, until they collectively became a pervasive and important personal symbol. However, unlike her male contemporaries, she does not sexualize her water women and instead presents them as figures of sorrow, regeneration, and joy.

The Wave, a watercolor from 1903, is Colman Smith's earliest known depiction of women in water who are clearly not mermaids (Figure 5.13). In it, seven women rise out of a towering wave on an otherwise calm, turquoise body of water. The women have recognizable facial features and hair, as well as in two cases arms and hands, but their bodies are long, sloping, and undifferentiated. Their coloration matches Colman Smith's depiction of the water that surrounds them. The two on the right, their hands covering their faces, are bent almost double, with tears streaming out of their eyes. Their pale blue hue marks them as poised to return to the water that gave them life and sets them apart from the others, who are pale green. The three in the center, with downcast eyes and somber expressions, gaze mournfully at their weeping sisters. The final pair face the rear but, rather than keep watch, they are lost in thought. Although water—that protean, ever-changing and life-giving force—is at the center of *The Wave*, the painting exudes sadness,

Figure 5.13 Pamela Colman Smith, *The Wave*, watercolor, 1903.
Courtesy of the Whitney Museum of American Art

as everything these women witness moves them to grief, rather than a joyous embracing of life.

Colman Smith returned to groups of water women several times, and at least five different versions were included in her first exhibition at Stieglitz's 291 gallery in 1907.[184] One recently discovered charcoal sketch held in a private collection features a large group of at least thirty-five women, rising, cresting, and then returning to the water (Figure 5.14). A small group in the top left appears to recreate the postures of the women in *The Wave*. However, the central grouping of women stand tall but connected, pushing back the rising waves with their outstretched hands. Furthermore, their expressions are far more peaceful and contemplative than the palpable grief in the earlier watercolor. This version also clearly conveys the sea's generative, cyclical nature.[185]

Colman Smith's most famous painting of women and water, *Sea Creatures*, is the cover image of this volume.[186] Also displayed at her 1907 Stieglitz exhibition, the painting details a veiled woman riding the crest of a wave on a vibrant purple, blue, green, and white sea. Eight female water sprites, some rising out of the water and others fully immersed, surround her. The

Figure 5.14 Pamela Colman Smith, untitled, 1907.
Private collection

canvas exudes playful joy. One woman, who consists entirely of white curly sea foam, rests her head on top of the water, staring intently with mock annoyance at the seemingly human woman who is seated on the surface of the water, her hands holding a translucent scarf as she appears to float away from the others. The women are enjoying each other's company, seemingly unaware of—or uninterested in—the silvery ships that float toward them on the horizon.

The clearest mythological connection in Colman Smith's "musical vision" paintings is with the Irish sidhe or fairy people.[187] As Lady Archibald Campbell outlined in the *Occult Review*:

> The armies of the mighty "Sidhe"—pronounced Shee—signify to the Irish the spirits of the ancient races, including the Divine race of the Tutha Dea Dänaan—the tribes of the Goddess Däna, who held sovereignty of Great Ireland prior to the arrival of the sons of Mil,

by whom they were dispossessed of earthy sway—mighty mystics, magicians, spiritualists, understanding the formative power of Nature, the principle of Life, the power which contains the essence of life and character in everything.[188]

Both Campbell and Yeats in his early folktale collections highlight the power and magic of these spirit-women of the earth, and it is this aspect of the mythological figure that Colman Smith emphasizes in her "music pictures." Explaining that the sidhe "feature prominently" in her art, M. Irwin MacDonald notes that several of these depictions are "all radiant and glowing and apparently 20 or 30 feet high."[189] This appears to refer to Colman Smith's 1907 musical vision inspired by Beethoven's Piano Sonata No. 11 in B flat major, in which a brown figure with a woman's head and pink scarf emerges from the side of a mountain (Figure 5.15).[190] Towering over the landscape, she stares past a lone traveler and out toward small boats floating in a pale sea. The power of her surveying gaze, which is placid rather than acquisitive, is readily apparent. Another Beethoven work, the Overture to Egmont, op. 84, inspired Colman Smith to create the head and torso of a large blue woman in deep contemplation as she looks down into a misty valley.[191] Her pose closely resembles that of August Rodin's *Thinker* and suggests that Colman Smith was attempting to make a space for intellectual, contemplative women, depicting them as the life-giving force that fuels the earth. Both works highlight women's close connection to and harmonious relationship with the natural world, as well as the power they hold over it.[192]

Other "music pictures" highlight the connection between earth and sky, both realms that the sidhe can inhabit. A recently discovered untitled painting from 1912 showcases a large, translucent, female figure on a hill of mist as she watches over a couple who traverse a barren landscape (Figure 5.16). Although not as solid as the mountain women, this painting better encapsulates the idea of a protective female spirit who, beyond the knowledge or awareness of most humans, watches over them. A 1909 painting entitled *Woman in Blue* features a giant woman who, with outstretched arms, appears poised to jump across the sky, prefiguring the poses of the dancers in Colman Smith's illustrations for Ellen Terry's 1913 *Russian Ballet* (Figure 5.17). The sky woman's movement, which is enhanced through Colman Smith's rare use of pointillism, is palpable, as the figure appears to vibrate along the sky, like passing clouds on a breezy summer day.[193] *Woman in Blue* highlights woman as a larger-than-life

Figure 5.15 Pamela Colman Smith, *Beethoven's Sonata No. 11*, 1907.
Courtesy Beinecke Rare Book and Manuscript Library, Yale University

FEMINIST SYMBOLIC ART 223

Figure 5.16 Pamela Colman Smith, untitled, 1912.
Private collection

Figure 5.17 Pamela Colman Smith, *Woman in Blue*, 1909.
Private collection

phenomenon that animates, captivates, and watches over the earth and its inhabitants, literally infusing all she surveys with the spirit of her presence.

The last, and by far the most expansive, symbolic representation of women in Colman Smith's musical visions is her depiction of women and trees. The first known example of this dates to November 1906 and, like her women in the mist, it appears to be a transitional image. It features a grouping of colossal women, the first two of whom are holding trees, while jets of water fall toward the ground (Figure 5.18). A fourth woman is bent over, protectively guarding a white city, and a fifth sits stoically in the distance gazing to the horizon. From five years later, an untitled watercolor depicts women as trees, their hands raised over their heads like branches (Figure 5.19). Some stand alone and others in groups of two or three stand in a reedy meadow surrounding a small pool. One with two trunk-like legs appears to be mid-stride. The face of a woman, her body submerged in the earth, reclines peacefully in the grass, the hint of a smile visible on her lips. Several of the clumps of trees sport white blossoms, signaling the imminent

FEMINIST SYMBOLIC ART 225

Figure 5.18 Pamela Colman Smith, untitled, 1906.
Private collection

Figure 5.19 Pamela Colman Smith, untitled, watercolor, 1911.
Private collection

rebirth of spring and its concomitant fertility. Both of these works were recently discovered in a private collection.

While there may be many more undiscovered images in this series, the final known painting dates to December 1943. Entitled *O, Pines of Sister Pines*, it features a cluster of three pine trees, their branches intertwined, situated together on a small hill set against a pale orange sky.[194] A closer inspection reveals that the branches consist of multicolored women, their long arms and legs holding onto each other, and their bushy hair providing the illusion of clumps of pine needles. Other groups of women form the trunks of the trees, crowding together and standing on each other's heads. The hundreds, if not thousands, of small women who make up the trees highlight a new focus on communality and interdependence among women that is generally not present in Colman Smith's early "music pictures," which most commonly depict androgynous figures alone or in smaller groups. The main exception to this is the paintings of women as water, where groups of women rise and fall like a living wave.

Even more so than her depictions of women in water and women in the earth and air, Colman Smith's representations of women as trees have no direct mythological link. There is a vague topical similarity to Greek myths that relate stories of women being turned into trees to protect their chastity, such as Apollo's pursuit of Daphne which leaves her confined to a laurel tree, and Myrrha, who is transformed into a myrrh tree after tricking her father into having sex with her and becoming pregnant with Adonis. Similarly, there is no clear allusion to Baucis and Philemon, the loving couple who, as a reward for their hospitality to Zeus and Hermes, are transformed into intertwined trees so that they do not have to be separated in death. None of Colman Smith's canvases that depict tree-women include men. Instead, she creates a landscape filled with women, who, irrespective of men, create life and find communality, stability, and seeming happiness with each other.

Colman Smith's work on the tarot, her early association with the works of Blake and Swedenborgianism, her time in Jamaica, her interest in myth and folklore, her friendship with Yeats, her suffrage activities, and her "music pictures" have all generally been viewed as separate activities. This chapter demonstrates that these disparate elements work together to help explain who Colman Smith was and what she accomplished. Even her otherwise surprising conversion to Catholicism in 1911 is understandable in terms of these other elements in her history. In a sense every activity of Colman Smith's upbringing and artistic career prepared her for her "big job for very little cash." Colman Smith perfectly complemented Waite and, although he was loth to admit it, she was the critical factor in the ultimate success of the tarot deck they both worked on. She infused his book-learning with a psychic energy that allowed the famous tarot deck to live and grow in the minds of a still expanding audience.

This chapter has also argued that she likely began working on designs for the deck earlier than previously believed, and that her "music pictures" of the 1907–08 period share several similarities with her tarot designs, including frequent use of the Rückenfigur technique and tower symbolism. In addition, her association with the women's suffrage movement, which commenced in earnest in 1909, was an important influence for both her tarot designs and the evolution of her feminist symbolic art. However, the culmination of Colman Smith's involvement in both the occult revival and the women's suffrage movement was the evolution of the symbolism regarding the female figures in her "musical vision" paintings. Moving from women in water, to women in the earth and sky, to, finally, women as trees, Colman Smith created her own symbolic lexicon that allowed her to highlight different aspects of womanhood such as rebirth, connection to the natural world, and the importance of communality. But despite her continued interest in tree-women over the course of thirty years, many things changed both for herself and for society—two world wars chief among them—and I will briefly discuss this later period of Colman Smith's life, of which comparatively little is known, in the Epilogue.

Epilogue

World War I

In April 1914 Pamela Colman Smith wrote in her visitors' book in which guests had recorded their names since 1901 that "she didn't care for people anymore."[1] She then gave the book to Frederick Allen King, the editor of the New York-based *Literary Digest*, who had been a supporter of her work.[2] It is unclear if this marked the end of her weekly gatherings or if she was just in a misanthropic mood when she made the decision to jettison the book. This change signaled a shift in her social demeanor and foreshadows the change in focus that many experienced during World War I.

One possible explanation of this mystery can be found in a letter Susan "Lily" Yeats, the sister of W. B. Yeats, sent to her father after spending a week with Colman Smith during a 1913 trip to London:

> Pixie is as delightful as ever and has a big-roomed flat near Victoria Station with black walls and orange curtains. She is now an ardent and pious Roman Catholic, which has added to her happiness but taken from her friends. She now has the dullest of friends, selected because they are R. C., converts most of them, half-educated people who want to see both eyes in a profile drawing. She goes to confession every Saturday—except the week I was there—she couldn't think of any sins, so my influence must have been very holy.[3]

Lily Yeats's assessment is full of stereotyped notions about the background and leanings of Roman Catholics, which are likely the result of her position as a member of Ireland's Protestant ascendancy.[4] Even though many of her conclusions appear wrong—such as her assertion that Colman Smith's black walls and orange curtains are due to her Roman Catholicism—the letter offers an interesting glimpse into Colman Smith's life. The comments also make clear that Colman Smith was no longer in close contact with W. B. Yeats and his extended family, and had distanced herself from his wide network of friends and associates. However, Lily continued to stay with Colman Smith during her annual shopping trip to London at least through 1917.[5]

Despite this shift in friends, Colman Smith appears to have developed a wide network of her own. In one of the most telling lines in the letter, Lily states that the conversion has "added to her happiness." While Joan Coldwell takes Lily's conclusions at face value and asserts that after her conversion Colman Smith "became conventionally staid and pious,"[6] I contend that she retained her trademark eccentricity and unpredictability, which her choice of paint and draperies appears to confirm, but had gained happiness. After her July 12, 1911 baptism at the Church of the Immaculate Conception, better known as the Farm Street Church, in Mayfair, she regularly attended Mass and was an involved parishioner.[7] After she moved to Westminster in 1913 she became a member of the Westminster Cathedral parish. The years following her conversion were busy ones. She was an active participant in the women's suffrage movement, had a major solo exhibition at the Berlin Photographic Company in New York, and completed several illustration projects that had a distinct feminist bent, none of which aligns with Coldwell's "staid and pious" assessment. However, there does appear to be a shift in Colman Smith's work from the 1910s away from the individual and toward the communal experience. Whether this was a result of her conversion to Roman Catholicism or her immersion in the suffrage movement is debatable.

Colman Smith worked on several illustration projects during this period. She contributed six color plates for Bram Stoker's 1911 novel *The Lair of the White Worm*. Although not nearly as successful as *Dracula*, Stoker's final novel shared an interest in the supernatural, and critics lauded Colman Smith's drawings as highlighting "the attractiveness as well as the weird character of the book."[8] The novel's central character, Lady Arabella, has the ability to transform into a serpent who wreaks havoc on all she encounters. Colman

Smith's illustration of a silver-clad Lady Arabella dancing with outstretched arms brings to mind a costume sketch she did with Edy Craig for Russell Vaun's *Nicandra*.[9] Like Stoker's novel, Vaun's 1901 play rewrites the Egyptian myth of the serpent-eyed goddess Hathor, "who embodies female power manifested by desire and anger."[10] However, Colman Smith's illustrations of Arabella's human and worm forms instead emphasize her boldness, strength, and power.[11]

Fairy tales of all types also became a persistent interest during this period. In "Susan and the Mermaid," a story Colman Smith wrote and illustrated for the December 1912 edition of *The Delineator*, she returns to her long-time interest in mermaids. The story describes a young girl's journey to a magical undersea world that she unlocks with her grandmother's magic pearl. Populated by polite mermaids, pompous dolphins, sociable seahorses, and excitable pugfish, the Coral City of Oceana also contains "great galleries of pictures, and the national theater, and a large concert-hall with notes painted outside that played themselves when you looked at them."[12] The ruler of the kingdom is the Queen of Tides, which is the title of Colman Smith's "music picture" inspired by Beethoven's Symphony No. 5 in C minor that depicts a floating queen, "who carries in her hand the pearl-like moon."[13] When Susan's mermaid guide abruptly leaves her to find her own way home, she is saved by her grandmother, highlighting the importance of close intergenerational ties between women.

Fusing her interest in both the magic of the fairy tale and the limitations of female agency, Colman Smith illustrated an edition of Charles Perrault's *Blue Beard* in 1912.[14] The stark cover design features a man's disembodied head, complete with vacant blue eyes and blue-tinged beard.[15] Later turned into a feminist masterpiece by Angela Carter,[16] the story highlights the dangers of unchecked patriarchal power and the irrational expectations imposed on women to obey their husbands over their own safety and welfare. It is easy to see why the fairy tale would have resonated with Colman Smith, who was participating in the women's suffrage movement at the time. Young and impoverished, the unnamed female protagonist marries a wealthy older man who soon needs to go away on business. Before leaving, he informs his wife that she can invite all her friends and gives her free range of the house and all his wealth, with the exception of a "little closet" on the ground floor. He directs her to "[o]pen them all; go into all and every one of them, except that little closet, which I forbid you, and forbid it in such a manner that, if you happen to open it, there's nothing but what you may expect from my just anger and resentment."[17] The woman quickly gives in to her curiosity, disobeys her spouse, and enters the secret closet, only to be confronted by quantities of clotted blood and the dead bodies of Blue Beard's previous wives. Interestingly, Colman Smith's illustration for this grisly scene superimposes elements from Stoker's *The Lair of the White Worm*. All of the wives have long, tube-like bodies and outstretched arms that are reminiscent of Lady Arabella in her serpent form.[18] Several of the women appear to have exchanged their humanity for patterned scales and serpent-like facial features. Blue Beard quickly recognizes his wife's disobedience due to a mark left by his magical key and sentences her to die. She manages to trick her husband and is rescued by her brothers, who kill him, allowing her to inherit her husband's wealth and live happily ever after.

The power of the body in motion is the subject of Colman Smith's illustrations for *The Russian Ballet* (1913).[19] Ellen Terry was listed as the author, but as she was in ill health, it was ghost written by Christopher St. John.[20] The book details the rise of the Ballets Russes, which was founded in 1909 by Sergei Pavlovich Diaghilev, the Russian ballet impresario and art critic. St. John's text focuses on the attention in the Russian system to developing the "virile agility of their steps" and the dramatic intensity of male dancers, in a profession that often privileged prima ballerinas and their seductive *en pointe* maneuvers.[21] Colman Smith's illustrations capture the lithe grace and emotional intensity of the company's principal male dancer, Vaslav Nijinsky. She highlights his ability to transform into his roles, contorting his body into a range of positions.

Colman Smith's major remaining illustration project from this period was her contribution of more than 100 black-and-white drawings to Eunice Fuller's *The Book of Friendly Giants*, which was published in October 1914.[22] Marketed for children, the book upends persistent stereotypes regarding the wickedness of ogres, prefiguring Roald Dahl's 1982 novel *The BFG*. Fuller collects folktales from Hungarian, Norse, Celtic, German, and Chinese sources to provide a new assessment of ogres.[23] Colman Smith's illustrations emphasize the beneficent nature of these mythical creatures and, in keeping with the focus on children, many of her drawings feature animals.[24] At least one of the stories, "The Giant Who Became a Saint," centrally deals with Catholic themes, in this case the origins of St. Christopher.[25] Furthermore, Fuller's collection calls on readers, primarily children, to believe unquestioningly in the myths included in its pages, offering an escape into magical realms at the outset of World War I.

Colman Smith, like many in England, turned her attention to charitable activities during the war. She hosted bazaars in her studio and donated the proceeds to the Red Cross and other groups. As Melinda Boyd Parsons has noted, "With [Colman Smith's] predilection for fantasy, she put her best efforts into making and selling imaginative toys at these bazaars, including according to Edward Carrick, some 'wonderful mermaids: with silver scales holding real combs and mirrors in their hands.'"[26] It is likely that these mermaid toys were sparked by Colman Smith's "Susan and the Mermaid." Christopher St. John recorded that Edy Craig joined Colman Smith in this endeavor, and "Pixie Pamela" frequently hosted "toy teas" at her flat that "were quite a fashionable gathering."[27] It is unclear how long she continued making toys, but her charitable activities extended into other areas. Colman Smith headed the picture makers' group at the June 1916 Chelsea Fair.[28] Later that month she took part in the art tent at a Temple of Magic bazaar featuring "high class astrology plus demonology."[29] She also gave benefit performances of her Anansi stories, such as one at the Savoy Hotel in support of the Women Wartime Workers.[30] She also gave private art lessons to help supplement her meager income, as she spent a large part of her time on charitable work.[31] In addition, she designed a poster in support of the Bulldog Soldiers & Sailors club.[32]

The influence of Colman Smith's conversion to Roman Catholicism is evident in several of her wartime projects. Her poster for the Polish Victims' Relief Fund implores the Blessed Virgin Mary, through her title of Most Holy Virgin of Czestochowa, for aid and assistance.[33] This poster resembles an earlier group of paintings Colman Smith exhibited at the Berlin Photographic Company in New York. As the *New York Sun* pointed out, "The designs for the Litany of Loreto— Rosa mystica, Turria Davidica, Turris Eburnea—demonstrate an imagination of no common order. They are decorative, spiritual and with a touch of the hieratic that may be noted in Byzantine art."[34] The Byzantine description would appear to identify the poster as being part of this series, or as art created in its likeness after the fact. A popular prayer of supplication, the Litany of Loreto was a medieval prayer first used at the famous Marian shrine at Loreto, Italy, and calls on the Virgin Mary with many of the titles Colman Smith gives to her paintings.[35] Several of these titles, such as *Rosa mystica* and *Stella matutina*—the mystic rose and the morning star—highlight the overlap between mystical Catholicism and the occult revival.[36]

Colman Smith's 1917 illustrations for an English edition of French writer Paul Claudel's *The Way of the Cross* is another Catholic project from this period.[37] Her thirty black-and-white woodcut illustrations map Jesus' passion and death, and Christ's suffering is the center of the work. Like several of her suffrage postcards, Colman Smith's illustrations are notable for their use of areas of darkness to emphasize the figure of Jesus. Interestingly, the last image does not depict Jesus' empty tomb or even the risen Christ himself, but instead a priest giving communion to a row of communicants, emphasizing the connection between Jesus' ultimate sacrifice and contemporary Catholics. While it is unclear how Colman Smith became involved in this project, her close friend Edy Craig directed Claudel's *The Tidings Brought to Mary* in London that same year.[38] This demonstrates that although Colman Smith had distanced herself from Yeats and his circle, she remained in close contact with Craig, St. John, and Terry. Indeed, she continued to contribute program covers and stage designs to Pioneer Player productions until she moved to Cornwall.

Colman Smith's 1912 exhibition at the Berlin Photographic Company in New York received less press attention than had her last Stieglitz show. The *New York Sun* asserted that "she has much improved technically," but "fantasy ruins these singularly attractive paintings…"[39] The *Brooklyn Daily Eagle* was more complimentary, stating that "the drawings are strong and full of the mystic impressive power."[40] The article also noted that several tarot designs were included in the exhibition, which was her last known U.S. show, and gives rise to the possibility that the designs were purchased and are still held in private collections.[41] Later in the decade she participated in the Ghent Exhibition of 1913 and the British Arts and Crafts Exhibition of 1914.[42] Her last known exhibition was at John Baillie's London gallery in 1915.[43]

Even though Colman Smith did not exhibit widely during World War I, Thomas Gerard thoughtfully discussed her "music pictures" in an essay on "Art After the War" in *The Living Age*. Alluding to the rise of surrealism, Gerard notes that "of late there has been an art development taking place in which music is illustrated by painting."[44] He then notes that Colman Smith had been inspired by music for many years and enthuses about her art, especially her painting inspired by Debussy's "Sunken Cathedral," emphasizing the connections between the music that inspired her paintings and the paintings themselves.[45] Stating that her work is "poetic and highly artistic," Gerard's praise is measured: "the soul of the hearer, whilst delighted for the time being, never gets higher than sense and emotion."[46] He concludes that "the hope of the future" for art lies not in Colman Smith's "music pictures" but in dance, specifically the Russian Ballet and Nijinsky.[47] However, Gerard does not mention, and possibly was not aware of, Colman Smith's illustrations for *The Russian Ballet*, which capture the power, majesty, and "reawakening to the respective claims of both body and spirit" that he praises in Nijinsky.[48] Gerard's article appears to have been one of the last critical appraisals of Colman Smith's art.

Move to Cornwall

Near the end of World War I, Colman Smith received a bequest from her Uncle Teddy Smith in New York. In March 1919 she used the funds to buy a permanent lease on Parc Garland, a large house with two additional buildings and two acres of land, on the Lizard at the tip of Cornwall in southwestern England. She had first visited Cornwall in 1899 with her father, shortly before his death; the memory of that visit and her interest in Cornish folklore may have spurred her return. It is unclear if she had connections with anyone in western Cornwall before embarking on this relocation.[49] Dawn Robinson suggests that the location, like Colman Smith's later move to Bude, was proposed by Catholic priests she knew who were eager to make inroads into predominantly Protestant Cornwall.[50]

Once Colman Smith arrived on the Lizard, she began a project to re-establish a disused Catholic chapel.[51] The upkeep of this chapel, and the securing of priests to say Mass there, became an ongoing focus of her next several years.[52] In an August 29, 1919 letter to the Plymouth diocese, Colman Smith states that she was a member of the Confraternity of the Blessed Sacrament and a Child of Mary in London, and asks permission to move furniture from the old chapel to a building in her garden, where she intended to "re-erect the stations of the cross."[53] She adds that she had been taking care of the chapel for the previous five weeks and, during that time, there had been "four masses daily." She concludes, "I feel sure that if the chapel were cared for that more Catholics would come to the district."[54] By November 1920 there were thirty-one local Catholics associated with the chapel, which she named Our Lady of the Lizard, and more than two hundred Masses had been said during that year alone.[55] However, in February 1922 Colman Smith wrote the Bishop of Plymouth to state that she was having difficulty covering the costs associated with visiting priests and asked for help from the diocese and the other members of the congregation.[56] The bishop wrote in *The Tablet*, England's Catholic newspaper, in February 1923, that "for some years, through the personal devotion and very difficult struggle of two ladies, this chapel (recently renewed) has been kept open."[57] The bishop explained that, although there were few Catholics in this "out-of-the-world-spot," summer holiday folk, "the Coastguard, oddments of military and naval forces, and the Marconi employees of Poldhu" all utilized it.[58] He announced the establishment of an Our Lady of the Lizard fund through which to purchase a cottage for a permanent priest and to establish Foundation Masses to celebrate the Eucharist regularly.[59] Despite this announcement, the fund appears not to have been successful.

It is unclear whether Colman Smith at some point operated a vacation home for priests in order to supplement her income and support the chapel, but she may have hosted a few vacationing priests she had known in London. During 1926 and 1927 she contacted the Plymouth diocese several times, asking for monies to help in the operation of the chapel, primarily to pay the fees of a visiting priest. The funds appear not to have been given, and in an October 1927 letter, the bishop termed her "a neurotic."[60] In a September 1927 letter to Ellen Terry and Edy Craig, Colman Smith, who by then used her given name of Corinne, was frantic. She suggests that as a Catholic church had been established in nearby Mullion, "it seems quite hopeless to go on here [at the Lizard]," and that she might sell Parc Garland and buy a bungalow in Penzance, moving the chapel with her.[61] However, she did not move from the Lizard until 1939.

Unlike her struggles with Our Lady of the Lizard chapel, far less is known about Colman Smith's daily life on the Lizard; there are far fewer extant letters from this period than from earlier periods of her life. Parc Garland was within walking distance of the rugged Atlantic coast, with a nearby secluded beach, and was just around the corner from the local Landewednack Primary School. In the December 1919 issue of *Drama Magazine*, Colman Smith recounted her experience of putting on a Nativity play in a village hall with local schoolchildren. She likely drew on her experience making costumes for Craig's *Early English Nativity Play* the previous year, which she does not mention in the article.[62] As Colman Smith notes about the Lizard production, "There were no stage directions. They had to be made, and the play written and made actable and speakable."[63] She adds that, while the children learned their parts relatively quickly, she called regular rehearsals because she "tried to make it as like the real thing as one could, and the children felt that it was like a 'real, live' play, though, I think, not one of them had ever been in a theatre."[64] She goes on to describe the play in detail, scene by scene, discussing everything from scenery and stage props to the placement of the child actors and even patterns for the various costumes. She concludes by discussing her substantial costs.[65] While it is unclear whether Colman Smith ever attempted to produce another such play on the Lizard, it is likely that, given the relatively substantial costs in time and labor required to mount such a venture, she viewed it as prohibitive.

For a brief period in the mid-1920s Colman Smith might have been poised for a comeback. In 1924 a small article on her "music pictures" appeared in an Australian newspaper, signaling that she was attempting to make inroads into that country.[66] As discussed earlier, the Hon. Mrs. Forbes-Sempill's article on her musical visions appeared in the *Illustrated London News* of February 12, 1927, and was accompanied by two full pages of black-and-white illustrations.[67] She also contributed twelve black-and-white illustrations for Edith Lyttelton's 1925 novel, *The Sinclair Family*, which was loosely based on the author's travels in the Far East and India.[68]

The late 1920s appear to have been beset with financial hardship for Colman Smith. A March 1927 letter to the American art dealer, critic, and author Martin Birnbaum reveals both how dire her financial situation really was and the fact that her artistic output had slowed considerably. Informing him of Forbes-Sempill's recent article, she first inquires as to whether "you know of someone who will buy some drawings?" She confides that "I am really in need now—I have a house & 2 acres of ground—poultry &c—and need money badly—to tide things over until I get the work going again."[69] With a note of bitterness, she adds: "People here [in England] are all enthusiastic but have not the brains to see the practical side…"[70] When Ellen Terry died the following year, Colman Smith wrote to Edy Craig to express her condolences but also to give voice to her financial distress.[71] She said that despite turning a small room in her house into a shop, "I am badly in need of money just now. I have sold *nothing* this year."[72] She asked Craig to help her sell either some small or large prints of Terry or even the original signed drawing of Terry as Mistress Page, which Colman Smith was willing to part with for ten pounds. Craig's response is not recorded, but the friendship continued, and photos reveal that Craig and St. John visited Colman Smith on the Lizard around 1932 and that the group went to the beach.[73]

The cause of Colman Smith's financial distress is unclear. Letters reveal that she was not selling work and she was having difficulty paying the expenses for the Our Lady of the Lizard chapel. A note in *The Collected Letters of W. B. Yeats* states that "in later life she [Colman Smith] took to drink, and embarrassed her friends over a series of unpaid loans."[74] A timeframe is not given, but this alleged alcoholism might potentially explain her financial hardships. However, she was also living in a remote location with a large property to maintain, and that, coupled with changing artistic tastes, might explain her financial situation.

The constant in Colman Smith's life during these last decades was the presence of Nora Lake. However, the exact nature of their relationship is unclear. Lake, who was three years older than Colman Smith, was the wife of the handyman for Parc Garland, though estranged from him.[75] According to a note on the inside cover of a hymnal in Colman Smith's collection, Alfred Hugh Lake died on December 5, 1943, in Bude.[76] In a September 1927 letter to Craig and Terry, Colman Smith notes that "Mrs. Lake is sure you will make a good suggestion. She is still in bed and sends greetings."[77] Why Lake was still in bed, possibly due to illness, is not explained. At that point at least, their relationship appears to have been relatively formal. By February 1939, however, matters seem to have changed. Nora's niece Alice sent a letter and gift to Colman Smith with "her very best wishes for happy or happier returns of the day," and hoped that her heart had improved.[78] The nature of this ailment is unknown, but Colman Smith died of "myocardial disintegration," so it is possible that her heart problems began in the late 1930s, if not before.[79] She appears to have recovered sufficiently to attend a Prayer Healing Fellowship in Dorset, a significant distance from the Lizard, in April 1939.[80]

An undated letter from Nora's sister (also apparently named Alice), written after the beginning of World War II, sends Colman Smith birthday wishes and expresses a desire to purchase a fountain pen for her as a present, but such an item could not be found in the shops due to war rationing.[81] Alice notes that she is thankful to have been spared in a recent German bombing campaign and "hopes poor Nora is a little better from the shock," presumably from the bombing as well.[82] The Luftwaffe conducted extensive bombing of Cornwall, especially along the coast. Books in Colman Smith's private library from the 1930s and 1940s reveal that she and Lake gave each other volumes, which they inscribed with pet names and sometimes adorned with drawings. Colman Smith was Mole, sometimes P. Mole, and Lake was generally

Growly Bear but sometimes Badger.[83] All of this would indicate that Colman Smith and Lake's relationship was close and intimate—definitely closer than between an employer and employee—but its exact nature, like so much in her later life, is unclear.

Last Years

In August 1939 Colman Smith sold Parc Garland, her home for twenty years. She then moved with Nora Lake first to Exeter, where Lake had family, and then to Gorseland at Upton Cliff, just outside Bude, settling there in 1942.[84] After the relocation, Colman Smith appears to have resumed her efforts at writing and illustrating books. A 1942 receipt shows that she employed a local service to type four manuscripts: *The Railings of Drift*, *The Cuckoo Bird*, *Greenfinger*, and *Fisher of Men*.[85] She attempted to place *Greenfinger* with the London publishing firm of George G. Harrap, but was rejected. Colman Smith also continued to paint throughout the 1940s. A 1946 "music picture" inspired by Stravinsky's "Duet" depicts a slumping hooded figure beside a denuded tree. A small animal, reminiscent of the moles she drew in her book notes to Lake, peers at the figure. The tree, as in the previously discussed painting, *O, Pines of Sister Pines*, appears to be made up of individual figures. However, while in the earlier picture the women are multicolored and form a large, branching tree, this one is completely brown and much smaller. The sense of death is emphasized by the barren landscape. Colman Smith became a fellow of the Royal Society of the Arts in 1941 and thereafter wrote the letters F.R.S.A. on the back of all her canvases.

A Catholic until her death, Colman Smith's Bible and hymnal reveal that she frequently perused these texts, copying down key passages—she particularly liked the Psalms—and doodling images of angels as well as both the crucified and risen Christ. However, she often mixed the religious iconography with references to the occult and other topics that had interested her earlier in her career. For example, there is a reproduction of William Blake's "When the morning Stars sang together, & all the Sons of God shouted for Joy" pasted on the inside cover of one of her hymnals.[86] This image, part of a twenty-two-plate series that Blake published in 1825 on the Book of Job, shows the mystical ecstasy Job and his family experienced after witnessing the power of God. The opposite page in Colman Smith's hymnal contains a quotation from St. Augustine, and a few pages later she sketched Blake's morning stars.[87] One of the volume's final pages includes the quotation, "Five fingers of the hand of prayer," evidently derived from a 1938 event at Scarborough Cathedral.[88] However, the bottom of the page has a hastily scrawled question about whether a spriggan is a Cornish pixie.[89] Another hymnal contains drawings of a stage with actors in the back while scripture verses and notations on the death of friends are inscribed in the front. A tucked-in piece of paper appears to be a sketch of the X of Cups from the tarot deck.[90] Similarly, the inside covers of her Bible present scriptural quotations alongside drawings of pentacles.[91]

On September 18, 1951 Colman Smith died in her apartment on the second floor of Bencoolen House in Bude, which she shared with Lake.[92] She was 73. Her friend and neighbor, Elsie Bates, who occasionally helped the largely bed-bound Colman Smith with cleaning and other household tasks, discovered the body.[93] Her burial record states that her Catholic burial Mass was said by the Rev. Joseph du Moulin Browne, but it does not contain a burial location.[94] Browne was a parish priest assigned to St. Peter's Church in Bude, but Colman Smith lacked the financial means to pay for a burial plot and headstone in the closest Catholic cemetery in Launceston. Instead, she was buried in an unmarked grave in the cemetery of St. Michael's, Bude's Anglican parish church. However, all the relevant burial records from this period were destroyed in a fire, making it impossible to determine her final resting place. Her will, dated February 23, 1951, left her entire estate "to my friend Nora Lake."[95] Unfortunately, Colman Smith had many debts, the majority being many years of unpaid income taxes, and even after her possessions were auctioned off and proceeds from a trust fund in New York were added into the estate, only about 25 percent of her debts were paid.[96] As a result, her last wish went unheeded and Lake received nothing.

Legacy

When Colman Smith died in significant debt in 1951, almost all her work was out of print and it appears to have been decades since she had published anything new or exhibited her work. Ironically, the publication of Eden Gray's *The Tarot Revealed*, which helped popularize the cards and led to the resurgence of the Smith-Waite deck, was less than a decade away. As Mary K. Greer has noted, "The number one legacy of Pamela Colman Smith resides in the millions of people around the world who over the past hundred plus years have been drawn to and continue to draw inspiration from her tarot deck."[97] Writers and musicians from Sylvia Plath to Madonna, and TV shows and movies from *Mad Men* to *A Walk on the Moon*, have included references to Colman Smith's famous images.[98] Some writers, like Thomas Pynchon in *Against the Day*, even immortalized Colman Smith herself.[99]

Arguably, the most famous of all the literary references to the Smith-Waite deck appears in T. S. Eliot's 1922 poem *The Waste Land*.[100] Eliot was obviously intrigued by the tarot but was also aware of the overtones of charlatanry that hung over practitioners of the psychic arts. Although he professed little knowledge of tarot reading, *The Waste Land* exhibits a close acquaintance with the unique elements of many of the Smith-Waite cards. Eliot knew Waite and it has been shown that the tarot deck that he references was the Smith-Waite deck.[101] Clearly, his medium, Madame Sosostris, and her "wicked pack of cards" provides more than a few hints that she is actually a fraud, yet Eliot shows that the cards can still provide accurate knowledge of the future. In this way, the poem implies that the Smith-Waite cards can overcome the limitations of the reader and offer real insight.

The power of Colman-Smith's tarot images to convey deep meaning is definitely a major component of the deck's popularity. Unlike many previous decks, the purpose of the Smith-Waite cards is clearly divinatory. As the first tarot deck ever to be printed in English, it has been a global phenomenon, growing in influence since its first publication in December 1909. It has never gone out of print, and its current publisher, Stuart Kaplan, says that demand for the deck is steady. It is now the most famous and popular tarot deck in the world.

But what about Colman Smith herself? In addition to putting her tarot images in closer conversation with her "music pictures," *Pamela Colman Smith: Feminist, Artist, Mystic* hopes to have shed more light on the many facets of her life and work. It highlights how she was consistently viewed as a racial Other—at times seen as Black, at other times as Asian, or even as an indeterminate creature—and it demonstrates how this prejudice affected her career and influenced her artistic choices. Incredibly prolific in the thirty years during which she produced the bulk of her oeuvre, Colman Smith wrote and illustrated Afro-Jamaican Anansi stories, edited her own little magazine, operated a feminist press, had three exhibitions at Alfred Stieglitz's 291 gallery in Manhattan, was active in the women's suffrage movement, and created hundreds of synesthetic "music pictures." However, these achievements did not meet with sustained critical or commercial success, an outcome shared by countless women writers and artists in the early twentieth century. Her tarot images continued to circulate and gain in popularity, helping to draw more attention to the full body of her work. Today, almost seventy years after her death, we are poised to appreciate more fully the unique vision and groundbreaking contributions made by this extraordinary artist, a woman who was truly ahead of her time.

Notes

Introduction

1. Pamela Colman Smith to George Pollexfen, February 17, 1902, Stony Brook University, William Butler Yeats Collection, box 53, 120, folder 44.
2. Jessica Berman, "Practicing Transnational Feminist Recovery Today," *Feminist Modernist Studies* 1, nos. 1–2 (2018): 10.
3. Anne Fernald, "Women's Fiction, New Modernist Studies, and Feminism," *Modern Fiction Studies* 59, no. 2 (2013): 231.
4. In 1918 the Representation of the People Act allowed women over 30 and men over 21 to vote. Women had to own property, be married to a property owner, occupy property with annual rent of £5, or have graduated from a British university. In 1928 everyone over the age of twenty-one was allowed to vote.
5. "Events," *The Observer* [London], January 24, 1904, 3.
6. Colman Smith to Pollexfen, February 17, 1902, box 53, 120, folder 44.
7. J. B. Yeats, *Letters to His Son W.B. Yeats and Others, 1869–1922*, ed. Joseph Hone (New York: E.P. Dutton, 1946), 61. See also Pamela Colman Smith to Albert Bigelow Paine, August 7, 1899, Huntington Library, Manuscripts Department, Albert Bigelow Paine Letters, AP 1672.
8. Ellen Terry to Audrey Campbell, no. 1088, in *The Collected Letters of Ellen Terry, Volume 4*, ed. Katharine Cockin (London: Taylor and Francis, 2015), 119.
9. Regina Armstrong, "Representative American Women Illustrators: The Decorative Workers," *The Critic*, June 1900, 528–29. See also "Who's Who," *Public Opinion* 28, no. 2, (June 14, 1900): 768.

10 Elazar Barkan and Ronald Bush, "Introduction," in *Prehistories of the Future: The Primitivist Project and the Culture of Modernism*, ed. Elazar Barkan and Ronald Bush (Stanford, CA: Stanford University Press, 1995), 2.
11 Barkan and Bush, "Introduction," 1.
12 Barkan and Bush, "Introduction," 14.
13 Qtd. in Barkan and Bush, "Introduction," 14.
14 Barkan and Bush, "Introduction," 14.
15 Qtd. in Melinda Boyd Parsons, "Pamela Colman Smith and Alfred Stieglitz: Modernism at 291," *History of Photography* 29, no. 4 (1996): 291 n.1.
16 Henry Wood Nevinson, *Changes and Chances* (London: Nisbet & Co., 1923), 303.
17 Nevinson, *Changes and Chances*, 303.
18 Nevinson, *Changes and Chances*, 303.
19 Earnest Elmo Calkins, *"Louder Please": The Autobiography of a Deaf Man* (Boston, MA: The Atlantic Monthly Press, 1924), 170.
20 Calkins, *"Louder Please"*, 170.
21 Marianna Torgovnick, *Gone Primitive: Savage Intellects, Modern Lives* (Chicago: University of Chicago Press, 1990), 189, 227; see also Jamie Hovey, "Sapphic Primitivism in Gertrude Stein's *Q.E.D.*," *Modern Fiction Studies* 42, no. 3 (1996): 549.
22 Qtd. in Melinda Boyd Parsons, *To All Believers: The Art of Pamela Colman Smith*, exhibition catalogue, Delaware Art Museum, September 11–October 19, 1975, and The Art Museum, Princeton University, November 4–December 7, 1975 (Wilmington, DE: Delaware Art Museum, 1975), unpaginated, n.101.
23 George Russell (AE) to Sarah Purser, March 5, 1902, in *Letters from AE*, ed. Alan Denson (London: Abelard-Schuman, 1961), 39
24 R.R.G. "Pamela Colman Smith: She Believes in Fairies," *The Delineator*, November 1912, 320.
25 R.R.G. "Pamela Colman Smith," 320.
26 Arthur Ransome, *Bohemia in London* (New York: Dodd, Mead, 1907), 56–57.
27 Sonita Sarker, "A Position Embedded in Identity: Subalternity in Neoliberal Globalization," *Cultural Studies* 30, no. 5 (2016): 818.
28 John Masefield, *Some Memories of W.B. Yeats* (Dublin: Cuala Press, 1940), 16.
29 Nora Chesson, *Aquamarines* (London: Grant Richards, 1902), 81.
30 Pamela Colman Smith to Alfred Stieglitz, March 18, 1908, Georgia O'Keeffe Collection, Beinecke Library, Yale University, YCAL MSS 85, box 45.
31 Sally Ledger, *The New Woman: Fiction and Feminism at the Fin de Siècle* (Manchester: Manchester University Press, 1997), 64.
32 Ledger, *The New Woman*, 64.
33 Deborah Cohler, *Citizen, Invert, Queer* (Minneapolis, MN: University of Minnesota Press, 2010), xii.
34 Jane Garrity, *Step-Daughters of England: British Women Modernists and the National Imaginary* (Manchester: Manchester University Press, 2003), 3.

35 Cohler, *Citizen, Invert, Queer*, xiii.
36 Cohler, *Citizen, Invert, Queer*, x.

Chapter One: Naming and Identity: Family, Miniature Theater, and Jamaican Residence

1   "Bobby" Reed, July 25, 1896, Pamela Colman Smith Collection, Canaday Library, Bryn Mawr College, box 1, folder 1.
2   Colman Smith to Reed, box 1, folders 1–17. The way Colman Smith addresses her cousin changes. September 9, 1898 begins "Dear Maysie," but December 7, 1899 is "Dear old Bobby Mary." February 25, 1900 begins "Dear old Mary," but in December 7, 1900 reverts to "Dear Bobby." The final letter on December 28, 1900 commences "Dear Mary."
3   "The Week," *The Theater* 4 (1889), 51; and William Winter, *The Wallet of Time: Containing Personal, Biographical, and Critical Reminiscence of the American Theatre*, vol. 2 (New York: Moffat, Yard, & Co., 1918), 75.
4   "Wins by Witchery in London Drawing Rooms: Remarkable Success of a Heights Girl in Folk-Lore Tales: A Remarkable Personality: Pamela Coleman [sic] Smith, Closely Related to Many Prominent Brooklyn Families, and Her Strange Career," *Brooklyn Daily Eagle*, November 1, 1904, 9.
5   Colman Smith to Reed, July 25, 1896, box 1, folder 1.
6   "Corinne Colman Smith," Jamaica Civil Registration, Birth, Marriage, and Death Records, 1878–1930, FHL 0538821, 1838 [database online], Provo, UT: Ancestry.com Operations, 2014; "Death Notice," *Brooklyn Daily Eagle*, August 1, 1896, 13; "Leg of Corinne Smith Amputated," Green-Wood Cemetery Burial Registry, burial date November 2, 1896, lot 416, section 36.
7   Colman Smith to Reed, July 25, 1896, box 1, folder 1.
8   Colman Smith to Reed, September 17, 1896, box 1, folder 2. The only time she signs her name Constance.
9   Colman Smith to Reed, December 7, 1899, box 1, folder 14.
10 Paul Manning, "Pixies' Progress: How the Pixie Became Part of the Nineteenth-Century Fairy Mythology," in *The Folkloresque: Reframing Folklore in a Popular Culture World*, ed. Michael Dylan Foster and Jeffrey A. Tolbert (Logan, UT: Utah State University Press, 2016), 81–103.
11 Lawson M. Smith, "Life After Death as Presented in *Heaven and Hell* by Emanuel Swedenborg," in *Annual Conference Proceedings* (Belphre, OH: Academy of Spirituality and Paranormal Studies, 2007), 120–28.
12 M. Irwin MacDonald, "The Fairy Faith and Pictured Music of Pamela Colman Smith," *The Craftsman* XXIII, no. 1 (1912): 32.
13 Howard Pyle, *The Garden Behind the Moon* (Mineola, NY: Dover, 2005). Reprinted from first edition published by Charles Scribner's Sons in New York in 1895.

14 See Jill P. May and Robert E. May, *Howard Pyle: Imagining an American School of Art* (Urbana, IL: University of Illinois Press, 2011), 4.
15 Jane Williams-Hogan, "Emanuel Swedenborg's Aesthetic Philosophy and Its Impact on Nineteenth-Century American Art," *Toronto Journal of Theology* 28, no. 1 (2012): 108.
16 Williams-Hogan, "Emanuel Swedenborg's Aesthetic Philosophy," 108.
17 Smith, "Life after Death," 120–21.
18 May and May, *Howard Pyle*, 70.
19 Perry Nodelman, "Pyle's Sweet, Thin, Clear Tune: *The Garden Behind the Moon*," *Children's Literature Association Quarterly* 8, no. 2 (1983): 22. See also May and May, *Howard Pyle*, 40, 70.
20 May and May, *Howard Pyle*, 70–71.
21 Pyle, *The Garden Behind the Moon*, 44–45.
22 Pyle, *The Garden Behind the Moon*, 44–45.
23 May and May, *Howard Pyle*, 4; Williams-Hogan, "Emanuel Swedenborg's Aesthetic Philosophy," 105–6.
24 Williams-Hogan, "Emanuel Swedenborg's Aesthetic Philosophy," 106; May and May, *Howard Pyle*, 4–5. See also Peter Otto, "Organizing the Passions: Minds, Bodies, Machines and the Sexes in Blake and Swedenborg," *European Romantic Review* 26, no. 3 (2015): 37–77; Jane Williams-Hogan, "Drawing on the Living Centre: The Creative Spirit and Emanuel Swedenborg," in *Seeking the Centre: 2001 Australian International Religion, Literature and the Arts Conference Proceedings*, ed. Colette Rayment and Mark Levon Byrne (Sydney: RLA Press, 2002), 85–103.
25 Jane Williams-Hogan, "The Place of Emanuel Swedenborg in the Spiritual Saga of Scandinavia," *Western Esotericism* 20 (2008): 254, 256.
26 See Williams-Hogan, "Emanuel Swedenborg's Aesthetic Philosophy," 106.
27 Charles Eldredge, *American Imagination and Symbolist Painting* (New York: Grey Art Gallery and Study Center, New York University, 1979), 43.
28 Eldredge, *American Imagination and Symbolist Painting*, 43.
29 Eldredge, *American Imagination and Symbolist Painting*, 45.
30 Colman Smith to Reed, December 7, 1899, box 1, folder 14.
31 Colman Smith to Reed, December 28, 1900, box 1, folder 17.
32 Colman Smith to Reed, October 5, 1896, box 1, folder 3.
33 Colman Smith to Reed, October 5, 1896, box 1, folder 3.
34 "Wins by Witchery," 9.
35 Joyce Purnick, "A Dig for Artifacts From the Days of Old Bruecklen," *The New York Times*, September 1, 1985, 42. In 1883 the poet William Cotter Wilson imagined "proud Iphetonga" as a princess who lifted her head to meet Henry Hudson as he sailed into the pristine wilderness to unleash centuries of white destruction. See William Cotter Wilson, *Poems of Two Worlds* (Kansas City, MO: Tiernan-Have Printing Co., 1893), 24.

36 "No More, No More," *The Brooklyn Daily Eagle*, November 16, 1899, 8. See also "Old Families Ruled in Own Communities," *The Brooklyn Daily Eagle*, April 8, 1934, 130.

37 Henry T. Tuckerman, *American Artist Life* (New York: G. P. Putnam & Sons, 1867), 559. In the *New York Times* obituary for his son, Samuel Colman, the elder Colman is described as "in his time, a well-known etcher." "Samuel Colman, Painter, Dies at 88," *The New York Times*, March 30, 1920, 11.

38 "Samuel Colman, Painter," 11.

39 Pamela Chandler Colman, *The Mother's Present: A Holiday Gift for the Young* (Boston, MA: S. Colman, 1847); Colman, ed., *Stories for Children: A Book for Little Girls and Boys* (New York: Samuel Raynor, 1856); Colman, ed., *The Juvenile Forget-Me-Not: A Christmas and New Year's Present* (Boston, MA: S. Colman, n.d.).

40 Miss (Pamela Atkins) Colman, *The Lulu Alphabet* (New York: Howe and Ferry, 1867).

41 There is much dispute regarding Corinne Colman's age. Her death certificate records that she was born in 1846, but this is at odds with census data. See "Corinne Colman Smith," Jamaica Civil Registration, Birth, Marriage, and Death Records, 1878–1930. The 1865 U.S. Census states that she is 28 and living with her sister, Katharine Howard's family in Brooklyn, which would indicate that Corinne was born in 1836. See Population Census, Sixth Ward, Kings County, New York, 40–41 [database online], Provo, UT: Ancestry.com Operations, 2014. By the 1870 U.S. Census Corinne was living with her husband Charles E. Smith in Manhattan, and she is listed as 35, which would indicate she was born in 1835. See U.S. Census, 1870, New York City Registry, 42 [database online], Provo, UT: Ancestry.com Operations, 2014. In the 1881 English Census, she is living with her husband Charles E. Smith and three-year-old daughter, Corinne Pamela, in Didsbury, Lancashire. Corinne's age is listed as 30, which would indicate she was born in 1851. See "Corinne Colman Smith," 1881 England Census, Chorlton, Didsbury, 4, 3890, 99, 23 [database online], Provo, UT: Ancestry.com Operations, 2014.

42 Mrs. Colman, editor, *Stories for Corinne: A Book for All Little Girls and Boys* (Boston, MA: S. Colman, 1847), 90–91.

43 Mrs. Colman, *Stories for Children: A Book for All Little Girls and Boys* (New York: Samuel Raynor, 1849, 1856), 91–92.

44 "Society," *Brooklyn Daily Eagle*, January 20, 1900, 3; and "Wins by Witchery," 9.

45 "Samuel Colman, Painter," 11.

46 Wayne Craven, "Samuel Colman (1832–1920); Rediscovered Painter of Far-Away Places," *The American Art Journal* 8, no. 1 (1976): 16–17, 32. See also Grace Guleck, "The Poetic Landscapes of Samuel Colman," *The New*

York Times, May 14, 1999, http://www.nytimes.com/1999/05/14/arts/art-in-review-the-poetic-landscapes-of-samuel-colman.htm.

47 Craven, "Samuel Colman," 31.
48 Craven, "Samuel Colman," 33.
49 Craven, "Samuel Colman," 33; see also the Metropolitan Museum of Art, Heilbrunn, "Timeline of Art History," http://www.metmuseum.org/toah/works-of-art/1992.125. For Colman and Tiffany decorating the Vanderbilt mansion, see "Wins by Witchery," 9. See also Dylan Landis, "A Tale of Treasures Lost and Memories Rekindled," *The New York Times*, March 25, 1993, 10.
50 "Wins by Witchery," 9.
51 "A Busy Life Ended: Death of Hon. Cyrus P. Smith," *The New York Times*, February 14, 1877, 5.
52 "A Busy Life Ended," 5.
53 "Wins by Witchery," 9.
54 U.S. Census, 1870, New York City Registry, 42. Charles and Corinne Smith were living in the 20th district of the 18th ward of New York City. The record was taken on December 21, 1870.
55 Baptismal record of Charles E. Smith,1845–46 [database online], Provo, UT: Ancestry.com Operations, 2014.
56 Mrs. C. E. Smith travelling alone from Kingston, Jamaica on the *Rising Star*, arrived at the port of New York on October 17, 1871. On April 2, 1874, Mrs. C.E. Smith returned to the port of New York on the *Acapulco*, sailing from Kingston, Jamaica, *New York Passenger and Crew Lists, 1820–1957* [database online], Provo, UT: Ancestry.com Operations, 2014.
57 "Heavy Failures in Manchester and New York, The Affairs of Messrs. Cowlishaw and Co," *Manchester Courier and Lancashire General Advertiser*, October 4, 1888, 3.
58 The transfer may well have overlapped with the beginning of Corinne's pregnancy and it is possible that the move was made to avoid gossip and uncomfortable speculation.
59 Eldredge, *American Imagination and Symbolist Painting*, 40.
60 "Corinne Pamela C. Smith," *Births Registered in January, February, and March 1878*, SM1, 480 [database online], Provo, UT: Ancestry.com Operations, 2014. Colman Smith was born on February 16, 1878, but her birth was not registered until March 29, 1878, nearly six weeks later, which was unusual. "Birth Announcements," *London Evening Standard*, February, 19, 1878, 1. For a reproduction of the birth certificate, see Stuart Kaplan, Mary K. Greer, Elizabeth Foley O'Connor, and Melinda Boyd Parsons, *Pamela Colman Smith: The Untold Story* (Stamford, CT: U.S. Games Systems, 2018), 388.
61 It was registered on March 29, 1878, 44 days after her birth.
62 "Wins by Witchery," 9.
63 "Corinne Colman Smith," 1881 England Census, 23.

64 Pamela Colman Smith to George Pollexfen, February 17, 1902, Stony Brook University, William Butler Yeats Collection, SC 294, box 53, 120, folder 44.
65 Colman Smith to Pollexfen, February 17, 1902, box 53, 120, folder 44.
66 Colman Smith to Reed, November 2, 1896, box 1, folder 5.
67 "Miss Pamela Coleman [sic] Smith," *The Reader: An Illustrated Monthly Magazine*, September 1903, 331.
68 Colman Smith to Pollexfen, February 17, 1902, box 53, 120, folder 44. See also Regina Armstrong, "Representative American Women Illustrators: The Decorative Workers," *The Critic*, June 1900, 527.
69 "Wins by Witchery," 9.
70 Colman Smith to Reed, October 19, 1896, box 1, folder 4. See Colman Smith to Reed, December 8, 1896, box 1, folder 7; and Colman Smith to Reed, January 5, 1898, box 1, folder 11.
71 Elazar Barkan, "Victorian Promiscuity," in *Prehistories of the Future: The Primitivist Project and the Culture of Modernism*, ed. Elazar Barkan and Ronald Bush (Stanford, CA: Stanford University Press, 1995), 71.
72 See Colman Smith to Reed, October 20, 1896, box 1, folder 4.
73 For reference to her time in Chislehurst from 1879 to 1881, see Pamela Colman Smith to Albert Bigelow Paine, May 28, 1901, Albert Bigelow Paine Letters, Manuscripts Department, Huntington Library, AP 1678. See also Colman Smith to Paine, December 13, 1900, AP 1675.
74 "Re Cowlishaw, Nicol, and Co. Meeting in Manchester," *Manchester Courier and Lancashire General Advertiser*, August 29, 1888, 7; "Bankruptcy," *Preston-Herald*, October 6, 1888, 10.
75 "Heavy Failures," 3.
76 "Manchester Bankruptcy-Court Yesterday (Before Mr. Registrar Lister)," *Manchester Courier and Lancashire General Advertiser*, August 16, 1888, 6; "Bankruptcy Receiving Orders," *Western Daily Press*, August 18, 1888, 8; "Bankruptcy Notice," *Huddersfield Chronicle*, August 18, 1888, 8.
77 "Heavy Failures," 3.
78 "Heavy Failures," 3. Using a calculation for inflation and a current dollars to pounds conversion rate, this would be approximately $428,486. In reality it was likely quite a bit more.
79 "The Bankruptcy of Messrs. Cowlishaw, Nicol & Co.," *Manchester Courier and Lancashire General Advertiser*, December 17, 1888, 3.
80 "Bankruptcy of Messrs. Cowlishaw, Nicol & Co.," 3.
81 "Bankruptcy of Messrs. Cowlishaw, Nicol & Co.," 3.
82 Charles E. Smith, Corinne Colman Smith, and Corinne Pamela (named Amelia on the manifest) Smith all arrived in the Port of New York on the *Etruria* on December 17, 1888. They had sailed from Liverpool, England, with a stop at Queenstown, Ireland. Corinne is listed as 42, which would mean she was born in 1846. *NY Passenger Lists, 1820 to 1957* [database online], Provo, UT: Ancestry.com Operations, 2014.

250   NOTES TO PAGES 33–35

83 Supreme Court Appellate Division of New York, First Department, "Central Trust Company of New York against The West India Improvement Company, The Manhattan Trust Company, James P. McDonald, Alfred Bishop Mason, and James Irvine," *Cases and Exemptions, Vol. 1* (June 1903), 518.
84 "An Interesting Social Event," *The New York Times*, August 14, 1878, 1. See also "Wins by Witchery," 9.
85 "Busy Life Ended," 5.
86 "History of Railroads in Jamaica," National Library of Jamaica, https://nlj.gov.jm/history-notes-jamaica/.
87 James Robertson, "Opening the Railway Line at Porus, 1885," in *Victorian Jamaica*, ed. Tim Barringer and Wayne Modest (Chapel Hill, NC: Duke University Press, 2018), 89.
88 Robertson, "Opening the Railway Line," 89.
89 "History of Railroads in Jamaica," National Library of Jamaica, https://nlj.gov.jm/history-notes-jamaica/.
90 Testimony by Fredric Wesson states that part of the Montego Bay line was contracted to James P. MacDonald & Company. Supreme Court Appellate Division of New York, First Department, "Central Trust Company of New York against The West India Improvement Company," 206.
91 "News of the Railroads," *The New York Times*, July 13, 1898, 4.
92 "News of the Railroads," 4.
93 "News of the Railroads," 4.
94 "Railroads in Jamaica," *The New York Times*, April 11, 1898, 4.
95 "Railroads in Jamaica," 4.
96 "Jamaica Railway to be Sold," *The New York Times*, July 12, 1898, 9.
97 Supreme Court Appellate Division of New York, First Department, "Central Trust Company of New York against The West India Improvement Company," 518.
98 Supreme Court Appellate Division of New York, First Department, "Central Trust Company of New York v. West India Improvement Company," 643.
99 Colman Smith to Reed, January 26, 1897, box 1, folder 10.
100 Tim Barringer and Wayne Modest, "Introduction," in Barringer and Modest, eds., *Victorian Jamaica*, 3.
101 Barringer and Modest, "Introduction," 4.
102 W.F.E. "The Consul in Kingston," *The New York Times*, August 17, 1895, 16.
103 Barringer and Modest," Introduction," 4. See also Belinda Edmonson, "'Most Intensely Jamaican': The Rise of Brown Identity in Jamaica," in Barringer and Modest, eds., *Victorian Jamaica*, 553–76.
104 Anna Arabindan-Kesson, "Picturing South Asians in Victorian Jamaica," in Barringer and Modest, eds., *Victorian Jamaica*, 395.
105 W.F.E. "The Consul in Kingston." See also Arabindan-Kesson, "Picturing South Asians," 395–419.
106 Barringer and Modest, "Introduction," 5.

107 Brian A. Moore and Michele A. Johnson, *Neither Led Nor Driven: Contesting British Cultural Imperialism in Jamaica, 1865–1920* (Mona, Jamaica: University of the West Indies Press, 2004), 1–2.
108 Moore and Johnson, *Neither Led Nor Driven*, 2.
109 See Diana Paton, "State Formation in Victorian Jamaica," in Barringer and Modest, eds., *Victorian Jamaica*, 236–37
110 Moore and Johnson, *Neither Led Nor Driven*, 2.
111 Moore and Johnson, *Neither Led Nor Driven*, 3.
112 Moore and Johnson, *Neither Led Nor Driven*, 3.
113 See Gad Heuman, "The View from the Colonial Office," in Barringer and Modest, eds., *Victorian Jamaica*, 152–53.
114 W.F.E. "The Oranges of Jamaica," *The New York Times*, March 29, 1895.
115 Moore and Johnson, *Neither Led Nor Driven*, 8–9.
116 Mark Nesbitt, "Botany in Victorian Jamaica," in Barringer and Modest, eds., *Victorian Jamaica*, 233.
117 W.F.E. "The Oranges of Jamaica."
118 Moore and Johnson, *Neither Led Nor Driven*, 11.
119 Nesbitt, "Botany in Victorian Jamaica," 233.
120 Nesbitt, "Botany in Victorian Jamaica," 234.
121 Brian L. Moore and Michele A. Johnson, *'They Do As They Please': The Jamaican Struggle for Cultural Freedom after Morant Bay* (Mona, Jamaica: University of the West Indies Press, 2011), 2.
122 Barkan and Bush, "Introduction," 3.
123 Colman Smith to Reed, October 19, box 1, folder 4.
124 Colman Smith to Reed, September 17, 1896, box 1, folder 2.
125 Colman Smith to Reed, January 26, 1897, box 1, folder 10.
126 Wayne Modest, "'A Period of Exhibitions': World's Fairs, Museums, and the Laboring Black Body in Jamaica," in Barringer and Modest, eds., *Victorian Jamaica*, 542–43. See Henry Blake, "The Jamaica Exhibition of 1891," *North American Review* 152, no. 411 (1891): 182–93.
127 Qtd. in Krista Thompson, *Eye for the Tropics* (Durham, NC: Duke University Press, 2006), 31.
128 Modest, "'A Period of Exhibitions,'" 543.
129 David Scott, "Modernity that Predated the Modern: Sidney Mintz's Caribbean," *History Workshop Journal* 58, no. 1 (2004): 191–210.
130 Qtd. in Scott, "Modernity that Predated the Modern," 192. See also Sidney Mintz, "Foreword," in Jean Besson, *Martha Brae's Two Histories: European Expansion and Caribbean Culture—Building in Jamaica* (Chapel Hill, NC: University of North Carolina Press, 2002), 15.
131 Barringer and Modest, "Introduction," 23.
132 Barringer and Modest, "Introduction," 1.
133 Nadia Ellis, "Jamaican Performance in the Age of Emancipation," in Barringer and Modest, eds., *Victorian Jamaica*, 630.

134 Ellis, "Jamaican Performance in the Age of Emancipation," 626–29.
135 Dianne M. Stewart, "Kumina: A Spiritual Vocabulary of Nationhood in Victorian Jamaica," in Barringer and Modest, eds., *Victorian Jamaica*, 615–16 n.2.
136 Colman Smith to Pollexfen, February 17, 1902, box 53, 120, folder 44.
137 "Wins by Witchery," 9. Corinne Colman Smith and Pamela Colman Smith are listed as passengers on the *Alene*, which departed Kingston, Jamaica, and arrived at the port of New York on October 4, 1893. Pamela and her mother did the same trip a year later on the same ship, arriving in the port of New York on September 25, 1894. *New York Passenger and Crew Lists, 1820–1957*, Microfilm Roll 619, line 33 [database online], Provo, UT: Ancestry.com Operations, 2014.
138 Colman Smith to Reed, November 15, 1896, box 1, folder 6.
139 Colman Smith to Reed, September 17, 1896, box 1, folder 2b.
140 Colman Smith to Reed, October 5, 1896, box 1, folder 3.
141 Colman Smith to Reed, November 2, 1896, box 1, folder 5.
142 Colman Smith to Reed, September 17, 1896, box 1, folder 2b.
143 Colman Smith to Reed, September 17, 1896, box 1, folder 2b.
144 Colman Smith to Reed, July 25, 1896, box 1, folder 1.
145 See Colman Smith to Reed, October 19, 1896, box 1, folder 4. See also *Jamaica in 1896: A Handbook of Information for Intended Settlers and Others* (Kingston, Jamaica: Institute of Jamaica, 1896), 16.
146 Colman Smith to Reed, July 25, 1896, box 1, folder 1; and Colman Smith to Reed, September 17, 1896, box 1, folder 2.
147 Colman Smith to Reed, July 25, 1896, box 1, folder 1.
148 Colman Smith to Reed, July 25, 1896, box 1, folder 1.
149 Colman Smith to Reed, July 25, 1896, box 1, folder 1.
150 Colman Smith to Reed, January 26, 1897, box 1, folder 1; see also "St. Andrew Sketching Club," *The Daily Gleaner* [Kingston], March 7, 1936, 34.
151 Colman Smith to Reed, September 17, 1896, box 1, folder 2b.
152 Colman Smith to Reed, September 17, 1896, box 1, folder 2a. See also Kaplan et al., *Pamela Colman Smith: The Untold Story*, 18.
153 Colman Smith to Reed, September 17, 1896, box 1, folder 2a.
154 "A Jamaica Spider," *The Washington Times*, January 15, 1899, 17.
155 I. A. Haskell, "The Decorative Work of Miss. Pamela Colman Smith," *Pratt Institute Monthly* 6, no. 3 (1897): 67.
156 "A Jamaica Spider," 17.
157 "A Jamaica Spider," 17.
158 Gardner Teall, "Cleverness, Art, and the Artist," *Brush and Pencil* 6, no. 3 (1900): 140. See also Kaplan et al., *Pamela Colman Smith: The Untold Story*, 20.
159 Lucy France Pierce, "The Littlest Theatre," *The Drama Magazine* 4, nos. 13–16 (1914): 84.
160 Pierce, "The Littlest Theatre," 84–87.

161 Pierce, "The Littlest Theatre," 89.
162 Pierce, "The Littlest Theatre," 85.
163 Albert Bigelow Paine, "A Miniature Theater," *The Puritan* VII, no. 3 (1899): 376.
164 Paine, "A Miniature Theater," 376.
165 See Colman Smith to Reed, September 17, 1896, box 1, folder 2a for references to *The Magic Carbuncle*, and Colman Smith to Reed, October 5, 1896, box 1, folder 3 for reference to *The Guardsman*.
166 Colman Smith to Reed, November 15, 1896, box 1, folder 6.
167 Colman Smith to Reed, December 15, 1896, box 1, folder 8.
168 Colman Smith to Reed, October 19, 1896, box 1, folder 4.
169 Colman Smith to Reed, October 19, 1896, box 1, folder 4.
170 Colman Smith to Reed, October 5, 1896, box 1, folder 3.
171 Colman Smith to Reed, October 19, 1896, box 1, folder 4.
172 Stephan Talty, *Empire of Blue Water: Captain Morgan's Great Pirate Army* (New York: Crown Publishers, 2007), 9–19.
173 Talty, *Empire of Blue Water*, 266–67.
174 Talty, *Empire of Blue Water*, 266–81.
175 May and May, *Howard Pyle*, 41.
176 Colman Smith to Reed, September 17, 1896, box 1, folder 2b.
177 Colman Smith to Reed, September 17, 1896, box 1, folder 2b.
178 For example, the account of *Henry Morgan* that Alfred Bigelow Paine gives differs quite substantially, although almost all the characters are the same, from the version Colman Smith relates to her cousin. See Paine, "A Miniature Theater," 369–76.
179 Colman Smith to Reed, September 17, 1896, box 1, folder 2b.
180 Colman Smith to Reed, September 17, 1896, box 1, folder 2b.
181 Colman Smith to Reed, September 17, 1896, box 1, folder 2b.
182 Colman Smith to Reed, September 17, 1896, box 1, folder 2b.
183 Paine, "A Miniature Theatre," 369–76.
184 Colman Smith to Reed, September 17, 1896, box 1, folder 2b.
185 Colman Smith to Reed, September 17, 1896, box 1, folder 2b.
186 Colman Smith to Reed, October 5, 1896, box 1, folder 3.
187 Colman Smith to Reed, October 5, 1896, box 1, folder 3.
188 Colman Smith to Reed, October 5, 1896, box 1, folder 3.
189 Colman Smith to Reed, October 5, 1896, box 1, folder 3.
190 Colman Smith to Reed, October 5, 1896, box 1, folder 3.
191 Colman Smith to Reed, October 5, 1896, box 1, folder 3.
192 Charles II died in 1685, and although he knighted Henry Morgan in 1674, he did so in England. See Talty, *Empire of Blue Water*, 266–67.
193 Paine, "A Miniature Theater," 376.
194 "School Entertainment at Half-way Trees," *The Daily Gleaner* [Kingston], December 14, 1896, 3.

195 Colman Smith to Reed, December 8, 1896, box 1, folder 7.
196 "School Entertainment at Half-way Trees," 3.
197 Colman Smith to Reed, December 15, 1896, box 1, folder 8.
198 "Teachers-Students-and-Things-," *Pratt Institute Monthly* 6, no. 4 (1898): 148.
199 "Teachers-Students-and-Things-," 148.

Chapter Two: Forging a Path: Critical Reception, Key Influences, and Emergence as an Artist

1 "Teachers-Students-and-Things-," *Pratt Institute Monthly* 6, no. 4 (1898): 148; "American Studio Talk," *International Studio: An Illustrated Magazine of Fine and Applied Art* 2, no. 1 (1898): xii.
2 "In Local Studios," *The Brooklyn Daily Eagle*, February 13, 1898, 12.
3 "American Studio Talk," xii.
4 See "Teachers-Students-and-Things-," 148. The article states that an unnamed New York newspaper reviewed Colman Smith's exhibit and termed her a "young English girl," but clarifies "(though, in fact, Miss Smith is an American)."
5 R.R.G, "Pamela Colman Smith: She Believes in Fairies," *The Delineator*, November 1912, 320.
6 Charles C. Eldredge, *American Imagination and Symbolist Painting* (New York: Grey Art Gallery and Study Center, New York University, 1979), 38.
7 Pamela Colman Smith to Mary "Bobby" Reed, January 5, 1898, Pamela Colman Smith Collection, Canaday Library, Bryn Mawr College, box 1, folder 11.
8 I. A. Haskell, "The Decorative Work of Miss. Pamela Colman Smith," *Pratt Institute Monthly* 6, no. 3 (1897): 65–67.
9 See Stuart Kaplan, Mary K. Greer, Elizabeth Foley O'Connor, and Melinda Boyd Parsons, *Pamela Colman Smith: The Untold Story* (Stamford, CT: U.S. Game Systems, 2018), 22.
10 Haskell, "The Decorative Work," 65.
11 *Our Pets* is very similar to Colman Smith's *Recess*, which was part of the Russell portfolio. Pamela Colman Smith, "Recess," in *Portfolio* (New York: R. H. Russell, 1898). The painting is also included in a 1912 *Craftsman* article. The placement of the figures is identical but there are deviations in the children's clothing and hair color. There is an interesting addition on the exterior wall of the schoolhouse of a small drawing of a woman, which is a characteristic part of Colman Smith's signature in letters beginning in 1900. See M. Irwin MacDonald, "The Fairy Faith and Pictured Music of Pamela Colman Smith," *The Craftsman* XXIII, no. 1 (1912): 25.
12 Nadia Ellis, "Jamaican Performance in the Age of Emancipation," in *Victorian Jamaica*, ed. Tim Barringer and Wayne Modest (Durham, NC: Duke University Press, 2018), 628.

13 Ellis, "Jamaican Performance," 628.
14 Henry Wansbrough, *The New Jerusalem Bible* (Garden City, NY: Doubleday, 1999), Num. 13:27.
15 Haskell, "The Decorative Work," 65. See also "Educational Notes," *Brooklyn Daily Eagle*, December 5, 1897, 30.
16 Haskell does temper her praise somewhat, saying, "Doubtless from an academic and conventional point of view her drawing may be severely criticized; but as she is still very young, there is time for her to develop on that side, as well as on others." Haskell, "The Decorative Work," 65–66.
17 Haskell, "The Decorative Work," 65.
18 Arthur Wesley Dow, *Composition: A Series of Exercises in Art Structure for the Use of Students and Teachers* (Oxford: Benediction Classics, 7th edn, 1913), 38.
19 Melinda Boyd Parsons points out that Marcus Ward and his family were neighbors of Colman Smith and her parents when they lived in Chislehurst on the outskirts of London when she was a toddler. Melinda Boyd Parsons, "Influences and Expression in the Rider-Waite Tarot Deck," in Kaplan et al., *Pamela Colman Smith: The Untold Story*, 355–56.
20 Haskell, "The Decorative Work," 65.
21 Nancy E. Green, "Arthur Wesley Dow, Artist & Educator," in *Arthur Wesley Dow and American Arts & Crafts*, ed. Nancy E. Green and Jessie Poesch (New York: The American Federation of the Arts, 1999), 59.
22 Green, "Arthur Wesley Dow," 55.
23 Green, "Arthur Wesley Dow," 60.
24 Qtd. in Green, "Arthur Wesley Dow," 60–61.
25 See Betty Lou Williams, "Japanese Aesthetic Influences on Early 20th-Century Art Education: Arthur Wesley Dow and Ernest Fenollosa," *Visual Arts Research* 39, no. 2 (2013): 104–15.
26 Dow, *Composition*, 7. See also Green, "Arthur Wesley Dow," 55–56, 66.
27 Arthur Warren Johnson, *Arthur Wesley Dow, Historian, Artist, Teacher* (Ipswich, MA: Ipswich Historical Society, 1934), 87.
28 See Kathleen Pyne, *Modernism and the Feminine Voice: O'Keeffe and the Women of the Stieglitz Circle* (Berkeley, CA: University of California Press, 2007).
29 Williams, "Japanese Aesthetic Influences," 105.
30 Green, "Arthur Wesley Dow," 57; Pyne, *Modernism and the Feminine Voice*, 47.
31 Green, "Arthur Wesley Dow," *Arthur Wesley Dow*, 57; Pyne, *Modernism and the Feminine Voice*, 47.
32 "Fine Arts: The Influence of our Normal Classes," *Pratt Institute Monthly* 4, no. 6 (1896): 179.
33 Jessie Morse, "Teachers-Students-and-Things," *Pratt Institute Monthly* 4, no. 7 (1896): 209.

34 Arthur W. Dow, "A Note on a New System of Art-Teaching," *Pratt Institute Monthly* 4, no. 3 (1896): 93.
35 Arthur W. Dow, "Some Results of a Synthetic Method of Art Instruction," *Pratt Institute Monthly* 5, no. 3 (1897): 69.
36 Colman Smith, Pratt Institute report card, private collection of Stuart R. Kaplan, U.S. Games, Inc.
37 Pamela Colman Smith correspondence to Alfred Bigelow Paine, February 7, 1904, Albert Bigelow Paine Letters, Manuscripts Department, Huntington Library, AP 1682.
38 In 1912 Colman Smith made tapestry designs that were executed by her maternal aunt, Mrs. George Notman, and her friends. See "Reviving Home Industries," *New York Sun*, March 24, 1912, 33; "Reviving Home Industries," *The Idaho Statesman*, March 31, 1912, 6; "Revival of Old Industries," *Oswego Palladium*, June 8, 1912, 11; "Revival of Old Industries," *Watertown Reunion*, July 17, 1912, 8.
39 "Founder's Day," *Pratt Institute Monthly* 4, no. 2 (1895): 42; "Fine Arts," *Pratt Institute Monthly* 4, no. 2 (1895): 52; "Teachers-Students-and-Things," *Pratt Institute Monthly* 4, no. 4 (1895): 112–13.
40 Dow, *Composition*, 5.
41 The Hon. Mrs. Forbes-Sempill, "Music Made Visible: An Unmusical Artist's Lightning Impressions Recorded While Listening to Music," *The Illustrated London News*, February 12, 1927, 3.
42 Colman Smith to Reed, January 5, 1898, box 1, folder 11.
43 "Reviews," *The Studio: An Illustrated Magazine of Fine & Applied Art* 20 no. 89 (1900): 199.
44 Regina Armstrong, "Representative American Women Illustrators: The Decorative Workers," *The Critic*, June 1900, 527.
45 Pamela Coleman [sic] Smith, illustration for "A School Girl Song of Spring," *Pratt Institute Monthly* 5, no. 7 (1897): 199.
46 See Dow, *Composition*, 22, 24–26.
47 Betty Botticelli, "A School-Girl Song of Spring," *Pratt Institute Monthly* 5, no. 7 (1897): 199.
48 Betty Botticelli, "A Schoolgirl Song of Spring," *The New York Times*, March 18, 1897, 6.
49 Dow, *Composition*, 38.
50 Arthur W. Dow, "Appreciation," *Pratt Institute Monthly* 7, no. 5 (1899): 62.
51 "Miss Pamela Coleman [sic] Smith," *The Reader: An Illustrated Monthly Magazine*, September 1903, 331. See also Armstrong, "Representative American Women Illustrators," 527.
52 Jill P. May and Robert E. May, *Howard Pyle: Imagining an American School of Art* (Urbana, IL: University of Illinois Press, 2011), ix, 36.
53 May and May, *Howard Pyle*, x.
54 Colman Smith to Reed, January 5, 1898, box 1, folder 11.

55 Colman Smith to Reed, January 5, 1898, box 1, folder 11.
56 Colman Smith to Reed, January 5, 1898, box 1, folder 11.
57 May and May, *Howard Pyle*, 62, 64. Wuanita Smith studied with Pyle between 1897 and 1899. Jessie Wilcox Smith was part of Pyle's first class and was one of his "protégés." See also May and May, *Howard Pyle*, 88, 106.
58 Richard Wayne Lykes, "Howard Pyle Teacher of Illustration," *The Pennsylvania Magazine of History and Biography* 80, no. 3 (1956): 341.
59 Qtd. in Lykes, "Howard Pyle Teacher of Illustration," 342.
60 Lykes, "Howard Pyle Teacher of Illustration," 345–46.
61 Qtd. in Lykes, "Howard Pyle Teacher of Illustration," 346.
62 Colman Smith to Reed, January 5, 1898, box 1, folder 11.
63 Colman Smith to Reed, January 5, 1898, box 1, folder 11.
64 Colman Smith to Reed, January 5, 1898, box 1, folder 11.
65 May and May, *Howard Pyle*, 76.
66 May and May, *Howard Pyle*, 76.
67 Colman Smith to Reed, March 9, 1898, box 1, folder 12.
68 Colman Smith to Reed, June 13, 1898, box 1, folder 13.
69 Colman Smith to Reed, June 13, 1898, box 1, folder 13.
70 Colman Smith to Paine, December 13, 1900, AP 1675.
71 The full-page note is found on a blank page near the beginning of Katharine Pyle's *The Counterpane Fairy* (New York: E. P. Dutton & Co., 1898). The initials P.C.S. are at the top of the page along with her address, 2 Bencoolen House, Bude, and the year, 1948, along with the request to "please return sometime." The book is in the private collection of Stuart R. Kaplan, U.S. Games Systems, Inc.
72 Colman Smith to Reed, March 9, 1898, box 1, folder 12.
73 Colman Smith to Reed, March 9, 1896, box 1, folder 12. See also Katharine Pyle, illustrations for Maud Wilder Goodwin, *Head of a Hundred* (Boston, MA: Little, Brown, 1892); and Katharine Pyle, illustrations for Maud Wilder Goodwin, *White Aprons: A Romance of Bacon's Rebellion, Virginia 1676* (Boston, MA: Little, Brown, 1897).
74 May and May, *Howard Pyle*, 16, 26–27.
75 May and May, *Howard Pyle*, 29.
76 May and May, *Howard Pyle*, 53.
77 May and May, *Howard Pyle*, 52. See also Helen Goodman, "Women Illustrators of the Golden Age of American Illustration," *Woman's Art Journal* 8, no. 1 (1987): 14.
78 See Lykes, "Howard Pyle Teacher of Illustration," 349–52, 355; May and May, *Howard Pyle*, 64.
79 Colman Smith to Paine, March 17, 1901, AP 1677.
80 Charlotte Herzog, "A Rose by Any Other Name: Violet Oakley, Jessie Wilcox Smith, and Elizabeth Shippen Green," *Women's Art Journal* 14, no. 2 (1993–94): 11.

81. See Herzog, "A Rose," 12.
82. Herzog, "A Rose," 11.
83. May and May, *Howard Pyle*, 183–84.
84. Goodman, "Women Illustrators," 13–21.
85. Armstrong, "Representative American Women Illustrators," 520.
86. Goodman, "Women Illustrators," 14.
87. Armstrong, "Representative American Women Illustrators," 526.
88. Armstrong, "Representative American Women Illustrators," 528.
89. Armstrong, "Representative American Women Illustrators," 529.
90. "Ida Haskell," *Benezit Dictionary of Artists* (Oxford: Oxford University Press, 2006).
91. "Ida Haskell," *Benezit Dictionary of Artists*.
92. Ida Haskell, "Summer in Holland from an Artist's Point of View," *Pratt Institute Monthly* 5, no. 6 (1896): 165–66. See also "Tell me how you spend your leisure, and I will tell you what you really are," *Pratt Institute Monthly* 5, no. 9 (1896): 322.
93. Haskell, "The Decorative Work," 65.
94. Colman Smith to Reed, January 5, 1898, box 1, folder 11.
95. Colman Smith to Reed, March 9, 1898, box 1, folder 12.
96. Colman Smith to Reed, June 13, 1898, box 1, folder 13.
97. Colman Smith to Reed, August 10, 1898, box 1, folder 14.
98. According to Census records and other documents available on "Brookhaven/South Haven Hamlets & Their People," Haskell and Boughton lived together in New York and Brookhaven for at least twelve years. Boughton was the executrix of Haskell's will and the recipient of almost all of her possessions. See http://brookhavensouthhaven.org/hamletpeople/tng/getperson.php?personID=I9383&tree=hamlet.
99. For a contemporaneous discussion of Colman Smith and Käsebier, see Sadakichi Hartmann, "Gertrude Käsebier," *Photographic Times* 32, no. 5 (1900): 198.
100. See Pyne, *Modernism and the Feminine Voice*, 21–47.
101. Colman Smith to Reed, June 13, 1898, box 1, folder 13.
102. "The Lounger," *The Critic* 34, no. 859 (January 1899): 15.
103. Colman Smith to Reed, June 13, 1898, box 1, folder 13. See also Colman Smith to Reed, September 9, 1898, box 1, folder 19; and "Progress of One Student of the Regular Art Class," *Pratt Institute Monthly* 7, no. 5 (1899): 71.
104. Julia Briggs, "Transitions: 1890–1914," in *Children's Literature: An Illustrated History*, ed. Peter Hunt (New York: Oxford University Press, 1995), 182.
105. See Colman Smith to Reed, March 9, 1898, box 1, folder 12, where she gives an almost complete alphabetical list of possibilities.
106. Pamela Colman Smith, watercolor of Caliban, Special Collections, Folger Shakespeare Library, 006205.jpg. https://www.folger.edu/file/006205jpg.
107. Dow, *Composition*, 48.

108 Colman Smith to Reed, June 13, 1898, box 1, folder 13. See also Colman Smith to Paine, August 7, 1899, AP 1671.
109 The Shakespearean Alphabet book is mentioned in "The Progress of One Student," 71, and "A Jamaica Spider," 17. No publisher is given in either article.
110 See Kaplan et al., *Pamela Colman Smith: The Untold Story*, 128.
111 Pamela Colman Smith, *Portfolio* (New York: R. H. Russell, 1898).
112 Johanna Drucker, "Modern Publishing Transformations: Libraries, Globalization, Corporatization, and Artists' Publications," in *The History of the Book* (UCLA Special Collections), ch. 10, https://hob.gseis.ucla.edu/HoBCoursebook_Ch_10.html.
113 Drucker, "Modern Publishing Transformations."
114 See Dow, *Composition*, 15. See also "Books and Authors," *The New York Times*, December 10, 1898, 834; "Literature," *The Washington Times*, December 25, 1898, 15; and "The Progress of One Student," 71.
115 Qtd. in Williams, "Japanese Aesthetic Influences," 109.
116 Arthur W. Dow, "A New System of Art Teaching," *Pratt Institute Monthly* 4, no. 4 (1896): 94.
117 See Haskell, "The Decorative Work," 65; MacDonald, "The Fairy Faith," 25; and Kaplan et al., *Pamela Colman Smith: The Untold Story*, 22,
118 See Kaplan et al., *Pamela Colman Smith: The Untold Story*, 24.
119 See Kaplan et al., *Pamela Colman Smith: The Untold Story*, 27.
120 William Butler Yeats, *The Land of Heart's Desire* (Chicago: Stone and Kimball, 1894), unpaginated, https://en.wikisource.org/wiki/The_Land_of_Heart%27s_Desire.
121 See Carol Silver, *Strange and Secret Peoples: Fairies and the Victorian Unconscious* (New York: Oxford University Press, 1999), 149–83.
122 Colman Smith, "The Land of Heart's Desire," in *Portfolio.*
123 Yeats, *Land of Heart's Desire*. See also W. B. Yeats, *The Land of Heart's Desire Manuscript Materials*, ed. Jared Curtis (Ithaca, NY: Cornell University Press, 2002).
124 Ann Saddlemyer, "Designing Ladies: Women Artists and the Early Abbey Stage," *The Princeton University Library Chronicle* 68, nos. 1–2 (2007): 184. See also John Kelly and Ronald Schuchard, eds., *The Collected Letters of W.B. Yeats, Volume Three, 1901–1904* (Oxford: Clarendon Press, 1986), 251 n.2.
125 Birgit Bramsbäck, "William Butler Yeats and Folklore Material," *Béaloideas* 39, no. 41 (1971–73), 59.
126 See Kaplan et al., *Pamela Colman Smith: The Untold Story*, 26.
127 William Shakespeare, *Macbeth*, 1.4.22–23, The Folger Shakespeare, https://shakespeare.folger.edu/shakespeares-works/macbeth/
128 "The Progress of One Student," 71, quotes a Russell circular advertising Colman Smith's December 1898 portfolio: "The quotation is from Macbeth,

Act 1., Scene 4, the picture from Act 1., Scene 6. The quotation is apt and suits the composition admirably." The distinction is not made anywhere else.
129 Cristina León Alfar, *Fantasies of Female Evil: The Dynamics of Gender and Power in Shakespearean Tragedy* (Newark, DE: University of Delaware Press, 2003), 112.
130 Samuel Taylor Coleridge, *Coleridge's Essays and Lectures on Shakespeare and Other Poets and Dramatists*, ed. Ernest Rhys (London: J. M. Dent, 1907), 162. See also Mary Balestraci, "Shakespeare's 'Wonderful Woman': A Victorian Defense of Lady Macbeth," *Victorians Institute Journal* 43 (2015): 163–66.
131 Qtd. in Georgianna Ziegler, "Accommodating the Virago: Nineteenth-Century Representations of Lady Macbeth," in *Shakespeare and Appropriation*, ed. Christy Desmet and Robert Sawyer (London: Routledge, 2013), 17.
132 Madeleine Leigh-Noel Elliott, *Lady Macbeth: A Study* (London: Wyman, 1884). See Balestraci, "Shakespeare's 'Wonderful Woman,'" 161–88.
133 Qtd. in Sandra M. Gilbert, "'Unsex Me Here': Lady Macbeth's 'Hell Broth'" (March 2016), in *Discovering Literature: Shakespeare & Renaissance* (London: British Library), https://www.bl.uk/shakespeare/articles/unsex-me-here-lady-macbeths-hell-broth. See also William C. Carroll, "The Fiendlike Queen: Recuperating Lady Macbeth in Contemporary Adaptations of *Macbeth*," *Borrowers and Lenders: The Journal of Shakespeare and Appropriation*, http://www.borrowers.uga.edu/1077/show.
134 Gilbert, "'Unsex Me Here.'"
135 See also Michael Holroyd, *A Strange Eventful History: The Dramatic Lives of Ellen Terry, Henry Irving, and Their Remarkable Families* (New York: Picador, 2008), 194–201.
136 John Singer Sargent, *Ellen Terry as Lady Macbeth*, 1889, Tate Gallery, https://www.tate.org.uk/art/artworks/sargent-ellen-terry-as-lady-macbeth-n02053. Nina Auerbach, *Woman and the Demon: The Life of a Victorian Myth* (Cambridge, MA: Harvard University Press, 1982), 207.
137 Boyd Parsons, "Influences and Expression," 356.
138 "American Studio Talk," *The International Studio* 6, no. 1. (1899): xx.
139 "The Lounger," *The Critic*, January 1899, 15.
140 See Kaplan et al., *Pamela Colman Smith: The Untold Story*, 27–39.
141 "Annancy Stories—A Literary Event," *New York Herald*, December 11, 1898, 7. This full-page spread contained nine black and white drawings by Colman Smith and reproduced the text of three stories: "Bull-Garshananee," "Paarat, Tiger, An' Annancy," and "Mr. Titman." Another full-page spread appeared in the *New York Herald*, December 25, 1898, 7. This included "Ticky-Picky Boom Boom" and "Mother Calbee." See also "Mother Calbee and Her Cruel Present," *Pittsburgh Daily Post*, December 25, 1898, 16. "The World of Books," *The Seattle Post-Intelligencer*, February 25, 1900, 32, combined a review of Colman Smith and *Annancy Stories* with three of her pictures, and the text of "De Man an de Six Poach Eggs."

142 Colman Smith to Paine, August 7, 1899, AP 1671.
143 Colman Smith to Paine, March 17, 1901, AP 1677.
144 "The Newest Books," *St. Louis Post-Dispatch*, October 14, 1899, 4. The same article appeared in "Literary Notes," *The Washington Times*, October 22, 1899, 20; "More Irish Folk Tales," *Brooklyn Life*, November 18, 1899, 12; and "Children's Gift-Books," *Pall Mall Gazette*, November 28, 1899, 9.
145 "Children's Gift-Books," 9.
146 "Modern Irish Art," *Dublin Daily Express*, November 11, 1899, 3.
147 Pamela Colman Smith, *The Golden Vanity and The Green Bed* (New York: R. H. Russell, 1899).
148 Colman Smith, *The Golden Vanity*, n.p.
149 See Kaplan et al., *Pamela Colman Smith: The Untold Story*, 115–17.
150 Dow, *Composition*, 118.
151 Elkin Mathews republished *The Golden Vanity and The Green Bed* in 1903 in London.
152 "Bookland," *The Philadephia Inquirer*, October 22, 1899, 6.
153 Colman Smith, *The Golden Vanity*, n.p.
154 Jonathan Cott, "A Dialogue with Maurice Sendak," in *Victorian Color Picture Books*, ed. Jonathan Cott (New York: The Stonehill Publishing Company in Association with Chelsea House Publishers, 1983), ix.
155 Pamela Colman Smith, *Widdicombe Fair* (New York: Doubleday and McClure, 1899), unpaginated.
156 Cott, "A Dialogue with Maurice Sendak," xi.
157 Sabine Baring-Gould collected more than twenty variations on the song; apparently "Tom Cobley was a real farmer from Spreyton, where he lies in an unmarked grave." See Theo Brown, "The Folklore of Devon," *Folklore* 75, no. 3 (1964): 158.
158 Colman Smith, *Widdicombe Fair*.
159 Colman Smith, *Widdicombe Fair*.
160 For example, Mildred Howells's portfolio included "six further prints and cards." See Pamela Colman Smith, *Widdicombe Fair*, Museum of Fine Arts Boston, Americas Prints and Drawings, Accession Number 53.2212, https://collections.mfa.org/objects/160916.
161 Martin Graebe, "Devon by Dog Cart and Bicycle: The Folk Song Collaboration of Sabine Baring-Gould and Cecil Sharp, 1904–1917," *Folk Music Journal* 9, no. 3 (2008): 292–348. See also "Literature," *The Philadelphia Inquirer*, October 22, 1899, 46; and "Literature," *The Washington Times*, October 22, 1899, 20.
162 "Guide for the Christmas Book Buyer: Art," *The Critic* 32, no. 6 (December 1899): 1145.
163 A. V. M. Horton, "Reverend Sabine Baring-Gold: 'Squarson Dilettante' (1834–1924)," *Borneo Research Bulletin* 37 (2007): 65–67.
164 David J. Skal, "Something in the Blood, Part One," *The Paris Review*, October 27, 2016.

165 "Literature," *The Philadelphia Inquirer*, October 22, 1899, 46; and "Literature," *The Washington Times*, October 22, 1899, 20. See also Colman Smith to Paine, August 23, 1899, AP 1673.
166 Colman Smith to Paine, August 7, 1899, AP 1672.
167 Colman Smith to Paine, August 7, 1899, AP 1672.
168 Colman Smith to Paine, August 7, 1899, AP 1672.
169 "Literature," *The Philadelphia Inquirer*, 46; and "Literature," *The Washington Times*, 20. The notice also appeared in Anne Pendleton, "About Books & Authors," *The Tennessean*, November 5, 1899, 20.
170 "Charles Edward Smith," *Brooklyn Daily Eagle*, December 2, 1899, 18; and "Died," *The New York Times*, December 3, 1899, 3.
171 "Charles Edward Smith," 18; and "Died," 3.
172 Ellen Terry to Edward Gordon Craig, no. 1067, in *The Collected Letters of Ellen Terry, Volume 4*, ed. Katharine Cockin (London: Taylor and Francis, 2015), 88; Colman Smith to Reed, February 25, 1900, box 1, folder 15.

Chapter Three: Becoming Pixie: Friendship, Synaesthesia, and *The Green Sheaf*

1 "Ocean Travel," *Brooklyn Life*, May 26, 1900, 19; Ellen Terry, no. 1086, in *The Collected Letters of Ellen Terry, Volume 4*, ed. Katharine Cockin (London: Taylor and Francis, 2015), 118.
2 Terry, no. 1086, in *The Collected Letters of Ellen Terry, Volume 4*, 118.
3 Pamela Colman Smith to Mary "Bobby" Reed, December 7, 1899, Pamela Colman Smith Collection, Canaday Library, Bryn Mawr College, box 1, folder 14. See also Terry, no. 1081, in *The Collected Letters of Ellen Terry, Volume 4*, 112.
4 Colman Smith to Reed, February 25, 1900, box 1, folder 15.
5 Colman Smith to Reed, December 7, 1899, box 1, folder 14.
6 Sheila Kineke, "'Like a Hook Fits an Eye': Jean Rhys, Ford Madox Ford, and the Imperial Operations of Modernist Mentoring," *Tulsa Studies in Women's Literature* 16, no. 2 (1997): 281–301; Caroline Zilboorg, "H.D. and R.A.: Early Love and the Exclusion of Ezra Pound," *The H.D. Newsletter* 3, no. 1 (1989): 26–34.
7 Terry, no. 1067, in *The Collected Letters of Ellen Terry, Volume 4*, 88. See also no. 1072, 97.
8 Terry, no. 1067, in *The Collected Letters of Ellen Terry, Volume 4*, 88. In a January 27, 1900 letter to her son, Terry terms Colman Smith "the sharpest little creature I ever met." Terry, no. 1072, in *The Collected Letters of Ellen Terry, Volume 4*, 97.
9 Paul Manning, "Pixies' Progress: How the Pixie Became Part of the Nineteenth-Century Fairy Mythology," in *The Folkloresque: Reframing Folklore in a Popular Culture World*, ed. Michael Dylan Foster and Jeffrey

A. Tolbert (Logan, UT: Utah State Press, 2016), 82; Carole Silver, *Strange and Secret Peoples: Fairies and Victorian Consciousness* (New York: Oxford University Press, 1999), 3. See also Jonathan Roper, "Thoms and the Unachieved 'Folk-Lore' of England," *Folklore* 118 (August 2007): 203–16.
10 Silver, *Strange and Secret Peoples*, 3, 37–43.
11 Lee O'Brien, "Uncanny Transactions and Canny Forms: Rosamund Marriott Watson's 'Marchen,'" *Victorian Poetry* 46, no. 4 (2008): 431.
12 Silver, *Strange and Secret Peoples*, 3.
13 Silver, *Strange and Secret Peoples*, 33–34.
14 See Victor Roman Mendoza, "'Come Buy': The Crossing of Sexual and Consumer Desire in Christina Rossetti's *Goblin Market*," *ELH* 73, no. 4 (2006): 913–47; Paul Ellis, "Radical Myths: Eliza Keary's *Little Seal-Skin and Other Poems* (1874)," *Victorian Poetry* 40 no. 4 (2002): 387–408.
15 See Silver, *Strange and Secret Peoples*, 3–32.
16 Silver, *Strange and Secret Peoples*, 33.
17 Silver, *Strange and Secret Peoples*, 47–48.
18 Silver, *Strange and Secret Peoples*, 49.
19 See Pamela Colman Smith to Alfred Bigelow Paine, August 7, 1899, Albert Bigelow Paine Letters, Manuscripts Department, Huntington Library, AP 1672; and Colman Smith to Paine, August 23, 1899, AP 1673. See also Terry, no. 1072, in *The Collected Letters of Ellen Terry, Volume 4*, 97.
20 Thomas Keightly, in the second edition of *Fairy Mythology* (1850), notes that "In short, everything that is done elsewhere by fairies, boggarts, or other like beings, is done in Devon by Pixies." Qtd. in Manning, "Pixies' Progress," 98.
21 Anna Eliza (Mrs.) Bray, *A description of the part of Devonshire bordering on the Tamar and the Tavy; its natural history, manners, customs, superstitions, scenery, antiquities, biography of eminent persons, &c. &c. in a series of letters to Robert Southey, Esq.* (London: J. Murray, 1836), 172–73. Bray repeated almost the identical description in her *A Peep at the Pixies; or, Legends of the West* (London: Grant and Griffith, 1854), 12.
22 Lady Rosalind Northcote, "Devonshire Folklore, Collected Among the People near Exeter within the Last Five or Six Years," *Folklore* 11, no. 2 (1900): 212.
23 See Colman Smith to Reed, September 17, 1896, box 1, folder 2.
24 See Michael Holroyd, *A Strange Eventful History: The Dramatic Lives of Ellen Terry, Henry Irving, and Their Remarkable Families* (New York: Picador, 2008), 257–58, 263–66.
25 "Society Continued," *Brooklyn Life*, January 20, 1900, 30.
26 Pamela Colman Smith, *William Gillette in Sherlock Holmes: as produced at the Garrick Theatre, New York* (New York: R. H. Russell, 1900), unpaginated. See also Anne Pendleton, "About Books and Authors," *The Tennessean*, April 22, 1900, 20; and Terry, no. 1174, in *The Collected Letters of Ellen Terry, Volume 4*, 197.

27 Stuart Kaplan, Mary K. Greer, Elizabeth Foley O'Connor, and Melinda Boyd Parsons, *Pamela Colman Smith: The Untold Story* (Stamford, CT: U.S. Game Systems, 2018), 39, 138–42.
28 Heather Campbell Coyle, "The Curious Case of the Stolen Composition," *Illustration History: An Educational Resource and Archive*, September 18, 2015, http://www.illustrationhistory.org/essays/the-curious-case-of-the-stolen-composition.
29 Coyle, "The Curious Case of the Stolen Composition."
30 Colman Smith to Paine, August 23, 1899, AP 1673.
31 See Kaplan et al., *Pamela Colman Smith: The Untold Story*, 36, 104–9.
32 "Literary Chat," *The Courier-Journal* [Louisville, Kentucky], November 18, 1899, 7. The same notice also appeared in "Literary World," *The Farmer and Mechanic* [Raleigh, North Carolina], November 21, 1899, 8; "Theatrical World," *The Record-Union* [Sacramento, California], November 26, 1899, 7; "Literary Notes: Interesting News Concerning New Publications," *Virginia-Pilot* [Norfolk, Virginia], November 26, 1899, 11; "Literary Clippings," *The Tennessean*, December 3, 1899, 20.
33 Colman Smith, "Sir Henry Irving and Miss Ellen Terry"; for more on Terry as "Our Lady of the Lyceum," see Holroyd, *A Strange Eventful History*, 119–26.
34 Godwin was the father of Terry's two children, Edith and Gordon Craig. See Holroyd, *A Strange Eventful History*, 72–76.
35 Terry, no. 1067, in *The Collected Letters of Ellen Terry, Volume 4*, 88–89; and Terry, no.1071, 95–97.
36 Terry, no. 1068, in *The Collected Letters of Ellen Terry, Volume 4*, 90.
37 Terry, no. 1067, in *The Collected Letters of Ellen Terry, Volume 4*, 88.
38 Ellen Terry and George Bernard Shaw, *Ellen Terry and Bernard Shaw: A Correspondence*, ed. Christopher St. John (London: Putnam & Sons, 1931), xviii.
39 Katherine Cockin, "Bram Stoker, Ellen Terry, Pamela Colman Smith and the Art of Devilry," in *Bram Stoker and the Gothic: Formations to Transformations*, ed. Catherine Wynne (Basingstoke: Palgrave Macmillan, 2016), 161.
40 Terry, no. 1088, in *The Collected Letters of Ellen Terry, Volume 4*, 119.
41 In *Edy was a Lady*, Ann Rachlin states that Terry and Edy Craig became interested in Japanese culture during their time living with the architect Edward Godwin (Edy's father). Both owned and wore kimonos; Edy's was given her by James McNeill Whistler. See Ann Rachlin, *Edy was a Lady* (Leicester: Matador, 2011), 6, 12.
42 See Charles C. Eldredge, *American Imagination and Symbolist Painting* (New York: Grey Art Gallery and Study Center, New York University, 1979), 38–48.
43 Rachlin, *Edy was a Lady*, 124–25. See also Terry, no. 1319, in *The Collected Letters of Ellen Terry, Volume 4*, 321.
44 Terry, no. 1067, in *The Collected Letters of Ellen Terry, Volume 4*, 88.

45 Both portfolios are housed at Smallhythe Place in Tenterdon, Kent, a National Trust site, EC_T10. See also Katharine Cockin, *Edith Craig (1869–1947): Dramatic Lives* (London: Cassell, 1998), 52–53.
46 "The two little devils Pixie and Puck," in *Ellen Peg's Book of Merry Joys*, 1900, Smallhythe Place, EC-T10.
47 See Cockin, "Stoker, Terry, Colman Smith and the Art of Devilry," 159–71.
48 Pamela Colman Smith, "Mr. Norman Hapgood," in "The Lounger," *The Critic* XXXVI, no. 6 (1900): 490. See Terry, nos. 1079 and 1081, in *The Collected Letters of Ellen Terry, Volume 4*, 109, 111.
49 Another possible slang usage of "peg," which was in circulation at the *fin de siècle*, was to refer to an alcoholic drink. However, nothing in Colman Smith's drawing or the accompanying description would suggest this meaning.
50 Colman Smith, *Ellen Peg's Book of Merry Joys*, EC_T10.
51 Colman Smith, *Ellen Peg's Book of Merry Joys*, EC_T10.
52 Colman Smith, *Ellen Peg's Book of Merry Joys*, EC_T10.
53 Elizabeth Emery, "Viral Marketing: Mariani Wine Testimonials in Early French and American Newspaper Advertising," *Nineteenth-Century Contexts* 39, no. 2 (2017): 119–20. See also David Smith, "Hail Mariani: The Transformation of Vin Mariani from Medicine to Food in American Culture, 1886–1910," *Social History of Alcohol and Drugs* 23, no. 1 (2008): 50.
54 "Every test proves uniformly excellent reputation for this French Tonic"; *Harper's Weekly*, December 15, 1894, 1196. See also Emery, "Viral Marketing," 120.
55 Colman Smith, Green Portfolio, EC-T9.
56 Colman Smith, Green Portfolio, EC-T9.
57 Colman Smith, Green Portfolio, EC-T9.
58 Colman Smith, Green Portfolio, EC-T9.
59 "Grantham Industrial Exhibition," *Grantham Journal*, January 25, 1902, 2.
60 See also Rachlin, *Edy was a Lady*, 140.
61 See also Terry, no. 1101, in *Collected Letters of Ellen Terry, Volume 4*, 134. See also Terry, no. 1149, 179; and no. 1229, 247.
62 Colman Smith to Reed, December 28, 1900, box 1, folder 17.
63 Colman Smith to Paine, December 13, 1900, AP 1675.
64 The Hon. Mrs. Forbes-Sempill, "Music Made Visible: An Unmusical Artist's Lightning Impressions Recorded While Listening to Music," *The Illustrated London News*, February 12, 1927, 260.
65 See Silver, *Strange and Secret Peoples*, 149–83.
66 M. Irwin MacDonald, "The Fairy Faith and Pictured Music of Pamela Colman Smith," *The Craftsman* XXIII, no. 1 (1912): 32–33.
67 Forbes-Sempill, "Music Made Visible," 260.
68 Donielle Johnson, Carrie Allison, and Simon Baron-Cohen, "The Prevalence of Synesthesia: The Consistency Revolution," in *The Oxford Handbook of*

Synesthesia, ed. Julia Simner and Edward M. Hubbard (Oxford: Oxford University Press, 2013), 3.
69   Johnson et al., "The Prevalence of Synesthesia," 3.
70   Julia Simner, "The 'Rules' of Synesthesia," in Simner and Hubbard, eds., *The Oxford Handbook of Synesthesia*, 151.
71   Simner, "The 'Rules' of Synesthesia," 151.
72   Charles Baudelaire, *Fleurs du Mal, The Complete Text of the Flowers of Evil* (Boston, MA: Godine, 1983), 15. See also Melinda Boyd Parsons, "Theatrical Productions, Symphonic Music, and the Rise of 'Musical Painting' in the Late Nineteenth Century," *Nineteenth Century Studies* 1 (1987): 50; and Henri Dorra, ed., *Symbolist Art Theories: A Critical Anthology* (Berkeley, CA: University of California Press, 1994), 1–11.
73   Dorra, ed., *Symbolist Art Theories*, 11.
74   Arthur Wesley Dow, *Composition: A Series of Exercises in Art Structure For the Use of Students and Teachers* (Oxford: Benediction Classics, 2010), 5.
75   Dow, *Composition*, 5. See Judith Zilczer, "'Color Music': Synaesthesia and Nineteenth-Century Sources for Abstract Art," *Artibus et Historiae* 8, no. 16 (1987): 104.
76   Private Collection of Stuart R. Kaplan, U.S. Games, Inc.
77   See Parsons, "Theatrical Productions," 49–72; and Zilczer, "'Color Music,'" 101–26.
78   James McNeill Whistler, "The Red Rag," in "Celebrities at Home, no. XCII. Mr. Whistler at Cheyne-Walk," *The World*, May 22, 1878, 4–5. Included in *The Correspondence of James McNeill Whistler*, University of Glasgow, System Number 13153.
79   Whistler, "The Red Rag."
80   Judith Zilczer, "Music for the Eyes: Abstract Painting and Light Art," in *Visual Music: Synaesthesia in Art and Music Since 1900*, exhibition held at the Hirshhorn Museum and Sculpture Garden, Smithsonian Institution, Washington, D.C. and The Museum of Contemporary Art, Los Angeles, organized by Kerry Brougher, Jeremy Strick, Ari Wiseman, and Judith Zilczer, exhibition catalogue (London: Thames and Hudson, 2005), 26.
81   Zilczer, "'Color Music,'" 102.
82   Zilczer, "'Color Music,'" 102–3. See also Melinda Boyd Parsons, "'Moonlight on Darkening Ways': Concepts of Nature and the Artist in Edward and Lillian Steichen's Socialism," *American Art* 11, no. 1 (1997): 68–87.
83   Qtd. in Zilczer, "'Color Music,'" 103.
84   Zilczer, "'Color Music,'" 103.
85   Qtd. in Zilczer, "'Color Music,'" 104.
86   See Zilczer, "'Color Music,'" 110–24.
87   See Terry, no. 1214, in *The Collected Letters of Ellen Terry, Volume 4*, 235.
88   Parsons, "Theatrical Productions," 53.
89   Parsons, "Theatrical Productions," 53.

90 See Rachlin, *Edy was a Lady*, 5.
91 Edward Craig, *Gordon Craig: The Story of Life* (New York: Alfred A. Knopf, 1968), 130–42.
92 Qtd. in Roy Foster, *W.B. Yeats: A Life, vol. I: The Apprentice Mage, 1865–1914* (Oxford: Oxford University Press, 1998), 251. See Ronald Schuchard, *The Last Minstrels: Yeats and the Revival of the Bardic Arts* (Oxford: Oxford University Press, 2008), 47.
93 Foster, *Yeats: A Life, vol. I*, 251–66; Schuchard, *The Last Minstrels*, 47, 77, 124–25.
94 Craig, *Gordon Craig*, 183–94. See also Terry, no. 1214, *The Collected Letters of Ellen Terry, Volume 4*, 236.
95 Pamela Colman Smith, "The Wind" and "Turkle and Pigeon," *The Page* IV, no. 2 (1901), unpaginated.
96 Pamela Colman Smith, *The Golden Vanity and The Green Bed* (London: Elkin Matthews, 1903). See also "Reviews," *Studio International* 27 (1903): 232.
97 Pamela Colman Smith, *The Basket Maker and Other Tales* (London: n.p., 1901), unpaginated. Held at Cornell University, Kroch Library Rare & Manuscripts, PZ1.B31 ++.
98 William McCarthy, "Introduction: Anna Letitia Barbauld Today," in *Anna Letitia Barbauld: New Perspectives*, ed. William McCarthy (Lewisburg, PA: Bucknell University Press, 2013), 1.
99 McCarthy, "Introduction: Anna Letitia Barbauld Today," 1–20.
100 Colman Smith to Paine, January 16, 1901, AP 1676.
101 Colman Smith to Bigelow Paine, May 28, 1901, AP 1678. Punctuation as original.
102 Colman Smith to Bigelow Paine, August 1901, AP 1679.
103 Colman Smith to Bigelow Paine, May 28, 1901, AP 1678.
104 See Cockin, *Edith Craig*, 44–46.
105 Holroyd, *A Strange Eventful History*, 344–47.
106 Holroyd, *A Strange Eventful History*, 344. See Terry, no. 1299, in *The Collected Letters of Ellen Terry, Volume 4*, 305–6. See also Colman Smith, "Miss Ellen Terry, As 'Hjordis' in Ibsen's play *The Vikings*," *The Reader* II, no. 4 (1903): 331–33. A color lithograph and another pose as the same character is in the Victoria and Albert Museum, Gabrielle Enthoven Collection, S.913-2012 and S.1414-2010.
107 Pamela Colman Smith, "Peg Woffington," *Kensington* 2 (April 1901): 46; Pamela Colman Smith, "Strolling Players" and "Our Adventures," *Kensington* 4 (June 1901): 97–99; Pamela Colman Smith, "L'Aiglon: Sarah Bernhardt," *The Kensington* 5 (July 1901): 173; Pamela Colman Smith, "The Faithful Wife Dancing Before the Robbers," *The Kensington* 6 (August 1901): 196.
108 "The Kensington: A Magazine of Art, Literature, and the Drama," *Art History Research net*, http://www.arts-search.com/review/the-kensington-a-

magazine-of-art-literature-and-the-drama.html. See also Foster, *Yeats: A Life, vol. I,* 234.
109 Colman Smith to Paine, March 17, 1901, AP 1677.
110 Schuchard, *The Last Minstrels,* ix, 39.
111 Schuchard, *The Last Minstrels,* 53, 20–79.
112 Schuchard, *The Last Minstrels,* 53–55.
113 W. B. Yeats, "Speaking to the Psaltery," in *Ideas of Good and Evil* (London: A. H. Bullen, 1903), 17.
114 See Schuchard, *The Last Minstrels,* 35–46, 55–66. See also John Butler Yeats, *Letters From Bedford Park: A Selection from the Correspondence (1890–1901) of John Butler Yeats,* ed. William M. Murphy (Dublin: Cuala Press, 1972), 47.
115 Alan Wade, ed., *The Letters of William Butler Yeats* (London: Hart Davis, 1954), 444. See also Joan Coldwell, "Pamela Colman Smith and the Yeats Family," *The Canadian Journal of Irish Studies* 3 no. 2 (1977): 28–29.
116 Schuchard, *The Last Minstrels,* 40, 46, 72, 124. See also "The Week," *The Speaker: The Liberal Review,* May 8-16, 1903, 152.
117 Pamela Colman Smith to Lady Augusta Gregory, June 12, 1902, New York Public Library, Berg Special Collection, BERG COLL MSS Gregory.
118 Schuchard, *The Last Minstrels,* 102–3, 108–9, plate 6.
119 Annie Horniman to Florence Darragh, August 18, 1906, National Library of Ireland, Manuscripts Departments, Yeats Abbey Theatre Collection, MSMS, 13, 068 (6/2). See also Mary K. Greer, *Women of the Golden Dawn: Rebels and Priestesses* (Rochester, VT: Park Street Press, 1995), 301.
120 W. B. Yeats, *Collected Letters of W.B. Yeats, vol. III, 1901–1904,* ed. John Kelly and Ronald Schuchard (Oxford: Clarendon Press, 1994), 329. See also Cockin, *Edith Craig,* 73–75.
121 Kelly and Schuchard, eds., *Collected Letters of W.B. Yeats, vol. III,* 329. See also Schuchard, *The Last Minstrels,* 122–23.
122 Schuchard, *The Last Minstrels,* 128–29.
123 "The Week," *The Speaker,* 152; see also Schuchard, *The Last Minstrels,* 128–29, 136.
124 Pamela Colman Smith to William Butler Yeats, December 16, 1903, Stony Brook University Special Collections, William Butler Yeats Manuscript Collection, box 53, folder 120. See also Richard J. Finneran, George Mills Harper, and William M. Murphy, eds., *Letters to W. B. Yeats,* vol. 1 (New York: Columbia University Press, 1977), 132. For more on the Dancers, see Schuchard, *The Last Minstrels,* 151–90.
125 Pamela Colman Smith to William Butler Yeats, December 16, 1903, box 53, folder 120.
126 Finneran et al., eds., *Letters to W. B. Yeats,* vol. 1, 132.
127 For a discussion of the edition of mythology, see Colman Smith to Gregory, June 12, 1902, BERG COLL MSS Gregory. For a discussion of the Blake project, see Pamela Colman Smith to W. B. Yeats, February 3, 1904, SC 294,

box 53, 120, folder 115. See also Coldwell, "Pamela Colman Smith and the Yeats Family," 29.
128 Schuchard, *The Last Minstrels*, 101–2, 114–17, 148, 164–68.
129 Wade, ed., *The Letters of William Butler Yeats*, 444.
130 Foster, *Yeats: A Life, vol. I*, 317–25.
131 "The Rambler," *The Lamp* 28 (1904): 59–62.
132 Pamela Colman Smith, "William Butler Yeats as Seen by Pamela Colman Smith," *The Lamp* 28 (1904): 60; and Alice Boughton, "William Butler Yeats as Seen by the Camera," *The Lamp* 28 (1904): 62.
133 Nicola Gordon Bowe, "Two Early Twentieth-Century Irish Arts and Crafts Workshops in Context: An Tur Gloine and the Dun Emer Guild and Industries," *Journal of Design History* 2, nos. 2/3 (1989): 201 n.59, 206. See also Joan Hardwick, *The Yeats Sisters: A Biography of Susan and Elizabeth Yeats* (London: Harper Collins, 1996), 122, 130
134 Hilary Pyle, *Jack B. Yeats: A Biography* (London: Routledge and Kegan Paul, 1970), 66–67.
135 William Michael Murphy, *Family Secrets: William Butler Yeats and His Relatives* (Syracuse, NY: Syracuse University Press, 1995), 287. See also "By the Way," *Freeman's Journal*, January 30, 1902, 5.
136 Pamela Colman Smith, "The Recitation," *A Broad Sheet*, February 1902. See also Kaplan et al., *Pamela Colman Smith: The Untold Story*, 167.
137 Pamela Colman Smith illustration for A.E.'s "The Gates of Dreamland," *A Broad Sheet*, June 1902. See also Kaplan et al., *Pamela Colman Smith: The Untold Story*, 171.
138 Schuchard, *The Last Minstrels*, 81–82.
139 Mrs. Barbauld, "It is September," *A Broad Sheet*, September 1902; and Mrs. Barbauld, "How many legs have fishes?" *A Broad Sheet*, December 1902. See also Kaplan et al., *Pamela Colman Smith: The Untold Story*, 174, 177.
140 Pamela Colman Smith, illustration, "The Better Horse is the Old Grey Mare, or Married to a Pirate's Widow," *A Broad Sheet*, March 1902; Colman Smith, "The merry wind" and accompanying illustration, *A Broad Sheet*, April 1902; Colman Smith, illustration for "In Cawsand Bay," *A Broad Sheet*, April 1902; Colman Smith, illustration for "All Around my Hat I will wear a Green Willow," April 1902; Colman Smith, illustration for Paul Fort's "The Sailor and the Shark" (translated by F. York Powell), *A Broad Sheet*, May 1902; Colman Smith, illustration for "Health to the Outward Bound," *A Broad Sheet*, November 1902; Colman Smith, illustration for John Masefield's "sand-bagging and throat-slitting," *A Broad Sheet*, December 1902. See also Kaplan et al., *Pamela Colman Smith: The Untold Story*, 166–77.
141 Pamela Colman Smith, "A cobweb cloak of time…," poem and illustration, *A Broad Sheet*, July 1902.
142 Pamela Colman Smith, illustration to A.E. "The Enchantment of Cathvah," *A Broad Sheet*, November 1902. See also Schuchard, *The Last Minstrels*, 88–89.

143 A lengthy discussion of Colman Smith only briefly mentions that Jack Yeats is a co-editor of *A Broad Sheet*, but instead focuses on the "celebrities" Colman Smith is acquainted with, her work for the theater, and her interest in Irish myth. See "By the Way," 4.
144 "A Literary Letter," *The Sphere*, November 29, 1902, 192.
145 Murphy, *Family Secrets*, 287–88.
146 Murphy, *Family Secrets*, 288.
147 See "By The Way," 4.
148 In late December 1902 Colman Smith wrote to Lady Gregory regarding an Irish translation she had given her: "there is not time to put it in 'The Hour Glass'—I mean there is too much time! O-dear! I should like to have it in the January ABS." It appeared in the January issue of the *Green Sheaf*. Colman Smith to Gregory, December 23, 1902, BERG COLL MSS Gregory.
149 Jack Yeats, "The wren!", *The Green Sheaf* 10 (October 1903), 2; and Hardwick, *The Yeats Sisters*, 142.
150 Schuchard, *The Last Minstrels*, 96–97, 120–22; see W. B. Yeats, *Rewriting the Hour-Glass: A Play Written in Prose and Verse Versions*, ed. Wayne K. Chapman (Clemson, SC: Clemson University Press, 2016).
151 Wade, ed., *The Letters of William Butler Yeats*, 389.
152 This description is on the title page of each of the thirteen issues.
153 Pamela Colman Smith, unpublished prospectus sheet for *The Green Sheaf*, private collection of Stuart R. Kaplan, U.S. Games, Inc. See also Kaplan et al., *Pamela Colman Smith: The Untold Story*, 181.
154 Pamela Colman Smith to George Pollexfen, February 17, 1902, Stony Brook University, William Butler Yeats Collection, box 53, 120, 44. See also Rudolph de Cordova, "The Woman Editors of London," *Cassell's Magazine*, May 1903, 684.
155 de Cordova, "The Woman Editors of London," 684.
156 See Lev. 23:10–14
157 "Sheaf," n.5, *Oxford English Dictionary*.
158 George Schoolfield, *A Baedeker of Decadence: Charting a Literary Fashion, 1884–1927* (New Haven, CT: Yale University Press, 1992), 32–33.
159 Richard Le Gallienne, "The Boom in Yellow," *British and European Aesthetes, Decadents, and Symbolists in the Victorian Web*, http://www.victorianweb.org/decadence/lagalliene1.html.
160 Oscar Wilde, "Pen, Pencil, and Poison" (1889), http://www.ajdrake.com/etexts/texts/Wilde/Works/pen_pencil_1889.pdf.
161 See *Martial's Epigrams*, 3.82, "To Rufus," Bohn's Classical Library (1897), http://www.tertullian.org/fathers/martial_epigrams_book03.htm.
162 Michael Patrick Gillespie, *Oscar Wilde and the Poetics of Ambiguity* (Miami, FL: University of Florida Press, 1996), 78.
163 Karl Beckson, "Oscar Wilde and the Green Carnations," *English Literature in Translation* 43, no. 4 (2000): 387–97.

164 Liz Constable, Dennis Denisoff, and Mathew Potolsky, "Introduction," in *'Perennial Decay': On the Aesthetics and Politics of Decadence*, ed. Liz Constable, Dennis Denisoff, and Mathew Potlosky (Philadelphia, PA: University of Pennsylvania Press, 1999), 11.
165 Laurence Irving, "Prince Siddartha," *The Green Sheaf* 4 (April 1903): 12–14; Mrs. (Anna Laetitia) Barbauld, "Charles, do you not remember the caterpillar...," with Pamela Colman Smith illustration, *The Green Sheaf* 4 (April 1903): 2; W. B. Yeats, "The Lake of Coole," *The Green Sheaf* 4 (April 1903): 14.
166 Sally Ledger, "Wilde Women and *The Yellow Book*: The Sexual Politics of Aestheticism and Decadence," *English Literature in Transition* 50, no. 1 (2007): 7.
167 Ledger, "Wilde Women and *The Yellow Book*," 9.
168 Ann Ardis and Patrick Collier, eds., *Transatlantic Print Culture, 1880–1940* (New York: Palgrave Macmillan, 2000), 2.
169 Carolyn Burdett, "Aestheticism and Decadence," *The British Library*, March 15, 2014, https://www.bl.uk/romantics-and-victorians/articles/aestheticism-and-decadence.
170 Ann Ardis, "Staging the Public Sphere: Magazine Dialogism and the Prosthetics of Authorship at the Turn of the Twentieth Century," in Ardis and Collier, eds., *Transatlantic Print Culture, 1880–1940*, 42.
171 Ardis, "Staging the Public Sphere," 42.
172 Leonard Koods, "Improper Names: Pseudonyms and Transvestites in Decadent Prose," in Constable, Denisoff, and Potlosky, eds., *'Perennial Decay'*, 198–214.
173 Kathleen Jones, *Kathleen Mansfield: The Story-Teller* (London: Penguin, 2010).
174 "Gelukiezanger," *The Green Sheaf* 6 (October 1903): 16.
175 E. Monsell, "The Book-Worm," *The Green Sheaf* 1 (January 1903): 2.
176 Edward Gordon Craig and Martin Shaw. "Harvest Home Masque," *Green Sheaf* 3 (March 1903): 2–3.
177 Alix Egerton, "The Lament of the Dead Knight," *The Green Sheaf* 3 (March 1903): 4.
178 Cecil French, illustration to Egerton, "The Lament of the Dead Knight," 5.
179 Pamela Colman Smith, "Once, in a dream...," *The Green Sheaf* 2 (February 1903): 7.
180 Pamela Colman Smith, "Alone," *The Green Sheaf* 4 (April 1903): 9.
181 Pamela Colman Smith, "The Town," *The Green Sheaf* 12 (January 1904): 5.
182 "Literary Notes," *The Academy and Literature* 66, no. 1657 (February 1904): 137.
183 "Art Notes," *The Academy and Literature*, 66, no. 1663 (March 1904): 307.
184 Pamela Colman Smith to William Macbeth, April 25, 1903, Macbeth Gallery Records, Smithsonian Institute Library, NMc11.
185 Colman Smith to Macbeth, April 25, 1903, NMc11.

186 Colman Smith to Bigelow Paine, February 7, 1904, AP 1682.
187 Colman Smith to Yeats, February 3, 1904, SC 294, box 53, 120, folder 115.
188 In his "Foreword" to the edition of Calvert that he published in 1913, Thomas Bird Mosher notes that the planned Unicorn Press edition, evidently advertised with copy by W. B. Yeats, never materialized. Edward Calvert, *Ten Spiritual Designs: Enlarged From the Proofs of the Originals on Copper, Wood, and Stone* (Portland, ME: Thomas Bird Mosher, 1913), vii.
189 Colman Smith to Yeats, February 3, 1904, SC 294, box 53, 120, folder 115.
190 "The Green Sheaf," *The Green Sheaf* 13 (February 1904): 12.

Chapter Four: Art on Her Own Terms: Anansi Stories, the Green Sheaf Press, and "Music Pictures"

1 Pamela Colman Smith, "A Protest Against Fear," *The Craftsman* XI, no. 6 (1907): 728. See also Stuart Kaplan, Mary K. Greer, Elizabeth O'Connor, and Melinda Boyd Parsons, *Pamela Colman Smith: The Untold Story* (Stamford, CT: U.S. Games Systems, 2018), 216.
2 Filippo Tommaso Marinetti's *Manifesto of Futurism* was published in January 1909 in Italian, and in French in the newspaper *Le Figaro* in February 1909. The first edition of Ezra Pound's and Wyndham Lewis's *Blast* was published on July 2, 1914.
3 Colman Smith, "A Protest Against Fear," 728.
4 Colman Smith, "A Protest Against Fear," 728.
5 The Hon. Mrs. Forbes-Sempill, "Music Made Visible: An Unmusical Artist's Lightning Impressions Recorded While Listening to Music," *The Illustrated London News*, February 12, 1927, 260.
6 Pamela Colman Smith, "Two Negro Stories from Jamaica," *Journal of American Folklore* 9, no. 35 (1896): 278; Pamela Colman Smith, *Annancy Stories* (New York: R. H. Russell, 1899).
7 Pamela Colman Smith, *Chim-Chim: Folk Stories from Jamaica* (London: Green Sheaf Press, 1905).
8 Carl Gustav Jung, *Four Archetypes: Mother, Rebirth, Spirit, Trickster*, trans. R. F. C. Hull (London: Routledge, 2014).
9 Jung, *Four Archetypes*, 165.
10 Emily Zobel Marshall, *American Trickster: Trauma, Tradition, and Brer Rabbit* (Lanham, MD: Rowman and Littlefield International, 2019), 1.
11 Cynthia James, "Searching for Anansi: From Orature to Literature in the West Indian Children's Folk Tradition—Jamaican and Trinidadian Trends," *Children's Literature Association Quarterly* 30, no. 2 (2005): 176.
12 Lieke van Duin, "Anansi as Classical Hero," *Journal of Caribbean Literature* 5, no. 1 (2007): 38.
13 Colman Smith, "Two Negro Stories from Jamaica," 278. See also Kaplan et al., *Pamela Colman Smith: The Untold Story*, 100.

14 Zobel Marshall, *American Trickster*, 45.
15 See "Our Anancy Stories," *The Daily Gleaner* [Kingston], February 4, 1899, 16.
16 Ada Wilson Trowbridge, "Negro Customs and Folk-Stories of Jamaica," *The Journal of American Folklore* 9, no. 35 (1896): 79–80.
17 Zobel Marshall, *American Trickster*, 45.
18 Mary Pamela Milne-Home, *Mamma's Black Nurse Stories* (Edinburgh: William Blackwood and Sons, 1890), 1–2.
19 Thomas Nelson Page, "Introduction," in Colman Smith, *Annancy Stories*, n.p.
20 Zobel Marshall, *American Trickster*, 48.
21 Private collection of Stuart R. Kaplan, U.S. Games, Inc.
22 Colman Smith, *Annancy Stories*, 2. See Kaplan et al., *Pamela Colman Smith: The Untold Story*, 131.
23 Walter Jekyll, ed., *Jamaican Song and Story: Anancy stories, digging songs, ring tunes, and dancing tunes* (London: Published for the Folk-lore Society by D. Nutt, 1907).
24 Wona, *A Selection of Anancy Tales* (Kingston, Jamaica: Aston W. Garner, 1899), 6–7.
25 "Wona's Anancy Stories," *The Daily Gleaner* [Kingston], March 19, 1900, 2. See Victoria Hamilton qtd. in Vivian Yenika-Agbaw, "'Rumpelstiltskin': A Picture Book Multicultural Retelling," *Callaloo* 36, no. 2 (2013): 432.
26 Martha Beckwith, *Anansi: Jamaican Stories of the Spider God*, rev. edn (Amsterdam: VAMzzz Publishing, 2016).
27 See Zobel Marshall, *American Trickster*, 52; Richard Wright, "Between Laughter and Tears," *New Masses*, October 5, 1937, 22–23; Cynthia Ward, "Truth, Lies, Mules, and Men: Through the 'Spy-Glass' of Anthropology and What Zora Saw There," *The Western Journal of Black Studies* 36 no. 4 (2012): 301–13.
28 See Kaplan et al., *Pamela Colman Smith: The Untold Story*, 71, 211.
29 Colman Smith, "Introduction," in *Chim-Chim*, n.p.
30 Beckwith, *Anansi*, 450.
31 "Wona's Anancy Stories," 2.
32 "Minutes of Meetings," *Folklore* 15, no. 3 (September 29, 1904): 243.
33 Colman Smith, *Annancy Stories*, 3, 9, 18, 26–29, 35, 37, 43, 45, 51–54, 59, 61, 69, 77, 79; Milne-Home, *Mama's Black Nurse Stories*, 3. See Kaplan et al., *Pamela Colman Smith: The Untold Story*, 131–34.
34 Colman Smith, *Chim-Chim*, 9, 14–16; Kaplan et al., *Pamela Colman Smith: The Untold Story*, 28–29.
35 Colman Smith, *Chim-Chim*, 17. In the background of a full-color illustration for "Chim-Chim," the first story in the collection, two Afro-Jamaican women cry. Their depiction is somewhat similar, although less pronounced, to her depiction of Afro-Jamaican characters in *Annancy Stories*.

36 Bram Stoker, *The Lair of the White Worm* (London: William Rider & Son, 1911), 148.
37 Kofi Boukman Barima, "Cutting Across Space and Time: Obeah's Service to Jamaica's Freedom Struggle in Slavery and Emancipation," *Africology: The Journal of Pan African Studies* 9, no. 4 (2016): 17–18.
38 Faith Smith, "'A Mysterious Murder': Considering Jamaican Victorianism," in *Victorian Jamaica*, ed. Tim Barringer and Wayne Modest (Durham, NC: Duke University Press, 2018), 665.
39 Smith, "'Mysterious Murder,'" 665.
40 See Sasha Turner Bryson, "The Art of Power: Poison and Obeah Accusations and the Struggle for Dominance and Survival in Jamaica's Slave Society," *Caribbean Studies* 41, no. 2 (2013): 61–90.
41 "Obeah," *Africana: The Encyclopedia of the African and African American Experience, Second Edition*, https://oxfordaasc.com/.
42 "Why Toad Walk 'Pon Four Leg," "Haylefayly An' Pretty Peallope," "Bull-Garshananee," "Annancy An' De Nyam Hills," and "The Three Sisters" all feature an "Obeah woman" who is identified as Mother Callbee. Colman Smith, *Annancy Stories*, 14–16, 47–50, 55–58, 59, 72–74.
43 Colman Smith, *Annancy Stories*, 31–34.
44 Kathleen Pyne, *Modernism and the Feminine Voice: O'Keeffe and the Women of the Stieglitz Circle* (Berkeley, CA: University of California Press, 2007), 8.
45 "More Irish Folk Tales," *Brooklyn Life*, November 18, 1898, 12.
46 Colman Smith, *Annancy Stories*, 19.
47 James, "Searching for Anansi," 176.
48 Pamela Colman Smith, "The Land of Heart's Desire," in *Portfolio* (New York: R. H. Russell, 1898); Seumas MacManus, *In Chimney Corners: Merry Tales of Irish Folklore, with illustrations by Pamela Colman Smith* (Garden City, NY: Doubleday, 1899).
49 Colman Smith, *Annancy Stories*, 37; Colman Smith, "The Land of Heart's Desire." See Kaplan et al., *Pamela Colman Smith: The Untold Story*, 27.
50 Colman Smith, *Annancy Stories*, 35.
51 Colman Smith, *Annancy Stories*, 35.
52 Colman Smith, *Annancy Stories*, 19, 49, 65, 67, 73.
53 MacManus, *In Chimney Corners*, 11, 43, 113.
54 MacManus, *In Chimney Corners*, 11.
55 Her posture and depiction is similar to Nanny in "Nanny and the Coin," in MacManus, *In Chimney Corners*, 198. See also Kaplan et al., *Pamela Colman Smith: The Untold Story*, 111–12.
56 Colman Smith, *Annancy Stories*, 15, 31, 38.
57 MacManus, *In Chimney Corners*, 267.
58 For a preliminary discussion, see Elizabeth O'Connor, "Pamela Colman Smith's Performative Primitivism," in *Caribbean Irish Connections: Interdisciplinary*

Perspectives, ed. Allison Donell, Maria McGarrity, and Evelyn O'Callaghan (Mona, Jamaica: University of the West Indies Press, 2015), 157–73.
59 MacManus, *In Chimney Corners*, 260.
60 MacManus, *In Chimney Corners*, n.p.
61 Pamela Colman Smith to Albert Bigelow Paine, August 7, 1899, Albert Bigelow Paine Letters, Manuscripts Department, Huntington Library, AP 1672, 2.
62 M. Irwin MacDonald, "The Fairy Faith and Pictured Music of Pamela Colman Smith," *The Craftsman* XXIII, no. 3 (1912): 32.
63 MacDonald, "The Fairy Faith," 33,
64 "Gelukiezanger," *The Green Sheaf* 6 (October 1903): 16.
65 Beckwith, *Anansi*, 49–50, 452. See also Elsie Clews Parsons, "Monkey, Rabbit, and Elephant," in *Folk-tales of Andros Island, Bahamas* (Lancaster, PA and New York: American Folk-lore Society, 1918), 116. See also the West African variant, Elphinstone Dayrell, "Concerning the Leopard, the Squirrel, and the Tortoise," in *Folk Stories from Southern Nigeria, West Africa* (London: Longmans, 1910), 87–90.
66 Beckwith's version gives Anansi's name as "Che-che-bun-da," a close variant to Colman Smith's. They also agree on the name Parrot tells his mother, "Greencornero." Beckwith, *Anansi*, 49; Colman Smith, *Annancy Stories*, 52.
67 Colman Smith, *Annancy Stories*, 52.
68 Colman Smith, *Annancy Stories*, 52.
69 Philip M. Sherlock, *Anansi: The Spider Man* (London: Macmillan Caribbean, 1979), 1–2.
70 Colman Smith, *Annancy Stories*, 54.
71 Colman Smith, *Chim-Chim*, 14.
72 Colman Smith, "Introduction," in *Chim-Chim*, n.p.
73 Colman Smith, *Chim-Chim*, 16
74 Colman Smith, *Annancy Stories*, 78; Colman Smith, *Chim-Chim*, 48–52.
75 Sharon Barcan Elswit, *The Caribbean Story Finder: A Guide to 438 Tales from 24 Nations* (West Jefferson, NC: McFarland, 2017), 18–19.
76 Colman Smith, *Chim-Chim*, 33. See Kaplan et al., *Pamela Colman Smith: The Untold Story*, 205–6.
77 Colman Smith, "Two Negro Stories from Jamaica," 278. See Kaplan et al., *Pamela Colman Smith: The Untold Story*, 100.
78 Colman Smith, "Two Negro Stories from Jamaica," 278. See also Beckwith, "Yam Hills," in *Anansi*, 92–93, 450.
79 Pascale de Souza, "Creolizing Anancy: Signifyin(g) Practices in New World Spider Tales," in *A Pepper-Pot of Cultures: Aspects of Creolization in the Caribbean*, ed. Gordon Collier and Ulrich Fleischmann (Amsterdam: Rodopi, 2003), 360–61.
80 Colman Smith, *Annancy Stories*, 59.

81 Colman Smith, *Annancy Stories*, 59.
82 Colman Smith, *Annancy Stories*, 59.
83 Colman Smith, *Chim-Chim*, 62.
84 Colman Smith, *Chim-Chim*, 61.
85 "Art Notes," *Pall Mall Gazette*, December 28, 1905, 3.
86 For a selection of the covers of these books, which were all designed by Colman Smith, see Kaplan et al., *Pamela Colman Smith: The Untold Story*, 57.
87 Katharine Cockin, *Edith Craig (1869–1947): Dramatic Lives* (London: Cassell, 1998), 75.
88 Cockin, *Edith Craig*, 76.
89 Headnote to Hadland Davis, "The Way of a Japanese Mystic," *The Aryan Way*, March 1931, 170. See Kaplan et al., *Pamela Colman Smith: The Untold Story*, 214–15.
90 Alphaeus Philemon Cole and Margaret Ward Cole, *Saints Among the Animals* (London: Green Sheaf Press, 1906).
91 For excerpts from Colman Smith's visitors' book, see Kaplan et al., *Pamela Colman Smith: The Untold Story*, 149–59.
92 *The Ellesmere Chaucer Reproduced in Facsimile. 2 vols. Preface by Alix Egerton* (Manchester: Manchester University Press, 1911); John Milton, *Milton's Comus, being the Bridgewater Manuscript with notes and a short family memoir by Alix Egerton* (London: J. M. Dent, 1910).
93 Laurence Alma-Tadema, *Tales from My Garden* (London: Green Sheaf Press, 1905), 93–94.
94 Frances Hodgson Burnett to Laurence Alma-Tadema, July 4, 1907, papers of Miss Laurence Alma-Tadema, Bodleian Archives and Manuscripts, University of Oxford, MS Eng let. X. 528, box 3—MSS Eng Misc c 790.
95 Colman Smith to Paine, February 7, 1904, AP 1682.
96 Colman Smith to Paine, April 1, 1906, AP 1683.
97 Giles Edgerton, "Is America Selling her Birthright in Art for a Mess of Pottage? Significance of This Year's Exhibit at the Pennsylvania Academy," *The Craftsman* XI, no. 6 (1907): 663.
98 "Theatre Notes," *Morning Post* [London], July 7, 1906, 5; "Arrangements," *Morning Post* [London], July 9, 1906, 7; "Arrangements," *Morning Post* [London], July 10, 1906, 10; "An Afternoon of Folklore," *The Sunday Times* [London], July 15, 1906, 6; "Aeolian Hall—An Afternoon of Folk Lore," *Morning Post* [London], September 9, 1906, 1.
99 Very few of the Green Sheaf Press's books were reviewed. *The Guardian* reviewed *Tales from My Garden* and termed Tadema "too thoroughly and completely grown up ever to show the light heartedness and dash which children demand." "Children's Books," *The Guardian*, November 17, 1906, 6.
100 Colman Smith to Paine, October 31, 1906, and December 24, 1906, AP 1684, AP 1685.

101 "Als Ik Kan: Notes: Reviews," *The Craftsman* XI, no. 6 (1907): 769. See also Melinda Boyd Parsons, "Pamela Colman Smith and Alfred Stieglitz: Modernism at 291," *History of Photography* 29, no. 4 (1996): 287.
102 "Women's Clubs," *Brooklyn Life*, February 16, 1907, 38.
103 "West Indian Folklore Stories," *The Winfield Daily Free Press* [Winfield, Kansas], October 21, 1904, 3.
104 For photos of her during these performances, see Kaplan et al., *Pamela Colman Smith: The Untold Story*, 70–73.
105 "The Week in Society," *Brooklyn Life*, January 26, 1907, 27.
106 "The Week in Society," January 26, 1907, 27. See also "The Week in Society," *Brooklyn Life*, February 9, 1907, 16; and "Packer Alumnae at Home," *The Brooklyn Daily Eagle*, February 24, 1907, 36.
107 "Looker-On," *Brooklyn Life*, January 12, 1907, 9; see also "The Week in Society," January 26, 1907, 27; and "The Week in Society," February 9, 1907, 16.
108 "The Week in Society," *Brooklyn Life*, March 2, 1907, 16.
109 "Jamaican Folk Lore: From *The London Mail*," *New York Tribune*, July 10, 1904, 22.
110 "The Week in Society," *Brooklyn Life*, March 26, 1907, 27; "The Week in Society," March 23, 1907, 17.
111 "Italian Officials Guests: Many Prominent Personages Attend Eight Event of Mrs. Hitchcock's Entertainments at the Waldorf," *The Brooklyn Daily Eagle*, January 30, 1907, 10; and "Mayor des Planches Honor Guest: Italian Ambassador Entertained by Entertainment Club at Waldorf," *New York Tribune*, January 30, 1907, 14; see also "Reading Club Anniversary," *The Brooklyn Daily Eagle*, March 17, 1907, 39.
112 "Women's Clubs," *Brooklyn Life*, February 16, 1907, 38.
113 "Made Veteran Humorist Laugh," reprinted from the *New York World* in *The Evening Statesman* [Walla Walla, Washington], February 27, 1907, 3.
114 "Mofussilite," "Weekly-Whispers," *Nelson Evening Mail* [New Zealand], May 4, 1907, 2.
115 Wendy Martin, "'Remembering the Jungle': Josephine Baker and Modernist Parody," in *Prehistories of the Future: The Primitivist Project and the Culture of Modernism*, ed. Elazar Barkan and Ronald Bush (Stanford, CA: Stanford University Press, 1995), 313.
116 "Made Veteran Humorist Laugh," 3.
117 Forbes-Sempill, "Music Made Visible," 260. For a reproduction of the article, see Kaplan et al., *Pamela Colman Smith: The Untold Story*, 346–48.
118 Forbes-Sempill, "Music Made Visible," 260.
119 Pamela Colman Smith to Alfred Stieglitz, February 21, 1908, Georgia O'Keeffe Collection, Beinecke Library, Yale University, YCAL MSS 85, box 45.
120 Forbes-Sempill, "Music Made Visible," 260
121 Forbes-Sempill, "Music Made Visible," 260.

122 Forbes-Sempill, "Music Made Visible," 260.
123 Forbes-Sempill, "Music Made Visible," 260.
124 MacDonald, "The Fairy Faith," 22.
125 "Visualizing Music by Means of Brush & Pad Is the Newest Psychological Pastime," *Boston Sunday Post*, April 25, 1909, 23.
126 William James, *Text Book of Psychology* (London: Macmillan, 1892), 12.
127 Pamela Colman Smith, draft manuscript from December 1907 given to Alfred Stieglitz, Georgia O'Keeffe Collection, Beinecke Library, Yale University YCAL MSS 85, box 105, scrapbook 4. See also "Pictures in Music," *The Strand Magazine* XXXV, no. 210 (June 1908): 635. For a reproduction of the article, see Kaplan et al., *Pamela Colman Smith: The Untold Story*, 276–80.
128 "Pictures in Music," 635.
129 Forbes-Sempill, "Music Made Visible," 260.
130 See Kaplan et al., *Pamela Colman Smith: The Untold Story*, 197.
131 Forbes-Sempill, "Music Made Visible," 259.
132 "Pictures in Music," 635.
133 For a selection of Colman Smith's paintings that were included in the 1907 Stieglitz exhibition, see Kaplan et al., *Pamela Colman Smith: The Untold Story*, 217–30, 251–75.
134 MacDonald, "The Fairy Faith," 27.
135 MacDonald, "The Fairy Faith," 27.
136 See Richard Whelan, *Alfred Stieglitz: A Biography* (New York: Little, Brown, 1995), 218–20.
137 "'291' The Mecca and the Mystery of Art in a Fifth Avenue Attic," *The New York Sun*, October 24, 1915, 6. See also Dorothy Norman, *Alfred Stieglitz: An American Seer* (New York: Random House, 1960), 71–72.
138 Lillian K. Cartwright, "Alfred Stieglitz and '291': A Laboratory for Fostering Creativity," *Art Criticism* 24, no. 2 (2009): 48.
139 Penelope Niven, *Steichen: A Biography* (New York: Clarkson Potter, 1997), 220.
140 Alfred Stieglitz, "The Editor's Page," *Camera Work* 18 (April 1907): 37.
141 "'291' The Mecca and the Mystery," 6.
142 James Huneker, "Some Special Exhibitions," *The New York Sun*, January 15, 1907, 6.
143 Dennis Denisoff, "Pamela Colman Smith, Symbolism, and Spiritual Synaesthesia," in *The Occult Imagination in Britain, 1875–1947*, ed. Christine Ferguson and Andrew Radford (New York: Routledge, 2018), 155.
144 See Whelan, *Alfred Stieglitz*, 219.
145 Colman Smith, *Chim-Chim*, 45.
146 Huneker, "Some Special Exhibitions," 6.
147 "Als Ik Kan: Notes," 769–70.
148 Alfred Stieglitz qtd. in Boyd Parsons, "Pamela Colman Smith and Alfred Stieglitz," 288.

149 "Als Ik Kan: Notes," 769.
150 Colman Smith to Stieglitz, April 27, 1907, YCAL MSS 85, box 45. See also Edgerton, "Is America Selling her Birthright," 657–70.
151 Colman Smith to Stieglitz, April 27, 1907, YCAL MSS 85, box 45.
152 For an assessment of the Academy show that quotes Colman Smith, but does not discuss her work, see Edgerton, "Is America Selling her Birthright," 657–70.
153 Colman Smith to Stieglitz, November 9, 1907, YCAL MSS 85, box 45, folder 3. For press references to the Baillie Gallery, see "Gallery Notes," *Morning Post* [London], November 8, 1907, 2; "The Baillie Gallery," *Morning Post* [London], November 26, 1907, 2; "Art Notes," *The Observer* [London], December 1, 1907, 8. For a brief discussion of the Edinburgh show with James Patterson, see Colman Smith to Stieglitz, December 27, 1907, YCAL MSS 85, box 45.
154 Colman Smith to Stieglitz, December 27, 1907, YCAL MSS 85, box 45.
155 "Miss Colman-Smith's Story-Telling," *The Times* [London], February 4, 1908, 9.
156 "The League of Mercy," *Morning Post* [London], April 14, 1908, 6; "Stone," *Bucks Herald* [Buckinghamshire], December 26, 1908, 5.
157 "Around the Galleries," *New York Sun*, January 14, 1908, 6; "Notes," *The Craftsman* XIII, no. 6 (1908): 727.
158 "The Photo Secession: Exhibitions," *American Art Annual* 8 (1908): 202; "Art Notes," *New York Tribune*, February 26, 1908, 7.
159 For reference to an unidentified "Uncle" and his advice not to return to the U.S. that winter for financial reasons, see Colman Smith to Stieglitz, November 9, 1907, YCAL MSS 85, box 45. See also Colman Smith to Stieglitz, December 27, 1907, December 31, 1907, January 1, 1908, and February 21, 1908.
160 "Around the Galleries," *New York Sun*, March 4, 1908, 6.
161 "Around the Galleries," 6.
162 "Art Notes," *New York Tribune*, March 10, 1908, 7; see also "Gallery Notes," *The New York Times*, February 26, 1908, 7.
163 Colman Smith to Stieglitz, December 27, 1908, YCAL MSS 85, box 45.
164 Program included in Alfred Stieglitz scrapbook, Georgia O'Keeffe Collection, Beinecke Library, Yale University YCAL MSS 85, box 105, scrapbook 4.
165 Edgerton, "Is America Selling her Birthright," 663.
166 "Around the Galleries," *The New York Sun*, February 25, 1908, 6
167 "Als Ik Kan: Notes," *The Craftsman* XVI, no. 1 (1909): 122–23.
168 "Notes on Fine Arts," *The Brooklyn Daily Eagle*, October 2, 1908, 7.
169 "The Looker-On." *Brooklyn Life*, January 12, 1907, 9.
170 Qtd. in Edgerton, "Is America Selling her Birthright," 663–64.
171 Pamela Colman Smith, "Should the Art Student Think?", *The Craftsman* XIV, no. 4 (1908): 418.

280 NOTES TO PAGES 169–79

172 Colman Smith, "Should the Art Student Think?", 419.
173 Colman Smith, "Should the Art Student Think?", 419.
174 "Art Notes Here and There," *The New York Times*, March 21, 1909, 56.
175 Benjamin De Casseres, "Pamela Colman Smith," *Camera Work* 27 (July 1909): 18.
176 De Casseres, "Pamela Colman Smith," 19–20.
177 "Drawings by Pamela Colman Smith," *Camera Work* 27 (July 1909): 27. See also Whelan, *Alfred Stieglitz*, 247.
178 Marius de Zayas, "Pamela Colman Smith," Metropolitan Museum of Art, Alfred Stieglitz Collection, accession number 49.70.221a, https://www.metmuseum.org/art/collection/search/488454.
179 "The Rodin Drawings the Photo-Secession Galleries," *Camera Work* 22 (April 1908): 35–41. See also George Heard Hamilton, "The Alfred Stieglitz Collection," *Metropolitan Museum Journal* 3 (1970): 371–92.
180 See Cartwright, "Alfred Stieglitz and '291,'" 38.
181 Qtd. in Boyd Parsons, "Pamela Colman Smith and Alfred Stieglitz," 288. See also Whelan, *Alfred Stieglitz*, 373, who suggests O'Keeffe was influenced by Colman Smith's work.
182 Boyd Parsons, "Pamela Colman Smith and Alfred Stieglitz," 288.
183 Boyd Parsons, "Pamela Colman Smith and Alfred Stieglitz," 285.
184 Colman Smith to Stieglitz, November 19, 1909, YCAL MSS 85, box 45.
185 Colman Smith to Stieglitz, November 19, 1909, YCAL MSS 85, box 45.
186 "Society News," *Brooklyn Life*, March 27, 1909, 15.
187 "A Lecture on Art: Pamela Colman Smith Talks to Pratt Art Club," *Brooklyn Daily Eagle*, March 25, 1909, 11. See also "Lecture at Pratt Institute," *Brooklyn Daily Eagle*, March 14, 1909, 12.
188 "Around the Galleries," *Boston Globe*, April 10, 1909, 7; "Around the Galleries," *Brooklyn Times Union*, April 13, 1909, 7.
189 "Visualizing Music by Means of Brush and Pad," 23.

Chapter Five: Feminist Symbolic Art: Tarot Designs, Suffrage Posters, and Representations of Women

1 Pamela Colman Smith to Alfred Stieglitz, November 19, 1909, Georgia O'Keeffe Collection, Beinecke Library, Yale University, YCAL MSS 85, box 45.
2 Colman Smith to Stieglitz, November 19, 1909, YCAL MSS 85, box 45.
3 A. E. Waite, *Shadows of Life and Thought: A Retrospective Review in the Form of Memoirs* (Dublin: Bardic Press, 2016), 184–85.
4 Lady Archibald Campbell, "Faerie Ireland," *The Occult Review* 6, no. 5 (1907): 265–66.
5 See Peter Ackroyd, *Blake: A Biography* (New York: Alfred A. Knopf, 1996).
6 Morton D. Paley, "'A New Heaven is Begun': Blake and Swedenborgianism," *Blake Quarterly* 13, no. 2 (1979): 82.

7   Alexander Gilchrist, *The Life of William Blake with Selections from his Poems and Other Writings* (London: Macmillan, 1863). See also Alexander Gilchrist, *The Life of William Blake*, ed. W. Graham Robertson (London: John Lane, 1907).
8   Leonard Trawick, "Blake's Empirical Occult," *The Wordsworth Circle* 8, no. 2 (1977): 163–66.
9   Trawick, "Blake's Empirical Occult," 161.
10 *Sketch of the History of the Boston Society of the New Jerusalem, with a list of its members* (Boston, MA: John C. Regan, 1873), 4.
11 Emanuel Swedenborg, *On the Divine Love and the Divine Wisdom from the Apocalypse Examined by Emanuel Swedenborg* (New York: S. Colman, 1841) and Swedenborg, *The Writings of Swedenborg: containing the following treatises viz. The last judgment, The earths in the universe, The Athanasian creed, and also Divine love and wisdom, from the "Apocalypse explained"* (New York: S. Colman, 1841).
12 Raymond H. Deck, "An American Original: Mrs. Colman's Illustrated Printings of Blake's Poems, 1843–44," *The Blake Quarterly* 11, no. 1 (1977): 16. See Mrs. [Pamelia] Colman, *Innocence of Childhood* (New York: D. Appleton, 1849). As late as 1850, Mrs. Samuel Colman wrote *The Innocence of Childhood*, which contained "fairly direct references to Swedenborg's teachings."
13 Deck, "An American Original," 16.
14 Deck, "An American Original," 4–18.
15 Deck, "An American Original," 4–11.
16 Deck, "An American Original," 8–11.
17 Deck, "An American Original," 5–6.
18 Edwin Ellis and W. B. Yeats, *The Works of William Blake* (1893), Bibliographic Studies 8 (Clemson, SC: Clemson University Press, 2014), https://tigerprints.clemson.edu/cudp_bibliography/8/.
19 Joan Coldwell, "Pamela Colman Smith and the Yeats Family," *The Canadian Journal of Irish Studies* 3, no. 2 (1977): 29.
20 Pamela Colman Smith to Alfred Bigelow Paine, February 7, 1904, Huntington Library, Manuscripts Department, Albert Bigelow Paine Letters, AP 1682.
21 Colman Smith to Paine, February 7, 1904, AP 1682.
22 Nicholas Goodrick-Clarke, *The Western Esoteric Traditions: A Historical Introduction* (Oxford: Oxford University Press, 2008), 13.
23 Christine Ferguson, "Introduction," in *The Occult Imagination in Britain, 1875–1947*, ed. Christine Ferguson and Andrew Radford (New York: Routledge, 2018), 1.
24 Ferguson, "Introduction," 2; and Leon Surette, *The Birth of Modernism: Ezra Pound, T.S. Eliot, W.B. Yeats, and the Occult* (Montreal: McGill-Queen's University Press, 1993), 12.
25 See Ferguson, "Introduction," 3.

26 Mark Morrison, "The Periodical Culture of the Occult Revival: Esoteric Wisdom, Modernity and Counter-Public Spheres," *Journal of Modern Literature* 31, no. 2 (2008): 3.
27 See Edward Bever, "Witchcraft, Female Aggression, and Power in the Early Modern Community," *Journal of Social History* 35, no. 4 (2002): 955–88.
28 Joy Dixon, *Divine Feminine: Theosophy and Feminism in England* (Baltimore, MD: Johns Hopkins University Press, 2001), 3. See also Surette, *The Birth of Modernism*, 232.
29 Dixon, *Divine Feminine*, 3.
30 Dixon, *Divine Feminine*, 3.
31 Dixon, *Divine Feminine*, 3.
32 Dixon, *Divine Feminine*, 12–13.
33 Israel Regardie, *What You Should Know about the Golden Dawn*, 6th edn (Tempe, AZ: New Falcon Publications, 1993), 10.
34 Mary Greer, *Women of the Golden Dawn* (Rochester, VT: Park Street Press, 1995), 47–49.
35 Dennis Denisoff, "The Hermetic Order of the Golden Dawn, 1888–1901," *Branch*, http://www.branchcollective.org/?ps_articles=dennis-denisoff-the-hermetic-order-of-the-golden-dawn-1888-1901.
36 Chic and Sandra Tabatha Cicero, *The Essential Golden Dawn: An Introduction to High Magic* (Woodbury, MN: Llewellyn Publishing, 2003), 50–51, 59.
37 Ferguson, "Introduction," 12.
38 Dixon, *Divine Feminine*, 8, 7.
39 Greer, *Women of the Golden Dawn*, 57.
40 Greer, *Women of the Golden Dawn*, 57.
41 Denisoff, "The Hermetic Order of the Golden Dawn."
42 Greer, *Women of the Golden Dawn*, 64.
43 Denisoff, "The Hermetic Order of the Golden Dawn"; Greer, *Women of the Golden Dawn*, 64.
44 Greer, *Women of the Golden Dawn*, 101–29.
45 Denisoff, "The Hermetic Order of the Golden Dawn"; Greer, *Women of the Golden Dawn*, 253–67.
46 Denisoff, "The Hermetic Order of the Golden Dawn"; Greer, *Women of the Golden Dawn*, 253–67.
47 Private collection of Stuart R. Kaplan, U.S. Games, Inc. See Christopher St. John to Ellen Terry, June 17, 1902, British Library, Ellen Terry Archive, ET 21, 412.
48 1901 England, Wales, and Scotland Census, 14 Milborne Grove, Kensington, RG13, 36, 100, 111 [database online], Provo, UT: Ancestry.com Operations, 2014.
49 1901 England, Wales, and Scotland Census.
50 "The Green Sheaf Press and Store," *The Green Sheaf* 13 (February 1904): 8. The advertisement notes a Mrs. Fortescue. Pamela's visitors' book notes both an

Ethel Fortescue and an Ethel Freyer-Fortescue, who is presumably the same person. See Stuart Kaplan, Mary K. Greer, Elizabeth Foley O'Connor, and Melinda Boyd Parsons, *Pamela Colman Smith: The Untold Story* (Stamford, CT: U.S. Game Systems, 2018), 150.

51 Private collection of Stuart R. Kaplan, U.S. Games, Inc. R. A. Gilbert correctly suggests that the Latin should be *Quod tibi id aliis*. See R. A. Gilbert, *The Golden Dawn Companion* (Wellingborough: Antiquarian, 1986), 161.

52 Arthur Ransome, *Bohemia in London* (New York: Dodd, Mead, 1907), 56, 60.

53 James Joyce, *Ulysses*, Gabler Edition (New York: Random House, 1986), 7.782–83. See Hugh Brogan, *The Life of Arthur Ransome* (London: Jonathan Cape, 1984), 31; and Vincent Deane, "From Swerve of Shore to Bend of Bay Area: The Afterlife of Opal Hush," *James Joyce Online Notes*, http://www.jjon.org/joyce-s-allusions/opal-hush.

54 See Kaplan et al., *Pamela Colman Smith: The Untold Story*, 149–51.

55 Waite, *Shadows of Life and Thought*, 172.

56 Surette, *The Birth of Modernism*, 7, 24.

57 W. B. Yeats, "Swedenborg, Mediums, and the Desolate Places," *Explorations I*, selected by Mrs. W. B. Yeats (New York: Macmillan, 1962), 40.

58 Yeats, "Swedenborg, Mediums, and the Desolate Places," 42.

59 Yeats, "Swedenborg, Mediums, and the Desolate Places," 43.

60 Yeats, "Swedenborg, Mediums, and the Desolate Places," 43.

61 Yeats, "Swedenborg, Mediums, and the Desolate Places," 34–35. See also Gregory Castle, *Modernism and the Celtic Revival* (Cambridge: Cambridge University Press, 2001), 86.

62 Yeats, "Swedenborg, Mediums, and the Desolate Places," 43.

63 Yeats, "Swedenborg, Mediums, and the Desolate Places," 30.

64 Yeats, "Swedenborg, Mediums, and the Desolate Places," 43–44.

65 James Huneker, "Some Special Exhibitions," *New York Sun*, January 15, 1907, 6.

66 Trawick, "Blake's Empirical Occult," 163.

67 William Blake, "The world of imagination is the world of eternity...," *The Green Sheaf* 2 (February 1903): 2.

68 Ellis and Yeats, *The Works of William Blake*, 394.

69 A. E. Waite, "The Tarot: A Wheel of Fortune," *Occult Review* X, no. 6 (1909): 311.

70 A. E. Waite, *The Pictorial Key to the Tarot: Being the Fragments of a Secret Tradition under the Veil of Divination* (New Hyde Park, NY: University Books, 1959), viii.

71 Kelly Richmond-Abdou, "The Spellbinding History of Tarot Cards, From a Card Game to a Magic Ritual," *My Modern Met*, April 19, 2020, https://mymodernmet.com/history-of-tarot-cards/

72 Stuart Kaplan, *The Encyclopedia of the Tarot*, vol. 3 (Stamford, CT: U.S. Game Systems, 2002), 30.

73 "Curator's Comments," British Museum, museum number 1845, 0825.485, https://www.britishmuseum.org/collection/object/P_1845-0825-485.
74 Ralph Shirley, "Notes of the Month," *The Occult Review* X, no. 6 (1909): 301; Ronald Decker and Michael Dummett, *The History of the Occult Tarot* (London: Duckworth, 2002), 131–33.
75 Gertrude Moakley, *The Tarot Cards Painted by Bonifacio Bembo for the Visconti-Sforza Family* (New York: New York Public Library, 1966). See also Melinda Boyd Parsons, "Influences and Expression in the Rider-Waite Tarot Deck," in Kaplan et al., *Pamela Colman Smith: The Untold Story*, 352; and Kaplan, *The Encyclopedia of the Tarot*, vol. 3, 30.
76 Manley P. Hall, *The Secret Teachings of All Ages: An Encyclopedic Outline of Masonic, Hermetic, Qabbalistic, and Rosicrucian Symbolic Philosophy* (San Francisco: H. S. Crocker, 1928), 129.
77 Ronald Decker, *The Esoteric Tarot: Ancient Sources Rediscovered in Hermeticism and Cabalah* (New York: Quest Books, 2013), 182–98.
78 Paul Huson, *Mystical Origins of the Tarot: From Ancient Roots to Modern Usage* (Rochester, VT: Destiny Books, 2004), 69.
79 Waite, "The Tarot," 309.
80 See Christopher McIntosh, *Éliphas Lévi and the French Occult Revival* (Albany, NY: SUNY Press, 2011); and Julian Strube, "Socialist Religion and the Emergence of Occultism: A Genealogical Approach to Socialism and Secularization in 19th-century France," *Religion* 46, no. 3 (2016): 359–88.
81 Waite, *Pictorial Key to the Tarot*, 32–34; Boyd Parsons, "Influences and Expression," 353.
82 Waite, *Pictorial Key to the Tarot*, 34.
83 Boyd Parsons, "Influences and Expression," 353–54; see also A. E. Waite, *The Hidden Church of the Holy Graal* (London: Reman, 1909).
84 R. A. Gilbert, *A.E. Waite: A Magician of Many Parts* (London: Thorsons, 1987), 128.
85 A. E. Waite, *The Life of Louis Claude de Sainte-Martin: The Unknown Philosopher* (London: Philip Wellby, 1901).
86 Waite, *Pictorial Key to the Tarot*, 7.
87 Gilbert, *Magician of Many Parts*, 16–18.
88 Gertrude Moakley, "Introduction," to Waite, *Pictorial Key to the Tarot*, x.
89 Kaplan et al., *Pamela Colman Smith: The Untold Story*, 159.
90 Waite, "The Tarot," 309.
91 Waite, "The Tarot," 309.
92 Waite, "The Tarot," 309.
93 On January 28, 1909, Pamela sailed from London to New York on the passenger ship *Minnetonka*. She returned to London on May 24. "Lists of Passengers for the United," January 1909 [database online], Provo, UT: Ancestry.com Operations, 2014.

94 Mary K. Greer, "Pamela's Legacy," in Kaplan et al., *Pamela Colman Smith: The Untold Story*, 372.
95 Colman Smith to Stieglitz, November 19, 1909, YCAL MSS 85, box 45.
96 Shirley, "Notes of the Month," 301
97 Boyd Parsons, "Influences and Expression," 361–68.
98 Boyd Parsons, "Influences and Expression," 361–62.
99 Marcus Katz and Tali Goodwin, *Secrets of the Waite-Smith Tarot: The True Story of the World's Most Popular Tarot* (Woodbury, MD: Llewellyn Publications, 2015), 98–109.
100 Katharine Cockin, "Bram Stoker, Ellen Terry, Pamela Colman Smith and the Art of Devilry," in *Bram Stoker and the Gothic*, ed. Catherine Wynne (Basingstoke: Palgrave Macmillan, 2016), 166.
101 Pamela Colman Smith, "Sketch for Glass," Yale University, Beinecke Library, Alfred Stieglitz/Georgia O'Keeffe Collection, YCAL MSS 85, box 159, folder 2912; see also Kaplan et al., *Pamela Colman Smith: The Untold Story*, 226.
102 Boyd Parsons, "Influences and Expression," 364; see also Kaplan et al., *Pamela Colman Smith: The Untold Story*, 207.
103 Waite, *Pictorial Key to the Tarot*, 27.
104 Waite, *Pictorial Key to the Tarot*, 140.
105 Kathleen Pyne, *Modernism and the Feminine Voice: O'Keeffe and the Women of the Stieglitz Circle* (Berkeley, CA: University of California Press, 2007), 48.
106 Jacqui Palumbo, "The Mysterious Appeal of Art that Depicts Figures from Behind," Artsy.net, April 23, 2020, https://www.artsy.net/article/artsy-editorial-mysterious-appeal-art-depicts-figures.
107 Elizabeth Prettejohn, *Beauty and Art: 1750–1800* (Oxford: Oxford University Press, 2005), 56.
108 Pamela Colman Smith, "Untitled," Yale University, Beinecke Library, Alfred Stieglitz/Georgia O'Keeffe Collection, YCAL MSS 85, box 159, folder 2912; see also Kaplan et al., *Pamela Colman Smith: The Untold Story*, 226.
109 "Pictures in Music," *The Strand Magazine* XXXV, no. 210 (June 1908): 635. For a reproduction of the article, see Kaplan et al., *Pamela Colman Smith: The Untold Story*, 276–80.
110 See also Pamela Colman Smith, "Time," Yale University, Beinecke Library, Alfred Stieglitz/Georgia O'Keeffe Collection, YCAL MSS 85, box 159, folder 2912; see also Kaplan et al., *Pamela Colman Smith: The Untold Story*, 229.
111 Kaplan et al., *Pamela Colman Smith: The Untold Story*, 254.
112 Waite, "The Tarot," 311.
113 Waite, "The Tarot," 311.
114 Pamela Colman Smith, *The Basket Maker: And Other Tales That Will Suit the Old and the Young*, unpublished printed manuscript held at Cornell University, PZ1.B31++, unpaginated; see also Kaplan et al., *Pamela Colman Smith: The Untold Story*, 165.

115 Waite, *Pictorial Key to the Tarot*, 206.
116 Waite, *Pictorial Key to the Tarot*, 178.
117 Waite, *Pictorial Key to the Tarot*, 210.
118 Waite, *Pictorial Key to the Tarot*, 194.
119 Waite, *Pictorial Key to the Tarot*, 193.
120 Waite, *Pictorial Key to the Tarot*, 8.
121 Waite, *Pictorial Key to the Tarot*, 286. See also Betsy Creekmore, "The Tarot Fortune in *The Waste Land*," *ELH* 49, no. 4 (1982): 921.
122 Waite, *Pictorial Key to the Tarot*, 26, 132.
123 Waite, *Pictorial Key to the Tarot*, 132–33.
124 Kaplan et al., *Pamela Colman Smith: The Untold Story*, 271.
125 Katz and Goodwin, *Secrets of the Waite-Smith Tarot*, 180.
126 Katz and Goodwin, *Secrets of the Waite-Smith Tarot*, 108–9.
127 Pamela Colman Smith, "Mozart's Sonata in F Major for Violin and Piano," Yale University, Beinecke Library, Alfred Stieglitz/Georgia O'Keeffe Collection, YCAL MSS 85, box 159, folder 2912; see also Kaplan et al., *Pamela Colman Smith: The Untold Story*, 288.
128 For other examples, see Kaplan et al., *Pamela Colman Smith: The Untold Story*, 253, 259, 260.
129 There is a brown tower on the X of Pentacles and a crest emblazoned with a white tower with two turrets.
130 Waite, *Pictorial Key to the Tarot*, 140.
131 Waite, *Pictorial Key to the Tarot*, 120.
132 Waite, *Pictorial Key to the Tarot*, 120.
133 A somewhat different white tower with red roofs and turrets appears in the background of several cards of the Smith-Waite deck. These include the Chariot, the King of Pentacles, the IX, VIII, VI, and IV of Pentacles, the VIII of Swords, and the IV of Wands. See also Pamela Colman Smith, illustration for Lucilla, "At Departing," *The Green Sheaf* 2 (February 1903): 4.
134 M. Irwin MacDonald, "The Fairy Faith and Pictured Music of Pamela Colman Smith," *The Craftsman* XXIII, no. 1 (1912): 24; see also Kaplan et al., *Pamela Colman Smith: The Untold Story*, 298.
135 Boyd Parsons, "Influences and Expression," 350, 367.
136 Laurence Houseman, *The Anti-Suffrage Alphabet*, stencils by Alice B. Woodward, Pamela Colman Smith, and Ada P. Ridley, ed. Lenora Tyson (Lambeth/Southwark Women's Social and Political Union, 1911); see also Katharine Cockin, "Pamela Colman Smith, Anansi, and the Child: from *The Green Sheaf* (1903) to the *Anti-Suffrage Alphabet* (1912)," in *Literary and Cultural Alternatives to Modernism*, ed. Kostas Boyiopoulos, Anthony Patterson, and Mark Sandy (New York: Routledge, 2019), 71–84.
137 Katharine Cockin, *Edith Craig and the Theatres of Art* (London: Bloomsbury, 2017), 86.
138 Cockin, *Edith Craig and the Theatres of Art*, 84.

139 Cockin, *Edith Craig and the Theatres of Art*, 84.
140 Katherine Cockin, "St. John, Christopher Marie [née Christabel Gertrude Marshall] (1871–1960)," *Oxford Dictionary of National Biography* (Oxford: Oxford University Press, 2004), https://doi.org/10.1093/ref:odnb/57057.
141 Cockin, *Edith Craig and the Theatres of Art*, 95.
142 Cockin, *Edith Craig and the Theatres of Art*, 95.
143 See Katherine Cockin, "Cicely Hamilton's Warriors: Dramatic Reinventions of Militancy in the British Women's Suffrage Movement," *Women's History Review* 14, nos. 3–4 (2005): 530. See also Harriet Blodgett, "Cicely Hamilton: Independent Feminist," *Frontiers: A Journal of Women Studies* 11, nos. 2/3 (1990): 100.
144 Cockin, *Edith Craig and the Theatres of Art*, 96–107; Cockin, "Cicely Hamilton's Warriors," 538.
145 Cockin, "Cicely Hamilton's Warriors," 531.
146 Lisa Tickner, *The Spectacle of Women: Imagery of the Suffrage Campaign 1907–1914* (Chicago: University of Chicago Press, 1988), 24.
147 Cockin, *Edith Craig and the Theatres of Art*, 96–107.
148 Cockin, *Edith Craig and the Theatres of Art*, 108–32.
149 Cockin, *Edith Craig and the Theatres of Art*, 124–25.
150 Ellen Terry Archive, ET-SC9, box 62, 8005 D; Cockin, "Stoker, Terry, Colman Smith and the Art of Devilry," 168.
151 Cockin, *Edith Craig and the Theatres of Art*, 118, 128; Ellen Terry Archive, EC PION, PION3 (BL), EC-D118, EC PION, PION 4 (BL), EC-D113, EC LIBRARY (SMA), EC-N380; "Our London Letter," *Derby Daily Telegraph*, February 7, 1913, 4; "Events," *The Observer* [London], February 23, 1913, 7. See also "The Travelers," *Brooklyn Life*, March 28, 1914; see ET DZ 179 for the program for the 1914 event.
152 Tara Morton, "Changing Spaces: Art, Politics, and Identity in the Home Studios of the Suffrage Atelier," *Women's History Review* 21, no. 4 (2012): 623–37; and Miranda Garrett and Zöe Thomas, *Suffrage and the Arts: Visual Culture, Politics, and Enterprise* (London: Bloomsbury, 2018), 66, 71–72.
153 Garrett and Thomas, *Suffrage and the Arts*, 67.
154 See Garrett and Thomas, *Suffrage and the Arts*, 78.
155 Morton, "Changing Spaces," 623–37.
156 See Garrett and Thomas, *Suffrage and the Arts*, 72.
157 Tickner, *Spectacle of Women*, 244; see also Garrett and Thomas, *Suffrage and the Arts*, 67.
158 Morton, "Changing Spaces," 626.
159 Tickner, *Spectacle of Women*, 69, 94, 117.
160 Morton, "Changing Spaces," 627.
161 Garrett and Thomas, *Suffrage and the Arts*, 79.
162 This one has a small P.S. in the left corner.
163 See Kaplan et al., *Pamela Colman Smith: The Untold Story*, 77.

288   NOTES TO PAGES 208–17

164 E. Sylvia Pankhurst, *The Suffragette: The History of the Women's Militant Suffrage Movement, 1905–1910* (New York: Sturgis and Walton, 1991), 239–40; see also Tickner, *Spectacle of Women*, 35.
165 Pankhurst, *The Suffragette*, 345–46.
166 Pankhurst, *The Suffragette*, 346.
167 Pankhurst, *The Suffragette*, 346–47.
168 Qtd. in Tickner, *Spectacle of Women*, 34.
169 Marian Sawer, "Cartoons for the Cause: Cartooning for Equality in Australia," *Ejournalist-Australian Media Traditions Conference 2001*, 6, https://ejournalist.com.au/public_html/v1n2/SAWER.pdf.
170 The black-and-white version of this has a clearly visible S. and lines that appear to be forming the bowl of a P. in the bottom righthand corner of the frame, but these have been damaged, likely in the printing process. A spot-color version of the same cartoon does not include any initials.
171 The label on the basket appears to be hand-lettered, and the G in George is very similar to the G in the "Vote for Women Bogies" and the "Comfortable Women" discussed below.
172 See Tickner, *Spectacle of Women*, 22, where it is reproduced as part of a sheet of postcards produced by the Suffrage Atelier in 1913.
173 See Tickner, *Spectacle of Women*, 22, where it is reproduced as part of a sheet of postcards produced by the Suffrage Atelier in 1913.
174 "Roll of Honor of Suffragette Prisoners, 1905–1914," London School of Economics, Women's Suffrage Library, ref. no. 7LAC/2, alt. ref. no. 7/XXX4/2, Box FL637.
175 P. Smith to Philippa Strachey, June 7, 1911, London School of Economics, Women's Library, ref. no. 9/09/144, microform TWL 6.1.
176 The letters reference Colman Smith staying with a Mrs. Smith who was an aunt. I have not been able to uncover any information on who this individual might have been and how she might have been related to Colman Smith's father, Charles Edward Smith. Colman Smith lived at 84 York Mansions, Battersea Park, London SW from at least April 1907 to November 1909, based on postmarks on her letters. I have not uncovered any other indication of where Colman Smith was living in 1911. The handwriting of the letters is identical to that of Colman Smith.
177 P. Smith to Strachey, June 7, 1911, microform TWL 6.1.
178 P. Smith to Strachey, June 7, 1911, microform TWL 6.1.
179 See Pyne, *Modernism and the Feminine Voice*, 50–51; see also Melinda Boyd Parsons, "Pamela Colman Smith and Arthur Stieglitz: Modernism at 291," *History of Photography* 20, no. 4 (1996), 285-292.
180 "Pictures in Music," *The Strand Magazine*, July 1908, 636.
181 Pamela Colman Smith, *The Golden Vanity and The Green Bed* (New York: R. H. Russell, 1899); see also Kaplan et al., *Pamela Colman Smith: The Untold Story*, 117.

182 H. Brink-Roby, "Siren Canora: The Mermaid and the Mythical in Late Nineteenth Century Science," *Archives of Natural History* 35, no. 1 (2011): 1–14.
183 See also Kaplan et al., *Pamela Colman Smith: The Untold Story*, 145.
184 See Pamela Colman Smith, "Untitled," 1909, Victoria and Albert Museum, National Art Library, box J4B1 for a striking gold-and-white drawing with similar positioning; see also Kaplan et al., *Pamela Colman Smith: The Untold Story*, 252, 266, 274.
185 See Kaplan et al., *Pamela Colman Smith: The Untold Story*, 274.
186 Pamela Colman Smith, "Sea Creatures," Yale University, Beinecke Library, Alfred Stieglitz/Georgia O'Keeffe Collection, YCAL MSS 85, box 159, folder 2912; see also Kaplan et al., *Pamela Colman Smith: The Untold Story*, 64.
187 W. B. Yeats, ed., *Fairy and Folk Tales of the Irish Peasantry* (London: Walter Scott, 1888), 1.
188 Campbell, "Faerie Ireland," 259.
189 MacDonald, "The Fairy Faith," 34.
190 Pamela Colman Smith, "Beethoven, Sonata, No. 11," Yale University, Beinecke Library, Alfred Stieglitz/Georgia O'Keeffe Collection, YCAL MSS 85, box 159, folder 2912. See also Kaplan et al., *Pamela Colman Smith: The Untold Story*, 223.
191 See Kaplan et al., *Pamela Colman Smith: The Untold Story*, 217.
192 See Kaplan et al., *Pamela Colman Smith: The Untold Story*, 221, 230, 262.
193 See Kaplan et al., *Pamela Colman Smith: The Untold Story*, 267, 268.
194 See Kaplan et al., *Pamela Colman Smith: The Untold Story*, 91.

Epilogue

1 Stuart Kaplan, Mary K. Greer, Elizabeth O'Connor, and Melinda Boyd Parsons, *Pamela Colman Smith: The Untold Story* (Stamford, CT: U.S. Games, 2018), 42.
2 Two of the paintings reproduced in the article are from the collection of Fredrick Allen King; see M. Irwin MacDonald, "The Fairy Faith and Pictured Music of Pamela Colman Smith," *The Craftsman* XXIII, no. 1 (1912): 24–25.
3 J. B. Yeats, *Letters to his Son W.B. Yeats and Others*, ed. Joseph Hone (London: Faber and Faber, 1944), 162.
4 Joan Hardwick points out that Lily viewed Catholics as inferior and often lumped them together with alcoholics. See Joan Hardwick, *The Yeats Sisters: A Biography of Susan and Elizabeth Yeats* (London: Harper Collins, 1996), 186.
5 Hardwick, *The Yeats Sisters*, 203.
6 Joan Coldwell, "Pamela Colman Smith and the Yeats Family," *The Canadian Journal of Irish Studies* 3, no. 3 (1977): 33.

290   NOTES TO PAGES 230-33

7   Pamela Colman Smith, baptismal record, July 12, 1911, Church of the Immaculate Conception (Farm Street Church), 114 Mount Street, Mayfair, given to the author on May 24, 2017.
8   "Literary Gossip," *Belfast Newsletter*, November 14, 1911, 10.
9   Bram Stoker, *The Lair of the White Worm* (London: William Rider & Son, 1911), 85; see also Katharine Cockin, *Edith Craig (1869–1947): Dramatic Lives* (London: Cassell, 1998), 44–45.
10 Cockin, *Edith Craig*, 45.
11 Cockin, *Edith Craig*, 45.
12 Pamela Colman Smith, "Susan and the Mermaid," reprinted by Corinne Kenner, Create Space Publishing, 2010, 16–17.
13 "Pictures in Music," *The Strand Magazine*, July 1908, 636.
14 "Pictures for Children," *The Brooklyn Daily Eagle*, November 29, 1913, 24.
15 Pamela Colman Smith, *Blue Beard* (New York: Duffield & Co., 1913), 4.
16 Angela Carter, *The Bloody Chamber* (New York: Penguin, 1990).
17 Colman Smith, *Blue Beard*, 6.
18 Colman Smith, *Blue Beard*, 8.
19 Ellen Terry, *The Russian Ballet*, illustrated by Pamela Colman Smith (New York: Bobbs-Merrill, 1913).
20 For the contract, see the British Library, Ellen Terry Archive, 125/26/3 Box 41, 8004E, ET 2000-2381, z157-Z215 and ET-Dz176.
21 Terry, *The Russian Ballet*, 10.
22 Eunice Fuller, *The Book of Friendly Giants*, illustrated by Pamela Colman Smith (New York: The Century Company, 1914).
23 "Books for Young Readers," *The Brooklyn Daily Eagle*, November 21, 1914, 21.
24 Marcus Katz and Tali Goodwin draw many connections between Colman Smith's illustrations for *The Book of Giants* and her designs for the Smith-Waite tarot deck. See Marcus Katz and Tali Goodwin, *Secrets of the Waite-Smith Tarot: The True Story of the World's Most Popular Tarot* (Woodbury, MD: Llewellyn Publications, 2015), 102–3, 117–18, 285.
25 Fuller, *The Book of Friendly Giants*, 215–31.
26 Melinda Boyd Parsons, *To All Believers: The Art of Pamela Colman Smith* (Newark, DE: University of Delaware Press, 1977), 6.
27 Christopher St. John to Ellen Terry, November 30, 1914, Ellen Terry Archive, British Library, Document ID ET-Z1, 433, Archive Location ET IN, St. John (BL) Loan 125/30/02.
28 "The Chelsea Fair," *Chelsea News and General Advertiser*, June 16, 1916, 2.
29 "Temple of Mystery," *Pall Mall Gazette*, June 29, 1916, 9.
30 "Tableaux at the Savoy Hotel," *The Times* [London], February 9, 1917, 3.
31 A 1917 advertisement notes that Miss Lilly B. A. Williams of Aarat, Victoria, had studied under "Miss. Pamela Colman-Smith R.A" in London. "Painting," *Aarat Advertiser* [Aarat, Victoria], July 21, 1917, 4. The Royal Academy does

Notes to pages 233–35 291

not list her as a member and Colman Smith is not known to have used the R.A. herself, so it is likely Williams added this in hopes of increasing her cachet as a prospective art teacher.

32 Pamela Colman Smith, "Buy a BullDog," https://en.wikipedia.org/wiki/File:Buy_a_Bulldog_on_June_16th_and_make_our_brave_boys_more_comfortable.jpg

33 Kaplan et al., *Pamela Colman Smith: The Untold Story*, 85.

34 "Drawings Suggested by Music by Pamela Colman Smith," *The New York Sun*, March 17, 1912, 15.

35 See Mary K. Greer, "Pamela Colman Smith 1912—Correspondences," https://marykgreer.com/2015/02/10/pamela-colman-smith-1912-correspondences/.

36 See Francis King, *Modern Ritual Magic: The Rise of Western Occultism* (Garden City, NY: Avery, 1989), 96.

37 Pamela Colman Smith, illustrations, *The Way of the Cross*, from the French of Paul Claudel, translated by Rowland Thurman and text by Beatrice Cualdram (London: Art and Book Co., 1917).

38 Cockin, *Edith Craig*, 122.

39 "Drawings, 'Suggested by Music,' by Pamela Colman Smith—Japanese Prints and English Book Plates—Germany's Exhibition of Applied Arts of To-day—Sir Joshua Reynolds as a Portrait Painter," *The New York Sun*, March 17, 1912, 55.

40 "Unusual Exhibit by Local Artist," *The Brooklyn Daily Eagle*, March 18, 1912, 24; see also "News and Notes of the Art World," *The New York Times*, March 17, 1912.

41 "Unusual Exhibit by Local Artist," 24.

42 Kaplan et al., *Pamela Colman Smith: The Untold Story*, 394–95.

43 Thomas Gerard, "Art After the War," *The Living Age* 288, no. 3741 (March 18, 1916), 721–23.

44 Gerard, "Art After the War," 721.

45 See Kaplan et al., *Pamela Colman Smith: The Untold Story*, 342–43.

46 Gerard, "Art After the War," 722.

47 Gerard, "Art After the War," 722.

48 Gerard, "Art After the War," 722–23.

49 A 1920 report from the Bishop of Plymouth references Colman Smith's Catholic relatives in the area. Who they might have been is unknown. Dawn Robinson, *Pamela Colman Smith—Tarot Artist—The Pious Pixie* (London: Fonthill, 2020), 162, 168.

50 Robinson, *Pamela Colman Smith*, 140–41.

51 "Plymouth," *The Tablet*, December 9, 1899, 954, qtd in Robinson, *Pamela Colman Smith*, 160–61.

52 Qtd. in Robinson, *Pamela Colman Smith*, 160–61.

53 Qtd. in Robinson, *Pamela Colman Smith*, 161.

54 Qtd. in Robinson, *Pamela Colman Smith*, 160.

55 Qtd. in Robinson, *Pamela Colman Smith*, 162.
56 Qtd. in Robinson, *Pamela Colman Smith*, 162–63.
57 "Plymouth," *The Tablet*, February 10, 1923, 32. See also "Plymouth," *The Tablet*, December 16, 1922, 15.
58 "Plymouth," *The Tablet*, February 10, 1923, 32.
59 "Plymouth," *The Tablet*, February 10, 1923, 32.
60 John Joseph Kelly, Roman Catholic Bishop of Plymouth, while in Rome, to his secretary Roberti, October 6, 1927, letter given to author by Dawn G. Robinson.
61 Qtd. in Robinson, *Pamela Colman Smith*, 164–65.
62 Cockin, *Edith Craig*, 118, 128.
63 Pamela Colman Smith, "Producing a Village Play," *Drama*, October 1919, 47.
64 Colman Smith, "Producing a Village Play," 47.
65 Colman Smith, "Producing a Village Play," 49.
66 Villette, "The Women's Column," *The Mercury* [Tasmania, Australia], March 25, 1924, 10.
67 The Hon. Mrs. Forbes-Sempill, "Music Made Visible: An Unmusical Artist's Lightning Impressions Recorded While Listening to Music," *The Illustrated London News*, February 12, 1927, 258–60. Colman Smith regularly received Christmas cards from Forbes-Sempill, which she kept. She recorded Forbes-Sempill's 1935 death in the front cover of the hymnal in which she noted Alfred Hugh Lake's passing. Private collection of Stuart R. Kaplan, U.S. Games, Inc.
68 Edith Lyttelton, *The Sinclair Family* (London: Heath, Cranton, 1925).
69 Pamela Colman Smith to Martin Birnbaum, 1927, Smithsonian Institution, Archives of American Art, Martin Birnbaum Papers, AAA birnmart, series 2, microfilm.
70 Colman Smith to Birnbaum, 1927, series 2, microfilm.
71 Pamela Colman Smith to Edith Craig, July 21, 1928, Ellen Terry Archive, British Library, Document ID EC-AZ3, 0373, Archive Location EC IN COND, C (BL) Loan 125/2/1.
72 Pamela Colman Smith to Edith Craig, October 29, 1928, Ellen Terry Archive, Document ID EC-Z3, 149, Archive Location EC IN COND, C (BL) Loan 125/2/1.
73 Photos were given to the author during a trip to Smallhythe Place in 2017. See also Robinson, *Pamela Colman Smith*, unpaginated photo section.
74 John Kelly and Ronald Schuchard, eds., *The Collected Letters of W.B. Yeats, Volume Three, 1910–1904* (Oxford: Clarendon Press, 1986), 251 n.2.
75 According to the England and Wales Death Registration Index, Nora Lake died in the spring of 1962 age 87. That would place her birth in approximately 1875 and make her three years older than Colman Smith.
76 The note was on the inside cover of *Hymns Ancient and Modern for Use in the Services of the Church* (London: William Clowes, 1920).

77 Colman Smith signs her given name as Corinne rather than Pamela. See Robinson, *Pamela Colman Smith*, unpaginated photo section.
78 Alice [last name not given] to Pamela Colman Smith, February 19, 1939, private collection of Stuart R. Kaplan Collection, U.S. Games, Inc.
79 Certified copy of an Entry of Death for Corinne Pamela Mary Coleman[*sic*]-Smith, HB 986561; reproduced in Kaplan et al., *Pamela Colman Smith: The Untold Story*, 388.
80 Private collection of Stuart R. Kaplan, U.S. Games, Inc.
81 Alice [last name not given] to Pamela Colman Smith, undated, private collection of Stuart R. Kaplan, U.S. Games, Inc.
82 The Germans bombed Cornwall in the spring and summer and then again throughout 1942.
83 Private collection of Stuart R. Kaplan, U.S. Games, Inc.
84 "General Info" dossier, private collection of Stuart R. Kaplan, U.S. Games, Inc.
85 Kaplan et al., *Pamela Colman Smith: The Untold Story*, 88–89.
86 Private collection of Stuart R. Kaplan, U.S. Games, Inc.
87 Private collection of Stuart R. Kaplan, U.S. Games, Inc.
88 Private collection of Stuart R. Kaplan, U.S. Games, Inc.
89 Private collection of Stuart R. Kaplan, U.S. Games, Inc.
90 Private collection of Stuart R. Kaplan, U.S. Games, Inc.
91 Private collection of Stuart R. Kaplan, U.S. Games, Inc.
92 Kaplan et al., *Pamela Colman Smith: The Untold Story*, 388.
93 "General info" dossier, private collection of Stuart R. Kaplan, U.S. Games, Inc.
94 Kaplan et al., *Pamela Colman Smith: The Untold Story*, 398.
95 Kaplan et al., *Pamela Colman Smith: The Untold Story*, 399–403.
96 Kaplan et al., *Pamela Colman Smith: The Untold Story*, 399–403.
97 Mary K. Greer, "Pamela's Legacy," in Kaplan et al., *Pamela Colman Smith: The Untold Story*, 371.
98 Greer, "Pamela's Legacy," 376–77.
99 Thomas Pynchon, *Against the Day* (New York: Penguin, 2007), 186.
100 T. S. Eliot, *The Waste Land* (New York: W. W. Norton & Co., 2000).
101 See Robert Currie, "Eliot and the Tarot," *ELH* 46, no. 4 (1979): 722–33; and Tom Gibbons, "*The Waste Land* Tarot Identified," *Journal of Modern Literature* 2, no. 4 (1972): 560–65.

Index

"A Bird in the Hand is Worth Two Mocking-Birds in the Bush" 208–9
A Pageant of Great Women 206–7
"A Protest Against Fear" 127–28, 167
A Selection of Anancy Stories 135
A Sheaf of Songs 151
Actresses Franchise League 207–8
Adams, Maud 194
Allen, Grant 136
Alliette, Jean-Baptiste (Etteilla) 188–89
Allison, Carrie 103
Alma-Tadema, Lawrence 152–53, n. 99 276
Alma-Tadema, Sir Lawrence 153, 218
"Alone" 121–22
Amber Heart, The 151
An Early English Nativity Play 36–37, 207
Anansi 2, 4, 6, 8, 9, 11, 12, 16, 17, 40, 51, 53, 55, 78, 83, 90, 109, 111, 112, 119, 126, 127, 129–40, 142–44, 146–49, 153–59, 161, 163, 165, 170–73, 176, 178, 185, 233, 241
Anansi: Jamaican Stories of the Spider God 136

Annancy Stories xiii, 51, 81–83, 107, 108, 125, 130, 132, 134–44, 147–50, 154, 163, 164
Anti-Suffrage Alphabet 205
archetype 132
Archibald Campbell, Lady 220–21
Ardis, Ann 4, 119
Armstrong, Regina 69–72
Art Nouveau 4, 56, 58, 117
Artist Suffrage League 207
Arts and Crafts movement 4, 5, 16, 32, 56, 58, 74, 127, 151, 234
Asquith, Herbert Henry 208–9
Atkins Colman, Pamela 28
Auerbach, Nina 80

Baillie Gallery 165, 234, 279 n.153
Baird, Dorothea "Dolly" 94
Baker, Constance 119
Baker, Josephine 156
Barbauld, Anna Laetitia 107, 108, 114, 118, 199
Baring-Gould, Sabine 86, 92, 100
Barkan, Elazar 8–9, 37
Baron-Cohen, Simon 103
Barrie, J. M. 92

295

Barringer, Tim 35
Basket Maker and Other Tales, The 108
Baudelaire, Charles 25, 104
Beach, Sylvia 131
Beardsley, Aubrey 81, 117, 162
Beethoven, Ludvig van 105, 159, 197, 200, 204, 221–22, 231
Bergson Mathers, Moina 183–84
Berlin Photographic Company 204, 230–33
Berman, Jessica 3
Bernhardt, Sarah 44, 100
Binyon, Laurence 125
Blake, Henry 37, 38, 42
Blake, William 25, 28, 108, 112, 118, 125–27, 131, 151, 162, 163, 166, 178–80, 185–87, 227, 239
Blavatsky, Helena Petrovna "Madame" 181, 184
"Blue Beard" 231
Boas, Franz 8
Bogle, Peter 35–36, 47
Boiardo Viti 187
Book of Friendly Giants, The 232
Book of Good Advice, The 152
Book of the Hours, The 152
Boughton, Alice 73, 113, 167, 171, 258 n. 98
Boyd Parsons, Melinda xv, 81, 106, 171, 189, 193, 233, 266 n.72
Bradley, Gertrude 151
Bramsbäck, Birgit 78
Bray, Eliza Anna 92–93
Brer Rabbit 134–35
Bridges, Victor 119
Briggs, Julia 74
Broad Sheet, A 2, 4, 17, 45, 51, 90, 109, 113–16, 118, 126
Brooklyn Daily Eagle, The 27, 29, 31, 53
Brown, Mary 119
Bruckins, Bruckins Party 39, 45, 49, 51, 55
Burnett, Vivian 153
Bush, Ronald 8–9, 37

Caldecott, Randolph 68, 87
Calkins, Earnest Elmo 10
Calmour, Alfred C. 151
Calvert, Edward 125, 151
Camera Work 162, 169
Campbell, Audrey 96
Campbell Coyle, Heather 95
Carbery, Ethna 146
Carrick, Edward A. 10–11
Cathleen ni Houlihan 111
Catholic Women's Suffrage Society 206
Central Trust Company of New Yok 34–35
Cezanne, Paul 74, 171
Chandler Harris, Joel 82, 135
Chesterton, G. K. 44
Chim-Chim: Folk Stories from Jamaica 51, 107, 130, 136, 138, 139, 142, 146, 147–50, 163, 164
Chopin, Frederic 159–60
Cicero, Sandra and Chic 182–83
Claudel, Paul 234
Clew Parsons, Elsie 147–48
"Closed Door, The" 210, 212
Cockin, Katharine 96, 193, 206
Cohler, Deborah 13–14
Colburn, Alvin Langdon 58
Coldwell, Joan 230
Cole, Alpheus Philemon 9, 152
Cole, Margaret 9, 152
Colman, Samuel (junior) 28–29
Colman, Samuel (senior) 27, 179
Colman Smith, Corinne 21–2, 27, 28, 30–31, 33, 41, n.6 245, n.41 247, n.82 249, n.137 252
Colman Smith, Pamela
  Cornwall 15, 18–19, 30, 78, 92, 234, 235–40
  early art 53–57, 70–72, 73–87, 94–95, 98–101, 107–8, 109–10
  family 21–23, 27–33, 97, 235–40
  Hermetic Order of the Golden Dawn 6, 17–18, 90–91, 110–11, 116, 126, 130, 176, 182–85, 189–90

Index

Irish influence 5, 82, 83, 86, 103, 110–12, 117, 143, 147, 177, 220
Japanese influence 7, 13, 29, 57–60, 70, 74, 75, 81, 84, 117, 134, 152, 171
life in Jamaica 20–24, 37–38, 41–43, 73, 129, 131–32
miniature theater 40, 43–51
"music pictures" 102–3, 157–73, 194–205, 217–28
Pixie nickname 2, 10, 11, 13, 16, 22, 89–93, 98–101, 104, 126, 130, 147
publishers 2, 14, 16, 57, 68–69, 73, 82, 107–9, 117, 127, 150–53, 209
racial identity 2, 6–12, 30–31, 38
Roman Catholicism 190, 227, 229–30, 233–34
signature 98, 183–84
suffrage involvement 4, 205–16
synesthesia 4, 60, 94, 102–4, 157–59, 163
see also entries for Colman Smith's individual works
Conan Doyle, Arthur 91, 94
Conciliation Bill 208–10
Constable, Liz 117
Countess Cathleen 111
Court de Gébelin, Antoine 188–89
Cowlishaw, Nicol & Company 30–35
Craftsman, The ix, 6–7, 12, 23, 127, 153, 158, 166–67, 172
Craig, Edith "Edy" 5, 10, 17, 97–100, 107, 109, 112, 126, 151, 190, 193, 205–8, 231, 233, 234, 236, 237
Craig, Edward Gordon 96–99, 101, 106–7, 119, 120, 126, 157
Crane, Walter 5, 16, 55, 56, 84, 112, 138
Critic, The 7, 13, 69, 73, 81, 99, 170–71
Crowley, Aleister 183–84

Dahl, Roald 232
Davies, Arthur B. 166
Davis, F. Hadland 152
De Casseres, Benjamin 169–70
de Saint-Martin, Louis Claude 190
De Zayas, Marius 171
Debussy, Claude 5, 159, 160, 234–35
Decadence 4, 8, 89, 116–18, 124
Decision: A Dramatic Incident, The 206
Delineator 11–12, 231
Denisoff, Dennis 117, 163
Dixon, Joy 181–82
Dolmetsch, Arnold 103, 110, 157
Doubleday 86, 95, 109, 145
Dow, Arthur Wesley 5, 16, 29, 55, 57–63, 65, 72, 73, 75, 83, 87, 104–6, 128, 131, 138, 142
du Maurier, George 32, 42
Duse, Eleonora, 100

Eckford, Quincey Oliver (U.S. Consul in Jamaica) 38, 42
Edward VII, King 5
Egerton, Lady Alix 119–20, 152, 177
Eldredge, Charles 25, 30
Eliot, T. S. 1, 4, 8, 241
Ellen Peg's Book of Merry Joys (Red Portfolio) 98–101, 108
Ellis, Edwin 180, 187
Ellis, Nadia 39, 55
Erskine, Beatrice 110–11

Farr, Florence 5, 19, 90, 103, 110–12, 114, 177, 183–85
Felkin, R. W. 185
Fenollosa, Ernest 58, 60, 104, 105
Ferguson, Christine 180
Fernald, Anne xiv, 4
Forbes-Sempill, Hon. Mrs. 237, n.67 292
Four Plays 153
Freemasons 91, 182, 190
French, Cecil 119–20
Freud, Sigmund 4
Frohman, Charles 94
Fryer-Fortescue, Ethel 125, 184–85
Fuller, Eunice 232

Garden Behind the Moon, The 21–24, 25, 26
Garrity, Jane 13–14
Gauguin, Paul 4, 25, 74
Geiger, Will 165
Gelukiezanger 119, 147, 148
George, David Lloyd 208–9
Gerard, Thomas 235
Gilbert, R. A. 190
Gillette, William 44, 94–95, 99
Gnostic Christianity 179, 190
Godwin, E. W. 95
Golden Vanity and The Green Bed, The 81, 83–5, 86, 100–101 (parody of), 107–8, 216
Gonne, Maud 183
Goodwin, Tali 193, 202
Gordon Kerby, Marion 206
Green, Nancy E. 57, 59
Green, significance of the color 93, 115–16
Green Portfolio 98, 100–101
Green Sheaf, The 2, 4, 5, 9, 11, 17, 45, 51, 60, 74, 85, 86, 89, 90, 93, 108, 109, 113–26, 130–31, 137, 147, 148, 151, 152, 184, 187
Green Sheaf Press 2, 9, 60, 86, 93, 126, 127, 131, 137, 148, 150–53, 164, 180, 184, 185, 208
Green Sheaf Store 130–31
Greenaway, Kate 5, 16, 55, 56, 75
Greer, Mary K. 183–84
Gregory, Augusta Lady 5, 111, 113, 118
Guardsman, The 44

Half Way Tree Infant Kindergarten (Jamaica) 49
Hamilton, Cecily 206
Hapgood, Norman 99
"Happy Townland, The" 112
Harcourt Williams, E. 119, 151
Harrods 130
"Harvest Home Masque, The" 120
Haskell, Ida 5, 16, 56–57, 72

H.D. 90
Heijerman, Herman 207
Henry Irving (biography) 151
Henry Morgan 40, 45–51, 55, 62
Hermetic Order of the Golden Dawn 6, 17, 18, 24, 31, 90, 91, 103, 110, 111, 116, 126, 130, 176, 182–85, 189, 190
Herne the Hunter 44–45
Herzog, Charlotte 69–70
Hodgson Burnett, France 154
Hogarth Press 131
Hokusai 57–58, 84
Hooker, Thomas 29
Horniman, Annie 183
Horton, W. T. 119, 184–85
Housman, Clemence 207
Housman, Laurence 205, 207
Huneker, James 162–66, 170, 186
Hurston, Zora Neale 4, 137

Illustrated London News 102–3, 15–19, 237
In Chimney Corners: Merry Tales of Irish Folklore 81–84, 86, 143–46
In the Valley of Stars There Is a Tower of Silence: A Persian Tragedy 151–52
Industrial and Fine Arts Exhibition 101
Inness, George 25, 28
Irish Literary Revival 5, 90, 103, 111, 113, 117, 126, 130, 146
Irving, Henry Jr., "Harry" 93
Irving, Sir Henry 5, 26, 44, 67, 81–82, 87, 89, 93–101, 151
Irving, Laurence 99, 118–19

Jamaica Exhibition 38–39
Jamaica Songs and Stories 136
James, Cynthia 132, 143
James, William 158, 167
Jeffrey-Smith, Una 135–37
Jekyll, Walter 136
Johnson, Donielle 103
Johnson, Michele 35–37
Journal of American Folklore 133

Joyce, James 111, 184
Jung, Carl Gustav 132

Kandinsky, Wassily 106
Kaplan, Stuart R. 241
Käsebier, Gertrude 5, 16, 57, 58, 70, 72–73, 165, 171
Katsushika 57
Katz, Marcus 193, 202
Keats, John 119
Kelmscott Press 86, 241
Kensington Magazine 109
Khamara, Samara 152
King, Frederick Allen 229
Koos, Leonard 119
Kumina 39–40
Kupka, Grantisek 105

Lair of the White Worm, The 109, 140, 230, 232
Lake, Nora 3, 18, 238–40
Land of Heart's Desire 74, 75, 77–79, 91, 102, 143, 144
Lang, Andrew 92
Le Gallienne, Richard 116
Ledger, Sally 13–14, 118
Leighton, Sir Frederic 32
Lévi, Éliphas 189
Lewis Hooker, Lydia 29
Little Galleries of the Photo-Secession 162, 171
Lyceum Theater, souvenir booklet 81, 94–96
Lykes, Richard Wayne 65

Macbeth, Lady 79–81
Macbeth, William 125
Macbeth Gallery 53
MacDonald, M. Irwin 160–61
Macdonald-Wright, Stanton 106
MacManus, Seumas 81, 86, 143, 145, 146
MacRitchie, David 92
Magic Carbuncle, The 44, 55
Mama's Black Nurse Stories 134

Manhattan Trust Company 34–35
Manning, Paul 91
Martin, Wendy 156
Masefield, John 12, 119
Masquers, The 5, 90, 103, 111–12, 126, 147, 185
Mathers, Samuel Liddell "McGregor" 182–83, 185, 188–89
Mathews, Elkin 107, 113, 117, 185
Matisse, Henri 170, 171
May, Jill and Robert 45, 66, 68–69
McLaughlin, D. S. 165
Méliès', George 197
Milne-Home, Pamela 134–37, 138, 143
Mintz, Sidney 39
Moakley, Gertrude 191
Modest, Wayne 35
Monsell, E. 120
Moore, Brian 35–37
Moore, George 113
Moore, Leslie 119
Moore, Sturge 112
Morant Bay Uprising 35–36, 47–48, 140
Morris, William 5, 16, 32, 56, 58–59, 79, 86, 138
Morton, Tara 207–8
Mozart, Wolfgang Amadeus 159, 202–4
Munch, Edvard 162, 163
"Music Pictures" 4, 5, 17, 18, 51, 60, 74, 102–7, 117, 126–28, 131, 151, 157–61, 172, 177, 187, 196, 197, 199, 200, 205, 217, 218, 221, 226, 227, 234, 235, 237, 241
Myal 40, 129

naming, importance of 21, 23, 51, 90
National Art Club's January 1908 Special Exhibition of Contemporary Art 165
"Negro Customs and Folk Stories of Jamaica" 133
Nesbitt, Mark 37
Nevinson, Henry Wood 9–10
New Woman 14, 96, 118
Nicandra 109, 231

Nietzsche, Friedrich 119
Noguchi, Yone 119

O'Brien, Lee 91
O'Keeffe, Georgia 58, 106, 171, 194
Oakley, Violet 64, 68–72
Obeah 16, 24, 40, 129, 132, 135, 140, 142, 144, 149, 156–57, 183, 184
Obeah Women 135, 140, 142, 144, 149, 156–57
Occult Review 177, 191, 193, 198, 220–21
Of Mules and Men 137
Our Lady of the Lizard 3, 235–37

Page, The 107–8
Page, Thomas Nelson 135–36
Paine, Alfred Bigelow 44, 49, 66, 82, 108–9, 125, 146–47, 153, 154
Pankhurst, Sylvia 208–9
Parrish, Maxfield 63
Pennell, Joseph 58, 86
Pennsylvania Academy Exhibition 165
Perrault, Charles 231
Picabia, Francis 105, 170
Picasso, Pablo 4, 8, 74, 170, 171
Pictorial Key to the Tarot, The 189–90, 194
Pioneer Players 205–6
pirates 23, 45–46, 49, 51, 64, 66, 83, 85, 114, 115, 117, 129–30
pixies 12, 13, 15, 22, 78, 91–93, 98, 102, 117, 120, 147
Pixie's Poetry Book 108
Plymouth Roman Catholic diocese 235–37
Pollexfen, George 3, 31, 116
"Polling Station" 215
Potolsky, Matthew 117
Pound, Ezra 90
Pratt Art Club 171
Pratt Institute 2, 4, 5, 10, 16, 21, 29, 41, 42, 50–51, 54, 55, 57–63, 72, 75, 138, 155, 167, 171–72,
Prettejohn, Elizabeth 197

primitivism 6, 8–10, 40, 91, 153–65
Pyle, Howard 5, 16, 23–26, 45, 46, 56–58, 63–68, 72, 75, 79, 83, 85, 87, 94, 107, 128, 217
Pyle, Katharine 5, 67–68, 72, n.71 257

Quinn, John 115

Radford, Dollie 151
Radford, Ernest 119–20, 151
Ransome, Arthur 11, 12, 109, 184
Reader, The 31, 63
Reddington, J. 44
Redon, Odilon 162
Reed, Mary "Bobby" 16, 20–23, 25, 26, 32, 37, 38, 46, 54, 64–66, 68, 94
Revival (Jamaican religious group) 40
Rhys, Jean 90
Rigby, Reginald 119, 152
Rising Sun, The 207
Robertson, W. Graham 117
Robinson, Dawn 235–36
Rockwell, Norman 64
Rodin, Auguste 162, 171, 197, 221
Roman Catholicism 3, 18, 24, 189, 190, 230, 233
Rosicrucians 91, 182
Rossetti, Dante Gabriel 56
Rückenfigur 177–78, 196–201, 216–27
Ruskin, John 162
Russell, George "AE" 5, 11, 114, 184
Russell, Morgan 106
Russell, R. H. 74, 82–83, 108–9, 135
Russell Portfolio 74–82
Russian Ballet, The 221, 232, 235

Sacrament of Judas, The 109
Saints Among the Animals 152
Savoy, The 117, 118
Sawyer, Marian 209
Schoolfield, George 116
"School-Girl Song of Spring, A" 60–61
Schuchard, Ronald 110

Schumann, Robert 159, 160, 197, 200–203
Scott, David 39
Second Sight 23, 103, 157–58, 177
Sendak, Maurice 85
"Servant's Tax" 210
Seven Lamps of Architecture 162
Shadow Rabbit: A Story of Adventure 151
Shadows of Life and Thought 176–77
Shakespeare & Company 131
Shakespeare's Heroines 74–75
Shaw, George Bernard 96
Shaw, Martin Fallis 106, 119–20
Shippen Green, Elizabeth 64–65, 68–72
Shirley, Ralph 193
"Should the Art Student Think" 128, 167, 169
Siddons, Sara 80
Silvers, Carol 92
Singer Sargent, John 112
Smith, Bryan 30, 33
Smith, Charles Edward 25, 30–31, 32–35, 65–66, 87
Smith, Cyrus Porter 29–30, 33, 167
Smith, Faith 140
Smith, Theodore "Teddy" 30
Smith-Waite tarot deck 1, 24, 74, 131, 175–78, 185, 187–92, 194–97, 199–202, 205, 217, 241
Sola Busca tarot deck 187
"Song of Wandering Aengus" 112
"Speaking to the Psaltery" 110–11
Sprengel, Anna 183–84
St. John, Chris (Christabel Marshall) 5–6, 97, 101, 110, 119, 151, 190, 205–8, 233
Stella Matutina 113, 182, 184–85
Stevenson, Robert Lewis 44, 63
Stewart, Dianne M. 40
Stieglitz, Alfred 1, 5, 17, 62, 73, 105, 128, 131, 154, 160–66, 170–72, 175, 186, 193, 194, 218, 219, 234, 241, 310
Stoker, Bram 5, 19, 26, 67, 86, 87, 99, 109, 140, 193, 230–32

Strand Magazine 159, 172
Suffrage Atelier 18, 172, 178, 205, 207–12, 216
Suffragette, The 208–9
Surette, Leon 186
"Susan and the Mermaid" 231, 233
Swedenborg, Emanuel 23–25, 57, 179, 185, 190
Swedenborgianism 15, 22–24, 26–28, 51, 94, 129, 179, 184, 227
Symbolism 56, 89, 94, 107, 117
Symons, Arthur 112, 117
Synge, John Millington 5, 112

Tales for Philip and Paul 151
Tales From My Garden 153
Teall, Gardner 43–44
Terry, Ellen 2, 5, 7, 10–12, 16–18, 22, 26, 44, 67, 70, 80–82, 87, 89–102, 106–8, 126, 151, 156, 184, 193, 206, 221, 232, 233, 236, 238
Their Eyes Were Watching God 137
Tickner, Lisa 208
Tidings Brought to Mary, The 234
Tiffany, Louis 29
"To the Girls' Christmas Tree" 210, 212–13
Todhunter, John 119
Toorop, Jan 166
Torgovnick, Marianna 10
"Town, The" 123–24
Trelawney of the Wells 81
Trickster 17, 129, 132, 143, 146
Twain, Mark 63, 155–56
Twentieth Century Club 172

Vikings at Helgeland 109
Vin Mariani 100
von Herkomer, Herbert 106
von Ketelhodt, Baron 36
Votes for Women 207

Wagner, Richard 159, 160
Wainwright, Thomas 116

Waite, A. E. 1, 5, 18, 19, 24, 113, 175–78, 182, 185, 188–92, 194, 199–202, 227, 240–41
Ward, Marcus 16, 55, 56
Warren Beckwith, Martha 136, 147
Waste Land, The 1, 2, 8, 241
Waterhouse, John William 218
Watty, Frederick 98–99
Waugh, Edwin 75–76
Way of the Cross, The 234
Weber, Max 58, 106
Well of the Saints, The 112
Wesson, Frederick 33
West India Improvement Society 33–35
"What a Woman may be, and yet not have the Vote" 214–15
"What May Happen" 210–11
Where There Is Nothing 112
Whistler, James 54, 58, 105
Widdicombe Fair 81, 85–86, 107–8
Wilcox Smith, Jessie 57, 64–65, 68–72
Wilde, Oscar 81, 116
William Rider & Sons 1, 175, 193
Wilson Trowbridge, Ada 133–37
Women's Freedom League 206

Women's Social and Political Union (W.S.P.U.) 207
Women Writers' Suffrage League 206
Wona *see* Jeffrey-Smith, Una
Woolf, Virginia 131
Woodman, William Robert 182
Wright, Frank Lloyd 59
Wyeth, N. C. 64
Wynn Westcott, William 182–84

Yeats, Cottie 113
Yeats, Elizabeth Corbet "Lolly" 113
Yeats, Jack 2, 17, 90, 113–15
Yeats, John 6–7
Yeats, Susan Mary "Lily" 113, 115, 229–30
Yeats, W. B. 4–5, 17, 19, 44, 62, 90, 110–13, 115–16, 130, 137, 154, 177, 184–86
  works 7, 77–78, 91, 102–3, 111–13, 118, 230
Yellow Book, The 117, 118
York Powell, Frederick 118, 137, 180, n.140 269

Zilczer, Judith 105
Zobel Marshall, Emily 132, 134

Printed and bound by CPI Group (UK) Ltd, Croydon, CR0 4YY
11/06/2025
14688103-0002